Population Aging

Population Aging

Is Latin America Ready?

Edited by Daniel Cotlear

THE WORLD BANK
Washington, D.C.

1 2 3 4 13 12 11 10

This volume is a product of the staff of the International Bank for Reconstruction and Development/The World Bank. The findings, interpretations, and conclusions expressed in this volume do not necessarily reflect the views of the Executive Directors of The World Bank or the governments they represent.

The World Bank does not guarantee the accuracy of the data included in this work. The boundaries, colors, denominations, and other information shown on any map in this work do not imply any judgement on the part of The World Bank concerning the legal status of any territory or the endorsement or acceptance of such boundaries.

ISBN-13: 978-0-8213-8487-9
eISBN: 978-0-8213-8469-5
DOI: 10.1596/978-0-8213-8487-9

Library of Congress Cataloging-in-Publication Data
Population aging: Is Latin America Ready? / Daniel Cotlear, editor.
    p. cm. — (Directions in development)
  Includes bibliographical references and index.
  ISBN 978-0-8213-8487-9 (alk. paper) — ISBN 978-0-8213-8469-5 (ebook)

  1. Population aging—Social aspects—Latin America—Congresses. 2. Population aging—Social aspects—Caribbean Area—Congresses. 3. Population aging—Economic aspects—Latin America—Congresses. 4. Population aging—Economic aspects—Caribbean Area—Congresses. 5. Population aging—Health aspects—Latin America—Congresses. 6. Population aging—Health aspects—Caribbean Area—Congresses. 7. Older people—Latin America—Economic conditions. 8. Older people—Caribbean Area—Economic conditions. I. Cotlear, Daniel.
  HQ1064.L29P67 2010
  305.26098—dc22

                                                                    2010031650

Cover design by Quantum Think
Cover photo by Gusjer@Flickr.

Contents

Figures

Tables

Preface

The World Bank had a significant role in the population field until the early 1990s. Since then, the Bank's work in general population and demographic matters has gradually ebbed.[1] The one exception to this trend was related to pension reform, where following the publication of *Averting the Old Age Crisis*, in 1994, much analytical and operational work was undertaken during the late 1990s and early 2000s.[2] Much of this work was done in Latin America and the Caribbean (LAC), which spearheaded many of the reforms on pension systems. The challenges of population, however, go beyond the area of pensions, and the Bank is seeking to reenter this field more broadly. Recently, the Bank published a book reviewing the process of demographic aging in Eastern Europe, which rekindled a broader interest in demographic issues by the Bank.[3] *Population Aging: Is Latin America Ready?* is an attempt to look broadly at issues related to population change in LAC, where the debate about population issues was fierce half a century ago, but later became silent.

The renewed interest in population is part of a growing awareness of the significance of population aging. Following on a 2002 World Conference on Aging in Madrid, the specialized agencies of the United Nations have been developing work programs related to aging in their areas of expertise. Several countries are already facing some of the consequences of aging. While the debate about fiscal liabilities related to pensions is far from over in many countries, new concerns are appearing in the press and in political discourse. Questions of old-age poverty and access to affordable higher-level health services are increasingly on the minds of specialized agencies, sectoral ministries, social security agencies, legislators, and even Constitutional courts, considering, for example, the need for social pensions for the elderly poor or explicit guarantees of access to health services. Ministries of Finance are being cautious about the potential fiscal impact these initiatives could have and about the expected effectiveness of some of the proposed interventions. A strong technical dialogue will have to develop among the parties, and the Bank has in the past been an effective catalyst for this sort of dialogue.

The LAC Region of the World Bank decided to launch a regional study on demographic change and its impact on social policy, with the objective of exploring the potential contributions that the Bank could make in this area. The idea was to have a small-scale exploratory effort to develop a better understanding of the field and its challenges. The study was planned in early 2009, when papers were invited for an authors' workshop in Washington, DC, in July 2009. This book contains a selection of the papers presented at the workshop and papers that further developed some of the ideas discussed there. The book aims to contribute to the growing debate about the demographic transition by exploring three topics that have not received much systematic attention in LAC and that are increasingly taking center stage in policy and politics in the region:

- Support of the aging and for alleviating poverty in the economic life cycle
- The sustainability of social expenditures in an aging world
- The impact of aging on health status and health care.

These topics were chosen because rapid progress could be made in understanding the issues by bringing to the attention of economic policy makers available data in the case of the economic status of the aging, newly available methods in the case of the sustainability of public expenditures or the insights of the economics of happiness, or the results of the technical debate among sector specialists in the case of health status.

We are pleased to contribute to the literature on issues related to aging and social policy in Latin America.

Keith Hansen
Sector Director, Human Development,
Latin America and the
  Caribbean Region
The World Bank

Augusto de la Torre
Regional Chief Economist
Latin America and the
  Caribbean Region
The World Bank

Notes

1. The topic of the 1984 *World Development Report* was "Population Change and Development." Two recent reviews of the Bank's work in health, nutrition, and population (HNP)—the diagnostic review contained in the HNP Strategy ("Healthy Development, The World Bank Strategy for Health, Nutrition, and Population Results," 2007, World Bank, Washington, DC), and the Independent Evaluation Group 2009 report on HNP (*Improving Effectiveness and Outcomes for the Poor in Health, Nutrition, and Population. An Evaluation of World Bank Group Support since 1997*, 2009, World Bank, Washington, DC)—have concluded that there is a need to reinvigorate the Bank's work in this area.

2. *Averting the Old Age Crisis*, World Bank Policy Research Report 1994, New York: Oxford University Press.

3. Mukesh Chawla, Gordon Betcherman, and Arup Banerji, 2007, *From Red to Gray: The Third Transition of Aging Populations in Eastern Europe and the Former Soviet Union*, Washington, DC: World Bank.

Acknowledgments

This book develops ideas first discussed at the World Bank-sponsored "Workshop on Demographic Change and Social Policy in Latin America" held in Washington, DC, in July 2009. It has benefited from the contributions of many people.

We are grateful to Evangeline Javier for her support, friendship, and guidance in the work leading to and defining the production of this book. Ariel Fiszbein, Augusto de la Torre, Francisco Ferreira, and Keith Hansen provided useful comments and guidance at different stages of the preparation of the book. Margaret Grosh deserves special thanks; she provided a careful, detailed assessment of the first draft of the book, making many useful suggestions. In addition, she was very helpful criticizing the story line of the overview chapter. Peer reviewers Emmanuel Jimenez and Ronald Lee provided guidance at all stages of the project. The authors of the papers discussed at the workshop were Diego Battiston, Ricardo Bebczuk, Daniel Cotlear, Carol Graham, Mauricio Holz, Bernardo Lanza Queiroz, Carl Mason, André Medici, Tim Miller, Paulo Saad, Leopoldo Tornarolli, and Cassio Turra. Comments on specific papers were provided at the workshop by Keith Hansen, Evangeline Javier, Emmanuel Jimenez, Tamar Manuelyan, and Julian Schweitzer as panel chairs: and by Francesco Billari, Pablo Fajnziylber, Francisco Ferreira, Rachel Nugent, Rafael Rofman, and Carolina Sanchez-Paramo as appointed commentators.

Cristian Aedo, Jorge Bravo, Mukesh Chawla, Tito Cordella, Pablo Fajnziylber, Marcelo Giugale, Michele Gragnolati, Jose Miguel Guzman, William Malloney, Helena Ribe, Edgard Rodriguez, Jaime Saavedra, Chris Scott, Enrique Vega, Ian Walker, and Xiaoqing Yu provided critical encouragement during the conceptualization phase. Dorothy Kronick provided valuable comments in addition to serving as the rapporteur for the workshop. Valuable organizational and logistical support were provided by Gabriela Moreno. We would like to thank Diane Stamm for her excellent work in editing these chapters, Mikhail Zaidman for his detailed work on the production of figures for chapter 1, and Emiliana Gunawan for her help in producing this volume. Production of the book was co-financed by the Latin America and the Caribbean (LAC) Chief Economist Office; the LAC Human Development Department; and the Health, Nutrition, and Population anchor of the World Bank.

The rapid preparation for the workshop on which this book is based was made possible by the support received from three entities, which we wish to acknowledge. The Economic Commission for Latin America and the Caribbean (ECLAC) provided two papers and general guidance on demographic matters. Within ECLAC we wish to acknowledge the support received from Dirk Jaspers, Tim Miller, and Paulo Saad. The University of La Plata's *Centro de Estudios Distributivos, Laborales y Sociales* (CEDLAS) provided access to its depository of household survey data and broad expertise in the use of these data. Within CEDLAS we wish to acknowledge especially Diego Battiston, Ricardo Bebczuk, Adriana Conconi, Leonardo Gasparini, and Leopoldo Tornarolli for their support. The National Transfer Accounts (NTA) project, a network of researchers who are introducing age into the National Accounts of almost 30 countries in the world (six in LAC), provided essential guidance and support. One of the co-directors of the NTA project, Ronald Lee, served as a peer reviewer of the book at all stages of the report; Cassio Turra provided guidance about NTA network findings and methodology, and he and Bernardo Lanza Queiroz presented papers at the workshop.

About the Authors

Daniel Cotlear is Lead Economist of the Health, Nutrition, and Population Unit in the Human Development Network of the World Bank. He holds a Ph.D. in Economics from Oxford University, a Master's degree from Cambridge University, and a Bachelor's degree from the Catholic University of Peru. Prior to his current appointment, he was the Lead Economist at the World Bank's Human Development Department for the Latin America and the Caribbean Region. At the World Bank, he has also served as Sector Leader for Human Development, covering the Andean countries; as health economist for Latin America; as macroeconomist in the Central America Department; and as Agricultural Economist in the Southern and Eastern Africa Department. Before joining the Bank, he was an advisor at the Ministry of Agriculture of Peru, a university lecturer, and author of several publications, including a book on poverty reduction in the Peruvian Sierra.

Carol Graham is Senior Fellow and Charles Robinson Chair at the Brookings Institution and College Park Professor in the School of Public Policy at the University of Maryland. From 2002 to 2004, she served as a Vice President at Brookings. She has also served as Special Advisor to the Vice President of the Inter-American Development Bank, as a Visiting

Fellow in the Office of the Chief Economist of the World Bank, and as a consultant to the International Monetary Fund and the Harvard Institute for International Development. She is the author of numerous books and articles. Her most recent book, published by Oxford University Press in 2010, is *Happiness around the World: The Paradox of Happy Peasants and Miserable Millionaires*. She has published articles in a range of journals, including the *Journal of Economic Behavior and Organization*; the *World Bank Research Observer; Health Affairs*, the *Journal of Socio-Economics*; the *Journal of Development Studies; World Economics*; the *Journal of Human Development*; and *Foreign Affairs*. She has an A.B. from Princeton University, an M.A. from Johns Hopkins, and a D.Phil. from Oxford University.

Mauricio Holz is a consultant at the Latin American and Caribbean Demographic Center (CELADE)–Population Division of the United Nations Economic Commission for Latin America and the Caribbean (UN ECLAC).

Carl Mason is a lecturer in the Department of Demography at the University of California, Berkeley; Director of the Demography Lab; and Director of Computing for the Center on the Economics and Demography of Aging. He holds a Ph.D. in Economics from the University of California, Berkeley.

André C. Medici is a Senior Health Economist with the World Bank, affiliated with the Human Development Network in the Latin America and the Caribbean Region. Before joining the World Bank he was, for 13 years, senior social development specialist at the Inter-American Development Bank. In Brazil, he held several public positions as Deputy Director of Population and Social Indicators of the Brazilian Institute of Geography and Statistics, Coordinator of Post-Graduate Courses of the National School, and Director of Social Policy Studies at the Institute of Public Sector Economy. He was also professor and researcher in the Department of Economy and Sociology of the Catholic University of Rio de Janeiro and the National School of Public Health (1981–91). He holds a Ph.D. in Economic History from the University of São Paulo and a Master's degree in Economics from the University of Campinas Brazil. He was also President of the Brazilian Association of Health Economics and a member of the Directory of the Brazilian Association of Population Studies.

Tim Miller is a Population Affairs Officer at the Latin American and Caribbean Demographic Center (CELADE)–Population Division of the United Nations Economic Commission for Latin America and the Caribbean (UN ECLAC). He holds a Ph.D. in Demography and a Master's degree in Economics from the University of California, Berkeley.

Paulo M. Saad is the Chief of the Population and Development Area at the Latin American and Caribbean Demographic Center (CELADE)– Population Division of the United Nations Economic Commission for Latin America and the Caribbean (UN ECLAC). He holds a Ph.D. in Sociology from the University of Texas at Austin, a Master's degree in Demography from El Colegio de México, and a Bachelor's degree in Statistics from the University of São Paulo. Before joining CELADE/ECLAC in 2007, he served as Population Affairs Officer for eight years at the Population Division of the United Nations Department of Economic and Social Affairs in New York.

Leopoldo Tornarolli is a Senior Researcher at the Centro de Estudios Distributivos, Laborales y Sociales (CEDLAS) and a Professor of Economics at the Universidad Nacional de La Plata, Argentina. He holds an M.A. in Economics from UNLP and a B.A. in Economics from the Universidad Nacional de Rosario, Argentina. He specializes in poverty, income distribution, and labor market topics. He has been a consultant to the World Bank, the Inter-American Development Bank, the United Nations Development Programme, and several Latin American national governments.

Cassio M. Turra is an Associate Professor of Demography in the Department of Demography/Centro de Desenvolvimento e Planejamento Regional (Cedeplar) at the Universidade Federal de Minas Gerais, in Belo Horizonte, Brazil, where he teaches graduate and undergraduate courses on demographic methods, population issues, and economic demography. After earning his Ph.D. in Demography from the University of Pennsylvania in 2004, Turra spent two years as a postdoctoral fellow at the Office of Population Research and the Center for Health and Wellbeing at Princeton University. Turra's research encompasses many aspects of aging, including the relationships among life challenges, social economic environment, health, and mortality in older populations.

Abbreviations

ADLs	Activities of daily living
AIDS	Acquired immune deficiency syndrome
AUGE	Plan de Atención Universal con Garantías Explícitas (Chile)
BGR	Benefit Generosity Ratio
BOD	Burden of disease
BONOSOL	Bolivia's universal old-age pension scheme (replaced in January 2008 by Renta Dignidad)
CCT	Conditional Cash Transfer
CDC	Centers for Disease Control
CEDLAS	Centro de Estudios Distributivos Laborales y Sociales, Universidad Nacional de La Plata
CELADE	Latin American and Caribbean Demographic Center (El Centro Latinoamericano y Caribeño de Demografía), a department of ECLAC
COPD	Chronic obstructive pulmonary disease
CVD	Cardiovascular disease
DALY	Disability-Adjusted Life Year

DESA	Department of Economic and Social Affairs (of the United Nations Population Division)
DG ECFIN	European Commission Directorate General for Economic and Financial Affairs, Economic Policy Committee and the European Commission
ECLAC	Economic Commission for Latin America and the Caribbean (United Nations) (Comisión Económica para América Latina y el Caribe)
EQ-5D	Euro-quality Five Dimensions
GBD	Global burden of disease
GDP	Gross domestic product
HIV	Human immunodeficiency virus
HNP	Health, nutrition, and population
IADLs	Instrumental activities of daily living
IDB	Inter-American Development Bank
INTERHEART	A study of 52 countries
LAC	Latin America and the Caribbean
MECOVI	Program for the Improvement of Surveys and the Measurement of Living Conditions in Latin America and the Caribbean
Mercosur	Southern Cone Common Market
NCDs	Noncommunicable diseases
NTA	National Transfer Accounts
OECD	Organisation for Economic Co-operation and Development
PAHO	Pan-American Health Organization
PAYGO	Pay-as-you-go
PLATINO	Latin American Project for the Investigation of Obstructive Lung Disease
PNAD	National Household Survey, Brazil
PPP	Purchasing power parity
SABE	Survey on Health, Well-being and Aging in Latin America and the Caribbean (Salud, Bienestar y Envejecimiento en America Latina y el Caribe)
SEDLAC	Socio-Economic Database for Latin America and the Caribbean
SUS	Universal single health system (Brazil)
SVD	Singular Value Decomposition
UN	United Nations

UNESCO	United Nations Educational, Scientific, and Cultural Organization
WHO	World Health Organization
YLD	Years Living with Disability
YLL	Years of Living Lost

CHAPTER 1

Population Aging: Is Latin America Ready?

Daniel Cotlear

Introduction

The past half-century has seen enormous changes in the demographic makeup of Latin America and the Caribbean (LAC). In the 1950s, LAC had a small population of about 160 million people, less than today's population of Brazil. Two-thirds of Latin Americans lived in rural areas. Families were large and women had one of the highest fertility rates in the world, low levels of education, and few opportunities for work outside the household. Investments in health and education reached only a small fraction of the children, many of whom died before reaching age five. Since then, the size of the LAC population has tripled and the mostly rural population has been transformed into a largely urban population. There have been steep reductions in child mortality, and investments in health and education have increased, today reaching a majority of children. Fertility has been more than halved and the opportunities for women in education and for work outside the household have improved significantly. Life expectancy has grown by 22 years. Less obvious to the casual observer, but of significance for policy makers, a population with a large fraction of dependent children has evolved into a population with fewer dependents and a very large proportion of working-age adults.

Most of the demographic changes of the recent past have been beneficial for the welfare of Latin Americans, and many of the changes constitute useful improvements for further development. Based on this experience, policy makers are less prone than they were in the past to react to scary "time bomb" announcements, especially since most of the scarier issues that occupied them in the past turned out to be more manageable than expected. Researchers have also become more cautious about relying on mechanistic projections, having learned that in the long run the initial impact of demographic change will be modified by feedback within social and economic systems. Researchers today tend to emphasize the relevance of compensating technology and institutions in moderating initial negative impacts of, for example, an aging population.[1]

But policy makers would be wrong to become complacent and to expect more of the same type of change. LAC is at a stage in the demographic transition when simple extrapolations from the past become a bad predictor of the future. Population growth has already slowed and the main features of the next half-century will be very different from the types of changes that occurred in the past. The main demographic trend of the next half-century will consist of a rapid aging of the population in most LAC countries. This prospect should be a source of concern for policy makers for two reasons: first, income growth may become harder to attain in countries with large populations of older people, and second, meeting the needs of a large old-age population may be especially difficult in low- and middle-income countries. This is partly because of lower incomes, but also because of the need to build economic and social institutions to realize income security, adequate health care, and other needs of the aging. Building appropriate institutions for an aging society cannot be postponed, because those reaching old age in 2050 are already entering the workforce, and decisions they make over their entire adult life will be framed by the existing and expected institutions providing economic security and health care in old age.

This overview seeks to introduce the reader to three groups of issues related to population aging in LAC. First is a group of issues related to the support of the aging and poverty in the life cycle. This covers questions of work and retirement, income and wealth, living arrangements, and intergenerational transfers. It also explores the relation between the life cycle and poverty. Second is the question of the health transition. How does the demographic transition impact the health status of the population and the demand for health care? And how advanced is the health transition in LAC? Third is an understanding of the fiscal pressures that are likely to accompany population aging and to disentangle the role of demography from the role of policy in that process. We seek to identify opportunities in these areas that may be missed by policy makers.

Individuals vary their economic behavior at different ages—adults tend to reduce their participation in the labor force as they grow older, and even while they remain in the labor force they often reach a point of declining productivity. The proportion of the aging is rapidly increasing in LAC; how will this impact the social fabric in the region? Is there a link between individual aging and poverty? How do the aging "retire" in LAC, where many have no access to a public pension? Are familial transfers a significant source of income for the aging in LAC? And what are the motivations leading families to move away from the type of living arrangements that facilitate families taking care of their members and into living arrangements that require more specialized institutions to provide for children and for the old? Remittances from international migrants are a significant source of income for recipient countries and for recipient families; are they also related to the life cycle and do they have an impact on the welfare of the aging?

The recent past has seen large improvements in the mortality of the population. Infant mortality, in particular, has fallen significantly, leaving a large population to grow up after being exposed at young ages to malnutrition, infectious diseases, and environmental risks. Since greater numbers of people are surviving, while remaining in poverty, is the population becoming healthier or is it increasingly suffering from disease and disability? It is important to understand whether the lower mortality achieved will facilitate further development or if it will become a drag on growth and on the welfare of the population. And how will the demographic and health transitions impact the demand for health services?

As population age structures change, the costs of education, health care, and public benefits will change dramatically. What fiscal impact will this have? To what extent will the fiscal impact depend on demography and to what extent on public policy? Many LAC countries have implemented pension reforms aimed at reducing the fiscal impact of aging; does this largely solve the fiscal problem or are there new fiscal challenges that require the attention of policy makers? Often the impact of demographic change is analyzed independently and in isolation for each of these sectors; what additional insight can be gained by looking at the interconnections and tradeoffs available to policy makers? Mindful of the impact of population aging, Australia, the European Union, New Zealand, and the United States have begun to issue official long-term budget projections. Is it also time for official budgets and for public expenditure studies in developing countries to consider the long-term impact of major policy decisions?

This chapter discusses some of the main conclusions reached by the papers contained in this book and seeks to provide additional contextual information about population aging in the region based on a review of the literature. It goes beyond the traditional role of an introductory chapter by presenting the results of some additional research designed specifically for this chapter. The chapter is not designed as a summary or a map of all the richness contained in each of the chapters of the book, and readers are encouraged to read the individual chapters. The chapter and the book also make no attempt to study the crucial question of how demography affects economic growth; this is an important topic for future research.

This chapter is divided into four sections. The rest of section 1 summarizes key concepts and data related to the demographic transition in LAC and presents some original data related to the economics of the life cycle in the region. It also describes the debate about pension reform in the region. Section 2 explains economic aspects of aging from the household's perspective. This includes discussions of poverty in the life cycle, sources of support for the elderly, labor force withdrawal among the aging, living arrangements, and familial transfers. It also includes a summary of new findings concerning the use of remittances from international migrants in the life cycle. Section 3 summarizes what is known about the health transition in LAC, and includes a discussion of the role of population aging on health status and health care utilization. It also highlights insights obtained from the economics of happiness in relation to health satisfaction and its possible implications for health-seeking behavior. Section 4 discusses the impact of population aging on public expenditures. Section 5 concludes the chapter with a discussion of several implications for policy makers and some lines of work for future data collection and research.

The Demographic Transition in LAC

Demographic transition is the process followed by a population moving from an initial state characterized by high fertility, high mortality, and the preponderance of a young population, to a different state characterized by low fertility, low mortality, and the preponderance of an old population. Most demographic transitions have been initiated by decreasing mortality of young children, leading to an increase in life expectancy. During an initial stage, usually lasting several decades, fertility rates remain high, so population grows increasingly rapidly. Children become increasingly plentiful. Eventually, as families recognize the drop in mortality, fertility begins to decline as well, leading to slower population growth and to a reduction in child dependency ratios. During this period, child dependency falls rapidly, and since the proportion of the elderly remains low, the total dependency ratio falls as each person of working age has fewer dependents to support. During this phase, the population experiences a "demographic dividend." This dividend, which results from reduced fertility, has been found to show up in the form of a mechanical acceleration in the rate of income growth per capita or in consumption. Eventually, this phase comes to an end when fertility levels find a floor and when the proportion of the elderly starts to rise. The initial stage of high child dependency and few elderly is replaced by a new stage of high old-age dependency and few children. Figure 1.1 shows the rapidly changing shape of the population in LAC.

Latin American demographers have begun to explore the history of the population in LAC, revealing considerable diversity. Argentina, southern Brazil, Chile, Cuba, and Uruguay, with populations that included very large European immigration during the 19th and early 20th centuries, did not follow the classical transition. Those countries initiated fertility transitions at the same time as the European countries of origin, but the fertility decline became stalled at moderate levels in the middle of the 20th century. Other countries in LAC, including those with large indigenous populations, did not see declines in mortality until well into the 20th century and did not initiate their fertility decline until the second half of the century.[2] Current demographic structures reflect this diverse past, with the high-immigration countries having a much older population than most other countries in the region.[3] Figure 1.2 shows life expectancy and the total fertility rate to illustrate some of the diversity of countries in the region.

Saad, in chapter 2, describes the demographic transition in LAC. By the middle of the 20th century, life expectancy at birth in LAC was only 52 and infant mortality was 128 per 1,000 births. There have been significant improvements since then; life expectancy at birth is now 73 and infant mortality has dropped to 22 per 1,000 births. Life expectancy in LAC is 8 years higher than the average for developing regions and only 1.2 years lower than the average life expectancy in Europe. Most of this improvement happened as a result of declines in infant mortality rates due

Figure 1.1 A Century of Changes in the LAC Population Structure

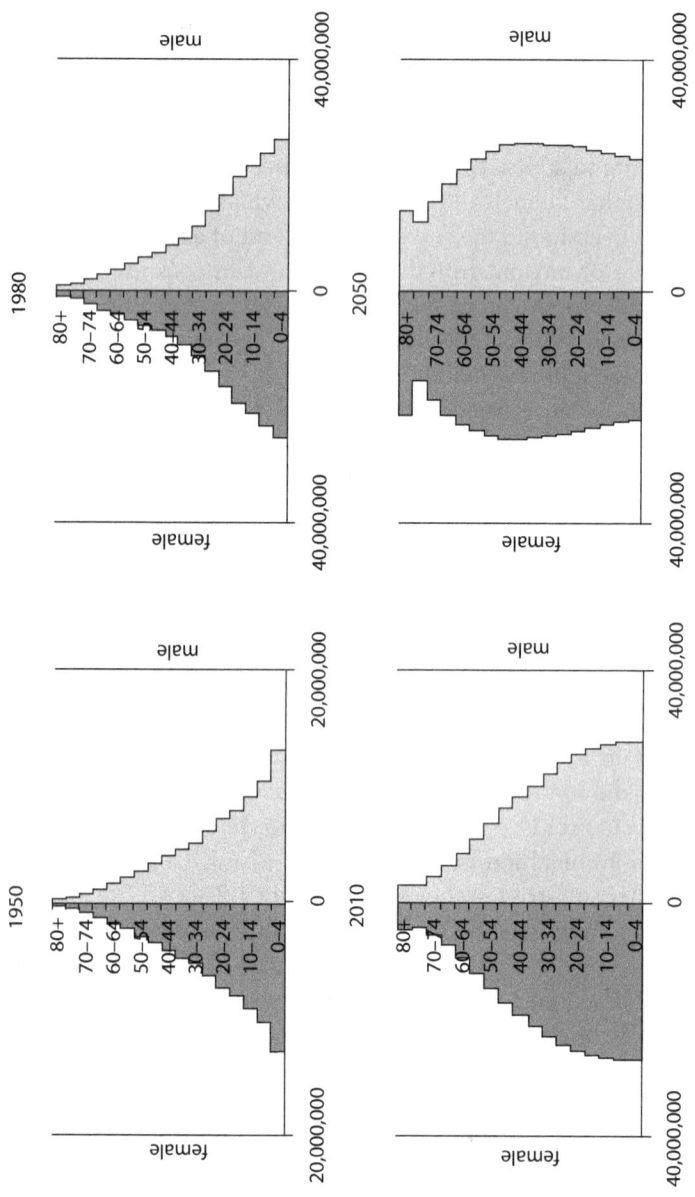

Source: CELADE/ECLAC.

Figure 1.2   Life Expectancy at Birth and Total Fertility Rate in LAC, 2005–10

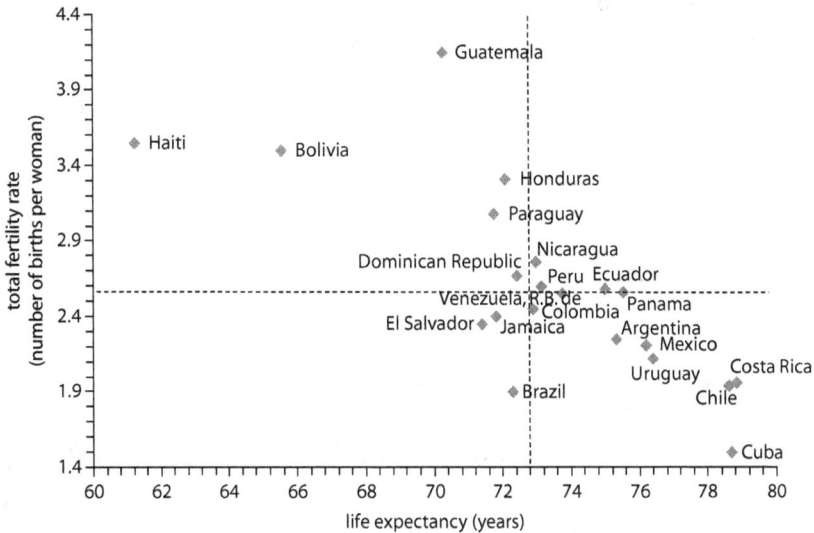

Source: UN Population Prospects Report 2008.
Note: Dotted lines represent the unweighted mean.

to improved control over infectious, parasitic, and respiratory diseases. During the last 60 years, female life expectancy has increased from being three years higher to six years higher than for males. There is great variation in life expectancy across LAC countries, ranging from 60 years in Haiti and 66 in Bolivia to more than 78 in Chile, Costa Rica, and Cuba. While all indications suggest that significant gaps in life expectancy between the poor and the nonpoor exist within LAC populations, we have not been able to find estimates of the magnitude of this important gap.

Despite the impressive declines in mortality, the strongest transformational force in LAC's demography has been the decline in fertility. Over the last 60 years, the total fertility rate has fallen from 5.9 children per woman during 1950–55 to 2.4 children per woman in 2005–10, and the average fertility over the next four decades is expected to hover around the replacement level of 2.1 children per woman. Three Caribbean countries and seven mainland countries are already at or below the replacement level. The fertility rate is one child or more above the replacement level in only five countries and falling rapidly. In the 30 years between 1960 and 1990, fertility levels in LAC decreased from among the world's highest to considerably below the global average.

Despite the decrease in fertility, the momentum generated by a large fraction of the population at reproductive age meant that the annual number of births continued to grow until the 1990s, when 11.5 million births took place each year. The number of annual births is now falling; population is now growing at half the rate of the mid-20th century, and the United Nations projects that most LAC countries will reach their largest population size between 2050 and 2070. Population growth is no longer the main trend in population in LAC: In the last 50 years, population in LAC tripled; in the next 50 years, the UN expects most countries to see population growth of less than 50 percent. For LAC as a whole, the projections are for a 40 percent increase, reaching 763 million in 2050.[4]

While in the past, the big population challenge was the growth in the total population, the big challenge ahead is the change in the structure of the population. In the last half-century, the number of children grew rapidly, but their proportion of the total has been declining since 1970, and it is now expected to decline by around 17 percent by 2050. The adult population was the fastest growing, expanding by almost four times in the first period, and is now projected to grow by only one-third during the second period. The older population grew slowly during the first period and is projected to grow very fast in the next few decades, matching that of the youth population in 30 years. The past is a bad predictor for the type of change that lies ahead: Between 1950 and 2000, the proportion of the population aged 60 and over increased only moderately, from 6 percent to 9 percent. Over the next 50 years, however, it will rise from 9 percent to 24 percent, or in absolute terms, from around 9 million to 180 million in the course of a century.

As the relative size of the different population groups continues to evolve, so will the dependency ratios. While fertility rates started to decline in the mid-1950s, the percentage of children in the total population continued to grow for another decade as a consequence of population momentum; as a result, the dependency ratio in Latin America continued to grow, peaking in the 1960s at 97 dependents per 100 working-age people. Starting in the 1970s, the percentage of children in the population has been falling while the proportion of adults (15–59) has been rising, leading to a continued decline in the dependency ratio. This decline is projected to continue until around 2020, when the ratio will reach a minimum of 60 before increasing again, now due to the growing proportion of older persons. The periods of decline in the dependency ratio, often termed "the demographic window of opportunity," vary by country as shown in table 1.1.

Table 1.1   Aspects of the Demographic Window of Opportunity

Countries	\multicolumn{6}{c}{Reduction period of dependency ratio}

Countries	Maximum value	Year of maximum value	Minimum value	Year of minimum value	Duration (years)	Magnitude (%)
Latin America						
Argentina	78	1989	63	2032	43	19
Bolivia	95	1974	57	2041	67	40
Brazil	97	1964	58	2007	43	41
Chile	92	1966	54	2011	45	41
Colombia	109	1965	56	2017	52	49
Costa Rica	115	1965	53	2014	49	54
Cuba	91	1974	53	1991	17	42
Dominican Republic	114	1965	63	2027	62	44
Ecuador	105	1965	61	2025	60	43
El Salvador	104	1968	57	2028	60	45
Guatemala	103	1988	55	2050	62	46
Haiti	92	1970	57	2039	69	38
Honduras	111	1972	56	2040	68	50
Mexico	110	1966	57	2022	56	49
Nicaragua	114	1965	59	2035	70	48
Panama	102	1968	61	2020	52	40
Paraguay	113	1962	58	2038	76	48
Peru	99	1967	59	2017	50	41
Uruguay	74	1989	67	2016	27	9
Venezuela, R.B. de	104	1966	61	2020	54	41
Caribbean						
Aruba	91	1961	50	1995	34	45
Bahamas, The	99	1966	54	2014	48	45
Barbados	101	1966	46	2007	41	55
Belize	117	1974	56	2035	61	52
Guyana	116	1960	59	2018	58	49
Jamaica	125	1971	63	2017	46	49
Netherlands Antilles	95	1959	55	2010	51	42
Puerto Rico	103	1959	65	2004	45	37
St. Lucia	134	1970	56	2011	41	58
St. Vincent and the Grenadines	135	1968	57	2019	51	58
Suriname	119	1963	59	2017	54	51
Trinidad and Tobago	96	1959	46	2007	48	53
U.S. Virgin Islands	102	1956	61	1992	36	40

Source: CELADE/ECLAC population estimates and projections 2007 for Latin America; Population Division of UN/DESA, "World Population Prospects: The 2006 Revision" for the Caribbean.

Whereas the demographic transition lasted over a century in developed countries, similar changes are occurring much more quickly in LAC and the developing world of today. This is due in part to the greater availability of means for controlling fertility and for reducing mortality. France had 115 years to accommodate a doubling of its elderly population from 7 percent to 14 percent; this relatively slow process was common in other European nations and in North America. Japan, the oldest country today, was unusual in that the same transition took place in only 26 years, from 1970 to 1996. Most developing countries are aging at the same rate as Japan or even faster—China is covering this change in 26 years. In LAC, the process is happening very fast. Chile is transitioning at the same pace as China, Brazil is projected to do it in 21 years, and Colombia is projected to be the fastest, in 19 years. The list of 25 countries with the fastest increase in population aged 65 and over includes seven from LAC (Brazil, Chile, Colombia, Costa Rica, Guatemala, Mexico, and Peru) (Kinsella and He 2009).

The Economic Life Cycle in LAC

The change in the population age distribution matters because individuals vary their economic behavior at different ages. Children are born and take years to mature and become economically independent; economic life tends to peak during the adult years and to decrease as people become older and frailer. Lee, Mason, and Cotlear (2010) point out that there are a number of factors beyond biology that shape the economic life cycle. Children may begin to work at very young ages in an agricultural society or may not start earning income until well into their 20s, depending on educational opportunity, family needs, and expectations. The elderly may continue to work until they die, despite illness and pain, or they may retire in their 50s and enjoy leisure while still in excellent health. The existence of public programs, the level of wealth, the availability of financial institutions, and cultural expectations all have an important influence. Likewise, the relative level of consumption across the life cycle combines biological needs, living arrangements, public programs for children and the elderly, fertility rates among the poor and the nonpoor, cultural expectations, and so on.

To appreciate the implications of the changes in population age distribution, it is useful to examine the shape of the economic life cycle in LAC. This can be done using some of the tools developed by the National Transfer Accounts (NTA) project.[5] The NTA project has developed a methodology to estimate income and consumption across the life cycle from birth to age 90 in a way that facilitates international comparisons. For labor income, it includes everyone in the population at each age, whether in the labor force or not. It includes salary and wages and two-thirds of any self-employment income, which in several LAC countries is very important. For consumption, it measures household expenditure data, allocating private educational and health expenditures for each age and assigning the remainder of consumption to all members in proportion to a simple set of equivalent adult consumer weights.[6] It then averages across all individuals at each age. For purposes of comparing the shape of the age profiles across countries, the age profiles are standardized by dividing all values of labor income and consumption by the average labor income for ages 30–49.

Figure 1.3 was created using the NTA methodology described above. It shows the age profiles for labor income and for consumption in Ecuador, Honduras, Mexico, Nicaragua, and Peru, and includes an average for the five countries.[7] The age profile for labor income has the shape of a bell curve; it is initially zero and then very low in the early ages and grows slowly as individuals enter the labor force and as their hourly wages increase. It peaks when workers are in their early or late 40s (depending on the country) and then slowly decreases. The NTA project has estimated labor income curves for developed countries; these are found to have steeper slopes both entering and exiting the labor market, which would be consistent with a sharper school-to-work transition as individuals enter the labor market, and a sharper exit from the labor market at a statutory retirement age at which workers become eligible for a pension. Labor income curves in developed countries also differ in that they peak 10 to 15 years later than they do in LAC.

Figure 1.3 makes clear that the withdrawal from the labor market in LAC is slow and there is no total exit—labor income remains significant even at age 80-plus. Compared with the earnings of the average adult aged 30–49, the average 60-year-old earns about two-thirds, and the average 70-year-old still earns more than a third of what prime-age adults earn.[8]

Figure 1.3 shows three consumption curves: (a) private consumption excluding private payments for health care and education; (b) private consumption including private payments for health care and education; and (c) total consumption, which includes public and private health care and education. Note that starting at about age 20, the private consumption curves become flat in most countries; by contrast, the total consumption curves have an upward slope in all countries except Mexico. This implies that the average consumption of people 60-plus is higher than the consumption of young adults in four of the five countries analyzed.

Figure 1.3   The Economic Life Cycle in LAC

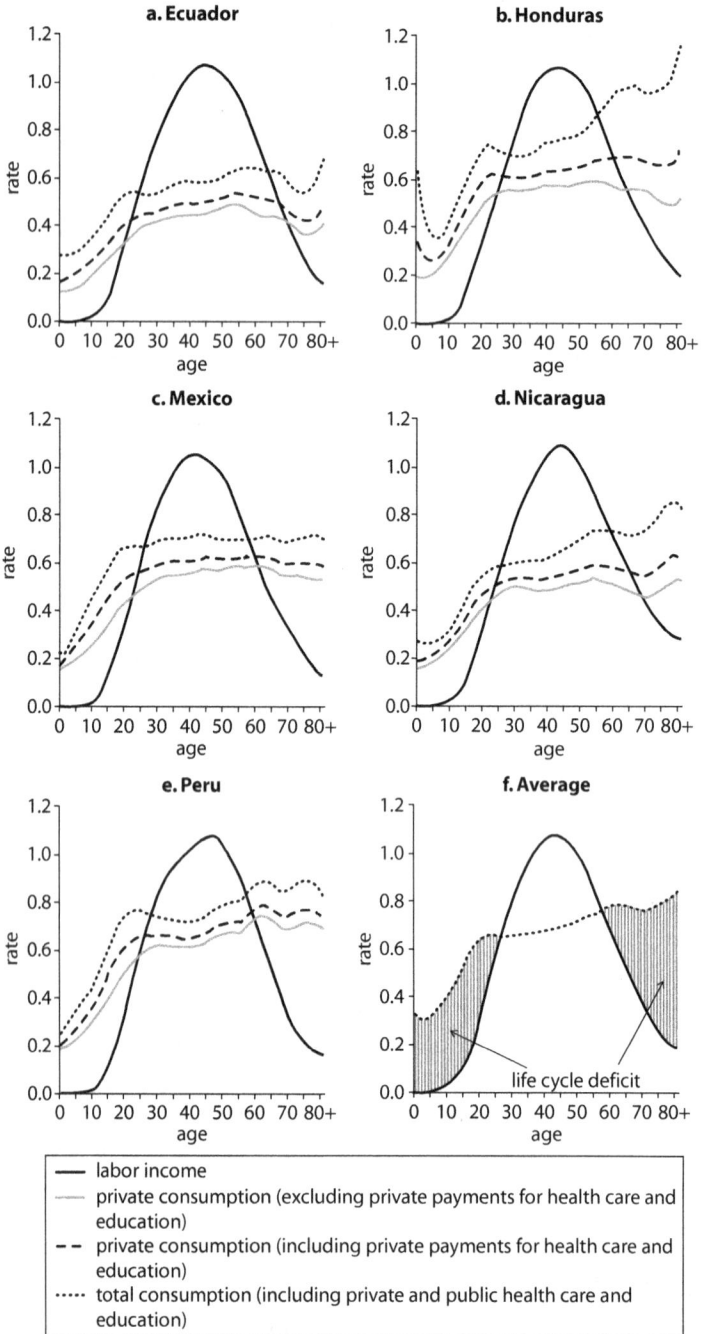

a. Ecuador

b. Honduras

c. Mexico

d. Nicaragua

e. Peru

f. Average

life cycle deficit

—— labor income

——— private consumption (excluding private payments for health care and education)

– – private consumption (including private payments for health care and education)

••••• total consumption (including private and public health care and education)

Source: Battiston, Conconi and Tornarolli 2009.

For both the young and the old, consumption is higher than labor income, which produces what the NTA project calls a "life cycle deficit" (the shaded area in the last graph of figure 1.3). In the five countries of our sample, individuals are in deficit for slightly less than half of their lives. In the five-country average, they begin to earn more than their private consumption at age 24 and they go into deficit again at age 63, so they are in surplus for 39 years. If the cost of education and health is included, the number of years of surplus drops to only 31.

Pensions, Pension Reform, and Social Pensions in LAC

During the last two decades, LAC has been at the forefront of pension reforms. Following a path initiated by Chile, a dozen countries in the region implemented reforms to introduce individual-funded accounts, moving away from the pay-as-you-go (PAYGO) system that prevailed before. Many countries also changed some of the key parameters of their pension systems, such as postponing the retirement age or raising the number of years of contribution needed to become eligible for a pension. The debate about many aspects of these reforms remains intense, but there is an emerging consensus that reforms had some positive effects and some shortcomings. The positive effects include reduced fiscal liabilities (discussed below) and a contribution to the development of the financial sector. At the same time, there were significant disappointments, chief among them the failure to extend access to social security to a broader segment of society (Gill, Packard, and Yermo 2005; Rofman, Lucchetti, and Ourens 2008; Mesa-Lago 2007; Kay and Sinha 2008; Levy 2008).

Figure 1.4, produced by Rofman, Lucchetti, and Ourens (2008), shows the evolution of the coverage of the old-age population between the 1990s and the early 2000s. On average, and despite intense reform efforts, coverage grew from 34 percent to barely 41 percent. The authors also find that the evolution of contributors to Social Security among the active workforce is flat. None of the countries has seen large increases in the coverage of contributory pensions, and in some of the countries that introduced reforms, coverage even fell.

In reaction to the concern about the lack of progress on increasing coverage, many countries are implementing or discussing the implementation of reforms aimed at expanding coverage by creating programs to pay *social pensions*—that is, cash transfers not linked to contributions—or to provide minimum income guarantees for old-age pensioners with some history of contributions. These programs have already been implemented as a complement to contributory pensions in all the high-coverage countries—Argentina, Brazil, Chile, Costa Rica, and Uruguay. As explained above,

Figure 1.4   Population Over 60 Receiving a Pension, Percent

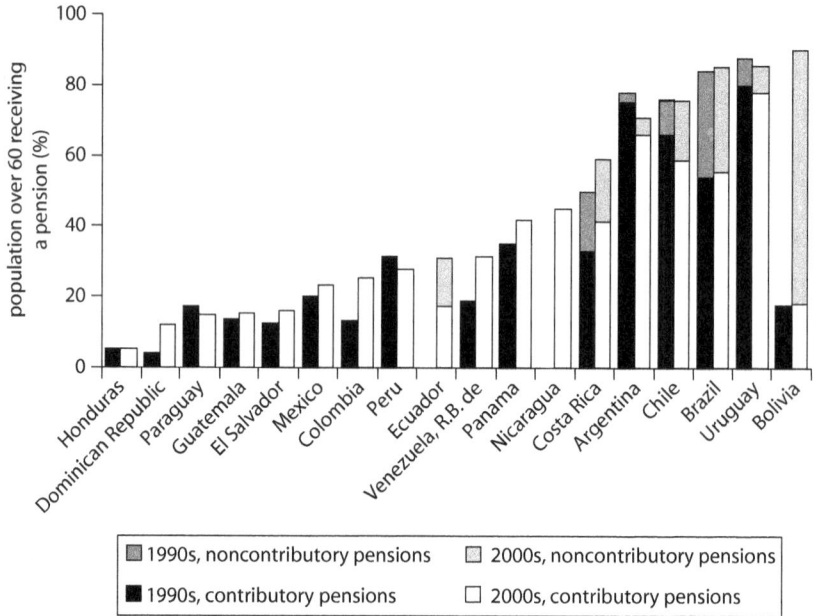

Legend:
- 1990s, noncontributory pensions
- 1990s, contributory pensions
- 2000s, noncontributory pensions
- 2000s, contributory pensions

Source: Rofman, Lucchetti and Ourens 2008.

these are the countries of heavy European immigration during the late 19th and early 20th centuries, and the culture and institutions that these immigrants brought with them probably explains why these countries contain both the oldest populations in the region and the most developed social insurance systems.

A more surprising development is the implementation of social pension programs in countries with younger populations and low contributory pension coverage. Social pensions in these countries were pioneered in Bolivia in the 1990s as a way to make the privatization of nationalized industries more palatable by sharing the revenues broadly. In the early 2000s, transfers to the aging were developed in Ecuador as part of a compensation package launched together with a reduction of fuel subsidies. More recently, social pension programs have been implemented in El Salvador, Panama, and in Mexico City; several other countries in the region are at different stages of piloting or considering the implementation of such systems. Many of these programs are being developed in a political context that begins to give more weight to the aging. The justification for the programs tends to emphasize a concern for old-age poverty and the assumption that it is widespread and that social pensions are the best way to address the problem.

There have been several attempts to estimate the likely impact of social pensions on poverty and the likely fiscal cost of these programs. A detailed and extensive attempt of estimation by Gasparini and others (2007) runs a number of microsimulations comparing two simple minimum pension schemes in 19 countries in LAC. The first scheme consists of a universal transfer equal to the poverty line granted to all people over age 60 (but excluding the beneficiaries of existing pension schemes). The second scheme targets the transfers to the poor over age 60. The study finds that these schemes have the potential to bring a substantial reduction of poverty among the aging, but that poverty is not completely eradicated in this age group since the total impact will depend on how the pension is shared within the household and how much labor supply is reduced in response to the pension transfers. They also find that there is a very small impact on the overall poverty rate, since poverty among the aging is only a small fraction of total poverty. In relation to the fiscal costs of financing these schemes with tax revenues, the estimates range from a regional average of 1 percent of gross domestic product (GDP) for the targeted scheme to about 2.5 percent of GDP for the universal scheme. The country averages for the universal scheme show that countries that already have a high coverage of contributory pensions would face relatively small costs of introducing social pensions (less than 0.5 percent of GDP in Brazil, Chile, and Uruguay); countries with low pension coverage would have larger costs, ranging around 3 to 4 percent of GDP in most of Central America and the Andean countries to 10 percent in Haiti.[9]

One publication explored potential risks of social pensions related to the creation of distortions in the labor market and in savings behavior and issues related to horizontal equity (Holzmann, Robalino, and Takayama 2009). It finds mixed evidence concerning distortions. In Brazil there is strong evidence that the rural social pension scheme reduced the labor supply in preretirement ages and induced retirement at early ages (de Carvalho and Evangelista 2008). By contrast in South Africa the overall effect on labor supply was positive since the elderly reduced the number of hours they worked, but the transfer facilitated financing the migration of younger members of the family, with a net positive effect on overall family employment.[10] The authors find evidence in Chile and Mexico that noncontributory arrangements can lead workers to the informal sector as they seek to avoid payment of social security contributions and to benefit from social pensions.[11] As for saving rates, evidence from the United

States and Spain suggests that eligibility for social pensions can induce workers to save less.

A separate concern relates to the need to maintain horizontal equity by giving equal consideration to the needs of all groups in poverty—the aging, children, persons with disabilities, and working families with low earnings. Grosh and Leite (2009) observe that in many LAC countries the total allocation to contributory social assistance programs is under 1 percent of GDP, so they emphasize the need to be very cautious before defining policies that would allocate a similar or greater amount to a subgroup of the poor. This concern leads to recommending that payments to the elderly be administered as part of the general social assistance system.

The debate about pensions and social pensions in LAC has been so intense that it has almost monopolized the attention of policy makers concerned with the welfare of the aging. The next section seeks to put the issue of pensions into proper perspective by broadening the understanding of the sources of income for the aging and of the relative poverty of the aging and the young in LAC. The section also asks, among other things, whether the existence of a life-cycle deficit increases the risk of poverty for the young and the aging, whether pensions are the main source of support for the aging, how the aging support themselves, and how living arrangements influence economic interactions among family members.

Support of the Elderly and Poverty in the Life Cycle

Poverty in Old Age and Among Children

How much poverty is there among children and among the aging? Cotlear and Tornarolli in chapter 3 examine the relation of poverty and the life cycle in 18 LAC countries using the international poverty line.[12] Readers are reminded of the wide differences that exist in national poverty levels across LAC countries, with low poverty levels in the Southern Cone countries and in Costa Rica and a poverty headcount more than three times higher in much of Central America and in the Andean countries. In that context, it is not surprising that the main determinant of poverty levels among the old or among children in any specific country is the national poverty level—children and the old may diverge from the average, but the level of poverty of any age group is strongly influenced by the national poverty rate.

Within this context, are children and the aging poorer than the rest of the population of their countries? Chapter 3 compares patterns for children (under 15), adults (15–60), and the aging (age 60 and over).[13] The main findings are summarized in figure 1.5, which compares the

Figure 1.5   Poverty among Children and the Aging

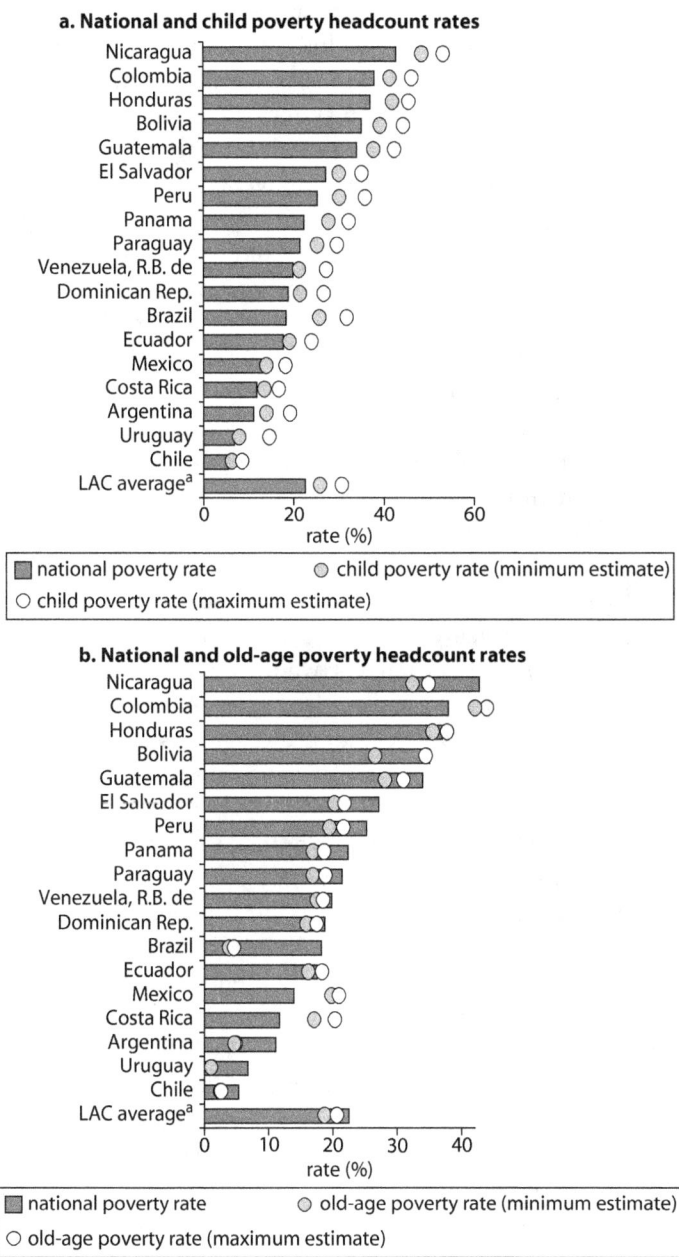

a. National and child poverty headcount rates

- ▨ national poverty rate
- ○ child poverty rate (minimum estimate)
- ○ child poverty rate (maximum estimate)

b. National and old-age poverty headcount rates

- ▨ national poverty rate
- ○ old-age poverty rate (minimum estimate)
- ○ old-age poverty rate (maximum estimate)

Source: Cotlear and Tornarolli (see chapter 3 of this book).
Note: Minimum and maximum poverty estimates for both young people and old-age individuals are estimated using different equivalence values and different measures of economies of scale.
a. Unweighted mean.

national poverty level with poverty of children and of the elderly. Chapter 3 explains the sensitivity of estimates to different methodological assumptions, and figure 1.5 includes the minimum and maximum estimates for each country. Two strong patterns are found.

First, in LAC countries, children systematically have higher levels of poverty than the rest of the population. This pattern is found to exist in all 18 LAC countries examined. On average, poverty levels among children are 20 to 40 percent higher than for the rest of the population. Children are disproportionately concentrated in the bottom quintiles of the income distribution. Note that this estimation is based on the use of an equivalence factor that already considers that children have lower consumption needs than adults and incorporates the existence of economies of scale that favor large families.

Second, the regional average for poverty among the aging is 10 to 20 percent lower than the overall poverty rate. This result, however, is the average of three different groups of countries.

Figure 1.5 shows the existence of a group of "pro-aging" countries where the aging are significantly better off than the rest of the population; these are the countries with the largest and most generous pension systems in LAC—Argentina, Brazil, Chile, and Uruguay—but also includes El Salvador and Nicaragua (two of the top receivers of international remittances in LAC) and Bolivia. At the other extreme, there are three countries where poverty among the aging is significantly higher than among the rest of the population—Colombia, Costa Rica, and Mexico.[14] For the rest of the countries, the aging have poverty levels similar to the national average (or the results vary depending on what methodological assumptions are chosen).

Why are the children concentrated in the lower-income groups? Does higher fertility lead to greater poverty? Or are children on average poorer because they are born to lower-income households? A simple microsimulation was applied in chapter 3 to explore how the income of the poorest 20 percent of households would change if these households had the demographic structure of the richest 20 percent of households while retaining their individual incomes. For the 18 countries in the sample, the incomes of the poorest would increase by 60 percent, on average. The simulation also emphasized that the demographic gaps between the richest and the poorest vary widely among countries, leading to a demographic "handicap" equivalent to a third of income for the poor in Chile (a low) to a high of about three-fourths of income in Argentina, Brazil, Peru, and Uruguay. The simulation also suggests that while demography does have a role explaining relative poverty, it accounts for less than 5 percent of the income gap between the bottom and top quintiles; differences in individual incomes accounts for most of the total gap.[15]

There is a common perception in LAC that the elderly tend to be poorer and that pensions are the main source of support for them. The findings reported here suggest the need to get a better grasp of the sources of income of the aging and of the role played by different living arrangements in alleviating or coping with elderly poverty. These topics are discussed next.

How Do the Aging Support Themselves?

Figure 1.6 shows the relative importance of the different sources of income for older adults by gender. As people age, their labor income becomes a smaller part of their total income. For young adults, labor income is on average around 90 percent of their total income (males 94 percent, females 82 percent). For the group over 60 this falls to 44 percent (males 54 percent, females 26 percent). If we look exclusively at the group over 80, labor income drops to 15 percent of the total (males 21 percent, females 5 percent).

What replaces labor income as people age? For the average older person in LAC, pensions grow in importance (from 34 percent to 49 percent) as do private transfers from outside the household (from 15 percent to 28 percent). While in most countries both pensions and private transfers grow in importance, in a few only transfers become relevant (Honduras and the Dominican Republic), and in six countries private transfers remain small and only pensions are significant (Argentina, Brazil, Colombia, Costa Rica, Panama, and Uruguay).[16] At all ages, women are more dependent on their family than are males, both in terms of transfers received from outside the household and in terms of net financial support within the household.

For people who receive pensions, this source of income is significant but, as was seen in figure 1.4, coverage is low in most LAC countries, and generally less than 40 percent of the older adults are pensioners. Coverage is higher in Argentina, Bolivia, Brazil, Chile, Costa Rica, and Uruguay. In Bolivia and Brazil, most beneficiaries receive "social" pensions. Chapter 3 shows that social pensions have a significant impact on poverty reduction. Social pensions also reduce inequality among the aging so that, while in most countries inequality at older ages is greater than at younger ages, in Bolivia and Brazil, inequality is lower at old age than for the population as a whole.

There are six countries where private transfers, mostly remittances from international migrants, reach more aging people than pensions do.

Figure 1.6   Sources of Income for the Aging Population, Percent

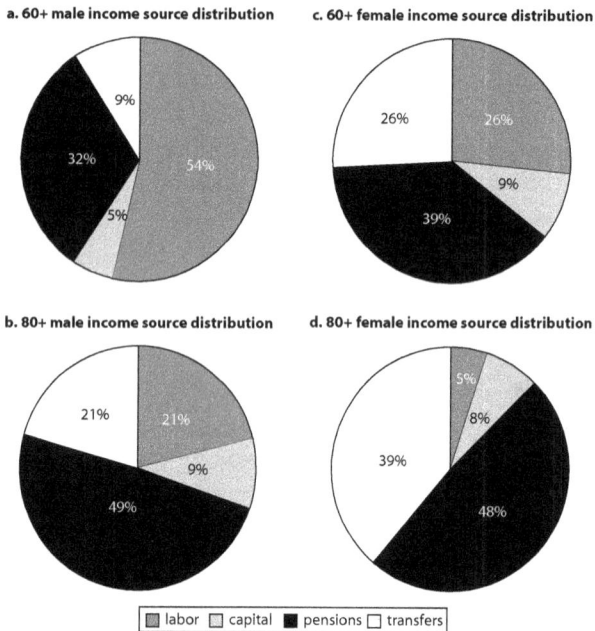

a. 60+ male income source distribution

c. 60+ female income source distribution

b. 80+ male income source distribution

d. 80+ female income source distribution

☐ labor ☐ capital ■ pensions ☐ transfers

Source: Cotlear and Tornarolli (see chapter 3 of this book).

In these countries, private transfers have a larger role than pensions in lifting older people above the poverty line. Contrary to common belief, transfers are more often directed to supporting aging relatives than they are to supporting young children (see chapter 3).

In conclusion, the labor market remains hugely important for the welfare of the aging. Among nonpensioners, typically over 40 percent of the over-60s remain active in the labor market (compared with a participation rate of young adults of 77 percent for men and women combined). And those who work do so for long hours—over 80 percent of the average hours worked by younger workers. There is some evidence pointing to the existence of specific challenges in the labor market for older adults. The aging have very low levels of declared unemployment, suggesting that small employment shocks to this group can have long-term effects as they get rapidly discouraged into leaving the labor market or (more likely given the high rates of participation among nonpensioners) into rapidly downgrading into lower-paying jobs when faced with employment problems. Little is known about labor market transitions in developing countries at old age. Do workers transition from the formal to the informal market or within activities in the informal market? Do they seek greater flexibility in their hours of work or greater proximity between work and residence? Are they discriminated against in the labor market? Does this push them into overcrowded niches of activity with low pay? Could training or microfinance policies be targeted to the aging? This book does not answer these questions, but they should feature prominently in future research in this area.

Living Arrangements and Familial Transfers

The choice of living arrangements has significant consequences for the welfare of family members and for the likely evolution of demand for public services with potentially large fiscal costs, including child care and long-term care for the elderly. Older people in developed countries tend to live on their own (alone or with a spouse), while living with kin in multigenerational households is still the norm in most of the developing world. In LAC, as in many other developing regions, this is rapidly changing, and in some countries it is increasingly common for the aging to live on their own. There are large differences in living arrangements among countries, with almost 90 percent of the aging living in multigenerational households in the young central American countries to around half of the aging doing so in Argentina and Uruguay.

The evidence from LAC discussed in chapter 3 shows a clear pattern by which higher incomes of the aging are associated with a preference for independent living arrangements. The poor and the near-poor tend to co-reside in multigenerational households, while the aging with higher incomes tend to live independently. Evidence also shows that in all countries, the probability of living on their own increases for people as they age into their 50s and 60s. But there is a clear turning point, usually in the mid-70s, when they return to living with their children. This is particularly common for women as they become widows, and less so for males, who tend to be survived by their spouses.

Since it is the poor and the near-poor elderly who are found to live with their children and grandchildren, it is tempting to assume that they live with their kin to receive a "net subsidy." This assumption is not correct. The evidence suggests that in most cases of co-residence, the elderly contribute more financially to their household than what they receive. Co-residence may be preferred by the poor for a variety of reasons, including a greater importance of economies of scale in consumption; caring arrangements for children, the sick, and the very old; and possibly as a strategy to pool risks (of employment, health, disability, poor harvests) with others.

The Impact of Population Aging on Health Status and Health Care Demand

How will the demographic transition affect the health status of the population? And what will be the impact on the demand for health care?

The Health Transition

Related to the process of demographic transition is a parallel process of "epidemiologic transition" or "health transition." The demographic transition is often triggered by a decline in infant mortality, which results primarily from the control of infectious and parasitic diseases at very young ages. That reduction in infant mortality also triggers a *health transition*. This refers to the long-term change in leading causes of death, from communicable, maternal, and perinatal diseases to noncommunicable diseases (NCDs), which include chronic and degenerative diseases. As children survive and grow into adults, they become increasingly exposed to risk factors associated with NCDs, raising the weight of NCDs in the leading causes of death. This shift in the nature of diseases and on the average age of the population suffering from disease is compounded by the decline in fertility, which increases the proportion of older adults, causing the preeminent causes of death to further shift from those associated with infant and childhood mortality to the NCDs associated with older age. Eventually, the increase in the number and proportion of adults shifts national morbidity profiles toward a greater incidence of chronic and degenerative diseases (Kinsella and He 2009).

How advanced is LAC in the health transition? By some measures, it is well advanced. Chapter 4 reviews results from the Disease Control Priority Project showing that in terms of the leading causes of mortality, LAC is much closer to Organisation for Economic Co-operation and Development (OECD) countries than it is to Sub-Saharan Africa (Jamison 2006). While communicable diseases and maternal and perinatal conditions account for most of the mortality in Sub-Saharan Africa (over 70 percent) and in South Asia (45 percent), these conditions account for only 22 percent of mortality in LAC. NCDs already dominate the causes of death in LAC, accounting for 62 percent of mortality. Compare this with 86 percent in high-income countries and with 21 percent in Sub-Saharan Africa. These results are further corroborated by disease-specific findings reported by the

Pan-American Health Organization (PAHO) in a study showing that cardiovascular diseases are the leading cause of death in 26 of 32 LAC countries (PAHO 2007, quoted by Kinsella and He 2009).

By other measures, however, LAC has made less progress than could be expected by international comparisons with other regions similarly advanced in the demographic transition. While there has been significant progress in reducing child mortality, mortality among young and middle-age adults remains high and in relative terms compares unfavorably with other middle-income regions, such as East Asia or Europe and Central Asia. This is reflected in figure 1.7, which shows the proportion of people, by region, who reach age 16 but die before reaching age 59.

A PAHO study found that early mortality from stroke in 2006 was in the 9-percent-to-16-percent range for the United States and Canada, and in the 32-percent-to-39-percent range in eight LAC countries. It is likely that the high adult mortality found in LAC is due to a combination of lack of prevention of risk factors and lack of access to treatment.

Risk factors are highlighted in chapter 4. Researchers have emphasized the possibility that especially high levels of abdominal obesity may be a special risk factor distinguishing LAC from other developing regions. A study of 52 countries (INTERHEART), including six LAC countries, found evidence consistent with this possibility. The study found that the population-adjusted risk for abdominal obesity was 49 percent in LAC compared with 31 percent in the other participating countries. It was also

Figure 1.7   Probability of Dying between the Ages of 5 to 59, (2001)

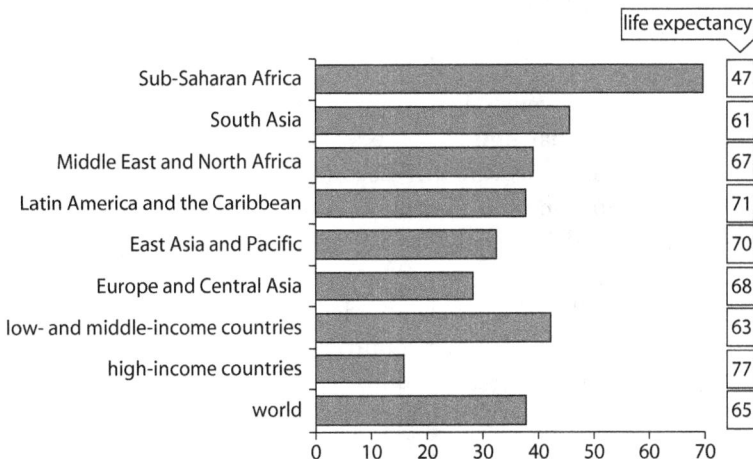

Region	life expectancy
Sub-Saharan Africa	47
South Asia	61
Middle East and North Africa	67
Latin America and the Caribbean	71
East Asia and Pacific	70
Europe and Central Asia	68
low- and middle-income countries	63
high-income countries	77
world	65

Source: Disease Control Priorities Project 2.

higher for high blood cholesterol (42 percent compared to 32 percent) and for hypertension (29 percent compared to 21 percent).

There is some evidence suggesting that early mortality from NCDs among the poor is significantly higher than among higher-income groups; a study in Santiago, Chile, comparing the bottom and top income quintiles found significantly large differences in early mortality and in morbidity for seven NCDs (ranging from 25 percent to 114 percent higher) and for trauma (119 percent higher).

Access to the type of measures needed to improve heart and circulatory conditions and visual limitations is often limited to a small segment of the population in LAC. Access to assistive technologies to help overcome early phases of disability in most countries is also limited. Medici, in chapter 4, warns that policy efforts in promotion, prevention, and treatment will be needed, with special emphasis on the poor.

The Impact on Health Status

Are people in LAC living healthier lives or are they spending their additional years of life in ill health and disability? The answer to this question will affect social welfare and will have a significant impact on national health systems, retirement and disability patterns, and the demand for long-term care for the aging.

Before attempting to answer this question for LAC, it is useful to review the situation in developed countries. Kinsella and He (2009) provide a careful literature review showing that researchers from developed countries report different answers ranging from pessimism ("a pandemic of chronic disease and disability") to optimism ("the compression of morbidity into a short period before death"). There is mounting evidence that disability rates have been declining in the United States.[17] Changes in the prevalence of heart and circulatory conditions and visual limitations played a major role in this decline. Positive factors included the increased use of assistive technologies and changes in socioeconomic characteristics such as higher education and decline in poverty. The nondisabled grew from 74 percent of over-65s in 1982 to 81 percent in 2004 (Manton, Gu, and Lamb 2006, quoted by Kinsella and He 2009). It is not clear, however, whether this trend is common to other developed countries since evidence is often inconclusive; a study of 12 OECD countries found this trend in only five of the countries (Denmark, Finland, Italy, the Netherlands, and the United States). Even less is known about this important topic in developing countries.

Studies from the United States also show that people with higher education tend to live longer. Life expectancy for better-educated people rose by about three years during 1981–2000, compared with half a year for less-educated people (Meara, Richards, and Cutler 2008). The pattern of disease at age 50 for people with less than a high school education is similar to that at age 60 for people with college degrees. Income is also related to health status; low-income people aged 55 to 84 in the United States are more likely than wealthier people to feel limited in basic physical activities, such as climbing stairs and lifting objects.

How will health status evolve in developing countries? Medici, in chapter 4, reports on World Health Organization (WHO) projections for trends in the burden of disease by age between 2004 and 2030. The projections assume that burden of disease among infants and youth younger than 15 will continue to decline. Projections are also optimistic for adults, for whom healthier lives are predicted at all ages.

Other researchers, however, take the opposite view. Many negative health conditions in adulthood stem from risks established early in life. The birth and development of today's older cohorts occurred during times characterized by generally poor nutrition and exposure to infectious diseases, such as polio, malaria, and tuberculosis. Early malnutrition in LAC has been found to be correlated with self-reported diabetes (Palloni and others 2006). Looking cross-nationally at data from two surveys of older populations—one in seven urban centers in LAC and one in Puerto Rico—researchers investigated the risk of being disabled according to conditions experienced early in life. In Puerto Rico, the probability of being disabled among people growing up in poor conditions was 60 percent higher than among people with better childhood socioeconomic levels. For the other seven cities, the corresponding figure was 22 percent (Monteverde and others 2007). The number of disabled people in developing countries seems certain to increase. Families in developing countries likely will be challenged to provide the future service and care requirements of older people.

The Impact on the Demand for Health Care

Medici, in chapter 4, reviews the evidence concerning service utilization and unit costs by age. Data are surprisingly scarce in this area, given its relevance for the management of health facilities, but the data that exist suggest rising utilization and rising costs with age, leveling out at a certain age. Studies for Brazil find that men's inpatient rates by age increase rapidly after about age 55. Unit costs for inpatient services also increase rapidly after age 45 but then flatten at about age 60. For Uruguay, Medici also reports on hospital costs that rise with age and then flatten at about age 70.

Some researchers from OECD countries argue that age is less of an influence over costs when the episodes ending in death are separated from the rest; that is, it is those episodes that have high costs and the rising age/cost curves simply reflect higher mortality with age. A recent study from Brazil investigates this hypothesis by reporting age-cost curves for episodes that end in death separately from the rest. A declining curve is found for episodes ending in death (implying that more is spent attempting to save the life of the young than of the aging). For episodes not ending in death, per capita costs still grow with age, but at a slower pace than if all episodes are aggregated. This suggests that the hypothesis may be correct and that the age profile of mortality may be the main driver of costs in health care.

Medici also discusses the perception of health care needs and of the self-perceived "need-use gap" using household survey data for 12 LAC countries. In all countries, the perception of medical needs increases with age after age 30. This pattern is found for both men and women and also for specific income groups. Perceived needs are higher in the bottom income quintile than in the top income quintile.

In relation to the declared need-use gap, survey data show large variations across countries. A very strong finding is that in all 12 countries, the gap is significantly larger for the poorest quintile than it is for the top quintile. This finding from data obtained through household surveys is consistent with findings from Gallup opinion polls, where the poor in LAC also report being less satisfied with their health than the higher-income population (see chapter 5).

While Medici in chapter 4 looks at objective measures of health status and tries to link them with health-care-seeking behavior, Graham, in chapter 5, looks at subjective determinants of health-seeking behavior, using innovative insights and instruments from the economics of happiness. Graham explores satisfaction with health status and with health care using the Gallup opinion poll that covers 18,000 respondents in 19 countries in the region. Satisfaction is important, both as an element of welfare and as a determinant of health-seeking behavior. The chapter finds that health satisfaction is remarkably high, given objective conditions, and displays several paradoxes. Respondents in Chile are less satisfied with their individual health than are those in Guatemala, even though objective indicators are better in Chile than in Guatemala. Within countries, the rich are more satisfied with their health than are the poor, but the gaps between their attitudes are smaller than the gaps between their outcomes.

The chapter suggests that different norms of health—the level, nature, and quality of health conditions and of health care that societies are accustomed to—play a role in determining health behaviors and health satisfaction. The difference in norms explains cross-country and cross-cohort differences in the levels of demand for health services. The chapter suggests that reference group norms may be significant, explaining some of the findings. The expectations of the poor in Chile may be based on comparisons with society at large, while in Guatemala, the poor may circumscribe their comparisons to other poor people. Taken together, the findings of Medici and Graham suggest that the poor feel underserved but that they may not feel dissatisfied as long as their group of reference remains other poor, equally underserved people. If development is accompanied by an enlargement of the reference group to the wider society, the poor could rapidly become dissatisfied with their current health care situation.

The Impact of Population Aging on Public Expenditures

As population age structures change, how will the fiscal costs of publicly provided education, health care, and pensions change? Miller, Mason, and Holz, in chapter 7, explore the fiscal impact of demographic change in 10 LAC countries. Most public expenditure studies measure social effort as a percent of GDP; this permits comparisons of expenditures among countries with vastly different levels of productivity. The chapter presents a simple framework that adds three innovations to traditional public expenditure reviews: (a) the conceptual separation of policy and demographic variables; (b) the use of an OECD policy path as a benchmark to be compared with the traditionally tacit assumption of a frozen policy framework; and (c) age-specific spending profiles for education, health care, and pensions.

Demography influences the "effort" of allocating a certain fraction of GDP to students, pensioners, and the population in need of health care. The size of each of these beneficiary populations will determine the total amount required to finance education, pensions, and health care. The effort of raising that amount in tax revenues is also influenced by demography. Raising 1 percent of GDP in a country where a large fraction of the population is of working age is less demanding than raising the same amount in a country with a small fraction of its population in the working ages and a larger fraction of retirees or of children. In

Japan, the school-age population is 10 percent of the working-age population, so each potential secondary student can rely on 10 workers to finance their education; in Nicaragua, potential students can rely on only 4 workers. The effect of demography on determining the effort of financing education, pensions, or health care is measured by the "support ratio"—the ratio of the population of beneficiaries to the working-age population.

Policy determines the "generosity" of the benefits that each society decides to assign to the potential beneficiaries of education, pensions, and health care. The Benefit Generosity Ratio (BGR) is the relative cost of benefits per person at risk (for example, potential pensioner or potential student). For example, the BGR for secondary education is the total spending on secondary education divided by the population aged 12 to 17. The BGR is measured in relation to the average productivity of the working-age population; it measures spending per person at the appropriate age for consuming education, health care, or pension benefits as a fraction of the average worker's productivity.

Using these concepts, the authors analyze data for 10 LAC countries and offer the following important insights.

Comparing **education** spending in LAC and the OECD, on average both groups of countries assign about 5 percent of GDP to educating the next generation. A closer inspection using the framework shows that this seemingly similar allocation implies vastly different levels of generosity due to the significantly higher proportions of children that exist in most LAC countries. The student-age population in LAC is about two-thirds the size of the working-age population, while in the OECD countries it is only about two-fifths. In terms of generosity, this implies that OECD secondary education spending per youth is about twice as high as it is in LAC.[18] Within LAC there are significant differences that are often not appreciated. Comparing LAC countries that spend similar amounts of GDP on education—say Brazil and Nicaragua at about 5 percent of GDP or Peru and Uruguay at about 3 percent—the model makes clear that because there are higher school dependency rates in Nicaragua and Peru, the same investment in education implies significantly lower generosity in spending per student. Brazil and Mexico spend about twice as much per student as Peru does (as a proportion of GDP per worker).

Comparing **pensions** spending, there is a large variation between the LAC average of about 5 percent of GDP and the OECD average of about 8 percent of GDP. The OECD has a much higher population of people over age 65 in relation to the working-age population than LAC, so clearly the demographic burden is higher there. The analysis provides two surprising insights. First, the average public pension benefit (as a percent of GDP per working-age adult) is slightly higher in LAC than in OECD countries, despite the low coverage rate prevailing in much of LAC. Second, in LAC the dispersion around the average BGR is huge: Brazil (with the highest levels in LAC and in the total sample) has 10 times the generosity level found in Mexico. The high BGR found in LAC does not mean that most seniors in LAC or even that most pensioners in LAC are better off than their OECD country cohorts. The high BGRs in LAC are a reflection of the fact that the wealthiest workers are most likely to be covered by the contributory public pensions.

Comparing **health care** spending, the authors find that the average BGR is slightly lower in LAC than the average for OECD countries. As with pensions, there exist wide variations across LAC countries; the high-generosity countries (Colombia, Costa Rica, and Cuba) have higher BGRs than OECD countries. At the other extreme, the low-BGR countries (Brazil, Peru, and Uruguay) have significantly lower BGRs than the OECD country average in health care.

Based on these findings, the authors make projections under two scenarios, both including the same changes in the age structure of the population but differing in the assumptions about policy. The first scenario assumes that policy remains "frozen," while the second scenario assumes policy converges to what is found today in OECD countries as income levels converge to current OECD levels. In the case of pensions, "a frozen policy framework" implies that the pre-funding reforms already under way in 6 of the 10 countries under review continue to be implemented.[19] Following are highlights from their findings.

Education: As the proportion of the student-age population falls, population aging with frozen policy would bring a significant reduction in educational spending in all countries in the range of 1 to 2 percent of GDP over the next 40 years. If policies converge to the OECD model, some of these gains would be applied to raise the benefit generosity ratios in education. This would allow achieving some combination of higher levels of enrollment in secondary and tertiary education, higher teacher salaries, and lower student-teacher ratios.

Pensions: The projections related to the fiscal cost of pensions lead to two significant conclusions. First, since the frozen policy scenario includes the continued implementation of the pre-funded pension reforms that are already under way, this scenario is less pessimistic than what a purely demographic projection would produce. Three of the

10 countries would see reductions in the costs of their public pension systems by 2050; several other countries would have greater costs but these would be below what the demographic ratio taken on its own would predict. Only two countries would see very large increases in fiscal cost (Brazil and Cuba would see their costs triple as a proportion of GDP). Second, in the scenario of OECD policy convergence, in 6 of the 10 countries the effect of aging is positive but *smaller* than that of the frozen policy scenario. These are countries in which the current generosity level is higher than the OECD mean. For these countries policy "convergence" implies a *reduction* in the BGR (Brazil, Chile, Costa Rica, Cuba, Peru, and Uruguay). For Chile and Colombia, both scenarios project a reduction in fiscal costs. Only for Argentina and Nicaragua is the combined effect positive and higher than the aging-only effect.

Brazil deserves a special comment as a result of this analysis. A recent study by the Center for Strategic and International Studies (CSIS) about retirement policy in LAC questions government projections that show pension benefits as a percent of GDP going from 7.2 percent in 2007 to "only" 8 percent in 2040 (Jackson, Strauss, and Howe 2009). Since these projections are based on promises of future parametric changes, CSIS considers these projections to be "highly optimistic" and makes an alternative projection assuming what we are calling a "frozen policy framework," which leads to an estimate of costs that more than doubles the government's projection. In the OECD scenario, Miller, Mason, and Holz (chapter 7), by assuming that Brazil will tend to converge to OECD-type policies, reach conclusions similar to those reached by the government of Brazil. The point is that a discussion of the political likelihood of the parametric changes can be seen in a different light if we only have past history to guide us, or if we use alternative benchmarks as a guide.

Health care: Aging alone—in a scenario of frozen spending levels by age—is projected to produce a modest increase in aggregate spending during the next four decades for the LAC average. If policy converges to the OECD model, the results are dramatically different. In health care, much more than in pensions or education, the impact of following the OECD benchmark policies would dramatically increase the aggregate cost of health care. The median increase in public spending projected by the study is a gigantic 3.5 percent of GDP. Why such drastic increases? While for pensions and education the projections of demographic change are partially counterbalanced by policy change, in health care the two effects are mostly compounding.

In summary, the study finds that while demography will play an important role in driving public expenditure growth, policy choices will have an even greater effect. For LAC as a whole, the aging-only scenario (where policy remains frozen) suggests a modest increase in social expenditures of 1 to 2 percent of GDP over the next 40 years—since the reduced pressure to spend on education can finance a significant part of the expected increase in the cost of pensions—at least in countries that have moved away from PAYGO, and the impact of demographics on health care is also relatively small.[20] A more likely path for policy is one of convergence toward the existing OECD model. In this scenario, the greatest challenge turns out to be health care. In part, this is because many countries have already reformed their pension systems in ways that shift future costs away from government budgets. The projections for the increase in pension costs in LAC are similar to those faced by the European Union—a mean increase of about 2.4 percent of GDP over the next 40 years. The projection for the increase in health care costs for LAC (4.3 percent of GDP), is even larger than for the European Union (3.2 percent of GDP).

Conclusions and Implications

Demographic change in LAC during the 21st century will be dominated by rapid population aging. Aging is being felt initially in the countries of high European immigration, which were the first to initiate the demographic transition during the early 20th century and which also have the most extended social security systems. The rest of LAC will continue to benefit from a falling dependency ratio for a few more years, but will then also face rapid aging. And this process will not take a century as it did in Europe; these changes in LAC will take place over two or three decades. Globally, a fourth of the countries that are aging most rapidly are in LAC.

The sources of support for the elderly in LAC and their vulnerability to poverty are often misunderstood. Most of the analytic and policy focus has been centered on pension reform. A growing consensus in this area suggests that the reform of pensions that many LAC countries have implemented has been largely successful at reducing fiscal pressures, but has not been successful in extending coverage to the elderly population; pension coverage of the elderly in most countries remains under 40 percent. That, however, does not automatically imply that the elderly live in poverty as is sometimes assumed. Most LAC elders avoid poverty by continuing to work into old age (especially men) and by relying on their families (especially women). In LAC it is the children, not the over 60s, who are (on average) the poorest age group. The "old old" (over 80) are different; they are more at risk of being poor and more dependent on family support than the over 60s; they are also overwhelmingly female.

Against the commonly held view of a society shaped by ageless institutions, this book describes how new social policy is often accompanied by significant changes in key features of the family and of social values. Extended family living arrangements are less common among higher-income groups or in countries that have acquired large and generous pension coverage. The tradition of long working lives by the elderly is abandoned in countries with large and generous pension coverage. Within countries, the elderly with pensions retire at early ages while the elderly without pensions continue to work. Familial transfers to the elderly are common in some countries with small pension systems and much less common in countries with extended pension systems. Reformers should be aware that changes to the key institutions of the social sectors discussed in this book, such as schools, public pensions, or health care may impact the organization of the family and life cycle behavior.

LAC shows clear progress in the health care transition; success in reducing mortality due to communicable and maternal and perinatal causes has increased the weight of noncommunicable diseases (NCDs) among the leading causes of mortality. NCDs have by now acquired such a large weight in the total that they constitute the main cause of mortality not just for high-income populations but also for the poor. The next challenge of the health care systems in LAC is to extend coverage to the population for NCDs. LAC shows relatively high adult mortality rates (for people aged 15–59). This high mortality reflects the existence of risk factors related to preventable unhealthy behaviors, but it also reflects lack of access of the population, and particularly of the poor, to treatment for NCDs.

The nature of fiscal pressures is likely to change. Population aging is likely to be accompanied by pressures for increased public spending. Economic policy makers in LAC have been dealing with one aspect of this—pension liabilities in PAYGO systems—during the last two decades and are very aware of these risks. They seem to be less aware of other aspects that are already accompanying the demographic transition and of new areas of impending risk. For example, the large increase achieved in most LAC countries in the coverage of public education and of basic health care has been celebrated widely, but it is seldom acknowledged that much of the increase has been financed not through greater national effort but from windfall gains generated by reduced fertility. Another example relates to options open to policy makers; some governments are responding to pressures related to population aging by prioritizing an expansion in health insurance coverage, while others are emphasizing income transfer programs, suggesting that there exists some degree of substitution between these programs.

Fiscal pressures accompanying population aging are likely to be strong in Latin America. Experience in OECD countries and the analysis in chapter 7 suggest that while demography will play a role in driving public expenditure, most of the fiscal pressure associated with population aging will be due to policy choices. Changes in the age structure of the population, together with income growth, are likely to create political pressures to direct a large fraction of the additional income to programs related to pensions and health care. It is not mainly the arithmetic of demography that reshapes public expenditure so much as the political economy that will change with demography.

While, on average, the fiscal pressures associated with population aging are likely to be substantial, this average obscures the significant heterogeneity in Latin America, due in part to demographic differences among the countries but also to substantial differences due to pension reforms undertaken in many of the countries. For countries that reformed their pension system toward higher participation in a defined-contribution system, the effect of aging on the public budget will be partly offset by a reduction in the obligations of the PAYGO system (unless of course new public programs develop in response to the lack of improvement in pension coverage).

Most LAC countries still have in their future agenda developing sustainable health care systems that respond to the new epidemiological needs of the population. The technical, institutional, and political complexities of the health sector have made it hard for economic policy makers in most of LAC to engage with this sector; a common reaction has been to attempt to cap explicit financial commitments to the sector while allowing the sectoral politics to define how any increase in resources is allocated. In the future, governments will find it harder to ignore the dynamics inside this sector. Three of the chapters of the book reach the conclusion—using very different routes—that there is a high likelihood that there will be growing pressure for expanded and improved health care services. This pressure is a likely effect of the combination of population aging, the greater weight of NCDs, and the high income elasticity of the demand for health care likely to accompany economic growth during the next several decades.

Miller, Mason, and Holz reach this conclusion in chapter 7 based on history, by noting the large expansion in health benefit generosity that occurred with economic growth in today's developed countries. Medici reaches the same conclusion in chapter 4 based on the observation that the medical needs of individuals in LAC grow in frequency and in cost as they age, and by detecting large unmet needs for medical care, particularly among the poor. In chapter 5 Graham reaches the same conclusion using instruments from the economics of happiness by noting that the level of satisfaction with health care depends on social norms that define expectations and that these norms may shift as the poor compare themselves not just with other poor people, but with their societies at large. The experience of the OECD and of many middle-income countries suggests that, unattended, the pressures over the health care sector will grow in possibly explosive ways. Health care financing should figure prominently in future debates about the sustainability of social protection systems in Latin America.

Policy makers in LAC generally discuss equity in relation to income, ethnic groups, regions, and gender. The generational dimension of equity has not been significant in LAC as it is in OECD countries. This is likely to change in LAC for many reasons. The elderly will no longer constitute a tiny group in relation to future generations; they will require an increasingly large fraction of fiscal revenues. In the past the elderly had markedly lower levels of education compared with the younger generation, and this limited their voice and political activism. Finally, there is an increasing public debate about decisions that favor one generation but can have a harmful impact over what future generations will inherit, be it in public debt, oil and mineral resources, or the environment.

Implications for Policy Making

Following is a list of areas that policy makers especially need to consider and where actions need to be taken.

A. Develop policies to support long productive lives of workers. The following are examples in this area.

- Avoid the unintended creation of incentives for early retirement by carefully screening proposed changes to norms related to social security and taxation. In countries where these incentives are already in place, actively promote a change of culture and, if appropriate, of the incentives themselves.

- Develop lifelong learning programs for people in their 50s and 60s, expanding them from their current target audience consisting of adults mostly in their 30s.

- Develop labor market policies for the informal sector. As workers become older and less mobile, the opportunities they face become more constrained to jobs closer to their residence and to physically less demanding work. This may force them into over-crowded occupational niches. Microfinance programs have been successful at overcoming similar obstacles faced by women; could microfinance programs be targeted to older workers to expand their options of activities?

- Modify labor market policies for the formal sector. LAC policy makers could explore adapting lessons from the now-extensive OECD country experience in this area by modifying some of the formal sector regulations. Also, antidiscrimination legislation should be explored, because in some countries there are indications that suggest there may be a problem of discrimination against elderly workers. A related effort would be to study whether the widespread perception that the old compete for jobs with younger workers is correct (studies of OECD countries suggest this is not a zero-sum game and studies in LAC may be useful to overcome this perception).

B. Incentivize greater labor participation by women. There is a large variation across LAC countries in the rate of labor participation by women; countries with low rates should think of this as an opportunity to expand their workforce in the context of population aging.

C. Continue to reform pension systems, seeking to achieve greater coverage of the population and to increase life savings. Consider the inclusion of international migrants in home-country social security systems in ways that continue to promote remittances and that find common ground with receiving countries in relation to guest worker programs. Countries considering social pensions should become cognizant of the differences between the "old" (over 60) and the "old old." Note that the justification for social pensions may be particularly strong in countries that have not made reforms to provide affordable access to health care for NCDs, because in these countries health spending among the elderly is likely to be especially high.

D. Develop health care policies to expand access to the prevention and treatment of NCDs, especially among the poor. In many countries, health insurance is restricted to the higher-income population while public health care services provide subsidized access to services focused on communicable diseases and maternal and child services, while treatment of NCDs is paid largely out-of-pocket and becomes the main cause of financial hardship related to health events. Poor health care status related to NCDs may increasingly become the key constraint to prolonging productive lives, and it is imperative for governments to invest in the surveillance of the prevalence of NCDs and disability in their populations. Equity considerations also make it important to measure the differences in life expectancy between the poor and the nonpoor and the magnitude and distribution of middle-age and old-age disability.

E. Countries considering social pensions should seek to transfer lessons learned by the conditional cash transfer programs (CCTs) to optimize living arrangements and healthy behavior by elders. While CCTs condition transfers on school attendance of children, social pensions could target healthy behavior, living arrangements, continued work outside the home, child care arrangements, and so forth.

F. Governments should consider incorporating long-term budget analysis into decisions related to areas impacted by population aging. This analysis should explicitly incorporate the impact of demography on public expenditures and should jointly consider investments in human capital with policies for the support of the elderly. Governments should also develop a capacity to monitor trends in programs of potentially high fiscal cost, such as long-term care services and high-cost health care procedures.

Notes

1. Birdsall and Sinding (2001) refer to this new emphasis as "revisionism."
2. We have not found studies about the demographic history of Afro-descendent groups in LAC. This is an important topic for future research.
3. See Lee (2010) for a description of the divergent paths and for a full description of the demographic transition in Mexico.
4. Population trends are also influenced by migration, and international migration has grown significantly in LAC. Migration tends to be selective by age and gender, so it affects not only the size, but also the age and gender structure of

populations at origin and destination. Most LAC countries are net exporters of migrants; five countries import about the same number of migrants as they export and three (Chile, Costa Rica, and Panama) are net importers of migrants.

5. The NTA project is led by Ronald Lee and Andrew Mason and is developing a data module designed to bring the age dimension into the National Accounts. As of end-2009, it covered 27 countries, including 5 countries in LAC. See www.ntaccounts.org for a description of the methodology.

6. See http://www.ntaccounts.org.

7. Publicly financed health care and education are estimated from the private data (Battiston, Conconi, and Tornarolli 2009) using an average coefficient for the public/private mix. The average was obtained from the Latin American countries in the NTA project. This assumes that the mix is constant at different ages, which is probably not factually correct.

8. The labor income curve includes all the population of a certain age, so the average earnings include active workers and people who do not participate in the labor market.

9. Other studies have further refined these estimations for LAC (Dethier, Pestisau, and Ali, 2010) and have done estimations for Sub-Saharan Africa (Kakwani and Subbarao 2007) and for all developing and transition countries (UN 2007).

10. Case and Deaton (1998) and Duflo (2003) found that the aging often share their social pensions for the benefit of children.

11. This possibility has been discussed at length for Mexico by Levy (2008).

12. The poverty line was updated in 2008. It uses US$2.50 a day in 2005 purchasing power parity terms as the poverty threshold (this replaces what formerly was the "two dollars a day" line.

13. The simpler poverty estimates, based on unadjusted per capita estimates for the different age groups, prove to be sensitive to methodological assumptions concerning economies of scale in the household and equivalence factors between children and adults. See chapter 3 for details.

14. These two groups of countries are significantly different from the average regardless of what assumptions are made in relation to economies of scale or of equivalence.

15. The simulation estimates average incomes for each age group in the bottom quintile and then estimates the average income that would exist if the age pyramid of the bottom quintile had the same proportions as the age pyramid of the top quintile. This cross-section simulation was inspired by a simulation comparing two points in time done by Paes de Barros, Firpo, and Guedes Barreto (2001) for Brazil.

16. We do not have data on private transfers for Chile.

17. Disability is most commonly measured using scales that assess the ability of individuals to perform activities of daily living, such as eating, dressing, toileting, and ambulation, as well as instrumental activities of daily living, such as shopping, doing housework, doing laundry, preparing meals, and using transportation.

18. Measured relative to GDP.

19. The projections focus on expenditures, ignoring fiscal issues pertaining to debt and taxation. More generally, the projections are not based on notions of equilibrium. Also important, the projections do not include any increase in productivity linked to the investment in human capital. The authors emphasize that these are not so much forecasts for what will happen in any particular country as they are illustrative projections that seek to uncover what features of the countries under consideration are likely to be significant.

20. This average, however, consists of an aggregation of countries where the impact will be small, countries where it will be beneficial, and countries where spending is projected to increase dramatically.

References

Baeza, C. C., and T. G. Packard. 2006. *Beyond Survival: Protecting Households from Health Shocks in Latin America.* Palo Alto: Stanford University Press.

Battiston, D., A. Conconi, and L. Tornarolli. 2009. *Tercera Edad. Patrones de consumo e ingresos en el ciclo de vida.* World Bank, Washington, DC.

Birdsall, N., A. C. Kelley, and S. W. Sinding. 2001. *Population Matters: Demographic Change, Economic Growth, and Poverty in the Developing World.* New York: Oxford University Press.

Birdsall, N., and S. W. Sinding. 2001. "How and Why Population Matters: New Findings, New Issues." In *Population Matters. Demographic Change, Economic Growth, and Poverty in the Developing World*, ed. N. Birdsall, A. C. Kelley, and S. W. Sinding. New York: Oxford University Press.

Caritas del Peru. 2009. *Pensiones No Contributivas para Reducir la Pobreza en el Peru.* Lima: Centro de Estudios y Publicaciones.

Case, A., and A. Deaton. 1998. "Large Cash Transfers to the Elderly in South Africa." *Economic Journal* 108 (450): 1330–61.

Chawla, M., G. Betcherman, and A. Banerji. 2007. *From Red to Gray: The Third Transition of Aging Populations in Eastern Europe and the Former Soviet Union.* World Bank, Washington, DC.

de Carvalho, F., and I. Evangelista. 2008. "Old-age Benefits and Retirement Decisions of Rural Elderly in Brazil." *Journal of Development Economics* 86 (1) (April): 129–46.

Dethier, J.-J., P. Pestisau, and R. Ali. 2010. "Universal Minimum Old Age Pensions: Impact on Poverty and Fiscal Cost in 18 Latin American Countries." World Bank, Washington, DC.

Duflo, E. 2003. "Grandmothers and Granddaughters: Old Age Pension and Intrahousehold Allocation in South Africa." *World Bank Economic Review* 17 (1): 1–25.

Fajnzylber, P., and J. H. Lopez. 2008. *Remittances and Development: Lessons from Latin America.* Washington, DC: World Bank.

Gasparini, L., J. Alejo, F. Haimovich, S. Olivieri, and L. Tornarolli. 2007. *Poverty among the Elderly in Latin America and the Caribbean.* (B. p. Situation, Ed.) La Plata: CEDLAS, Universidad Nacional de La Plata.

Gill, I. S., T. Packard, and J. Yermo. 2005. *Keeping the Promise of Social Security in Latin America.* Palo Alto: Stanford University Press and World Bank.

Grosh, M., and P. G. Leite. 2009. "Defining Eligibility for Social Pensions: A View from a Social Assistance Perspective." In *Closing the coverage Gap: The Role of Social Pensions and other Retirement Income Transfers,* ed. R. Holzmann and D. A. Robalino, and N. Takayama. Washington, DC: World Bank.

Hagist, C., and L. J. Kotlikoff. 2005. *NBER Working Paper Series: Who's Going Broke? Comparing Healthcare Costs in Ten OECD Countries.* Cambridge, MA: National Bureau of Economic Research.

Holzmann, R., and R. Hinz. 2005. *An International Perspective on Pension Systems and Reform: Old Age Income Support in the 21st Century.* World Bank, Washington, DC.

Holzmann, R., D. A. Robalino, and N. E. Takayama. 2009a. *Closing the Coverage Gap: The Role of Social Pensions and Other Retirement Income Transfers.* Washington, DC: World Bank.

———. 2009b. *The Role of Social Pensions and other Retirement Income Transfers.* Washington, DC: World Bank.

Jackson, R., R. Strauss, and N. Howe. 2009. *Latin America's Aging Challenge: Demographics and Retirement Policy in Brazil, Chile, and Mexico.* Washington, DC: Center for Strategic and International Studies.

Jamison, D. T. 2006. *Disease Control Priorities in Developing Countries.* Second Edition. New York: Oxford University and World Bank.

Kakwani, N., and K. Subbarao. 2007. "Poverty among the Elderly in Sub-Saharan Africa and the Role of Social Pensions." *Journal of Development Studies* 43 (6) (August 22): 987–1008.

Kay, S. J., and T. Sinha. 2008. *Lessons from Pension Reform in the Americas.* New York: Oxford University Press.

Kinsella, K., and W. He. 2009. *An Aging World: 2008 International Population Reports.* Washington, DC: U.S. Government Printing Office.

Lee, R. 2010. "Population Aging, Intergenerational Transfers, and Economic Growth: Latin America in a Global Context." Expert Group Meeting on Population Aging, Intergenerational Transfers and Social Protection, CELADE/ECLAC/DESA, Santiago, Chile.

Lee, R., A. Mason, and D. Cotlear. 2010. "Global Aging and Its Economic Consequences: An Issues Paper for the World Bank." World Bank, Washington, DC.

Levy, S. 2008. *Good Intentions, Bad Outcomes: Social Policy, Informality, and Economic Growth in Mexico.* Washington, DC: Brookings Institution Press.

Manton, K. G., X. Gu, and V. L. Lamb. 2006. "Change in Chronic Disability from 1982 to 2004/2005 as Measured by Long-Term Changes in Function and Health in the U.S. Elderly Population." *Proceedings of the National Academy of Sciences* 103 (48): 18374–79.

Meara, E. R., S. Richards, and D. Cutler. 2008. "The Gap Gets Bigger: Changes in Mortality and Life Expectancy by Education, 1981–2000." *Health Affairs* 27 (2): 350–60.

Mesa-Lago, C. 2007. *Reassembling Social Security: A Survey of Pensions and Healthcare Reforms in Latin America.* New York: Oxford University Press.

Monteverde, M., B. Novak, K. Norohna, and A. Palloni. 2007. "Obesity and the Loss of Life: A Comparison between the U.S. and Mexico." University of Wisconsin–Madison, Center for Demography and Ecology Working Paper No. 2007-12, Madison, Wisconsin.

National Institute of Aging, National Institutes of Health, U.S. Dept. of Health and Human Services, and U.S. Department of State. 2007. *Why Population Aging Matters: A Global Perspective.* Washington, DC: National Institute of Aging.

Nolte, E., and M. McKee. 2008. *European Observatory on Health Systems and Policies Series: Caring for People with Chronic Conditions: A Health System Perspective.* Berkshire: Open University Press.

Paes de Barros, R., S. Firpo, and R. P. Guedes Barreto. 2001. "Demographic Changes and Poverty in Brazil." In *Population Matters*, ed. N. Birdsall, A. C. Kelley, and S. W. Sinding. New York: Oxford University Press.

PAHO (Pan-American Health Organization). 2007. *Health in the Americas.* Washington, DC: Pan-American Health Organization.

Palloni, A., M. McEniry, R. Wong, and M. Pelaez. 2006. "The Tide to Come: Elderly Health in Latin America and the Caribbean." *Journal of Aging and Health* 18: 180–206.

Robalino, D. A., H. Ribe, and I. Walker. 2009. *From Right to Reality: Achieving Effective Social Protection for All in Latin America.* Social Protection Unit, Latin America and the Caribbean Region. Washington, DC: World Bank.

Rofman, R., L. Lucchetti, and G. Ourens. 2008. "Pension Systems in Latin America: Concepts and Measurements of Coverage." SP Discussion Paper No. 0616, Social Protection Unit. World Bank, Washington, DC.

United Nations. 2007. "Development in an Ageing World." World Economic and Social Survey. Department of Economic and Social Affairs. United Nations, New York.

World Bank. 1994. *Averting the Old Age Crisis.* World Bank Policy Research Report. New York: Oxford University Press.

———. 2007. *The World Bank Strategy for Health, Nutrition, and Population Results.* Washington, DC: World Bank.

CHAPTER 2

Demographic Trends in Latin America and the Caribbean

Paulo M. Saad

Introduction

Demographic changes have intensified in Latin America and the Caribbean (LAC) in recent decades. All countries in the region are experiencing substantial changes in the age structure of their populations as a result of the transition from high to low levels of mortality and fertility. These changes consist of a significant decrease in the share of the child population (those aged 0–14), and important increases in the share of the adult (those aged 15–59), and particularly the older (those aged 60 and over), population.

These changes in age structure mark the onset of a period in which the proportion of people in potentially productive ages grows steadily relative to the number of people in potentially unproductive (inactive) ages. This period, known as the "demographic dividend," "demographic bonus," or "demographic window of opportunity," creates a situation that is particularly conducive for development, because it increases the possibility of saving and investing in economic growth. Nearly all countries in the LAC region are currently in this favorable period of transition. Owing to the unevenness of demographic change, however, for some countries, this window of opportunity is beginning to close, whereas for others it is beginning to open.

Based on population estimates and projections produced by the Latin American and Caribbean Demographic Center/Population Division of the United Nations Economic Commission for Latin America and the Caribbean (CELADE/ECLAC) for the Latin American countries, and by the Population Division of the United Nations Department of Economic and Social Affairs (DESA) for the Caribbean countries, this chapter aims to provide an overview of past and future demographic dynamics in LAC, focusing on the opportunities and challenges posed by population changes and their effect on social and economic development.

Given the uncertainty of future demographic trends, the United Nations usually produces a number of projections based on different assumptions about the future paths of the demographic variables, fertility in particular. This chapter uses the medium-fertility variant, which is normally regarded as the most likely among the variants. Under the medium-fertility variant, total fertility in all countries is assumed to converge eventually toward a level of 1.85 children per woman. To provide an idea of the variation generated by different demographic assumptions, an exercise was performed comparing the medium-fertility variant with the extreme (and unlikely) cases of the low- and high-fertility variants. See Annex 2.1 for a detailed discussion.

This chapter is organized as follows: Section 2 examines recent and future trends in mortality, fertility, and migration levels. Section 3 analyzes the effects of the changes in the demographic variables on population size and age structure. Based on the changing balance among major age groups, section 4 shows the diversity that still prevails among countries in the region in terms of stage of demographic transition, calculates and analyzes past and future trajectories of dependency ratios, and discusses the opportunities provided by the demographic dividend and the challenges brought about by population aging in the countries of the region. Section 5 urges Latin American countries to take advantage of demographic dividends to prepare for the future.

Trends in Mortality, Fertility, and Migration

Mortality

During the first half of the 20th century, mortality declined slowly in LAC. During 1950–55, life expectancy at birth in the region was only 52 years, and infant mortality was 127.7 per thousand births (see table 2.1). From then on, life expectancy started increasing, and significantly, first due to the decline in infant mortality—mainly due to improved control

Table 2.1   Life Expectancy at Birth by Gender and Infant Mortality Rate in LAC, 1950–2025

Five-year period	Life expectancy (years)			Infant mortality (per 1,000 births)
	Total	Men	Women	
1950–55	51.8	50.1	53.5	127.7
1970–75	61.2	58.9	63.6	81.5
1990–95	69.1	65.9	72.5	38.3
2000–05	72.2	69.1	75.4	25.6
2005–10	73.4	70.4	76.6	21.7
2010–15	74.5	71.4	77.7	18.6
2020–25	76.3	73.3	79.5	13.8

Source: CELADE/ECLAC population estimates and projections 2007.

over infectious, parasitic, and respiratory diseases—and then as a product of declining mortality across the entire population. As a result, life expectancy in the region has increased by 21.6 years, on average, over the last 60 years, reaching 73.4 years in 2005–10. This means life expectancy is eight years longer than the average for developing regions and only 1.2 years shorter than the average life expectancy in Europe.

As in almost all societies, male mortality in LAC tends to be higher than female mortality, which is reflected in longer life expectancy for women. This difference has also widened as life expectancy increased over the last half-century (see table 2.1), mostly because of the joint effect of reduced mortality from female-specific causes such as those related to reproductive health, and increased mortality from causes that affect mainly men, such as accidents and violence. Between 1950–55 and 2005–10, the difference between female and male life expectancy increased from 3.4 years to 6.2 years. Population projections indicate that this difference should remain during the next decades, although a reduction is expected in the future, following a trend currently observed in developed countries.

Currently, there is a significant variation among LAC countries in terms of life expectancy, ranging from 60.6 years in Haiti and 65.5 in Bolivia to more than 78 years in Chile, Costa Rica, Cuba, and several Caribbean countries. Figure 2.1 shows life expectancy between 1950 and 2050 for selected LAC countries with different levels of mortality. Although it indicates a clear convergent trend, some important differences still exist among countries and are expected to remain at least until the middle of the 21st century.

Figure 2.1   Life Expectancy at Birth in Selected LAC Countries, 1950–2050

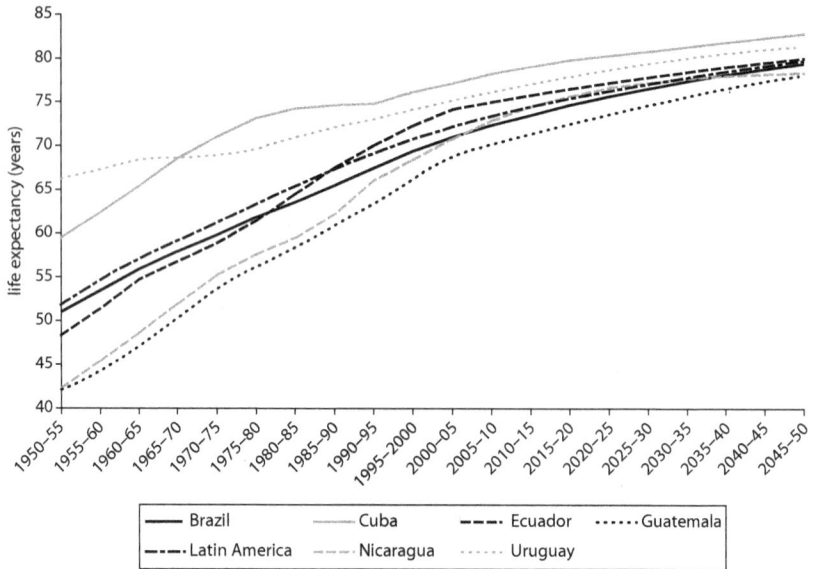

Source: CELADE/ECLAC population estimates and projections 2007.

Fertility

Despite the impressive decline in mortality, the decline in fertility has been the main factor affecting population size and age structure in LAC. Table 2.2 shows fertility trends in the region between 1950 and 2050, based on CELADE/ECLAC's population estimates and projections. Over the last six decades, the total fertility rate in the region dropped from 5.9 children per woman during 1950–55 to 2.4 children per woman during 2005–10. For the next four decades, it is expected to remain below but close to the replacement level of 2.1 children per woman.

Between 1950–1955 and 1990–1995, the annual number of births in the region increased from 7.5 million to 11.5 million, and then started decreasing as a consequence of the continuing decline in fertility. According to the most recent projections, a steady decrease in the annual number of births is expected in the future (see table 2.2). If fertility falls more than expected (which is not unlikely), the decline in the number of births in the region would be even steeper.

Fertility has played the most important role in the population dynamics of the majority of LAC countries. Since the age structure of

Table 2.2   Total Fertility Rate and Annual Births in LAC, 1950–2050

Five-year period	Total fertility rate (%)	Annual births (thousands)
1950–55	5.9	7,409
1970–75	5.1	10,548
1990–95	3.0	11,534
2000–05	2.5	11,424
2005–10	2.4	11,271
2010–15	2.2	11,017
2015–20	2.1	10,715
2020–25	2.0	10,462
2025–30	2.0	10,188
2030–35	1.9	9,855
2035–40	1.9	9,582
2040–45	1.9	9,321
2045–50	1.9	9,087

Source: CELADE/ECLAC population estimates and projections 2007.

the population is mainly a result of previous levels of fertility, those levels will continue to have an impact even when fertility levels have reached replacement.

It is possible to categorize LAC countries according to their current fertility levels as follows:

- Countries where fertility is at or below replacement level (2.1 children or fewer per woman), including those at a very advanced stage of transition, including Barbados and Cuba (1.5 children); Trinidad and Tobago (1.6 children); Puerto Rico (1.8 children); Chile, Martinique, and the Netherlands Antilles (1.9 children); The Bahamas (2.0 children); and Costa Rica, Guadeloupe, and Uruguay (2.1 children).
- Countries where the fertility rate is less than one child above the replacement level (between 2.2 children and 3.1 children per woman), including Brazil, Colombia, Mexico, and Saint Lucia (2.2 children); Argentina and Guyana (2.3 children); Jamaica and Suriname (2.4 children); the República Bolivariana de Venezuela and Peru (2.5 children); Ecuador and Panama (2.6 children); El Salvador (2.7 children); and the Dominican Republic (2.8 children).
- Countries where the fertility rate is one child or more above the replacement level (3.1 children and above), including Paraguay (3.1 children); French Guyana and Honduras (3.3 children); Bolivia and Haiti (3.5 children); and Guatemala (4.2 children).

Figure 2.2 shows trends in total fertility rates for selected countries with different levels of fertility between 1950 and 2050. Although fertility rates in all countries are expected to gradually converge around the replacement level over the projection period, current rates still show important variations, ranging from 1.5 children per woman in Barbados (not shown in figure) and Cuba to 4.2 children per woman in Guatemala.

Many studies on Latin America suggest that average levels of fertility do not provide a good insight into internal inequalities (that is, within-country variations between, for example, urban and rural areas, according to income and education, and so forth). In fact, although steady, the decline in fertility has shown to be uneven not only among countries but also between social groups within countries. For instance, significant variation has been reported by subnational region; between urban and rural areas, according to level of income and education; and by ethnic group (Chackiel and Schkolnik 1992; Schkolnik and Chackiel 1998; ECLAC 2005).

Trends in age-specific fertility rates, for example, show that reduction in fertility has been greatest among women in older age groups, especially

Figure 2.2   Total Fertility Rate in Selected LAC Countries, 1950–2050

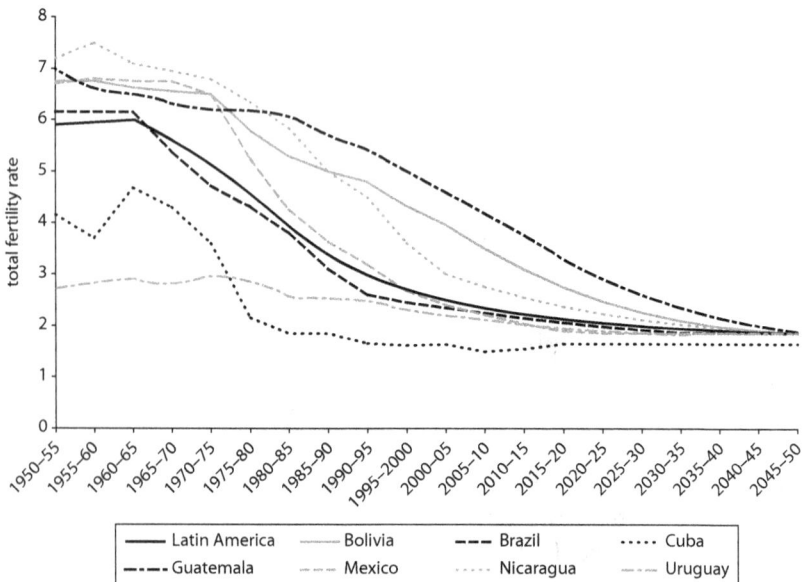

Source: CELADE/ECLAC population estimates and projections 2007.

those aged 35–49, and smallest among adolescents aged 15–19. As a result, the rate of adolescent fertility has almost doubled as a share of total fertility over the last half-century, from 8.5 percent in 1950–1955 to 14.3 percent in 2000–2005 (see table 2.3).[1] Given the health and social problems associated with adolescent fertility, this situation has become a source of concern in many countries across the region.

Migration

In LAC, both international immigration and emigration have played and continue to play an important role in terms of the size, growth, and social and economic characteristics of the region's countries.

Since migration tends to be selective by age and gender, it affects not only the size, but also the age structure and gender composition of populations at origin and destination. Immigrants may also influence fertility patterns and health conditions, thus affecting the levels of other demographic variables in both origin and destination populations.

By comparing natural growth rates (that is, the difference between births and deaths) and total population growth rates (which also takes

Table 2.3   Age-specific and Total Fertility Rate, Percentage Reduction, and Relative Distribution in LAC, 1950–2015

Period	15–19	20–24	25–29	30–34	35–39	40–44	45–49	Total fertility rate (%)
Age-specific fertility rate (births per 1,000 women)								
1950–55	100.1	264.0	289.0	241.0	173.0	84.0	30.0	5.9
1970–75	91.0	234.0	251.0	206.0	144.0	68.0	18.0	5.1
1990–95	83.0	165.0	150.0	105.0	63.0	24.0	4.5	3.0
2000–05	72.0	145.0	129.0	87.0	49.0	17.0	3.2	2.5
2005–10	69.0	138.0	122.0	82.0	45.7	16.0	2.9	2.4
2010–15	63.0	127.0	112.0	74.0	41.0	14.0	2.5	2.2
Reduction in fertility rate (%)								
1950–55 to								
2010–15	37.1	51.9	61.3	69.3	76.3	83.3	91.7	62.7
Relative distribution of rate by age (%)								
1950–55	8.5	22.3	24.5	20.4	14.6	7.1	2.5	100.0
1970–75	9.0	23.1	24.8	20.4	14.3	6.7	1.7	100.0
1990–95	14.0	27.7	25.2	17.6	10.6	4.1	0.8	100.0
2000–05	14.3	28.8	25.7	17.3	9.8	3.5	0.7	100.0
2005–10	14.5	29.0	25.7	17.2	9.6	3.4	0.6	100.0
2010–15	14.5	29.2	25.8	17.1	9.5	3.3	0.6	100.0

Source: CELADE/ECLAC population estimates and projections 2007.

migration into consideration), figure 2.3 identifies countries with positive net migration, that is, those in which the number of immigrants is higher than that of emigrants (total growth is higher than natural growth), and countries with negative net migration, that is, those in which the number of emigrants is higher than that of immigrants (total growth is lower than natural growth). Currently, total growth is below natural growth in most countries, including Colombia, the Dominican Republic, Ecuador, El Salvador, Guatemala, Haiti, Honduras, Mexico, Nicaragua, Paraguay, Peru, and Uruguay, as well as for LAC as a whole.

In contrast, population has increased due to the inflow of migrants in Chile, Costa Rica and, to a lesser extent, Panama. In the case of Chile, immigrants were mainly from Peru, while in Costa Rica they were mainly from Nicaragua (Cortes 2005, cited by Guzmán and others 2006). In countries like Argentina, Bolivia, Brazil, and República Bolivariana de Venezuela, migration balance has little effect on population size since total growth is similar to natural growth. In Argentina,

Figure 2.3   Natural and Total Growth Rates in LAC, by Country, 2005–10

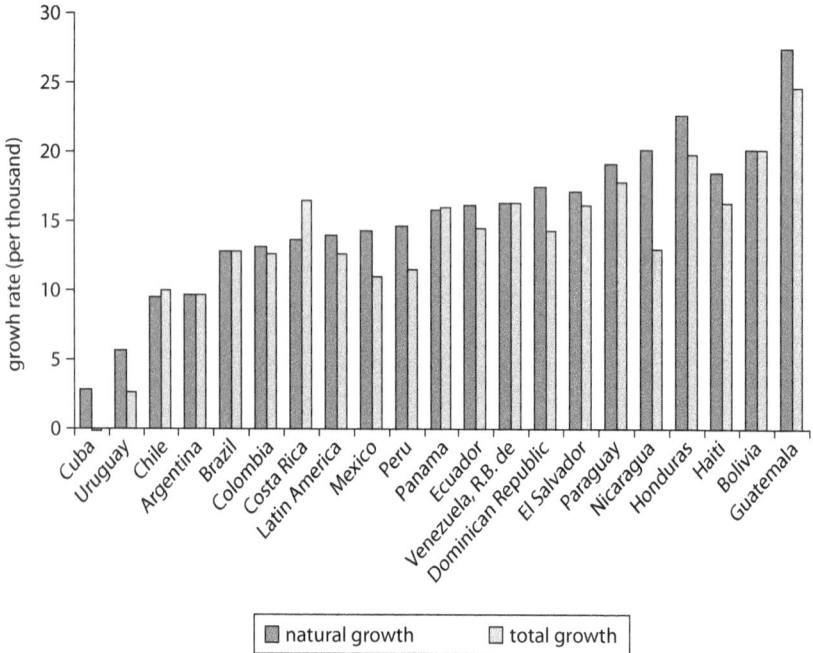

Source: CELADE/ECLAC population estimates and projections 2007.

in particular, European immigration in the early 20th century helped populate the country and was considered a key factor in the early decline in fertility. Although Argentina continues to receive migrants, especially from neighboring countries, it only offsets the effect of increasing emigration (Guzmán and others 2006). Other interesting cases are that of República Bolivariana de Venezuela, where population growth increased by around 40 percent during the 1970s as a result of immigration, and Cuba, where the negative total growth rate is due to emigration.

Although future migration is extremely difficult to predict over the long run due to its close link with short-term aspects of the economic conjuncture—that is, with economic crises or sudden job opportunities arising from a neighboring country—it will likely play an increasingly important role in national population dynamics, given the increasing globalization of economies, the increased access to labor markets, and greater opportunities for individual mobility.

Changes in Population Size and Age Structure

Changes in population size and structure are determined by changes in mortality, fertility, and migration levels. In addition, population tends to grow even beyond the point that replacement-level fertility is achieved due to the effect of population momentum (Bongaarts and Bulatao 1999). This phenomenon results from the large number of young people associated with former high fertility rates. As these youths grow older and move through reproductive ages, the greater number of births tends to exceed the number of deaths in the older populations for a certain period of time (World Bank 2003). This is already the case in some LAC countries such as Chile and Costa Rica, where fertility has reached or fallen below replacement level but the population continues to grow, due to the still relatively high proportion of young people and people of childbearing age.

Population Growth and Size

The LAC population has been growing at declining rates. In 1950, the average annual population growth rate in the region was 2.8 percent. Currently, the growth rate has dropped to 1.3 percent, and by 2050 population is expected to be growing at a rate close to zero (approximately 0.3 percent). However, opposing trends are observed if we look at specific age groups: while the adult population (aged 15–59) is growing at declining rates and the young population (aged 0–14) will soon start to decline in absolute numbers, the growth rate of the older population (aged 60 and over) is expected to follow an upward trend until 2010–15. After that, the growth rate might begin to fall, although remaining well above the growth rates of the other age groups (see figure 2.4).

In absolute numbers, the population increased 3.5 times over the last half-century—from 161 million in 1950 to 547 million in 2005—and is projected to increase an additional 40 percent over the next 45 years, to reach 763 million in 2050.

Considerable variation exists among different age groups. While the young population increased 2.5 times between 1950 and 2005 and is expected to decline by around 17 percent between 2005 and 2050, the adult population expanded 3.8 times in the first period and is projected to continue increasing over the second period, but only by 33 percent. Yet, the most significant change concerns the older population, which increased 5.4 times between 1950 and 2005, and will practically quadruple between

Figure 2.4   Population Growth Rates by Major Age Group in LAC, 1950–2050

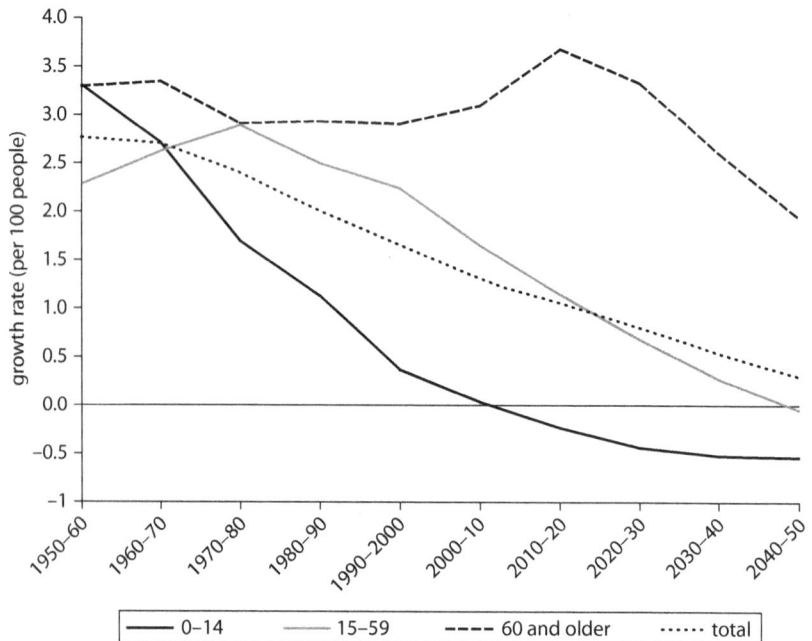

Source: CELADE/ECLAC population estimates and projections 2007.

2005 and 2050. The magnitude of the older population is expected to match that of the youth population for the first time in history around 2040. By 2050, the older population is expected to outnumber the youth population by 30 percent (see figure 2.5 and table 2.4).

According to figure 2.5, the youth population is expected to stop growing around 2020, while the working-age population is expected to expand up to 2045. After that, population growth in LAC will be entirely due to increases in the older population. This situation certainly

Figure 2.5   Population by Age Group in LAC, 1950–2050

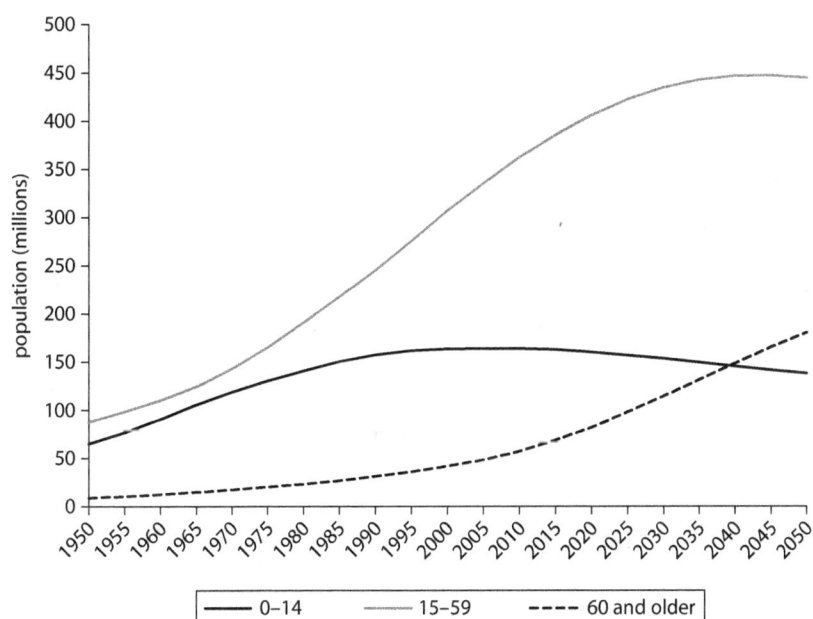

Source: CELADE/ECLAC population estimates and projections 2007.

Table 2.4   Population by Major Age Group in LAC, 1950, 2005, and 2050

Age group (years)	Population (thousands)		
	1950	*2005*	*2050*
Total	167,626	558,818	776,631
0–14	67,449	166,479	138,146
15–59	90,843	342,111	451,764
60 and older	9,334	50,228	186,721

Source: CELADE/ECLAC population estimates and projections 2007.

places population aging among the main demographic phenomena of this era.

Age Structure

The share of the distinct age groups in the total population in LAC has changed considerably over time as they grew at different rates. Although in absolute terms the youth population will continue to grow until 2020, its proportion has been declining since 1970 and is expected to continue declining. Similarly, the share of the adult population is expected to start declining after 2020 even though its magnitude will continue to expand until 2045. Whereas the share of the youth and adult populations are predicted to decrease, the share of the older population is expected to increase steadily over the entire period considered in this study (see figure 2.6).

Although current figures on the proportion of the older population seem to be at a reasonable level, they are deceptive if taken as an indication of the future, since the process of population aging should speed up considerably in the near future. In fact, between 1950 and 2000, the proportion of the population aged 60 and over increased only moderately, from 5.5 percent to 8.8 percent. Over the next 50 years, however, it will rise from 8.8 percent to 23.6 percent, which means, in

Figure 2.6   Population Distribution by Major Age Group in LAC, 1950–2045

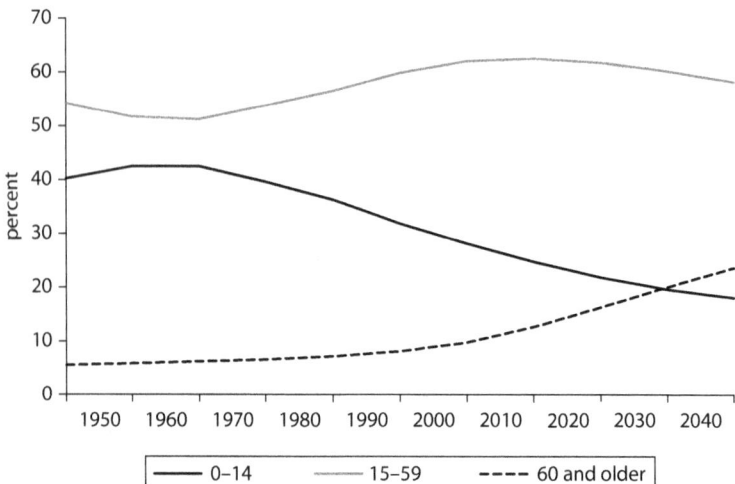

Source: CELADE/ECLAC population estimates and projections 2007.

absolute terms, an increase from around 9 million to 180 million in the course of a century.

Nevertheless, population aging in LAC will not be a homogeneous process across countries. In many countries of the region, the young and working-age populations will still play a major role in population growth well into the 21st century, thus continuing to constitute a considerable source of demand for social sectors and posing a challenge for public policy.

Demographic Transition, Dependency Ratios, and Demographic Dividend

Demographic Transition

Like other developing regions, LAC is going through a period of profound demographic changes known as the demographic transition (Zavala de Cosío 1995; Wong, Carvalho, and Aguirre 2000; Fígoli and Wong 2003; CEPAL 2008a). This is a relatively long process that starts with high mortality and fertility rates and ends with much lower ones. Population growth is low at both ends of the process, but tends to increase as the process unfolds and mortality rates decline, and then to decrease again when fertility rates come down. In LAC, the fact that the onset of the decline of the mortality and fertility rates did not coincide produced a relatively short period of rapid population growth in the middle of the 20th century that substantially altered the age structure of the population.

During the initial stage of the demographic transition—in which mortality, especially among children, falls, but fertility remains high—the region's population remained quite young and even became somewhat younger as a result of the growing proportion of children. Beginning in the mid-1960s, the joint effect of the decline in fertility and sustained increase in life expectancy gave rise to a gradual process of population aging that tends to intensify in the future as the larger generations born during the initial stage of the transition progress through the life cycle.

As noted, regional averages tend to conceal major differences at the country level in terms of the pace and intensity of demographic change. In order to analyze this variation and obtain a comprehensive view of the changes under way in the region, CEPAL (2008a) has classified LAC countries into four stages of demographic transition according to life expectancy and fertility rates: very advanced, advanced, full, and moderate (see Annex 2A.2).

Only Barbados and Cuba are classified in the very advanced stage of transition. Fertility in Cuba, which was already fairly low in the middle of the 20th century compared with the regional average, reached replacement level much earlier than any other country in the region (between the late 1970s and early 1980s). Since then, fertility in Cuba has continued to decline, reaching its current and well-below-replacement-level rate of 1.5 children per woman. Its population is currently growing at a natural rate of 0.29 percent, which is completely atypical for the region, while life expectancy at birth (78.3 years) ranks third among Latin American countries after Costa Rica (78.8 years) and Chile (78.5 years).

Latin American countries in the advanced stage of transition fall into three subgroups. The first includes Argentina and Uruguay. In these countries, reductions in both mortality and fertility rates started considerably earlier than in other countries (during the first half of the 20th century). By the middle of the 20th century, fertility rates there had already declined to about three children per woman. The second subgroup is Chile, which, despite having a fertility rate in 1950 similar to that of Cuba, has not experienced a fertility decline as sharply as Cuba. Chile is nonetheless the second subgroup in the region where fertility has fallen below the replacement level. As in Argentina and Uruguay, the current population growth rate in Chile is less than 1 percent. The third subgroup within advanced transition countries includes Brazil, Colombia, Costa Rica, and Mexico. Unlike the other countries at this stage of transition, fertility rates in these countries remained extremely high (between six and eight children per woman) until the mid-1960s. However, by the late 1980s to early 1990s, these rates had already halved or dropped even further. The natural population growth rate in this subgroup is currently between 1.3 percent and 1.4 percent.

Levels of mortality and fertility also vary among the Caribbean countries classified as in the advanced stage of transition. Trinidad and Tobago at one extreme shows the lowest levels of fertility, but a relatively low life expectancy. At the other end of the spectrum are Guadeloupe, Martinique, and Puerto Rico, where life expectancy has substantially increased in recent decades.

Two groups of Latin American countries are in the full transition stage. On the one hand, there are those where fertility had already declined considerably by the early 1980s (the Dominican Republic, Ecuador, El Salvador, Panama, Peru, and República Bolivariana de Venezuela). On the other hand, there are those where more significant reductions in fertility took place more recently (Honduras, Nicaragua, and Paraguay). Although fertility rates in both groups of countries have now leveled out around the regional average, their natural population growth rates still differ, ranging from 1.5 percent in Peru to 2.3 percent in Honduras.

Countries classified as in the full transition stage in the Caribbean are Belize, French Guiana, Guyana, Jamaica, and Suriname. Here again, mortality and fertility differences are noticeable among countries. Whereas mortality and fertility levels in Jamaica are close to the regional average, in Guyana and Suriname fertility levels are low, but mortality levels are considerably higher than the regional average. At the other extreme, Belize and French Guiana show relatively high levels of fertility but below-average levels of mortality (the longest life expectancy among the countries in this group).

Countries classified as in the moderate transition stage in Latin America are Bolivia, Guatemala, and Haiti. Fertility has dropped in all three countries but remains far above the regional average. The decline has been particularly slow in Guatemala, which now has the highest fertility rate in the region (4.2 children per woman) and the highest rate of population growth (2.8 percent). Haiti and Bolivia, on the other hand, have the highest levels of mortality in the region, with a life expectancy of about 61 and 66 years, respectively, well below the regional average of 73.

Despite the diversity of demographic situations among countries in the region, LAC can be said to have undergone a rapid process of demographic transition compared with that experienced by industrialized countries (ECLAC/CELADE/IDB 1996). Whereas the demographic transition lasted over a century in developed countries, similar changes are occurring at a much faster pace in Latin America, due in part to the greater availability of means for controlling fertility and reducing mortality in more recent times. In a period of approximately 30 years, between 1960 and 1990, fertility levels in Latin America decreased from among the world's highest to considerably below the global average. Consequently, changes in the age structure of the population, particularly aging, are occurring faster in Latin America than they did in the industrialized countries, which calls for the implementation of innovative measures to tackle the challenges and take advantage of the opportunities raised by the demographic changes.

Changes in Dependency Ratios in Latin America

Since people's economic behavior is strongly associated to the stage they are at in the life cycle, changes in age structure tend to have a major impact on economic development. A high proportion of economically dependent persons in the population (children and older persons, in general) usually constrain economic growth, because a significant portion of resources is allocated to attend to their needs. In contrast, a large share of working-age people can boost economic growth, since a larger proportion of workers and a lower level of spending on dependent persons tends to accelerate the accumulation of capital.

In this regard, the dependency ratio—which relates the number of people in dependent age groups (children under age 15 and persons over age 59, in this study) to that of people in the working-age group (aged 15–59, in this study)—is a valuable indicator of the potential effects of demographic changes on socioeconomic development. The dependency ratio can also be disaggregated into a child dependency ratio, which relates the number of children to that of people of working age, and the old-age-dependency ratio, which relates the number of older persons to that of people of working age. In general, dependency ratios are expressed in terms of the number of people in dependent age groups for every 100 people of working age.

It is important, however, to understand the limitations of dependency ratios expressed in terms of age ranges. First, in most populations, people do not automatically cease to be economically active at a specific age. In addition, not everyone in the working-age group is economically active, particularly among the female population (despite the increasing participation of women in the labor market). Similarly, as professional training becomes more lengthy, a growing number of young adults remain in the education system and outside the labor market longer (thereby extending the period of dependence far beyond adolescence). These observations suggest that trends in dependency ratios examined in this section offer only an indication of the economic impact of age structural changes.

Between 1950 and the mid-1960s, the dependency ratio in Latin America increased due to the relative increase in the child population, until reaching a maximum value of 97 dependents per 100 people of working age. Following the decline in fertility rates in the mid-1960s, the dependency ratio started a steady decline, which is expected to last until 2019, when the ratio will reach its minimum value of 60 before increasing again, due to the growing proportion of older persons. Although, in general, Latin American countries coincide with this model in terms of shape, there are huge variations from one country to another in terms of timing (see Annex 2A.3).

To illustrate this point, figure 2.7 shows the situation in three countries that are at different stages of the demographic transition: Cuba, in the very advanced stage; Mexico, in the advanced stage; and Guatemala, in the moderate stage. In Cuba, the period in which the dependency ratio declines (17 years) is much shorter than in the other countries (56 years in Mexico and 62 years in Guatemala), and after stabilizing at relatively low levels for a long period of time is expected to rise again much faster than in the other countries. In Mexico, the dependency ratio, which was extremely high at the beginning of the period due to the high proportion of children, started a steep downward trend by the mid-1960s that is expected to last until the middle of the 2020s, when it will gradually increase again. In Guatemala, the decline of the dependency ratio has been far more gradual because fertility rates have remained relatively high. In this country, the dependency ratio is projected to continue declining at least until the middle of the 21st century. As a result of these varying trends, a convergent trend is projected in child dependency ratios (figure 2.8) and a divergent trend in old-age dependency ratios (figure 2.9).

Figure 2.10 shows how the dependency ratio will vary over the next few decades in selected Latin American countries at different stages of the demographic transition. The year 2008 is taken as the base year (equal to 100) against which projections up to 2050 are compared. It

Figure 2.7   Dependency Ratio in Selected Countries, 1950–2050

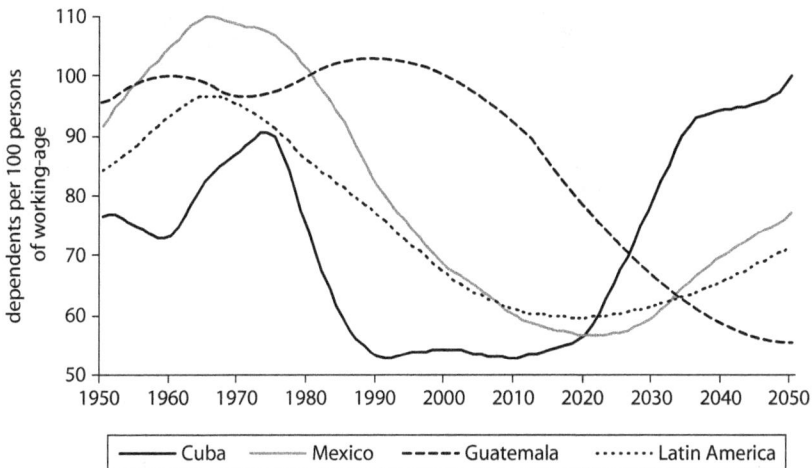

Source: CELADE/ECLAC population estimates and projections 2007.

Figure 2.8   Child Dependency Ratio in Selected LAC Countries, 1950–2050

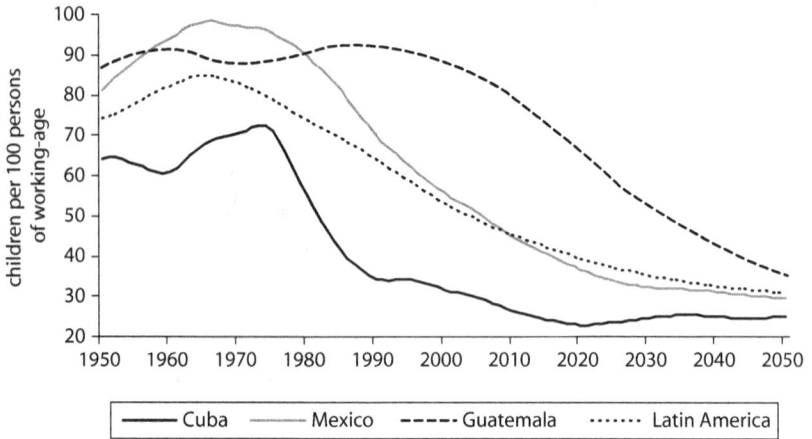

Source: CELADE/ECLAC population estimates and projections 2007.

Figure 2.9   Old Age Dependency Ratio in Selected LAC Countries, 1950–2050

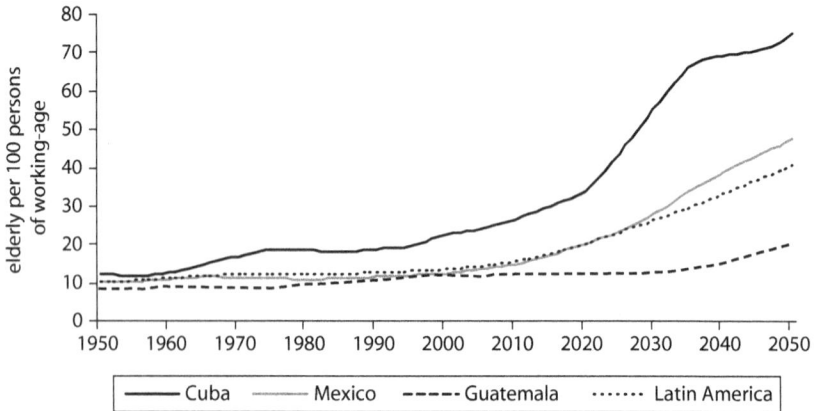

Source: CELADE/ECLAC population estimates and projections 2007.

clearly indicates a strong upward trend in countries at later stages of the transition (Chile and Cuba); a less accentuated upward trend in countries at intermediate stages of the transition (Brazil and Mexico); and a downward trend in countries furthest behind in the transition process (Bolivia and Guatemala). A comparison of the extreme cases

Figure 2.10   Future Trends in Dependency Ratio in Selected LAC Countries, 2008–50

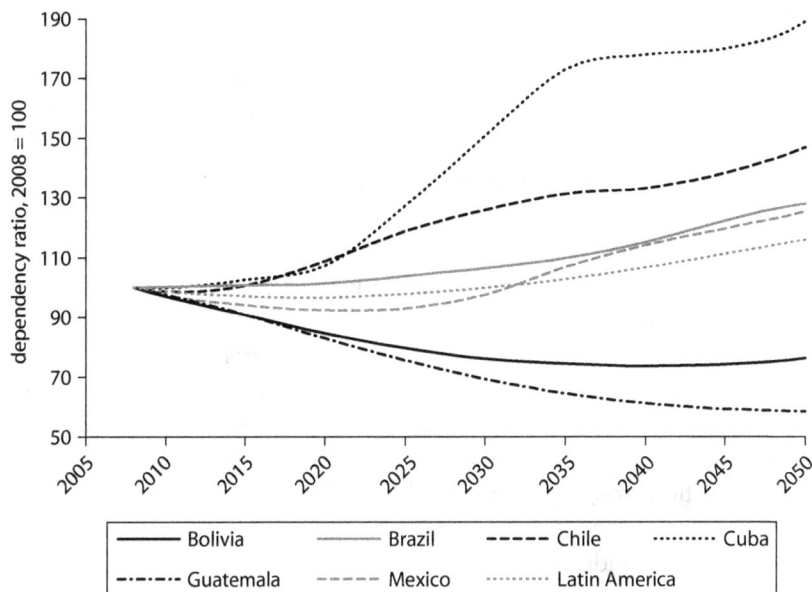

Source: CELADE/ECLAC population estimates and projections 2007.

of Cuba and Guatemala provides a clear picture of the diversity of demographic situations in the region: while in Cuba the dependency ratio is expected to practically double by 2050, in Guatemala it is expected to be nearly halved.

The Demographic Dividend

There is a period during the demographic transition in which the dependency ratio drops substantially as the share of the working-age population grows relative to the dependent-age population. During this period, the situation is particularly favorable for development because there are more possibilities for savings and investment in economic growth, and less pressure on primary education spending (CEPAL 2008b). Various terms have been coined to describe this period, including, as mentioned, "demographic dividend," "demographic bonus," or "demographic window of opportunity," which refers to the possibility of increasing rates of economic growth per capita and hence increasing levels of well-being of the population during this period (Bloom, Canning, and Sevilla 2003; Wong and Carvalho 2006a).

The benefits associated with this period do not accrue automatically. They are subject to the adoption of macroeconomic policies that encourage productive investment, increase employment opportunities, and promote a stable social and economic environment conducive to sustained development (Adioetomo and others 2005; Bloom, Canning, and Sevilla 2006; Wong and Carvalho 2006b). In particular, they require major investments in human capital in order to increase productivity.

The recent history of many Southeast Asian countries shows that the combination of a large pool of young workers with high job skills and a relatively small contingent of dependent older people creates a situation that is highly favorable for economic growth. The increase in productivity observed in these countries was due to a large extent to the considerable investments made in the education of young people during the period of the demographic dividend (UNFPA 1998; Mason 2002).

There is no exact measurement of the beginning and end of the demographic dividend, and its definition in terms of the dependency ratio tends to vary. In this study, the period corresponding to the demographic dividend has been subdivided into three phases. In the first phase, the dependency ratio declines but is still fairly high (above two-thirds, that is, two persons in dependent-age groups for every three persons in working-age groups). In the second phase, the dependency ratio falls below two-thirds and continues to decrease. In the third and final phase, the dependency ratio begins to rise as the proportion of older people increases, but is still below two-thirds. The two thirds cut-off point was chosen arbitrarily to serve as an illustrative benchmark.[2]

While the countries of the region show little difference as regards the onset of the demographic dividend,[3] the extent and duration of its different phases vary significantly (see figure 2.11). Generally speaking, countries more advanced into the demographic transition have a shorter period of dividend left than countries that are behind in the process. In Chile and Cuba, for example, the dividend is expected to come to an end sometime in the first quarter of this century. In Brazil and Costa Rica, it will last until the beginning of the 2040s, while in Ecuador and Peru it is expected to finish around 2050. In seven countries, the dividend should last beyond the middle of the century, including the extreme cases of Bolivia (2062) and Guatemala (2069).

Figure 2.11   Period and Stages of Demographic Dividend in Latin American Countries

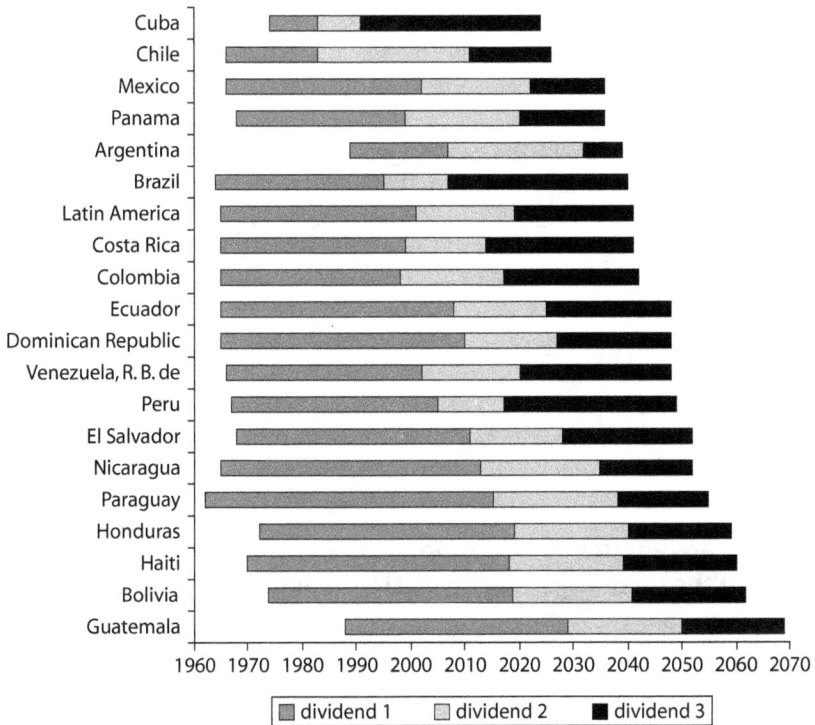

Source: CELADE/ECLAC population estimates and projections 2007.
Note: Dividend 1 = dependency ratio above two-thirds and declining; dividend 2 = dependency ratio below two-thirds and declining; dividend 3 = dependency ratio below two-thirds and increasing.

Uruguay represents a special case in which no demographic dividend as defined in this study takes place. While the dependency ratio in Latin America is expected to decrease by 38 percent on average, in Uruguay it is expected to decrease by only 9 percent. In addition, after reaching a maximum value (74 in 1989) significantly lower than the regional average (97 in 1965), the dependency ratio in Uruguay is expected to remain above two dependents per each three persons of working age during the whole projection period (see Annex 2A.3). This situation is in part associated with both the smoothness of fertility decline and the important out-migration flow of young people of working age.

Taken as a whole, the Latin American population is currently in the second and most favorable stage of the demographic dividend, in which the dependency ratio has already reached relatively low levels and continues to fall. This period started at the beginning of this century (2001) and is expected to last until the end of the next decade (2019), when the third stage starts, and should last until the beginning of the 2040s. Currently, only two countries are in the third phase of the demographic dividend: Cuba, since 1991; and Brazil, since 2007. Chile is expected to enter this final phase very shortly (2011), and eight other countries are already in the second phase: Argentina, Colombia, Costa Rica, Ecuador, Mexico, Panama, Peru, and República Bolivariana de Venezuela. The remaining Latin American countries are still in the first phase (see figure 2.11).

In the Caribbean, where transition to lower levels of fertility began earlier than in Latin America, almost all countries (with a few exceptions such as Jamaica) have already surpassed the first stage of the demographic dividend. Many countries, such as Aruba, Barbados, Puerto Rico, Trinidad and Tobago, and the U.S. Virgin Islands have already reached the third stage, while the others remain in the second stage.

Taking Advantage of the Demographic Dividend to Face the Challenges of Population Aging

Practically all LAC countries are in a period that is particularly conducive to economic development. In some countries, this period has already entered, or is about to enter, into a final phase, while in others it is just beginning and should last for the next five or six decades. Sooner for some countries and later for others, the advantage of a favorable ratio between the working-age population and the dependent-age population will disappear as the share of older persons steadily increases.

The demographic dividend period will then be followed by a period of rapid population aging that will pose new social and economic challenges to the society and require the implementation of public policies and programs in multiple areas, including the provision of long-term health care and the financing of pensions for a progressively aging population.

Population aging will take place in all countries across the region, inverting the dependency ratio as the number of older dependents steadily increases in relation to the number of children and working-age adults. If this phase is reached in adverse economic conditions, with little or no economic growth or accumulated savings, the burden placed by the dependent older population on the economically active population will require huge transfers of resources from the latter to the former, which might create not only intergenerational conflict, but also solvency problems that could jeopardize the financing of key systems, such as health care and social security.

The demographic dividend represents a unique opportunity to prepare for the future. Taking advantage of the demographic dividend by investing in education and creating productive jobs not only generates more opportunities for the young people of today, but the dividends of such investments are essential for creating the necessary savings and productive conditions to properly deal with the exponential increase in costs that is expected to come with society's inexorable aging.

Annex 2.1 Population Projection, Dependency Ratio, and Demographic Dividend under Different Demographic Assumptions[4]

A Brief Explanation of Low-, Medium-, and High-fertility Variants

The United Nations revises its official population estimates and projections every two years by incorporating all new and relevant evidence regarding the demographic dynamics in each country or area of the world and formulating detailed assumptions about the future paths of the demographic variables.[5]

However, because future trends cannot be known with certainty, a number of projection variants are produced, most of them differing exclusively in the assumptions made regarding the future path of fertility. For the purpose of this exercise, the medium-fertility variant, usually recommended as the most likely one, is compared with the extreme (and unlikely) cases of the low- and high-fertility variants.

The fertility assumptions are described in terms of three groups of countries: (a) high fertility: countries that until 2010 had no fertility reduction or only an incipient decline; (b) medium fertility: countries where fertility has been declining but whose level was still above 2.1 children per woman in 2005–10; and (c) low fertility: countries with total fertility at or below 2.1 children per woman in 2005–10.

Under the medium-fertility variant, total fertility in all countries is assumed to converge eventually toward a level of 1.85 children per woman. However, not all countries reach this level during the projection period, that is, by 2045–50. Projection procedures differ slightly depending on whether a country had a total fertility rate above or below 1.85 children per woman in 2005–10.

Fertility in high- and medium-fertility countries is assumed to follow a path derived from models of fertility decline established by the United

Nations Population Division on the basis of the past experience of all countries with declining fertility during 1950–2010. If the total fertility projected by a model for a country falls to 1.85 children per woman before 2050, total fertility is held constant at that level for the remainder of the projection period (that is, until 2050). If the model of fertility change produces a total fertility above 1.85 children per woman for 2045–50, that value is used in projecting the population.

Under the high-fertility variant, fertility is projected to remain 0.5 children above the fertility in the medium variant over most of the projection period. By 2045–50, fertility in the high variant is therefore half a child higher than that of the medium variant.

Under the low-fertility variant, fertility is projected to remain 0.5 children below the fertility in the medium variant over most of the projection period. By 2045–50, fertility in the low variant is therefore half a child lower than that of the medium variant.

Projection Variations Under Low-, Medium-, and High-fertility Variants

Figure 2.12 shows the absolute numbers of total population and broad age groups from 1950 to 2050 under the medium, high, and low variants of the UN population projections. Under the medium variant, the total population in the region is estimated to grow to approximately 729 million and would range between 626 million and 845 million under the high and low variants (see also table 2.5).

The major impact of the different variants can be seen in the group of children under age 15. The number of children would range somewhere between a low of 75 million and a high of 185 million in 2050, which illustrates how the different assumptions on fertility mostly affect the group of infants and children. Only under the high-fertility variant would the number of children keep growing during the entire projection period. In contrast, under the low and medium variants the number of children would start to fall around 2015. The number of the working-age population (aged 15–59) is estimated to keep growing steadily until around 2030, after which it would start to decline under the low and medium variants, but the growth would continue under the high variant. The total number of working-age people is estimated at between 365 million and 474 million in 2050. The number of older adults (aged 60 and over) does not vary under the different variants because the assumptions on mortality remain equal in all variants. The older population would outnumber the children around 2030 under the

Figure 2.12   Population by Major Age Groups under Different Projection Variants in LAC, 1950–2050

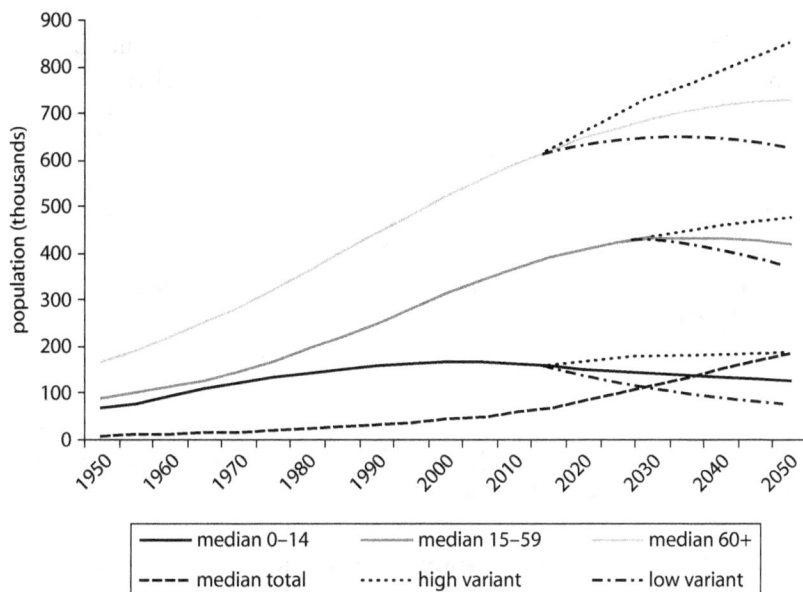

Source: United Nations Population Division, Department of Economic and Social Affairs (DESA), population estimates and projections 2008 revision.

Table 2.5   Population by Major Age Groups under Different Projection Variants in LAC, 1950–2050

Age group (years)	1950	2005	2050 Low	2050 Medium	2050 High
Population (thousands)					
Total	167,307	556,512	625,884	729,185	845,110
0–14	67,293	165,645	75,281	124,274	184,594
15–59	90,625	340,747	364,567	418,875	474,480
60 and older	9,389	50,120	186,036	186,036	186,036
Population (%)					
Total	100.0	100.0	100.0	100.0	100.0
0–14	40.2	29.8	12.0	17.0	21.8
15–59	54.2	61.2	58.2	57.4	56.1
60 and older	5.6	9.0	29.7	25.5	22.0

Source: United Nations Population Division, Department of Economic and Social Affairs (DESA), population estimates and projections 2008 revision.
Note: Figures in table differ slightly from ECLAC's estimates and projections because of adjustments made by DESA for international migration.

low variant, around 2040 under the medium variant, and around 2050 under the high variant.

The older persons' share of the total population does vary, however, and in 2050 would be somewhere between 22 and 30 percent, the most probable value being 26 percent (table 2.5 and figure 2.13). Under the low and medium variant, the share of older adults of the total population would double from around 10 percent in 2010 to 20 percent around 2035.

The percentage of children varies significantly under the three projection scenarios, ranging between 12 and 22 percent in 2050, depending on the fertility assumption. The share of children is estimated to keep declining under all three variants, the decline being slower under the high variant. The percentage of the working-age population would start to fall around 2020, independent of the fertility assumptions. By the end of the projection period, the share of population aged 15–59 is estimated to be lower than in 2010 under all three variants, which is also reflected in changes in the dependency ratios.

Figure 2.13   Population Distribution by Major Age Groups under Different Projection Variants in LAC, 1950–2050

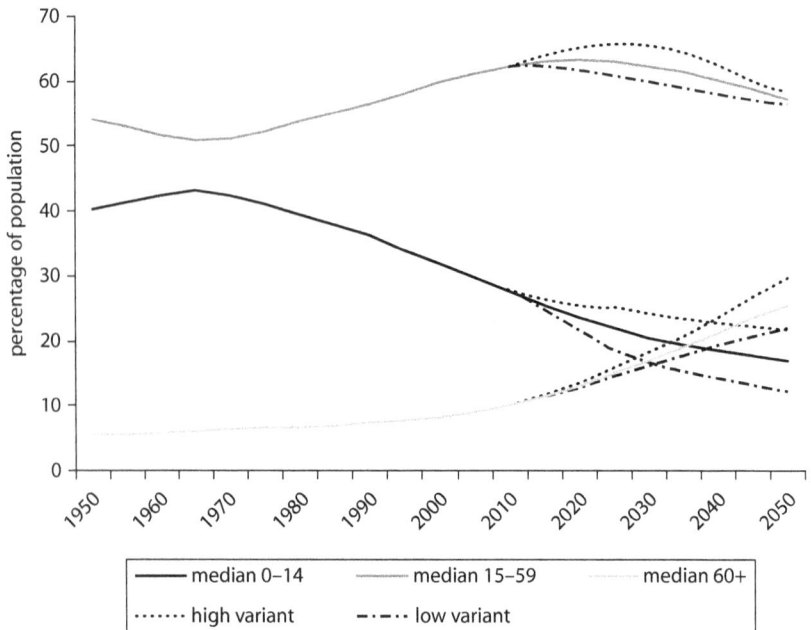

Source: United Nations Population Division, Department of Economic and Social Affairs (DESA), population estimates and projections 2008 revision.

The total dependency ratio is estimated to keep falling modestly until 2020, after which it would start to grow. In the high-fertility variant, the growth would start later, around 2025, and the variation between different assumptions on fertility would be largest between 2025 and 2035. By 2050, however, the differences in the total dependency ratio under the three variants are projected to be quite small, ranging from 72 to 78 dependents per 100 persons of working age. The major impact of using different projection variants is structural, which is illustrated by the increasing differences in child- and old-age dependency ratios (figure 2.14 and table 2.6).

The child dependency ratio is estimated to fall under all three variants, dropping from 44 dependents in 2010 to 30 dependents in 2050 under the medium variant. Under the high variant, the drop in child dependency ratio would be quite modest, reaching 40 dependents in 2050. Under the low variant the ratio would more than halve in the period. The old-age dependency ratio is estimated to more than double under all three variants. It is expected that in 2010 there will be about 16 persons 60 years and over per every 100 persons of working age. This number

Figure 2.14   Total Child and Old-age Dependency Ratios under Different Projection Variants in LAC, 2010–50

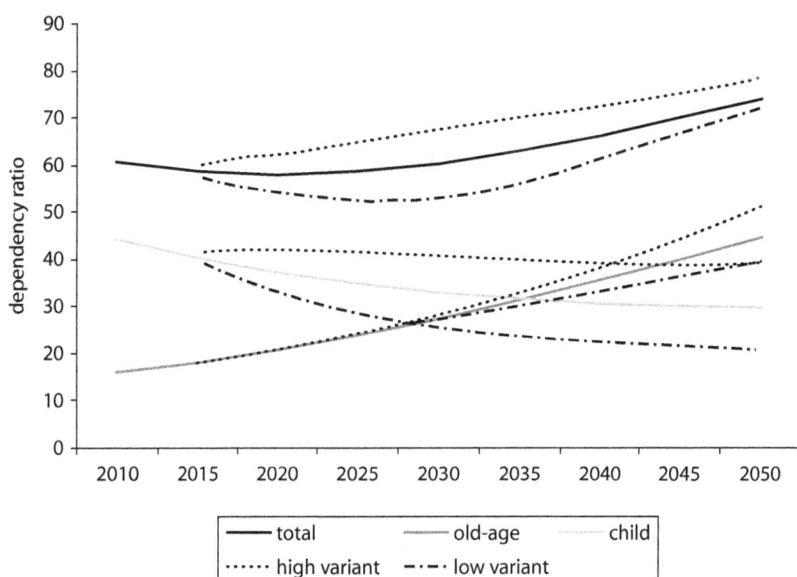

Source: United Nations Population Division, Department of Economic and Social Affairs (DESA), population estimates and projections 2008 revision.

Table 2.6   Total, Child, and Old-age Dependency Ratios under Different Projection Variants in LAC, 1950–2050

			Dependents per 100 persons of working age		
				2050	
Dependency ratio	1950	2005	Low	Medium	High
Total dependency	84.4	63.3	71.7	74.1	78.1
Child dependency	74.2	48.9	20.6	29.7	38.9
Old-age dependency	10.2	14.4	51.0	44.4	39.2

Source: DESA, population estimates and projections 2008 revision.
Note: Figures in table differ slightly from ECLAC's estimates and projections because of adjustments made by DESA for international migration.

would almost triple under the medium variant to 44 dependents in 2050 and could be as high as 51 dependents under the low-fertility variant.

Figure 2.15 shows the timing of the demographic dividend for Mexico, Guatemala, and Cuba under the three projection variants and the timing for Latin America under the medium variant. Of the three countries, Cuba is the most advanced in the aging process, and by the mid-1990s had already completed the first and second stages (as defined in this study) of the demographic dividend. Thus, population projections have no effect on the timing of the two first stages. In addition, the impact of using different fertility assumptions on the end date of the third and final stage (2024 under the medium variant) would be minimal (2022 under the high variant and 2027 under the low variant).

Because Mexico and especially Guatemala are less advanced than Cuba in the process of demographic transition, their demographic dividend would be more affected under the high and low projection variants, particularly regarding the duration of each of the different stages. The impact on the total duration, however, would be relatively small. In the case of Mexico, the impact of different variants can be seen in the duration of the second stage of the demographic dividend, which would be notably shorter under the high variant (lasting only 13 years) compared with the medium variant (20 years) and the low variant (24 years). The duration of the third stage of the dividend would remain fairly unchanged, ranging from 13 to 15 years.

For Guatemala, the impact of the different variants is more notable due to the younger population age structure and higher current fertility. In this case, the second stage of the demographic dividend would start somewhere between 2021 (low variant) and 2035 (high variant). Under the high-fertility variant, the second stage would be only 13 years long

Figure 2.15   Future Trends in Dependency Ratio in Selected LAC Countries, 2008–2070

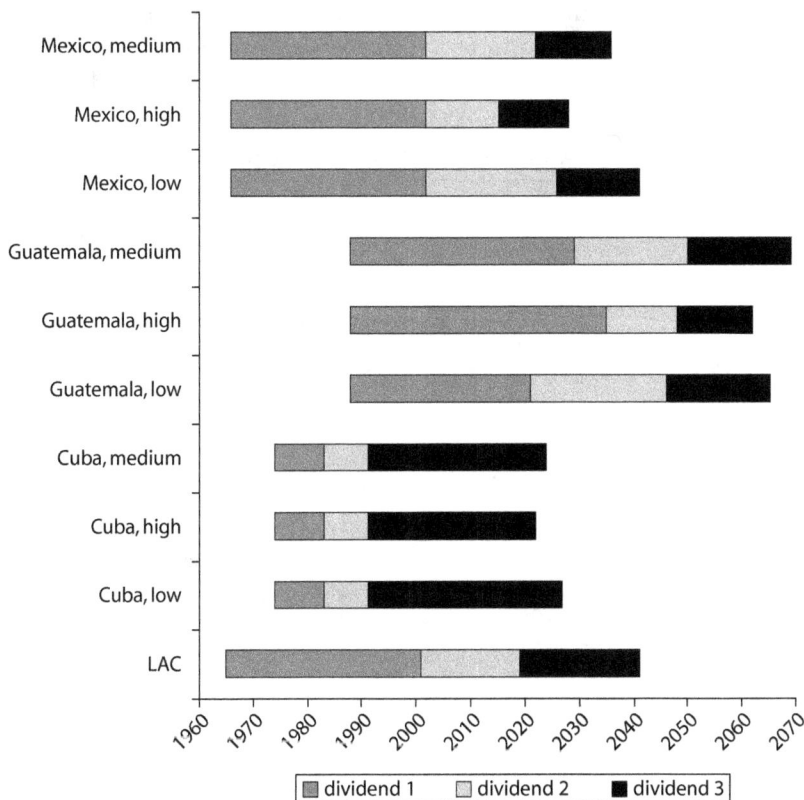

Sources: CELADE, Population Division of ECLAC (for Cuba, Guatemala, and Mexico); DESA, Population Division (for Latin America), population estimates and projections 2008 revision.
Note: Dividend 1 = dependency ratio above two-thirds and declining; dividend 2 = dependency ratio below two-thirds and declining; dividend 3 = dependency ratio below two-thirds and increasing.

compared to 21 under the medium variant and 25 under the low variant. Under the high variant, the third stage of the dividend would also be quite short in Guatemala, lasting only 14 years compared to 19 years under the other two variants. The second stage of the dividend would have the same duration in Mexico and Guatemala under the different variants but the onset would be about 25 years later in Guatemala, where the third stage is estimated to last beyond 2060.

In conclusion, experiments with the high-, medium- and low-fertility variants of the population projection show that population aging is an irreversible trend regardless of the assumptions on future fertility trends.

The effects of using different variants of population projection tend to be rather modest on the demographic dividend, especially in countries that are more advanced in the demographic transition process. Even assumptions on fertility that lead to fairly unlikely scenarios for the future produce only moderate changes in the timing of the demographic dividend.

Annex 2A.2   Countries According to the Stage of Demographic Transition in LAC

Stage of demographic transition	Economy	Life expectancy (years)	Total fertility rate (number of children born per woman)
Very advanced	Barbados	77.3	1.5
	Cuba	78.3	1.5
Advanced	Argentina	75.2	2.3
	Bahamas, The	73.5	2.0
	Brazil	72.4	2.2
	Chile	78.5	1.9
	Colombia	72.8	2.2
	Costa Rica	78.8	2.1
	Guadeloupe	79.2	2.1
	Martinique	79.5	1.9
	Mexico	76.1	2.2
	Netherlands Antilles	75.1	1.9
	Puerto Rico	78.7	1.8
	St. Lucia	73.7	2.2
	Trinidad and Tobago	69.8	1.6
	Uruguay	76.2	2.1
Full	Belize	76.1	2.9
	Dominican Republic	72.2	2.8
	Ecuador	75.0	2.6
	El Salvador	71.8	2.7
	French Guiana	75.9	3.3
	Guyana	66.8	2.3
	Honduras	72.1	3.3
	Jamaica	72.6	2.4
	Nicaragua	72.9	2.8
	Panama	75.6	2.6
	Paraguay	71.8	3.1
	Peru	71.4	2.5
	Suriname	70.2	2.4
	Venezuela, R.B. de	73.8	2.5
Moderate	Bolivia	65.5	3.5
	Guatemala	70.2	4.2
	Haiti	60.6	3.5

Sources: CELADE/ECLAC population estimates and projections 2007; Population Division of UN/DESA, "World Population Prospects: The 2006 Revision."

Annex 2A.3 Aspects of Dependency Ratio Trends in LAC

Country	Reduction period of dependency ratio						Period for which dependency ratio remains below two-thirds		
	Maximum value	Year of maximum value	Minimum value	Year of minimum value	Duration (years)	Magnitude (%)	Starting year	Final year	Duration (years)
Latin America									
Argentina	78	1989	63	2032	43	19	2011	2037	26
Bolivia	95	1974	57	2041	67	40	2021	2060	39
Brazil	97	1964	58	2007	43	41	1996	2038	42
Chile	92	1966	54	2011	45	41	1985	2024	39
Colombia	109	1965	56	2017	52	49	2000	2039	39
Costa Rica	115	1965	53	2014	49	54	2000	2038	38
Cuba	91	1974	53	1991	17	42	1983	2024	41
Dominican Republic	114	1965	63	2027	62	44	2015	2042	27
Ecuador	105	1965	61	2025	60	43	2010	2045	35
El Salvador	104	1968	57	2028	60	45	2013	2047	34
Guatemala	103	1988	55	2050	62	46	2031	2067	36
Haiti	92	1970	57	2039	69	38	2021	2057	36
Honduras	111	1972	56	2040	68	50	2021	2057	36
Mexico	110	1966	57	2022	56	49	2005	2034	29
Nicaragua	114	1965	59	2035	70	48	2015	2050	35
Panama	102	1968	61	2020	52	40	2003	2031	28
Paraguay	113	1962	58	2038	76	48	2018	2053	35
Peru	99	1967	59	2017	50	41	2006	2046	40
Uruguay	74	1989	67	2016	27	9	—	—	—
Venezuela, R.B. de	104	1966	61	2020	54	41	2003	2045	42

(continued)

Annex 2A.3 Aspects of Dependency Ratio Trends in LAC *(continued)*

Country	Reduction period of dependency ratio						Period for which dependency ratio remains below two-thirds		
	Maximum value	Year of maximum value	Minimum value	Year of minimum value	Duration (years)	Magnitude (%)	Starting year	Final year	Duration (years)
Caribbean									
Aruba	91	1961	50	1995	34	45	1976	2020	44
Bahamas, The	99	1966	54	2014	48	45	1989	2033	44
Barbados	101	1966	46	2007	41	55	1985	2023	38
Belize	117	1974	56	2035	61	52	—	—	—
Guyana	116	1960	59	2018	58	49	1996	2025	29
Jamaica	125	1971	63	2017	46	49	2010	2028	18
Netherlands Antilles	95	1959	55	2010	51	42	1978	2023	45
Puerto Rico	103	1959	65	2004	45	37	1992	2015	23
St. Lucia	134	1970	56	2011	41	58	2002	2043	41
St. Vincent and the Grenadines	135	1968	57	2019	51	58	2003	2036	33
Suriname	119	1963	59	2017	54	51	2002	2031	29
Trinidad and Tobago	96	1959	46	2007	48	53	1995	2037	42
U.S. Virgin Islands	102	1956	61	1992	36	40	1988	2002	14

Sources: CELADE/ECLAC population estimates and projections 2007; Population Division of UN/DESA, "World Population Prospects: The 2006 Revision."

Note: Dependency ratio in Uruguay does not decrease below two-thirds; in Belize, it does not remain below two-thirds for a continuous period. — = not available.

Notes

1. This age pattern of fertility decline is a classic pattern over the transition, with women increasingly reducing fertility after attaining their desired fertility, and with desired fertility levels dropping over time.

2. Another definition that is often used is based on the rate of change in the ratio and whether that rate of change is positive or negative.

3. Most countries reached the maximum dependency ratio between 1960 and 1975. In Latin America, the only exceptions are Argentina, Guatemala, and Uruguay, where maximum levels were reached around 1990. The Caribbean, the Netherlands Antilles, the U.S. Virgin Islands, Puerto Rico, and Trinidad and Tobago reached the maximum level just before 1960.

4. The author is grateful to Tuuli Pajunen for her support in the preparation of this annex.

5. A general description of the procedures used in revising estimates of population dynamics can be found in United Nations (2004).

References

Adioetomo, S. R., G. Beninguisse, S. Gultiano, Y. Hao, K. Nacro, and I. Pool. 2005. "Policy Implications of Age-structural Changes." CICRED Policy Papers Series, Paris.

Bloom, D., D. Canning, and J. Sevilla. 2003. "The Demographic Dividend: A New Perspective on the Economic Consequences of Population Change." RAND Population Matters Program, N° MR-1274, 2003. Santa Monica, California.

———. 2006. "Growth and the Demographic Transition." NBER Working Papers 6. National Bureau of Economic Research, Cambridge, MA.

Bongaarts, J., and R. A. Bulatao. 1999. "Completing the Demographic Transition." Policy Research Division, Working Paper 125. Population Council, New York.

CEPAL (Comisión Económica para América Latina y el Caribe). 2008a. *Transformaciones demográficas y su influencia en el desarrollo en América Latina y el Caribe.* LC/G.2378 (SES.32/14), Santiago, de Chile.

———. 2008b. "El bono demográfico: una oportunidad para avanzar en cobertura y progresión en educación secundaria." *Panorama social de América Latina 2008*, Capítulo III. (LC/G.2402-P/E), Santiago de Chile.

Chackiel, J., and S. Schkolnik. 1992. "La transición de la fecundidad en América Latina." *Notas de población* (55). Santiago, Chile: Latin American Demographic Center.

Cortes, P. 2005. "Mujeres migrantes de América Latina y el Caribe: derechos humanos, mitos y duras realidades." *Serie Población y Desarrollo* 61. Latin American and Caribbean Demographic Centre/Population Division of the United Nations Economic Commission for Latin America and the Caribbean (CELADE/ECLAC), Santiago, Chile.

ECLAC (Economic Commission for Latin America and the Caribbean). 2005. *Social Panorama of Latin America, 2005* (LC/L.2288-P/E). Santiago, Chile. United Nations publication, Sales No. E.05.II.G.161.

ECLAC/CELADE/IDB (Economic Commission for Latin America and the Caribbean/Latin American Demographic Centre/Inter-American Development Bank). 1996. "Impacto de las tendencias demográficas sobre los sectores sociales en América Latina." Contribución al diseño de políticas y programas, Serie E (45) (LC/DEM/G.161). Santiago, Chile.

Fígoli, M. G. B., and L. R. Wong. 2003. "El camino hacia la estabilización demográfica y el proceso de envejecimiento en América Latina: una ilustración a partir de algunos países seleccionados." *Papeles de población* (35). México, D.F.

Guzmán, J. M., J. Rodríguez, J. Martínez, J. M. Contreras, and D. González. 2006. "The Demography of Latin America and the Caribbean since 1950." *Population* 61: 5–6.

Mason, A., ed. 2002. *Population Change and Economic Development in East Asia: Challenges Met, Opportunities Seized*. Palo Alto, CA: Stanford University Press.

Schkolnik, S., and J. Chackiel. 1998. "América Latina: la transición demográfica en sectores rezagados." *Notas de población* (67/68) (LC/G.2048/E). Santiago, Chile: Economic Commission for Latin America and the Caribbean (ECLAC).

UNFPA (United Nations Population Fund). 1998. "Shift to Smaller Families Can Bring Economic Benefits." News features, http://www.unfpa.org/swp/1998/newsfeature1.htm. United Nations, New York.

United Nations. 2004. "Chapter VI. Methodology of the United Nations Population Estimates and Projections." In *World Population Prospects: The 2004 Revision, Volume III: Analytical Report*. New York: United Nations Department of Economic and Social Affairs/Population Division 99, 100–104.

Wong, L. R., and J. A. M. Carvalho. 2006a. "Age Structural Transition in Brazil: Demographic Bonuses and Emerging Challenges." In *Age Structural Transitions: Challenges for Development*, ed. I. Pool and L. R. Wong. Paris: Comité para la Cooperación Internacional en las Investigaciones Nacionales sobre Demografía (CICRED).

———. 2006b. "El rápido proceso de envejecimiento en los países del tercer mundo y las políticas sociales: el caso de Brasil." *Notas de población* (81): 1–31 (LC/G.2300-P). Santiago de Chile: Comisión Económica para América Latina y el Caribe (CEPAL).

Wong, L. R., J. A. M. Carvalho, and A. Aguirre. 2000. "Duración de la transición demográfica en América Latina y su relación con el desarrollo humano." *Estudios Demográficos y Urbanos* (043): 185–207. México, D.F.: El Colegio de México.

World Bank. 2003. "Population Momentum." *Glossary*. http://www.worldbank .org/depweb/english/modules/glossary.html.

Zavala de Cosío, M. E. 1995. "Dos modelos de transición demográfica en América Latina." *Perfiles latinoamericanos: revista de la Facultad Latinoamericana de Ciencias Sociales* (6): 29–47. Sede México, ISSN 0188-7653.

CHAPTER 3

Poverty, the Aging, and the Life Cycle in Latin America

Daniel Cotlear and Leopoldo Tornarolli

Introduction

This chapter explores how poverty is linked to the life cycle in Latin America and the Caribbean (LAC). Economic behavior varies across the life cycle. There are biological determinants to this variation: children take many years to become independent; the aging become less capable of supporting themselves as they age. Does this make them more vulnerable to poverty? Many of the new antipoverty programs are aimed at families with children and at the aging. Is this a reflection of the relatively higher poverty found among these groups? Much of the focus on antipoverty programs for the aging is on social pensions. Is this the best way to reach the aging poor? To respond to these questions, this chapter will also explore the sources of income of the aging, their living arrangements, and the economic dynamics between the aging and their extended family.

Several recent studies on old-age poverty have provided results for Africa and for LAC. Kakwani and Subbarao (2007) examined data for 14 African countries and concluded that poverty among older people in African countries tracks aggregate poverty rates fairly closely, but that in 10 out of 14 countries, the elderly are overrepresented among the poor, but not by a large margin. For LAC, Gasparini and others (2007), following a methodology first developed by Bourguignon and others (2006), found that poverty among the elderly compared to other age groups differs across countries: while in the countries with well-developed pension systems old-age poverty is substantially lower than the national mean, in many other countries it is similar or higher than the national average.

The methods for this study closely follow the paper by Gasparini and others (2007). Some of the empirical results differ because more recent surveys that were not available before have been incorporated into this study and the poverty line has been recalculated to fit the new international standard, as explained below. Also, this chapter expands the area of inquiry to include poverty among children, investigates in greater detail income sources for the aging beyond pensions, and explores the determinants of living arrangements. The data used in this chapter are drawn from a large database of household surveys from 18 LAC countries: the Socio-Economic Database for Latin America and the Caribbean (SEDLAC), assembled by the Centro de Estudios Distributivos Laborales y Sociales of the Universidad Nacional de La Plata, and the World Bank's poverty group. The surveys are described in table 3.1.

This chapter is organized as follows: Section 2 characterizes LAC countries in sociodemographic terms, paying special attention to the age structure of the population and the living arrangements of older people. After discussing poverty measurement issues in section 3, section 4 presents estimations on the incidence of poverty across age groups in LAC countries. Section 5 evaluates the role of pensions and private transfers in alleviating old-age poverty. Section 6 explores the role of the labor market as a source of income for the older population. Section 7 describes inequality among the aging and compares it with inequality among the rest of the population. Section 8 investigates the determinants for the living arrangements of the aging and discusses familial transfers. Section 9 summarizes the main findings and presents our conclusions.

Demographic and Residence Indicators in Latin America

The population aging process has been heterogeneous across LAC countries, as described in chapter 2. Consequently, the current population structure by age differs markedly among LAC countries. On average, the share of the aging in the total population is below 10 percent. However, the participation of older people in the population varies significantly among countries. That heterogeneity is illustrated in figure 3.1. While older people in Guatemala, Honduras, and Nicaragua represent about 7 percent of their total population, the share in Uruguay is about 20 percent.

Table 3.1 Description of Household Surveys

Country	Year	Name of survey	Coverage	Field work	Number	
					Households	Individuals
Argentina	2006	Encuesta Permanente de Hogares–Continua (EPH-C)	Urban	July–December	29,086	99,726
Bolivia	2005	Encuesta Continua de Hogares–MECOVI (ECH)	National	October	4,086	16,895
Brazil	2007	Pesquisa Nacional por Amostra de Domicilios (PNAD)	National	September	126,145	399,955
Chile	2006	Encuesta de Caracterización Socioeconómica Nacional (CASEN)	National	November	73,720	268,873
Colombia	2006	Gran Encuesta Integrada de Hogares (GEIH)	National	August–September	31,539	120,583
Costa Rica	2006	Encuesta de Hogares de Propósitos Múltiples (EHPM)	National	July	12,361	46,278
Dominican Republic	2006	Encuesta Nacional de Fuerza de Trabajo (ENFT)	National	October	7,649	28,469
Ecuador	2007	Encuesta Nacional de Empleo, Desempleo y Subempleo (ENEMDU)	National	December	18,933	76,922
El Salvador	2005	Encuesta de Hogares de Propósitos Múltiples (EHPM)	National	January–December	16,546	70,066
Guatemala	2006	Encuesta Nacional sobre Condiciones de Vida (ENCOVI)	National	June–December	13,686	68,739
Honduras	2006	Encuesta Permanente de Hogares de Propósitos Múltiples (EP-IPM)	National	May	21,076	99,645
Mexico	2006	Encuesta Nacional de Ingresos y Gastos de los Hogares (ENIGH)	National	August–November	20,875	83,624
Nicaragua	2005	Encuesta Nacional de Hogares sobre Medición de Nivel de Vida (EMNV)	National	July–October	6,884	36,614
Panama	2006	Encuesta de Hogares (EH)	National	August	12,865	48,762
Paraguay	2007	Encuesta Permanente de Hogares (EPH)	National	October–December	4,812	21,053
Peru	2007	Encuesta Nacional de Hogares (ENAHO)	National	January–December	22,204	95,469
Uruguay	2006	Encuesta Continua de Hogares (ECH)	National	January–December	85,316	256,866
Venezuela, R.B. de	2006	Encuesta de Hogares por Muestreo (EHM)	National	July–December	38,492	166,506

Source: SEDLAC, 2009.

Figure 3.1   Population Structure by Age

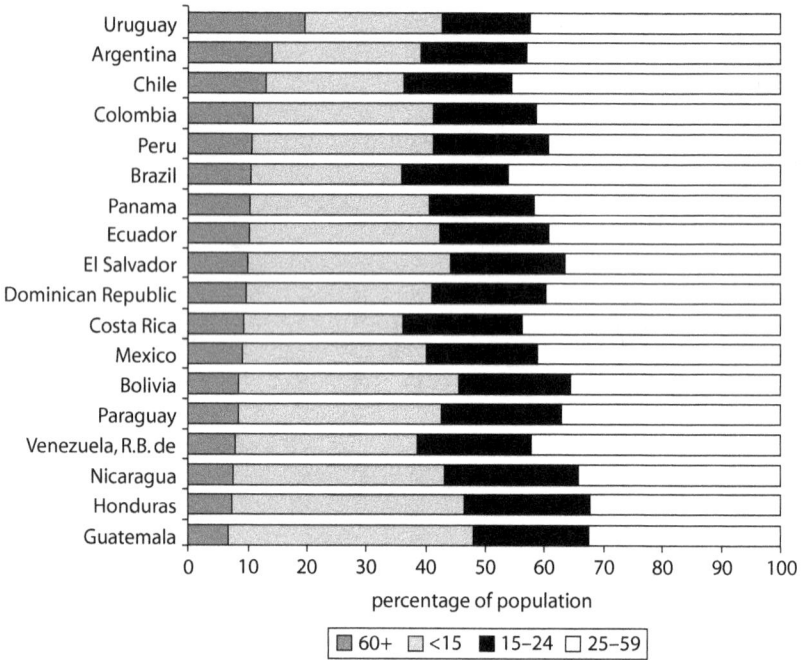

percentage of population

| 60+ | <15 | 15–24 | 25–59 |

Source: Authors' calculations.

Uruguay stands out among the countries for which data are available as the one in which the aging process is most advanced.[1] Besides Uruguay, Argentina (14 percent) and Chile (13 percent) have a high share of the aging in their populations.

The share of the aging in the population is slightly larger, on average, in rural areas than in cities. An intriguing feature is the existence of very different patterns in different countries, as can be seen in figure 3.2. The aging concentrate in rural areas in three Andean countries and in Mexico. By contrast, in most of Central America and in Paraguay, they concentrate in the cities. In the rest of countries their presence is similar in rural and urban areas.[2]

Women live longer than men. As a result, the gender structure differs by age group (see figure 3.3). In almost all countries, (Guatemala is the only exception), the share of women among the aging is substantially larger than the corresponding proportion of the nonaging. The average masculinity index, defined as the ratio between the male population and the female population, is 14 percent higher for the nonaging (0.97) than

Figure 3.2   Population Age 60+ in Urban and Rural Areas, Percent

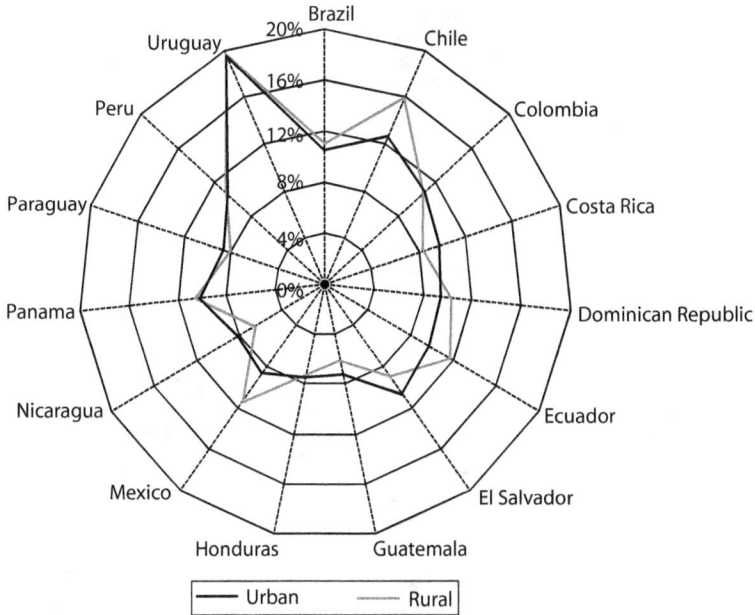

Source: Authors' calculations.

for the aging (0.85). Older countries have a higher proportion of women in their population.

In all Latin American countries, older people live in households of smaller size than younger people. On average, the aging live in households with 3.7 people, while the rest of the population live in households with 5.2 people. Figure 3.4 shows that in Nicaragua, Honduras, Guatemala, República Bolivariana de Venezuela, and Paraguay—the five youngest countries in our sample—the aging live in households of the largest size, while Uruguay and Argentina—the oldest countries in our sample—are at the other extreme of the ranking, with the aging living in households of the smallest size.[3]

Poverty at Different Ages: Methodological Notes

This section discusses methodological concepts and decisions used in the estimations of poverty. (The incidence of poverty at different stages of the life cycle in Latin America is described in the next section.) Data for 18 Latin American countries are drawn from the SEDLAC database, described

Figure 3.3   Male/Female Ratio by Age

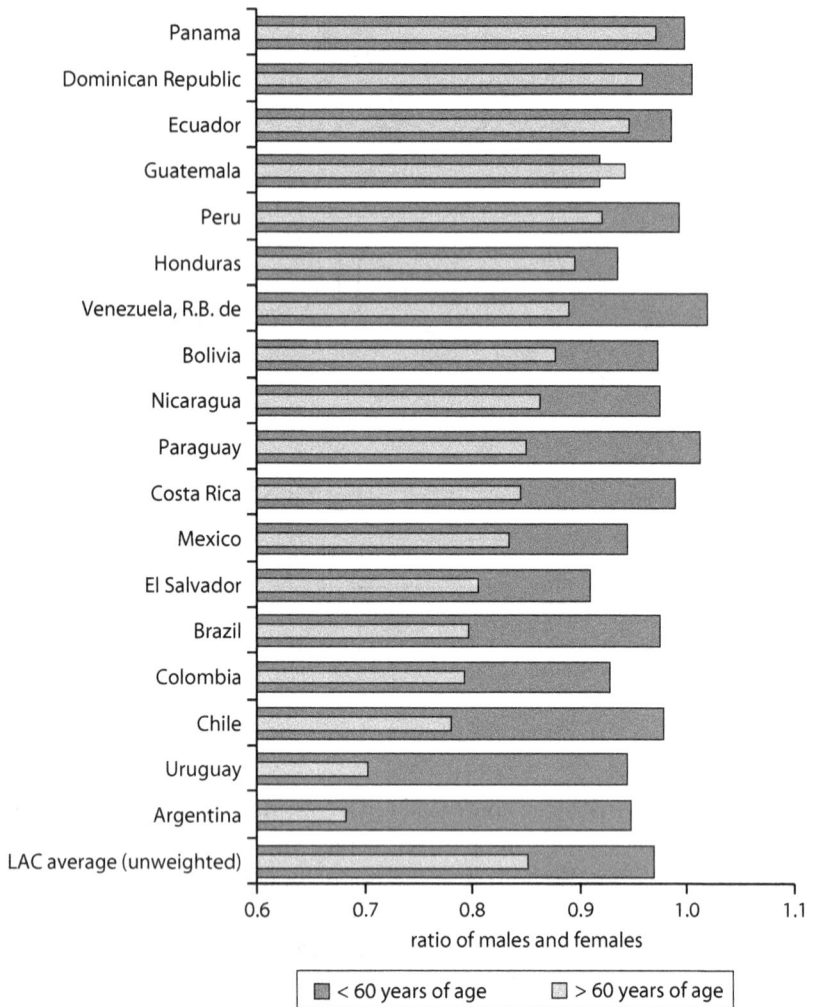

Source: Authors' calculations.

above. The most recent data available were chosen for each country, and all countries for which poverty data were deemed reliable were included. While we recognize poverty as a multidimensional issue, in section 4 the analysis will be restricted to the income dimension of poverty. We follow the common practice of defining an individual as poor if his or her welfare level does not reach a given threshold. The practical implementation of this definition involves selecting an indicator for the individual well-being

Figure 3.4   Average Family Size by Age

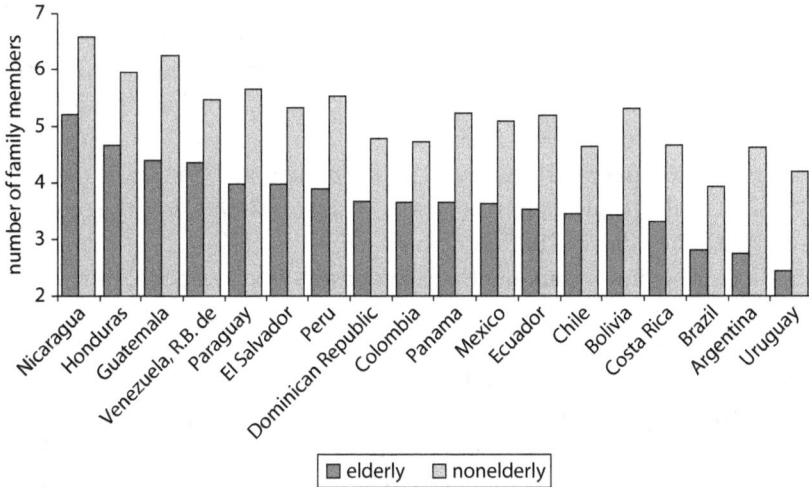

Source: Authors' calculations.

and a poverty line. Most of the literature on poverty estimation recommends using household consumption adjusted for demographics as the welfare indicator, and a poverty line that combines a certain threshold in terms of consumption of calories, with the consumption habits of the population, and the domestic prices of goods and services.

While household consumption is a better proxy for welfare than household income, the estimations in this paper use income as the wellbeing indicator. A practical reason explains this decision: Few countries in LAC conduct household surveys with questionnaires asking about household consumption/expenditures, while all of them include questions on individual and household income.

There are neither normative nor objective arguments to set a poverty line below which everybody is poor and above which everyone is non-poor. Therefore, societies differ in the criteria used to identify the poor, and each country has its own poverty lines. This creates serious comparability problems. For this reason, cross-country comparisons are usually made in terms of international poverty lines. The most popular one is the US$1-a-day line proposed in Ravallion, Gaurav, and Van de Walle (1991). It is a value measured in 1985 international prices and adjusted to local currency using purchasing power parity (PPP) to take into account local prices. The US$1-a-day standard was chosen as being representative of the national poverty lines found among low-income countries. The US$2-a-day line is also extensively used in comparisons across middle-income countries, the income range of most LAC countries. Although the US$1-a-day or US$2-a-day lines have been criticized, their simplicity and the lack of reasonable and easy-to-implement alternatives have made them the standard for international poverty comparisons. The lines have recently been updated using 2005 PPP dollars at US$1.25 a day and US$2.50 a day (Ravallion, Chen, and Sangraula 2008). In this study, we use US$2.50 a day in 2005 PPP terms.

Measuring poverty among the aging poses some additional difficulties. The first one relates to the use of income data in the absence of consumption data. The issue arises because labor income, a key component of total income, has a bell shape in relation to age (growing as individuals enter the labor force and falling as they age), while consumption tends to be relatively smooth across all ages. This implies that the aging tend to have a different composition of income sources than the young. Some older people may be living partly from the sale of assets they acquired during their lifetimes. The income from the sale of assets is not usually considered as current income, and hence is not taken into account in poverty estimations. This practice might be incorrect if we are considering the situation of an older person who periodically sells assets to keep his or her living standard.

A second problem arises from lack of information about the intra-household distribution of consumption. We are estimating individual poverty based on the income level of the household in which the individual lives. The typical information included in a household survey does not allow the measurement of the specific allocation scheme adopted by each household. For these reasons the usual practice is to assume complete intrahousehold equality in living standards.

Another important problem arises from the fact that older people usually live in households with a demographic structure that is significantly different from the rest of the population. That difference makes the poverty comparisons between the aging and the nonaging population highly dependent on the assumptions about the impact of the household structure on individual well-being. We discuss the implications of the use of different assumptions below.

In summary, although we believe that poverty is a multidimensional problem, due to data restrictions in this study we consider the poor to be those individuals living in households whose per capita income is lower than US$2.50 a day in terms of 2005 PPP dollars. Most researchers and practitioners seem to agree that this is a reasonable approximation for a complex problem. In this paper, we use that widely accepted definition and assess the robustness of the results with different methodological assumptions related to economies of scale and adult equivalence.

Poverty at Different Ages: Empirical Evidence

We begin with a brief review of the poverty landscape in Latin America. Table 3.2 contains the poverty headcount ratios by age group and region for the US$2.50-a-day poverty line. Poverty levels for the total population of each country vary greatly within the region. While the percentage of people in poverty is lower than 12 percent in the Southern Cone—Chile, 5 percent; Uruguay, 7 percent; Argentina, 11 percent—and Costa Rica, 12 percent, the share of people with household per capita income below that poverty line climbs to over 30 percent in most Central American countries—Nicaragua, 43 percent; Honduras, 37 percent; and Guatemala, 34 percent—and in Colombia, 38 percent and Bolivia, 35 percent.

As can be seen in table 3.2, poverty rates are substantially higher in rural areas. The largest rural-urban differences are in the Andean countries and in Panama, where poverty is more than three times higher in rural areas than in urban areas (in Peru it is 5.6 times higher). The least-unequal countries by region are the three small countries with the lowest incidence of poverty—Chile, Uruguay, and Costa Rica.[4]

Within this broader context we now turn to examining poverty by age group. The correlation between national poverty and poverty in any age group is very high. In the case of the aging (older than age 60),[5] the linear correlation coefficient is 0.892. This strong relationship is illustrated in figure 3.5. Note that most points in the figure lie close to but below the 45° line, implying slightly lower poverty rates for the aging compared to the rest of the population. Three exceptions are Colombia, Mexico and Costa Rica.[6] This evidence will be analyzed in detail later.

The correlation is even stronger between the national poverty rate and the poverty rate of the young (under age 15)—0.987—as depicted in figure 3.6. As can be observed in the figure, in *all* countries, the incidence of poverty is higher among young people than among the rest of the population.

This is not to imply that poverty is monotonically decreasing with age in most countries. Figure 3.7 provides additional information on the relationship of age to poverty. It exhibits age-poverty profiles, which are nonparametric (kernel) estimates of the poverty headcount ratio by age in

Table 3.2 Poverty: Headcount Ratio by Age and Region

Country	National						Urban						Rural					
	All	60+	65+	<15	15–24	25–59	All	60+	65+	<15	15–24	25–59	All	60+	65+	<15	15–24	25–59
Argentina	11.0	4.9	3.7	19.2	11.6	8.0	11.0	4.9	3.7	19.2	11.6	8.0						
Bolivia	35.0	26.6	25.3	44.5	28.4	30.7	19.4	9.0	8.1	27.4	16.1	16.1	62.7	46.0	42.2	67.9	61.1	62.1
Brazil	18.2	4.2	3.5	31.8	18.3	13.8	15.0	4.0	3.4	27.2	15.3	11.1	34.0	4.9	4.0	51.3	33.5	29.3
Chile	5.2	2.5	2.3	8.6	5.5	4.2	4.9	2.3	2.2	8.1	5.1	3.9	7.6	3.6	3.1	11.5	8.5	6.7
Colombia	37.8	42.2	44.3	46.3	36.3	31.0	30.8	35.6	38.2	38.2	30.4	24.5	57.3	60.7	61.9	65.3	53.8	50.7
Costa Rica	11.6	17.0	18.5	16.7	8.7	8.5	8.0	11.6	12.7	12.4	6.2	5.4	16.6	25.5	27.6	21.5	12.4	13.1
Dominican Republic	18.7	16.0	15.6	26.8	16.6	14.0	15.2	12.2	11.7	22.4	13.7	11.1	25.1	22.3	22.0	34.0	22.2	19.5
Ecuador	17.6	16.2	17.2	24.0	15.1	13.8	9.9	8.4	8.7	14.2	8.2	7.9	32.1	29.1	30.5	39.4	28.8	27.1
El Salvador	27.1	20.3	20.7	35.2	24.9	22.4	15.5	12.6	13.4	20.9	13.9	12.9	44.2	33.9	33.9	52.0	40.5	39.9
Guatemala	33.9	28.2	29.1	42.4	28.4	27.6	17.2	13.8	14.3	24.1	13.5	13.1	49.4	43.8	45.2	55.6	43.2	44.8
Honduras	36.9	35.6	37.1	45.7	30.1	31.3	20.5	21.4	23.1	27.4	15.8	16.7	56.7	54.8	56.2	63.2	50.2	51.9
Mexico	13.9	19.9	21.9	18.2	11.8	10.2	9.7	14.7	16.4	13.0	8.2	6.9	28.4	33.5	35.4	34.0	24.1	23.7
Nicaragua	42.7	32.5	32.5	53.2	38.5	36.6	25.3	20.1	21.1	34.1	21.9	20.7	64.6	51.9	51.2	72.6	61.1	59.5
Panama	22.3	17.0	18.2	32.4	21.8	16.6	10.0	8.0	9.4	15.3	9.9	7.2	43.9	32.2	32.7	55.7	43.7	36.1
Paraguay	21.4	16.9	17.2	29.7	18.1	16.5	12.1	11.3	11.1	18.2	9.4	8.9	34.3	25.4	26.4	42.8	30.3	29.0
Peru	25.2	19.5	20.1	36.0	21.4	20.1	9.6	5.9	5.7	14.9	8.9	7.5	53.8	44.3	45.5	64.1	46.8	49.2
Uruguay	6.7	1.1	0.9	14.6	7.2	4.8	6.8	1.1	0.9	14.9	7.3	4.8	5.5	1.8	1.2	10.9	5.4	4.3
Venezuela, R.B. de	19.8	18.2	19.4	27.3	17.5	15.5	19.8	18.2	19.4	27.3	17.5	15.5						
LAC average (unweighted)	22.5	18.8	19.3	30.7	20.0	18.1	14.5	12.0	12.4	21.1	12.9	11.2	38.5	32.1	32.4	46.4	35.4	34.2

Source: Authors' compilation.

Note: Poverty line = US$2.50-a-day purchasing power parity.

Figure 3.5   National and Old-age Poverty Headcount Ratios

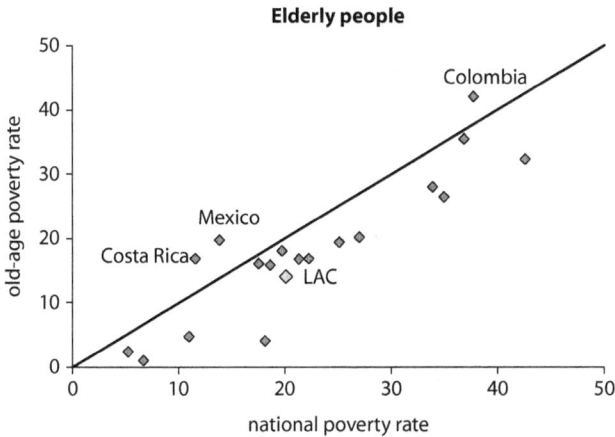

Elderly people

Source: Authors' calculations.

Figure 3.6   National and Young People's Poverty Headcount Ratios

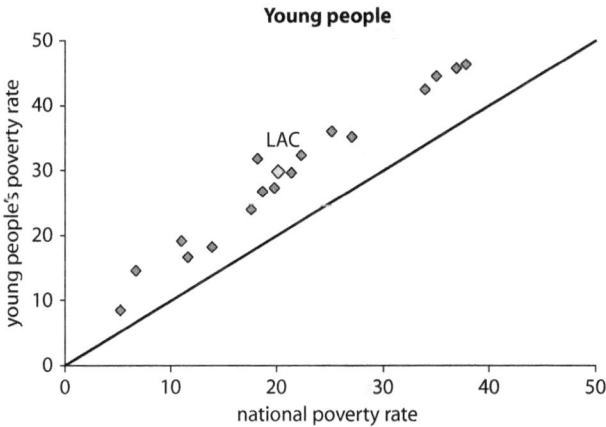

Young people

Source: Authors' calculations.

each LAC country. Using the figure, we can define a typology of countries on the basis of the situation of the aging relative to the rest of the population. The first group consists of "pro-aging" countries where poverty continuously falls with age—Argentina, Brazil, Chile, and Uruguay. This is the group relatively most favorable to the aging. The second (and most numerous) group consists of countries in which poverty falls with age until around age 40, and then becomes either

Figure 3.7 Poverty Headcount Ratio by Age

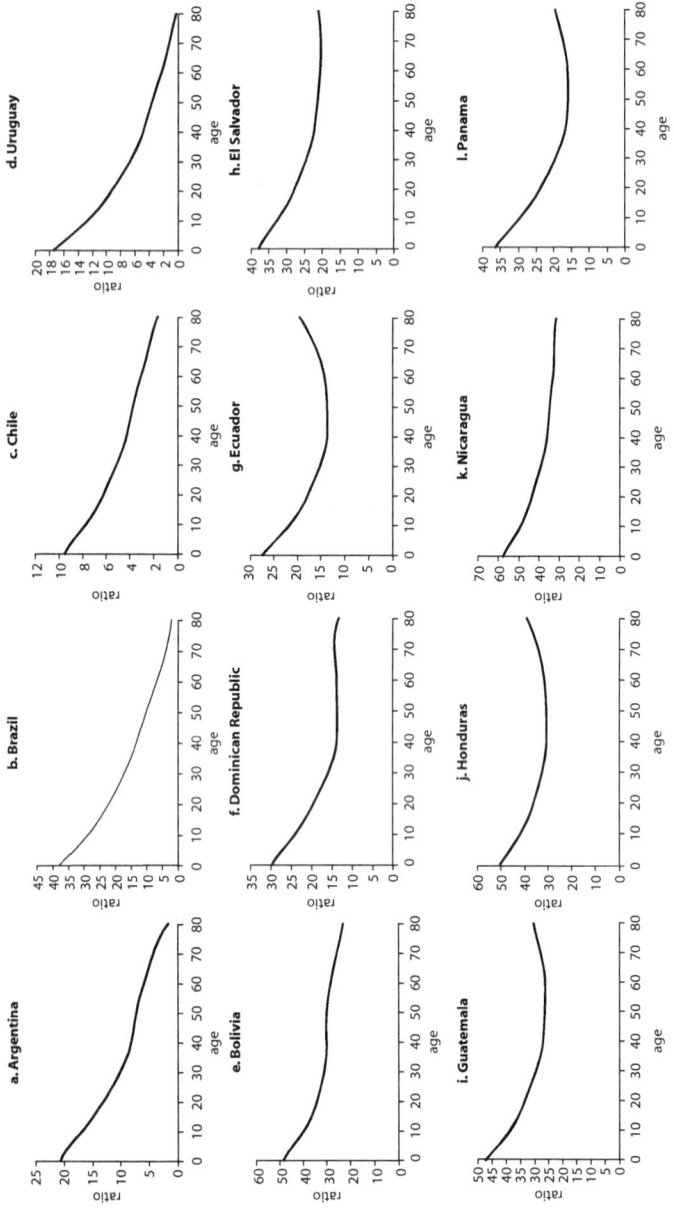

m. Paraguay

n. Peru

o. República Bolivariana de Venezuela

p. Colombia

q. Costa Rica

r. Mexico

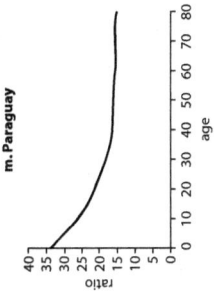

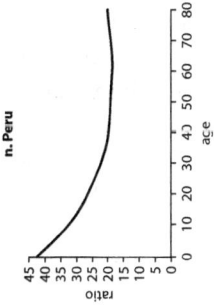

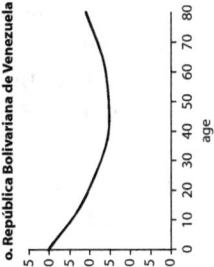

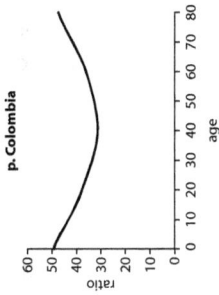

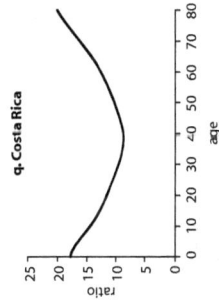

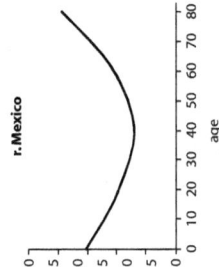

Source: Authors' calculations.

constant or slightly increases (for example, Bolivia, the Dominican Republic, Ecuador, El Salvador, Guatemala, Honduras, Nicaragua, Panama, Paraguay, Peru, and República Bolivariana de Venezuela). The third group consists of "anti-aging" countries where poverty first falls until around age 40 and then increases steeply with age in a U-shape. Only three countries are in this group—Colombia, Costa Rica, and Mexico—the least favorable to the aging.

Table 3.3 provides further detail on differences among the three groups. For the pro-aging countries, poverty reaches its minimum levels in the older age brackets. In Argentina and Chile, the poverty rate for those older than age 60 is around 40 percent of the poverty rate for the total population. The aging are relatively even better off in Brazil (where the poverty rate is only 21 percent) and in Uruguay (14 percent).

Note that the pro-aging countries exhibit the highest levels of relative poverty among the young compared to the rest of the population. While all other LAC countries have poverty rates among the young that are less than twice the poverty of the rest of the population, all pro-aging countries have poverty rates among the young that are more than twice those of the rest of the population.

For countries in the second group, poverty incidence among the aging is also slightly lower (between 10 percent and 30 percent) than the incidence of poverty in the rest of the population. Most of this difference, however, is due to the higher poverty rates found among the young. In contrast, for countries in the anti-aging group, old-age poverty rates are significantly higher than the national rates. While the first group combines the lowest relative poverty among the aging with the highest relative poverty among the young, the opposite is not true for the third group. The third group shows the highest relative poverty for the aging, but does not especially favor the young.

The poverty estimates presented in this section use a simple measure of income per capita. Could the conclusions reached so far be simply a methodological construction? Do the groupings of countries into *pro-aging* and *anti-aging* resist more rigorous forms of measurement? We now address these questions.

The Role of the Demographic Structure
Until now, we have estimated poverty rates for all individuals by dividing the household income by the number of household members. However, both the percentage of aging people and the percentage of children classified as poor depend on the assumptions about differences in needs

Table 3.3 Relative Poverty Ratio by Age and Region

Country	National			Urban			Rural		
	60+/<60	<15/15+	60+/<15	60+/<60	<15/15+	60+/<15	60+/<60	<15/15+	60+/<15
Argentina	0.41	2.40	0.25	0.41	2.40	0.25	—	—	—
Bolivia	0.74	1.52	0.60	0.45	1.81	0.33	0.71	1.16	0.68
Brazil	0.21	2.40	0.13	0.25	2.50	0.15	0.13	1.95	0.10
Chile	0.44	2.07	0.29	0.43	2.14	0.28	0.44	1.81	0.32
Colombia	1.13	1.37	0.91	1.18	1.39	0.93	1.07	1.23	0.93
Costa Rica	1.54	1.77	1.02	1.53	1.98	0.93	1.62	1.51	1.19
Dominican Republic	0.84	1.81	3.60	0.79	1.89	0.54	0.88	1.67	0.66
Ecuador	0.91	1.68	0.67	0.83	1.80	0.59	0.90	1.42	0.74
El Salvador	0.73	1.56	0.58	0.79	1.61	0.60	0.75	1.34	0.65
Guatemala	0.82	1.54	0.66	0.79	1.85	0.57	0.88	1.26	0.79
Honduras	0.96	1.46	0.78	1.05	1.63	0.78	0.96	1.22	0.87
Mexico	1.49	1.55	1.09	1.60	1.61	1.13	1.21	1.35	0.99
Nicaragua	0.75	1.47	0.61	0.78	1.66	0.59	0.79	1.23	0.71
Panama	0.74	1.84	0.52	0.79	1.94	0.53	0.71	1.51	0.58
Paraguay	0.78	1.77	0.57	0.93	1.99	0.62	0.72	1.50	0.59
Peru	0.75	1.79	0.54	0.58	2.01	0.39	0.81	1.35	0.69
Uruguay	0.14	3.49	0.08	0.13	3.53	0.07	0.27	2.92	0.16
Venezuela, R.B. de	0.91	1.69	0.67	0.91	1.69	0.67	—	—	—
LAC average (unweighted)	0.79	1.84	0.59	0.79	1.97	0.55	0.80	1.53	0.66

Source: Authors' compilation.
Note: Poverty line = US$2.50-a-day purchasing power parity. — = not available.

across people of different ages, and about the existence of economies of scale (Deaton and Paxson 1995).

First, consider the needs of people of different ages and of the situation of two households of the same size but of dissimilar demographic composition. If the cost of financing children's basic consumption is lower than the cost of financing the consumption of adults, then the household with more adults will need higher per capita income to reach a given welfare level. The effect of different assumptions about the cost of children on the absolute poverty rate of the adults and of the aging will depend on the particular family arrangements in each country. Second, consider the existence of economies of scale in the household. Economies of scale allow a couple to live on less than double the budget of a person living alone. Larger households share in the consumption of some goods and services such as electricity, heating, and others, where consumption by one family member does not reduce availability of the good for consumption by others in the household. Note that considering economies of scale in the analysis will affect both absolute and relative poverty rates of the aging.

In this section we will take into account both considerations and study how estimates of poverty incidence for different age groups change as the assumptions are modified. In our approach, we proxied individual well-being by total household income deflated by an equivalence scale, defined as a function of the size of the household and its demographic composition. There is long-standing literature on equivalence scales (see Deaton and Paxson 1998a). We follow the approach of Buhmann and others (1988) and Deaton and Paxson (1997) by assuming a parametric form for the equivalence scale and examining the consequences of changing the parameters. In particular, we assume that the living standard of an individual i living in household h is given by:

$$x_{ih} = \frac{Y_h}{(\alpha_1 C_1 + \alpha_2 C_2 + A)^\theta}$$

where. C_1 is the number of children under age 5, C_2 is the number of children aged 6–14, and A is the number of adults. Parameters α allow for different weights for younger and older children compared with adults, while θ regulates the degree of household economies of scale. When $\theta = 1$ there are no economies of scale, while at the other extreme, when $\theta = 0$, there are full economies of scale, meaning that all goods in the household could be shared completely (that is, they are all public goods, with no rivalry in consumption). In very underdeveloped economies where people spend nearly all their income on food, there is not much scope for economies of scale. In developed economies where a much larger share of the budget is spent on housing, energy, heating, transportation, entertainment, and other goods easier to share, consumption economies of scale are more important. Following the suggestion of Deaton and Zaidi (2002) for middle-income countries such as those in LAC, we take intermediate values of the αs ($\alpha_1 = 0.50$ and $\alpha_2 = 0.75$) and θ ($\theta = 0.8$) as the benchmark case.

In practice, it is convenient to work with a transformation of the above equation to make poverty estimates comparable to those obtained with household per capita income and the US\$2.50-a-day line. The need for an adjustment comes from the fact that by deflating by $(\alpha_1 C_1 + \alpha_2 C_2 + A)^\theta$ instead of by just the number of family members $(C_1 + C_2 + A)$, the indicator of individual welfare x_{th} increases, and without any adjustment in the poverty lines, poverty estimates go down. However, we are not trying to adjust the total percentage of people classified as poor; rather, we are comparing the relative situation of different age groups. We alleviate (although not eliminate) this nuisance by following the procedure suggested by Deaton and Paxson (1997) and multiplying the above equation by $(\alpha_1 C_1^0 + \alpha_2 C_2^0 + A^0)^\theta / (C_1^0 + C_2^0 + A^0)$, where C_1^0, C_2^0, and A^0 are the number of children under age 5, children aged 6–14, and adults in the "base" household, respectively. We take the average number of children and adults in each country to construct the base family.

The impact of considering different parameters for economies of scale is analyzed with the help of table 3.4. As the parameter goes from 1 to 0, consumption economies of scale internal to the household become more important, and relative old-age poverty increases in all countries. In many countries, the sign of the poverty comparison between the aging and the rest of the population does not depend on the parameter of economies of scale (given the adult-equivalent scale used). For instance, in Colombia and Mexico (third-group countries), old-age poverty is always higher than national poverty, (the same is true in almost all cases in Ecuador and Honduras), while the opposite is true in Argentina and Brazil, regardless of the degree of economies of scale. In some other countries, (all second-group countries), the sign of the difference depends on the parameter; that is the case of Bolivia, El Salvador, Guatemala, Nicaragua, Panama, Paraguay, Peru, and República Bolivariana de Venezuela. Old-age relative poverty is higher than 1 in some cases in Chile and Uruguay, although at improbable values of the parameter of economies of scale.

Table 3.4 Relative Poverty Ratio of the Aging with the Economie of Scale (60+/60<) Ratios by Poverty

	Argentina	Bolivia	Brazil	Chile	Colombia	Costa Rica	Dominican Republic	Ecuador	El Salvador	Guatemala	Honduras	Mexico	Nicaragua	Panama	Paraguay	Peru	Uruguay	Venezuela
Case 1																		
1.0	0.41	0.74	0.21	0.44	1.13	1.54	0.84	0.91	0.73	0.82	0.96	1.49	0.75	0.74	0.78	0.94	0.14	0.91
0.9	0.42	0.82	0.21	0.46	1.17	1.67	0.88	0.99	0.76	0.85	0.99	1.62	0.77	0.79	0.82	1.00	0.15	0.95
0.8	0.45	0.93	0.21	0.49	1.20	1.82	0.94	1.07	0.80	0.87	1.01	1.74	0.79	0.84	0.89	1.08	0.18	0.98
0.7	0.49	1.01	0.22	0.55	1.22	2.03	1.02	1.15	0.83	0.93	1.04	1.85	0.83	0.90	0.94	1.16	0.22	1.04
0.6	0.53	1.07	0.22	0.62	1.25	2.29	1.11	1.30	0.88	0.99	1.07	1.96	0.87	0.96	1.04	1.24	0.27	1.09
0.5	0.58	1.14	0.23	0.70	1.29	2.44	1.22	1.42	0.93	1.03	1.10	2.12	0.90	1.02	1.10	1.33	0.34	1.17
0.4	0.61	1.21	0.24	0.84	1.33	2.68	1.35	1.54	1.01	1.10	1.13	2.30	0.94	1.12	1.19	1.42	0.44	1.22
0.3	0.65	1.30	0.25	1.01	1.37	2.89	1.45	1.70	1.07	1.15	1.16	2.51	0.97	1.19	1.28	1.51	0.60	1.28
0.2	0.75	1.36	0.25	1.17	1.42	3.06	1.59	1.84	1.16	1.23	1.20	2.69	1.02	1.27	1.38	1.62	0.82	1.34
0.1	0.87	1.40	0.30	1.43	1.44	3.29	1.69	1.96	1.24	1.28	1.23	2.79	1.04	1.35	1.46	1.71	1.08	1.41
0.0	0.94	1.44	0.41	1.78	1.50	3.40	1.78	2.13	1.32	1.35	1.27	2.94	1.08	1.43	1.65	1.78	1.35	1.48
Case 2																		
1.0	0.45	0.91	0.25	0.51	1.20	1.86	0.96	1.07	0.82	0.92	1.04	1.75	0.83	0.82	0.89	1.03	0.19	1.03
0.9	0.48	1.01	0.25	0.54	1.23	1.97	1.01	1.13	0.85	0.95	1.06	1.85	0.84	0.87	0.96	1.10	0.21	1.07
0.8	0.51	1.05	0.25	0.57	1.26	2.11	1.09	1.23	0.88	0.98	1.08	1.93	0.86	0.91	0.97	1.17	0.26	1.09
0.7	0.54	1.11	0.26	0.64	1.28	2.35	1.14	1.34	0.92	1.03	1.10	2.04	0.89	0.96	1.05	1.24	0.30	1.14

0.6	0.58	1.16	0.26	0.70	1.31	2.49	1.25	1.45	0.96	1.08	1.12	2.16	0.92	1.02	1.11	1.33	0.35	1.20
0.5	0.61	1.21	0.24	0.78	1.33	2.64	1.36	1.55	1.02	1.11	1.15	2.32	0.95	1.09	1.18	1.41	0.43	1.26
0.4	0.66	1.28	0.25	0.92	1.37	2.85	1.46	1.65	1.08	1.16	1.17	2.48	0.97	1.15	1.24	1.49	0.53	1.30
0.3	0.75	1.36	0.25	1.07	1.40	3.02	1.59	1.82	1.12	1.22	1.20	2.64	1.01	1.25	1.31	1.57	0.71	1.36
0.2	0.79	1.38	0.30	1.24	1.44	3.16	1.63	1.90	1.21	1.26	1.22	2.76	1.02	1.31	1.41	1.66	0.90	1.39
0.1	0.88	1.41	0.31	1.49	1.45	3.32	1.70	2.01	1.26	1.28	1.25	2.82	1.05	1.36	1.51	1.74	1.13	1.43
0.0	0.94	1.44	0.41	1.78	1.50	3.40	1.78	2.13	1.32	1.34	1.27	2.94	1.08	1.43	1.65	1.78	1.35	1.48
Case 3																		
1.0	0.52	1.05	0.28	0.59	1.27	2.10	1.10	1.22	0.90	1.03	1.11	1.97	0.89	0.91	1.00	1.13	0.26	1.18
0.9	0.53	1.10	0.28	0.60	1.29	2.30	1.16	1.31	0.92	1.06	1.13	2.05	0.90	0.95	1.02	1.20	0.30	1.19
0.8	0.55	1.14	0.28	0.65	1.30	2.44	1.23	1.38	0.95	1.09	1.15	2.16	0.93	0.98	1.08	1.26	0.33	1.23
0.7	0.59	1.19	0.28	0.68	1.32	2.56	1.31	1.49	1.00	1.13	1.16	2.27	0.95	1.04	1.14	1.33	0.38	1.25
0.6	0.63	1.22	0.28	0.78	1.37	2.73	1.42	1.58	1.03	1.15	1.18	2.37	0.96	1.11	1.18	1.41	0.44	1.32
0.5	0.66	1.29	0.29	0.86	1.38	2.87	1.48	1.69	1.08	1.17	1.18	2.56	0.98	1.14	1.27	1.48	0.53	1.35
0.4	0.74	1.36	0.29	1.02	1.40	2.96	1.54	1.77	1.13	1.23	1.20	2.64	1.00	1.23	1.30	1.54	0.65	1.38
0.3	0.79	1.38	0.29	1.15	1.43	3.11	1.63	1.87	1.18	1.26	1.22	2.73	1.02	1.30	1.35	1.62	0.81	1.40
0.2	0.81	1.41	0.33	1.32	1.45	3.31	1.66	1.96	1.24	1.28	1.24	2.81	1.03	1.34	1.45	1.68	0.95	1.43
0.1	0.89	1.43	0.31	1.54	1.46	3.33	1.75	2.04	1.27	1.31	1.25	2.87	1.06	1.38	1.53	1.75	1.17	1.45
0.0	0.94	1.44	0.41	1.78	1.50	3.40	1.78	2.13	1.32	1.34	1.27	2.94	1.08	1.43	1.65	1.78	1.35	1.48

Source: Authors' compilation.

Note: Case 1: No adult equivalents; case 2: $\alpha_1 = 0.5$, $\alpha_2 = 0.75$; case 3: $\alpha_1 = 0.25$, $\alpha_2 = 0.5$.

Table 3.5 shows the absolute and relative poverty of aging people using four alternative income variables: (a) per capita household income, (b) household income per adult equivalent, (c) household income adjusted for economies of scale, and (d) household income per adult equivalent adjusted for economies of scale. The consideration of adjustments of adult equivalence or of economies of scale worsens the poverty ranking of the aging relative to other age groups: First, by definition, equivalizing income lowers child poverty and raises the incomes of households with many children. Since the aging on average live in households with a smaller number of children, they benefit less than the rest from this adjustment. Second, as seen above, older people live in smaller households than the rest of the population; this implies they are less able to take advantage of consumption economies of scale. Hence, both of these adjustments tend to reduce the relative position of the aging in relation to the rest of the population. How does this affect our initial findings?

Looking at table 3.5, we find that two of the patterns described above resist the change in methodology: First, the pro-aging group of countries continues to be the best for the aging and the worst for the young, and remains Argentina, Brazil, Chile, and Uruguay. Second, the anti-aging group continues to be the worse for the aging, and the use of equivalized income makes the relative disadvantage of the aging even sharper. This group continues to comprise Colombia, Costa Rica, and Mexico. Ecuador and Honduras become borderline members of this group. For the other 9 countries, the poverty-age profile becomes less defined; the relative differences in poverty for this group of countries seem to depend mostly on methodological assumptions.

The exercise above consisted of examining the robustness of poverty estimations with different methodological approaches to the demographic structure of the family. To conclude the discussion on the importance of the demographic composition of the family on income, we present a simple simulation that asks: How would the per capita income of the poorest quintile change if those families retained their current individual incomes but had the size and age composition of the top quintile?[7] Figure 3.8 shows the results of the simulation. Incomes of the poorest quintile would increase significantly in all countries by between 35 percent (in Chile) and 79 percent (in Argentina and Brazil). The size of the gain can also be thought of as the "demographic gap" that exists between the rich and the poor in LAC. While significant in absolute terms, the demographic gap between Q1 and Q5 explains only a small fraction of the

Table 3.5 Poverty Rates by Age Group

| | Per capita income | | | | Adult equivalents | | | | Household income adjusted for | | | | | | | |
| | | | | | | | | | Economies of scale | | | | Both | | | |
Country	60+	< 15	60+/ national	< 15/ national	60+	< 15	60+/ national	< 15/ national	60+	< 15	60+/ national	< 15/ national	60+	< 15	60+/ national	< 15/ national
Argentina	4.9	19.2	0.44	1.74	4.9	16.4	0.45	1.49	4.7	16.3	0.43	1.48	4.8	14.0	0.44	1.27
Bolivia	26.6	44.5	0.76	1.27	31.4	41.4	0.90	1.18	31.3	41.8	0.89	1.19	34.5	39.3	0.98	1.12
Brazil	4.2	31.8	0.23	1.75	4.6	28.1	0.25	1.54	3.9	29.0	0.21	1.59	4.3	25.8	0.24	1.42
Chile	2.5	8.6	0.48	1.63	2.6	7.1	0.49	1.35	2.5	7.4	0.47	1.42	2.6	6.3	0.49	1.20
Colombia	42.2	46.3	1.12	1.22	44.0	45.7	1.16	1.15	42.7	43.8	1.13	1.16	43.8	41.5	1.16	1.10
Costa Rica	17.2	16.7	1.48	1.44	18.9	14.4	1.63	1.24	18.8	15.2	1.62	1.31	20.4	13.5	1.76	1.16
Dominican Republic	16.0	26.8	0.86	1.43	17.1	23.5	0.91	1.26	15.9	23.7	0.85	1.27	17.5	21.5	0.94	1.15
Ecuador	16.2	24.0	0.92	1.37	17.3	20.7	0.99	1.18	17.0	21.3	0.97	1.21	18.4	19.1	1.05	1.09
El Salvador	20.3	35.2	0.75	1.30	21.8	32.4	0.81	1.20	20.4	31.9	0.76	1.18	21.8	30.1	0.81	1.11
Guatemala	28.2	42.4	0.83	1.25	30.4	39.7	0.89	1.17	28.5	40.0	0.84	1.18	31.0	37.8	0.91	1.11
Honduras	35.6	45.7	0.96	1.24	37.0	43.1	1.00	1.17	36.2	43.9	0.98	1.19	37.8	42.0	1.02	1.14
Mexico	19.9	18.2	1.43	1.31	20.7	15.2	1.49	1.10	20.4	15.7	1.47	1.13	21.0	13.9	1.51	1.00
Nicaragua	32.5	53.2	0.76	1.25	34.9	50.4	0.82	1.18	32.9	50.7	0.77	1.19	34.9	48.5	0.82	1.14
Panama	16.9	32.4	0.76	1.45	17.9	29.6	0.80	1.33	17.9	29.8	0.80	1.34	18.7	27.9	0.84	1.25
Paraguay	16.9	29.7	0.79	1.39	18.3	26.7	0.85	1.25	18.4	27.7	0.86	1.29	18.9	25.3	0.88	1.18
Peru	19.5	36.0	0.77	1.43	20.7	32.7	0.82	1.30	20.6	33.1	0.82	1.31	21.7	30.3	0.86	1.20
Uruguay	1.1	14.6	0.17	2.18	1.2	10.6	0.17	1.57	1.1	10.8	0.16	1.61	1.2	7.9	0.18	1.17
Venezuela, R.B. de	18.2	27.3	0.92	1.38	18.5	23.4	0.94	1.18	17.5	24.2	0.89	1.22	18.0	21.3	0.91	1.08
LAC average	18.8	30.7	0.80	1.40	20.1	27.7	0.90	1.30	19.5	28.1	0.80	1.30	20.6	25.9	0.90	1.20

Source: Authors' compilation.
Note: Poverty determined by headcount ratio. Poverty line = US$2.50-a-day purchasing power parity.

Figure 3.8   Simulating the Impact of Demography on the Income of the Poor

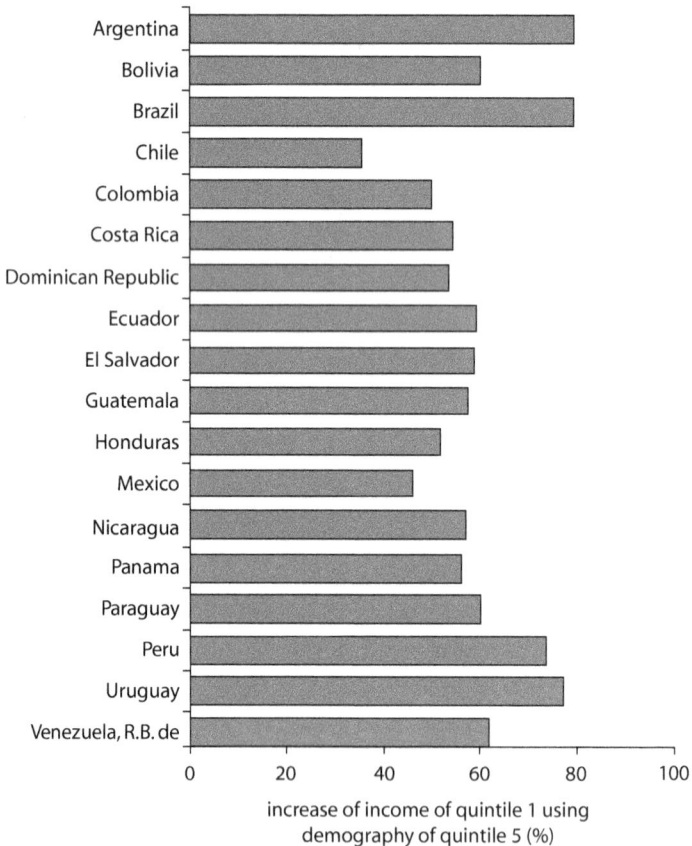

increase of income of quintile 1 using
demography of quintile 5 (%)

Source: Authors' calculations.

difference in income between these income groups—ranging from 1 percent (in Chile) to 6 percent (in Uruguay).

The analysis up to this point refers to the population over 60 as a homogenous group. But what if there exist significant differences between the "old" (60+) and the "old old" (80+)? Figure 3.9 compares the aggregate poverty level and poverty among these two groups. It shows that for the average in LAC and for most countries, poverty levels are slightly higher among the old old than they are among the over 60s. This pattern is particularly strong in the countries where the old are poorer than the rest of the population—Colombia, Costa Rica, Ecuador, Honduras, and Mexico. This suggests that in those countries, the main problem of poverty among the aging is concentrated among the over 80s.

Figure 3.9   Poverty Ratios for the 60+ and 80+ Populations

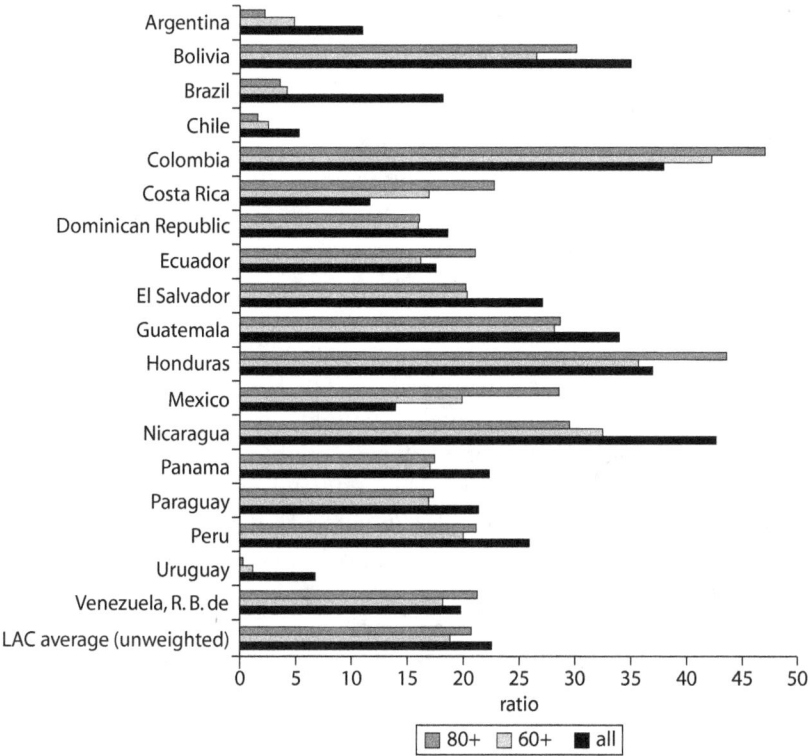

Source: Authors' calculations.

It is also interesting to note that the four countries where the elderly are significantly less poor than the average are all countries with low levels of poverty among the old old. This suggests that the main problems of poverty among the elderly are found among the old old, and that countries that have programs that target poverty among the old old have largely succeeded in reducing poverty among the elderly. (Notice that these comparisons are done on estimations based on per capita incomes, with no adjustments for economies of scale or adult equivalence.)

Drivers of Old-age Poverty and the Role of Pensions and Other Transfers

As explained in the previous section, the relative situation of the aging in terms of income poverty incidence varies among countries in LAC. In some countries, the aging are in a better situation than the rest of the population, regardless of the methodological decisions used for the estimations. In other countries, the aging are in a worse situation than the rest of the population regardless of methodological considerations. Finally, for one group of countries, the relative situation of the aging depends on the assumptions made about economies of scale and adult equivalent.

What are the drivers behind these heterogeneous results? Because in our estimations of poverty incidence, we are working with the concept of *income* poverty, the answer to the question must be strongly connected with the importance of several income sources for older people in the different countries.

Table 3.6 shows the relative importance of the different sources of income for young adults and for older adults by gender. As people age, their labor income becomes a smaller part of their total. For young adults, labor income is on average around 89 percent of their total income (males 94 percent, females 82 percent). For the group over 60, this falls to 44 percent (males 53 percent, females 26 percent). If we look exclusively at the group over 80, labor income drops to 15 percent of the total (males 21 percent, females 5 percent).

What replaces labor income as people age? For the average in LAC, pensions grow in importance (from 34 percent to 48 percent) as do private transfers from outside the household (from 15 percent to 28 percent). While in most countries both pensions and private transfers grow in importance, in a few only transfers become relevant (the Dominican Republic and Honduras), and in six countries private transfers remain small and only pensions are significant (Argentina, Brazil, Colombia, Costa Rica, Panama, and Uruguay).[8] At all ages, females are more dependent on their family than are males. Transfers are more important for females than for males at all ages.

In the next two subsections we analyze the influence of each of these sources of income on poverty in the life cycle.

Impact of Pension Systems on Poverty

In this subsection, we analyze in greater detail the impact of pension systems on poverty. After presenting information on the coverage of pension systems in LAC countries, we estimate the incidence of income poverty on two groups: people who are pension beneficiaries and people who are not pension beneficiaries. Then, we present a simple counterfactual by computing poverty incidence, excluding pension income from total household income.

Table 3.6 Percentage of Individual Income from Different Income Sources by Gender

Females and Males

Country	60+					80+					24–59				
	Labor	Nonlabor	Capital	Pension	Transfer	Labor	Nonlabor	Capital	Pension	Transfer	Labor	Nonlabor	Capital	Pension	Transfer
Argentina	35	64	2	53	3	2	97	1	81	8	93	6	1	2	2
Bolivia	37	63	11	39	12	8	91	5	62	24	89	10	2	0	6
Brazil	26	73	4	68	0	4	95	4	89	0	87	12	3	9	0
Chile	48	51	—	34	—	13	86	—	68	—	92	7	—	1	—
Colombia	37	63	11	48	5	13	86	14	61	10	92	7	2	4	2
Costa Rica	38	61	8	48	0	3	96	7	79	0	92	8	2	2	0
Dominican Republic	43	56	11	8	34	16	83	6	7	68	81	18	2	1	13
Ecuador	58	41	7	21	12	16	83	19	42	21	90	9	1	1	5
El Salvador	36	63	3	24	35	9	91	6	28	55	87	12	0	1	1
Guatemala	66	33	7	10	15	52	47	8	17	22	89	10	2	0	7
Honduras	44	55	7	14	46	14	85	14	11	74	84	15	1	0	20
Mexico	50	49.2	9.5	30.2	9.5	25.9	74.1	22.7	31.4	20.0	93.4	6.6	1.2	2.1	3.3
Nicaragua	62.3	37.7	2.2	12.2	23.3	36.0	64.0	4.3	21.9	37.7	91.2	8.8	1.1	0.4	7.2
Panama	29.8	70.2	4.7	56.5	7.2	6.2	93.8	6.9	72.3	12.5	89.3	10.7	1.4	4.1	2.7
Paraguay	58.8	41.2	5.2	14.1	18.4	13.2	86.8	3.5	24.3	58.7	90.1	9.9	1.4	1.3	6.6
Peru	39.6	60.4	6.1	23.6	8.9	10.1	89.9	3.2	36.7	19.4	81.5	18.5	1.9	1.3	4.3
Uruguay	25.1	74.9	6.4	64.1	4.4	2.6	97.4	6.9	84.8	5.6	89.2	10.8	2.1	4.9	3.9
Venezuela, R.B. de	44.2	55.8	3.1	40.5	12.2	14.8	85.2	3.1	49.4	32.7	92.5	7.5	0.8	2.8	3.9
LAC average	43.5	56.5	6.6	34.1	14.7	14.6	85.4	8.2	48.4	27.8	89.4	10.6	1.7	2.4	5.9

(continued)

Table 3.6 Percentage of Individual Income from Different Income Sources by Gender *(continued)*

Female	60+					80+					24–59				
Country	Labor	Nonlabor	Capital	Pension	Transfer	Labor	Nonlabor	Capital	Pension	Transfer	Labor	Nonlabor	Capital	Pension	Transfer
Argentina	20.5	79.5	2.3	65.2	5.0	0.8	99.2	1.5	81.9	9.6	88.0	12.0	2.0	3.3	6.5
Bolivia	28.6	71.4	19.6	33.0	18.8	5.3	94.7	2.0	54.6	38.1	80.1	19.9	3.3	1.0	15.5
Brazil	11.4	88.6	4.6	83.0	1.1	1.4	98.6	4.3	92.9	1.4	80.6	19.4	4.4	14.2	0.8
Chile	33.0	67.0	—	48.7	—	5.0	95.0	—	72.9	—	90.0	10.0	—	2.1	—
Colombia	21.7	78.3	17.6	54.7	10.7	3.3	96.7	11.1	69.8	13.6	88.1	11.9	2.4	4.1	5.0
Costa Rica	12.9	87.1	12.5	64.3	0.4	0.4	99.6	5.4	80.0	0.9	84.5	15.5	1.9	5.2	0.3
Dominican Republic	21.4	78.6	15.3	7.3	54.3	3.0	97.0	5.2	6.4	85.1	67.0	33.0	2.3	1.1	28.1
Ecuador	38.9	61.1	12.4	25.1	23.6	5.1	94.9	27.1	39.1	28.7	82.5	17.5	2.5	2.6	12.4
El Salvador	27.8	72.2	2.8	17.7	51.7	7.3	92.7	6.3	17.3	69.1	80.6	19.4	0.5	1.6	17.2
Guatemala	38.3	61.7	13.0	13.1	35.5	10.4	89.6	12.8	29.9	47.0	76.9	23.1	3.1	1.8	18.2
Honduras	26.4	73.6	9.5	11.7	71.7	8.3	91.7	6.2	10.6	89.5	70.3	29.7	1.8	1.1	41.5
Mexico	37.1	62.9	15.5	33.6	13.9	5.8	94.2	27.8	38.1	28.3	86.7	13.3	1.2	3.7	8.5
Nicaragua	37.9	62.1	1.7	17.7	42.7	11.3	88.7	4.2	38.0	46.4	86.1	13.9	1.7	0.4	11.8
Panama	14.6	85.4	3.3	66.7	15.1	1.7	98.3	2.5	72.2	23.4	84.0	16.0	1.8	6.3	5.9
Paraguay	35.2	64.8	8.2	14.2	32.7	7.2	92.8	0.4	23.3	69.1	81.8	18.2	1.5	2.1	13.8
Peru	27.4	72.6	5.3	20.1	24.6	9.2	90.8	2.1	18.7	43.1	78.4	21.6	2.2	1.5	10.9
Uruguay	15.1	84.9	5.8	73.7	5.4	0.7	99.3	5.8	86.8	6.6	84.5	15.5	1.8	8.9	4.8
Venezuela, R.B. de	26.7	73.3	2.7	43.3	27.2	4.9	95.1	2.6	35.7	56.8	87.2	12.8	0.9	4.5	7.4
LAC average	26.4	73.6	8.9	38.5	25.6	5.1	94.9	7.5	48.2	38.6	82.1	17.9	2.1	3.6	12.3

Male	60+					80+					24-59				
Country	Labor	Nonlabor	Capital	Pension	Transfer	Labor	Nonlabor	Capital	Pension	Transfer	Labor	Nonlabor	Capital	Pension	Transfer
Argentina	46.6	53.4	2.8	44.7	2.1	4.2	95.8	1.6	79.6	6.6	96.4	3.6	0.9	1.6	0.9
Bolivia	43.9	56.1	4.2	44.7	7.3	11.1	88.9	8.6	69.3	11.0	94.6	5.4	2.2	0.7	2.5
Brazil	36.8	63.2	4.3	58.7	0.2	9.0	91.0	5.3	85.6	0.1	91.6	8.4	2.2	6.0	0.2
Chile	56.5	43.5	—	28.2	—	20.8	79.2	—	63.9	—	93.4	6.6	—	1.7	—
Colombia	45.3	54.7	8.4	45.6	2.3	20.9	79.1	16.7	55.3	8.8	95.0	5.0	1.7	4.2	0.5
Costa Rica	50.2	49.8	6.6	40.5	0.1	5.3	94.7	8.4	79.3	0.0	95.7	4.3	2.2	1.6	0.0
Dominican Republic	52.6	47.4	9.8	8.4	25.9	21.0	79.0	7.0	8.2	62.5	89.9	10.1	2.3	1.1	4.5
Ecuador	67.7	32.3	5.1	19.8	7.4	24.0	76.0	13.5	45.4	17.0	95.4	4.6	1.6	1.3	1.7
El Salvador	43.8	56.2	4.1	30.0	22.0	10.5	89.5	7.4	38.3	43.9	94.0	6.0	0.8	1.2	4.0
Guatemala	77.9	22.1	5.5	9.6	7.0	67.5	32.5	7.1	12.7	12.7	95.2	4.8	1.8	1.0	2.0
Honduras	60.3	39.7	6.4	16.6	23.9	23.1	76.9	23.9	12.5	55.2	95.0	5.0	1.4	0.3	4.8
Mexico	57.2	42.8	6.7	28.6	7.5	37.1	62.9	19.9	27.7	15.4	96.7	3.3	1.1	1.4	0.8
Nicaragua	72.1	27.9	2.4	10.0	15.5	55.2	44.8	4.4	9.4	30.9	94.0	6.0	0.8	0.5	4.7
Panama	37.2	62.8	5.3	51.6	3.3	8.9	91.1	9.6	72.3	6.0	92.2	7.8	1.2	2.8	1.0
Paraguay	69.8	30.2	3.8	14.0	11.7	16.2	83.8	5.0	24.8	53.5	94.0	6.0	1.3	0.8	3.2
Peru	44.3	55.7	6.4	24.9	2.9	10.7	89.3	3.9	48.0	4.7	82.9	17.1	1.7	1.2	1.1
Uruguay	33.5	66.5	6.9	56.0	3.6	5.1	94.9	8.4	82.2	4.3	91.9	8.1	2.2	2.5	3.4
Venezuela, R.B. de	53.8	46.2	3.3	39.0	3.9	23.1	76.9	3.6	60.8	12.5	95.7	4.3	0.7	1.7	1.8
LAC average	52.8	47.2	5.4	31.7	8.6	20.8	79.2	9.1	48.6	20.3	93.5	6.5	1.5	1.8	2.2

Source: Authors' compilation.
Note: — = Data not available.

Figure 3.10 presents information on the percentage of people over age 60 who are receiving income from pensions at the national level. Pension coverage in LAC is very low: in 12 of the 18 countries for which data are available, the share of the aging receiving income from pensions is lower than 40 percent. Brazil, Uruguay, and Bolivia, have the highest coverage: 76 percent of the people age 60 and older receive a pension. The high coverage in Bolivia and Brazil results partly from large noncontributory programs that include the rural population. Slightly more than half of the aging populations in Argentina, Chile, and Costa Rica have pensions.

As a first approach to assessing the impact of pension systems on poverty, we present estimations of the incidence of poverty among beneficiaries and nonbeneficiaries of pensions. The results in table 3.7 are very clear: the incidence of income poverty among those who receive pensions is significantly lower than the incidence of poverty among those who do not receive pensions. The only three countries in which poverty rates for aging pensioners exceed 10 percent are Nicaragua (11.1 percent), Costa Rica (15.4 percent), and Bolivia (21.4 percent). The results in Bolivia reflect the fact that the amount paid by Bolivia's universal old-age social pension scheme is relatively small (US$18 monthly) while the poverty gap is very large.[9]

Next, we present a simple simulation of poverty rates, which excludes income from pensions from total household income. Note that this counterfactual exercise has an implicit assumption: If the pension system

Figure 3.10   People Over Age 60 Who Receive Income from Pensions, Percent

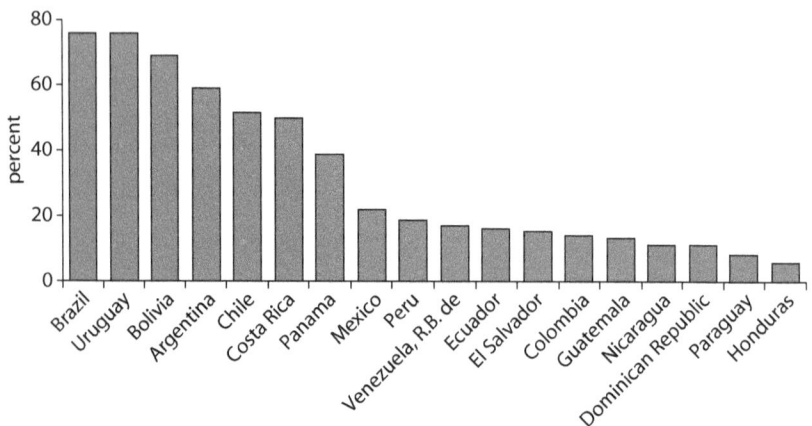

Source: Authors' calculations.

Table 3.7 Poverty Headcount Ratio of Pension Beneficiaries and Nonbeneficiaries

Country	All		60+		65+	
	Beneficiaries	Nonbeneficiaries	Beneficiaries	Nonbeneficiaries	Beneficiaries	Nonbeneficiaries
Argentina	1.7	13.4	1.1	11.2	1.1	11.3
Bolivia	20.6	35.9	21.4	38.0	22.9	46.0
Brazil	3.3	20.4	1.6	12.6	1.5	14.3
Chile	1.3	5.6	1.1	4.1	1.0	4.3
Colombia	2.4	38.6	2.1	48.9	2.4	51.4
Costa Rica	14.7	11.4	15.4	18.6	16.0	22.2
Dominican Republic	5.6	18.9	7.1	17.1	6.9	16.8
Ecuador	3.2	18.0	3.2	18.8	3.2	20.7
El Salvador	2.8	27.6	1.8	23.6	2.2	24.3
Guatemala	7.3	34.3	7.5	31.3	8.2	33.0
Honduras	5.5	37.1	6.4	38.0	7.8	39.6
Mexico	2.2	14.2	2.7	24.7	2.7	27.9
Nicaragua	12.5	43.0	11.1	35.1	10.4	35.4
Panama	8.0	23.6	1.7	26.7	1.9	29.7
Paraguay	0.0	21.6	0.0	18.5	0.0	18.8
Peru	0.3	26.5	0.4	24.5	0.4	26.0
Uruguay	1.6	8.0	0.6	2.6	0.5	3.0
Venezuela, R.B. de	6.0	39.3	6.1	38.6	6.3	40.4
LAC average (unweighted)	5.5	24.3	5.1	24.1	5.3	25.8

Source: Authors' compilation.

disappeared, older people's incomes would be reduced by the amount of the pensions they are now receiving. The assumption is strong, since it is likely that without pensions, behavior would change. Some older people could receive transfers from relatives, friends, or nongovernmental organizations, or decide to reenter the labor market. These behavioral changes would be even more important in the long run, because young adults would begin preparing for old age with the knowledge that social security will not be available. Given these caveats, the simulations of this section should be viewed as just the direct short-term effects of the pension system on poverty. A deeper analysis requires a behavioral model that is beyond the scope of this document.

Table 3.8 presents the results of this simple exercise: pension systems are the main factor that explains low old-age poverty rates in all four pro-aging countries (Argentina, Brazil, Chile, and Uruguay). The strongest impact occurs in Argentina and Brazil, where poverty among people over age 60 is less than 5 percent would increase by over 35 percentage points if pensions suddenly disappeared. In Bolivia, Chile, Costa Rica, Panama, and Uruguay the sudden disappearance of pensions would raise poverty among the aging by about 20 percentage points.

Figure 3.11 shows that for older people in all countries, the proportion of males receiving pensions is higher than for females. On average for the region, 45 percent of males over 80 receive pensions while only 35 percent of females do. Males have better pension coverage than females in every country in LAC. On average, males are 30 percent more likely than females to have access to a public pension, but there are large differences across countries. The greatest inequalities are found in Peru (where males are five times more likely than females to have a public pension), República Bolivariana de Venezuela (three times), Paraguay, the Dominican Republic and El Salvador.

Impact of Private Transfers on Poverty

We saw above how transfers from the family and from social networks are important income sources in several Central American and Caribbean countries: in the Dominican Republic, El Salvador, Guatemala, Honduras, and Nicaragua, income from transfers constitutes the main source of non-labor income for the aging.

Figure 3.12 presents the percentage of people over age 60 who receive income from private transfers.[10] The data refer only to transfers from outside the household. This includes remittances from migrants but does not include sharing of the income of relatives who reside with the aging.

Table 3.8 Poverty Headcount of Individuals with and without Pensions, Percent

Country	All With	All Without	60+ With	60+ Without	0–59 With	0–59 Without	65+ With	65+ Without	0–64 With	0–64 Without	0–14 With	0–14 Without	15–24 With	15–24 Without	25–59 With	25–59 Without
Argentina	11.0	18.6	4.9	40.0	12.0	15.1	3.7	46.5	11.8	15.4	19.2	21.9	11.6	15.1	8.0	11.1
Bolivia	35.0	38.1	26.6	48.6	35.8	37.1	25.3	52.8	35.6	37.1	44.5	45.6	28.4	30.1	30.7	31.9
Brazil	18.2	29.2	4.2	49.3	19.8	26.8	3.5	54.9	19.3	27.1	31.8	38.0	18.3	25.5	13.8	21.0
Chile	5.2	9.2	2.5	18.0	5.7	7.9	2.3	20.7	5.5	8.1	8.6	10.7	5.5	8.0	4.2	6.5
Colombia	37.8	40.6	42.2	52.0	37.3	39.2	44.3	54.2	37.3	39.5	46.3	47.5	36.3	38.5	31.0	33.4
Costa Rica	11.6	15.2	17.2	39.0	11.0	12.8	18.7	44.3	11.1	13.2	16.7	18.1	8.7	10.7	8.5	10.5
Dominican Republic	18.7	19.5	16.0	18.6	19.0	19.6	15.6	18.6	18.9	19.6	26.8	27.4	16.6	17.5	14.0	14.6
Ecuador	17.6	19.1	16.2	23.6	17.7	18.5	17.2	26.3	17.6	18.5	24.0	24.7	15.1	15.8	13.8	14.7
El Salvador	27.1	27.9	20.3	23.9	27.8	28.4	20.7	24.6	27.5	28.2	35.2	35.6	24.9	25.6	22.4	23.1
Guatemala	33.9	36.1	28.2	34.9	34.4	36.2	29.1	37.1	34.2	36.0	42.4	44.0	28.4	30.1	27.6	29.8
Honduras	36.9	37.3	35.6	37.4	37.0	37.2	37.0	38.9	36.9	37.2	45.7	45.8	30.1	30.4	31.3	31.6
Mexico	13.9	15.9	19.9	30.1	13.3	14.5	21.9	33.0	13.3	14.8	18.2	19.1	11.8	13.0	10.2	11.8
Nicaragua	42.7	43.2	32.5	34.5	43.5	43.9	32.5	34.8	43.2	43.7	53.2	53.7	38.5	38.8	36.6	37.1
Panama	22.3	27.9	16.9	36.0	22.9	26.9	18.1	39.3	22.7	27.0	32.4	36.5	21.8	25.6	16.6	20.5
Paraguay	21.4	22.1	16.9	20.4	21.8	22.2	17.2	21.2	21.7	22.1	29.7	30.0	18.1	18.5	16.5	17.0
Peru	21.0	22.0	19.9	23.1	21.2	21.8	20.4	24.2	21.0	21.7	28.9	29.4	21.6	22.3	20.5	21.1
Uruguay	6.7	14.8	1.1	23.5	8.1	12.6	0.9	26.4	7.7	12.7	14.6	19.6	7.2	12.2	4.8	9.0
Venezuela, R.B. de	38.7	41.4	32.9	44.6	39.1	41.2	34.1	46.9	38.9	41.1	49.7	51.1	36.0	38.3	32.2	34.6
LAC average (unweighted)	23.3	26.6	19.7	33.2	23.7	25.7	20.1	35.8	23.6	25.7	31.5	33.3	21.1	23.1	19.0	21.1

Source: Authors' compilation.

Figure 3.11   Pension Coverage by Age and Gender, Percent

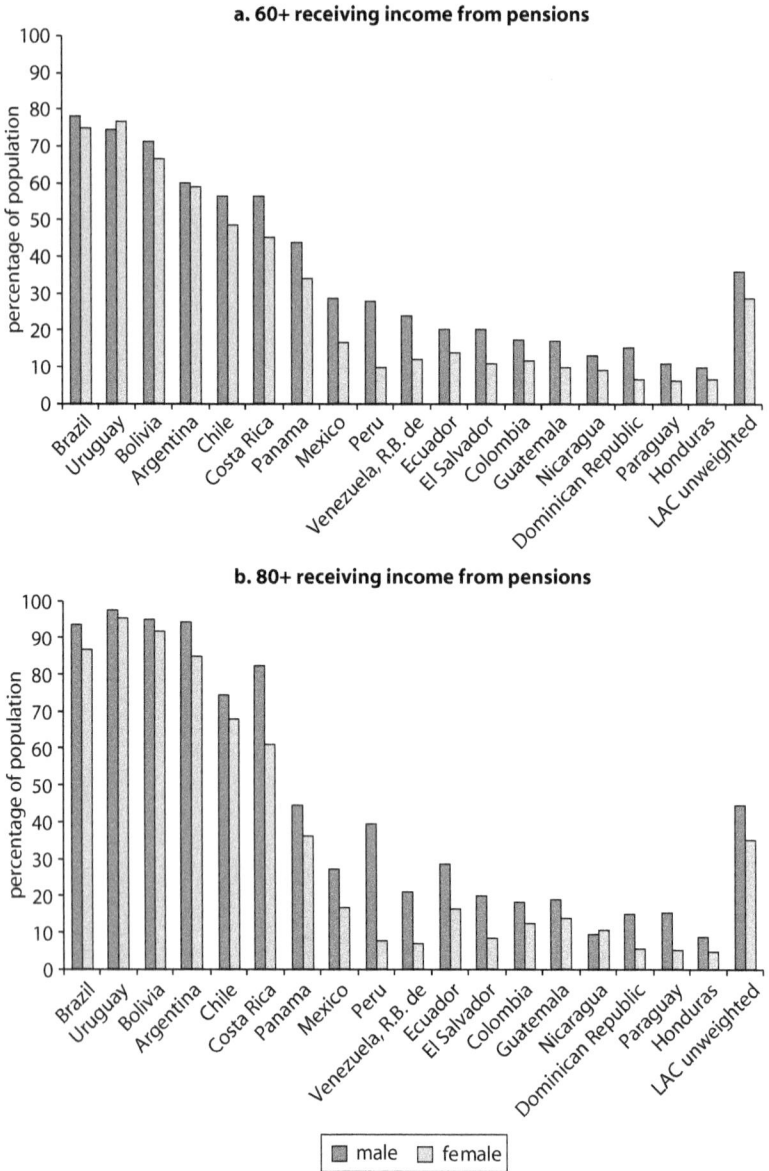

a. 60+ receiving income from pensions

b. 80+ receiving income from pensions

male   female

Source: Authors' calculations.

Figure 3.12   People over Age 60 Who Receive Private Transfers, Percent

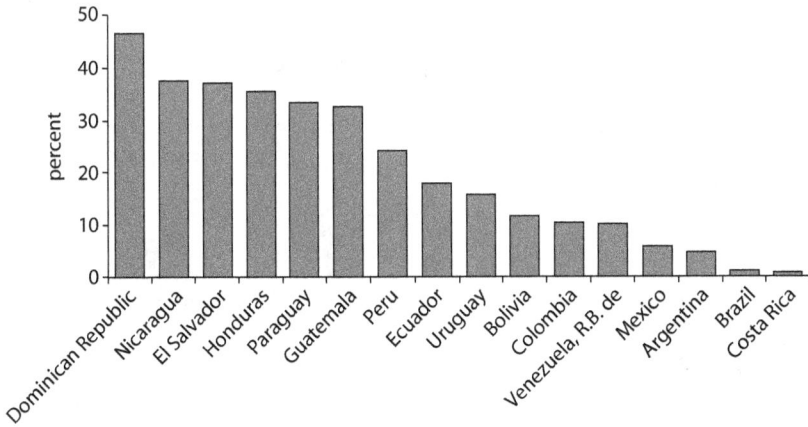

Source: Authors' calculations.

There are six countries where more than 30 percent of the aging receive familial transfers.

How useful are these transfers in helping the aging escape poverty? To answer that question, we estimate the incidence of poverty, excluding income from private transfers from total household income.[11] The outcomes of this exercise are presented in table 3.9.

Several results are worthy of mention. First, in those countries with the highest percentage of aging people receiving income from transfers, the impact on poverty of these transfers is very important: while 16.0 percent of Dominicans age 60 and older are poor, the percentage would climb to 33.5 percent if remittances were suddenly interrupted. The countries with the highest impacts after the Dominican Republic are, in descending order, Honduras, Guatemala, El Salvador, Paraguay, and Ecuador. In all these countries, poverty among the aging would increase by over 10 percent if remittances suddenly disappeared.

Second, the impact of remittances on poverty reduction is greater among the aging than among the young. Remittances reduce the poverty count by over 10 percentage points among the aging in six countries; the same effect is obtained for children (under age 15) in only three countries (El Salvador, Guatemala, and Honduras).

Third, in eight countries the impact of transfers on reducing old-age poverty is greater than the corresponding impact of pensions (see figure 3.13).

Table 3.9 Poverty Headcount Ratio of Individuals with and without Transfers

Country	All		60+		0–59		65+		0–64		0–14		15–24		25–59	
	With	Without	With	Without	With	Without	With	Without	With	Without	With	Without	With	Without	With	Without
Argentina	11.0	15.4	4.9	6.3	12.0	16.9	3.7	5.0	11.8	16.6	19.2	25.1	11.6	19.7	8.0	11.0
Bolivia	35.0	39.3	26.6	34.7	35.8	39.7	25.3	34.1	35.6	39.6	44.5	48.4	28.4	34.7	30.7	33.3
Brazil	18.2	18.5	4.2	4.5	19.8	20.2	3.5	3.7	19.3	19.7	31.8	32.2	18.3	18.9	13.8	14.0
Colombia	37.8	39.6	42.2	44.9	37.3	39.0	44.3	47.1	37.3	39.0	46.3	48.0	36.3	38.5	31.0	32.5
Costa Rica	11.6	12.0	17.2	17.4	11.0	11.4	18.7	19.0	11.1	11.5	16.7	17.1	8.7	9.2	8.5	8.8
Dominican Republic	18.7	25.9	16.0	33.5	19.0	25.1	15.6	35.6	18.9	25.2	26.8	33.4	16.6	23.8	14.0	19.2
Ecuador	17.6	23.8	16.2	26.8	17.7	23.4	17.2	29.8	17.6	23.3	24.0	30.9	15.1	20.9	13.8	18.4
El Salvador	27.1	36.5	20.3	36.8	27.8	36.5	20.7	39.4	27.5	36.3	35.2	45.2	24.9	34.7	22.4	29.3
Guatemala	33.9	43.0	28.2	41.4	34.4	43.1	29.1	43.7	34.2	42.9	42.4	52.5	28.4	36.3	27.6	35.2
Honduras	36.9	47.9	35.6	53.2	37.0	47.6	37.0	55.8	36.9	47.5	45.7	57.2	30.1	42.0	31.3	39.9
Mexico	13.9	18.0	19.9	26.2	13.3	17.2	21.9	29.0	13.3	17.2	18.2	23.4	11.8	15.6	10.2	13.2
Nicaragua	42.7	47.3	32.5	40.8	43.5	47.9	32.5	42.1	43.2	47.6	53.2	57.8	38.5	43.4	36.6	40.5
Panama	22.3	26.9	16.9	24.5	22.9	27.2	18.1	26.4	22.7	27.0	32.4	37.7	21.8	26.3	16.6	20.0
Paraguay	21.4	27.8	16.9	30.8	21.8	27.5	17.2	34.1	21.7	27.4	29.7	36.3	18.1	24.2	16.5	21.1
Peru	21.0	23.3	19.9	23.5	21.2	23.2	20.4	24.5	21.0	23.1	28.9	32.2	21.6	24.1	20.5	22.3
Uruguay	6.7	10.4	1.1	2.4	8.1	12.4	0.9	2.0	7.7	11.9	14.6	21.4	7.2	11.6	4.8	7.8
Venezuela, R.B. de	38.7	42.2	32.9	39.2	39.1	42.4	34.1	41.4	38.9	42.3	49.7	53.0	36.0	40.2	32.2	35.2
LAC average (unweighted)	24.4	29.3	20.7	28.6	24.8	29.5	21.2	30.2	24.6	29.3	32.9	38.3	22.0	27.3	19.9	23.6

Souce: Authors' compilation.
Note: Data not available for Chile.

Figure 3.13   Simulated Impact Pensions and Private Transfers on Old-age Poverty (percentage point increase of poverty)

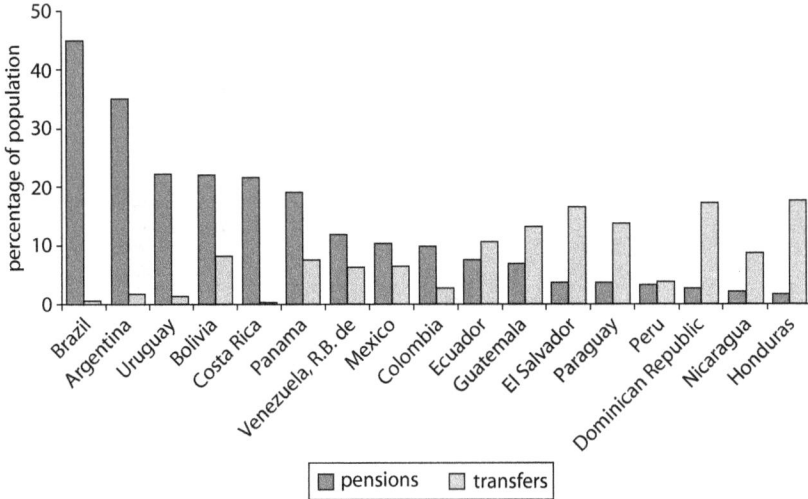

Source: Authors' calculations.

The Labor Market and Old-age Poverty

As shown in table 3.10, among young adults, males have homogeneously high rates of labor market participation in all LAC countries—practically all are over 90 percent. At age 60 and again at age 80 there are strong drops in male labor market participation in the four high-pension countries (Argentina, Brazil, Chile, Uruguay) and in Colombia and Costa Rica. The smallest drop in participation occurs in the Andean countries (Bolivia, Ecuador, and Peru) and Paraguay, in Central America (Guatemala, Honduras, Nicaragua), and in Mexico.

Young women have lower rates of participation than young males and there is considerably greater heterogeneity in participation rates across countries; participation rates of women aged 25–59 range mostly between 50 and 75 percent. The highest female participation rates are found in the Andean countries (Bolivia, Ecuador, and Peru) and Paraguay and in three of the four high-pension-coverage countries: Argentina, Brazil, and Uruguay.

In table 3.11, we present unemployment rates for different age groups at the national level. For almost all countries, (Mexico is the only exception), the aging are less likely to be unemployed. This could be interpreted favorably as meaning that older workers are less vulnerable

Table 3.10 Labor Force Participation

Country	Male (%)				Female (%)				Both genders (%)					
	All	60+	80+	25–59	All	60+	80+	25–59	All	60+	80+	25–59	60+ with pensions	60+ without pensions
Argentina	82.8	42.4	7.2	94.2	53.1	17.4	1.5	66.2	66.6	27.6	3.4	79.4	10.9	42.3
Bolivia	91.4	66.1	33.0	97.1	67.9	51.8	22.7	71.6	79.1	58.5	27.1	83.8	50.7	75.8
Brazil	83.1	44.0	16.2	91.4	58.6	19.8	5.7	68.0	70.2	30.5	9.7	79.2	25.8	45.5
Chile	82.5	43.0	10.1	92.8	47.2	15.4	1.9	57.0	63.8	27.5	5.0	74.2	19.1	36.4
Colombia	83.4	44.6	10.9	93.2	51.4	15.9	3.4	61.0	66.0	28.6	6.5	75.8	14.0	30.9
Costa Rica	86.1	41.4	6.0	95.0	45.7	10.6	1.1	53.4	64.9	24.7	3.2	73.3	12.1	37.2
Dominican Republic	82.3	51.8	17.4	89.8	43.8	12.4	1.8	51.4	62.6	31.7	8.9	70.2	17.3	32.9
Ecuador	91.2	69.2	28.8	97.1	66.8	38.0	12.8	74.3	78.5	53.1	20.2	85.2	27.4	58.1
El Salvador	84.5	52.3	20.5	93.5	49.7	21.3	7.5	57.3	65.0	35.1	13.1	73.1	16.3	38.5
Guatemala	93.2	73.1	40.4	97.7	50.2	28.8	9.3	54.4	69.7	50.2	23.6	73.7	33.8	52.8
Honduras	90.1	66.9	30.3	95.7	44.1	24.5	8.1	48.5	65.0	44.5	18.4	69.7	14.3	46.3
Mexico	89.5	60.6	28.7	95.9	52.2	25.1	9.2	58.4	69.3	41.2	17.2	75.6	25.1	45.7
Nicaragua	91.3	67.3	29.3	96.6	50.5	23.6	6.6	56.3	69.3	43.8	16.2	74.9	23.2	46.3
Panama	86.9	49.7	18.1	96.0	49.6	13.5	3.2	58.6	67.8	31.1	9.9	76.9	14.7	41.8
Paraguay	90.0	63.2	22.0	95.7	60.3	34.6	8.9	66.4	74.6	47.8	15.1	80.7	22.0	50.1
Peru	88.5	65.5	32.0	94.8	67.3	43.0	22.1	73.9	77.5	53.8	26.6	83.9	26.1	60.2
Uruguay	77.0	33.2	4.2	94.8	53.5	15.5	1.1	72.9	64.1	22.8	2.2	83.1	11.6	57.7
Venezuela, R.B. de	89.1	54.0	21.6	95.3	57.1	20.4	5.0	64.3	72.9	36.2	11.7	79.8	—	—
LAC average (unweighted)	86.8	54.9	20.9	94.8	53.8	24.0	7.3	61.9	69.3	38.3	13.2	77.4	21.4	47.0

Source: Authors' compilation.
Note: — = not available.

Table 3.11   Unemployment Rate by Age Group

Country	All (%)	60+ (%)	25–59 (%)	60+ with pensions (%)	60+ without pensions (%)
Argentina	6.6	6.2	6.6	4.7	6.5
Bolivia	2.9	1.2	3.4	59.4	12.9
Brazil	5.6	2.0	5.9	1.5	2.9
Chile	5.5	3.5	5.7	3.7	3.3
Colombia	8.8	5.4	9.1	4.9	5.4
Costa Rica	3.6	3.8	3.6	4.8	3.5
Dominican Republic	2.8	0.4	3.0	0.0	0.4
Ecuador	9.4	8.0	9.6	11.8	7.7
El Salvador	5.1	3.7	5.3	1.6	3.9
Guatemala	1.0	0.4	1.1	1.2	0.3
Honduras	1.4	0.4	1.6	0.0	0.4
Mexico	1.9	2.2	1.8	0.3	2.4
Nicaragua	5.0	3.1	5.3	2.2	3.1
Panama	5.5	2.5	5.8	1.3	2.8
Paraguay	3.3	2.1	3.5	9.2	1.8
Peru	2.9	1.4	3.1	3.8	1.2
Uruguay	7.4	5.7	7.6	8.6	4.0
Venezuela, R.B. de	7.4	5.6	7.6	—	—
LAC average (unweighted)	4.8	3.2	5.0	7.0	3.7

Source: Authors' compilation.
Note: — = not available.

to unemployment because of greater seniority or other factors that shelter these workers from shocks. More likely, however, it is due to the aging workers responding to such shocks either: (a) by dropping out of the labor force (perhaps as part of a family strategy that requires the older family members to engage in homecare activities to release younger family members for labor market activities) or (b) by rapidly accepting a downgrade in working conditions (for example, a pay cut or loss of security).[12]

Figure 3.14 depicts the hours worked by the aging at the national level as a percentage of the hours worked by those aged 25–59. The hours worked by the aging, while lower than those of other adults, are quite high, ranging from 93 to 94 percent of the hours worked by adults in Bolivia, República Bolivariana de Venezuela, and Chile, to 80 to 81 percent of the hours worked by adults in Costa Rica, Brazil, and Panama.

Hourly wages of the aging as a percent of the hourly wages of those aged 25–59 are presented in Figure 3.15. The table shows that in most countries, the hourly wage rate received by the over-60s is slightly below

Figure 3.14   Hours Worked by the Aging as a Percentage of the Hours Worked by Those Aged 25–59

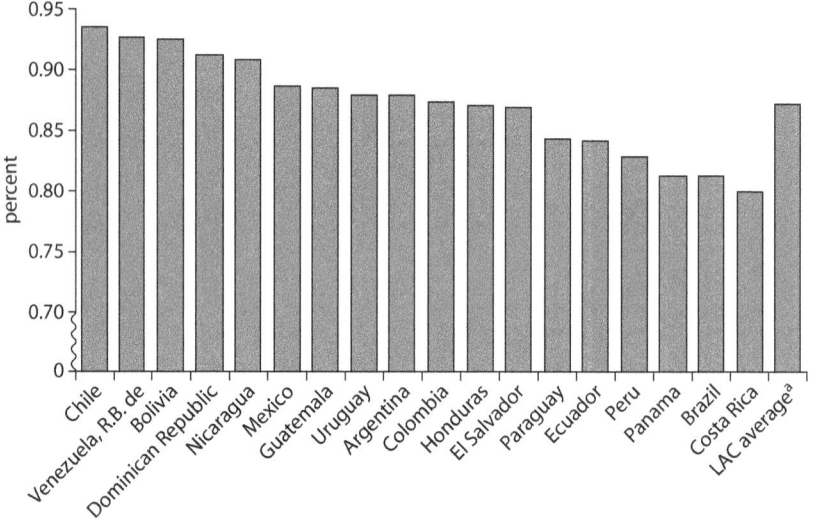

Source: Authors' calculations.
Note: a. Unweighted mean.

Figure 3.15   Hourly Wages of the Aging as a Percentage of the Hourly Wages of Those Aged 25–59

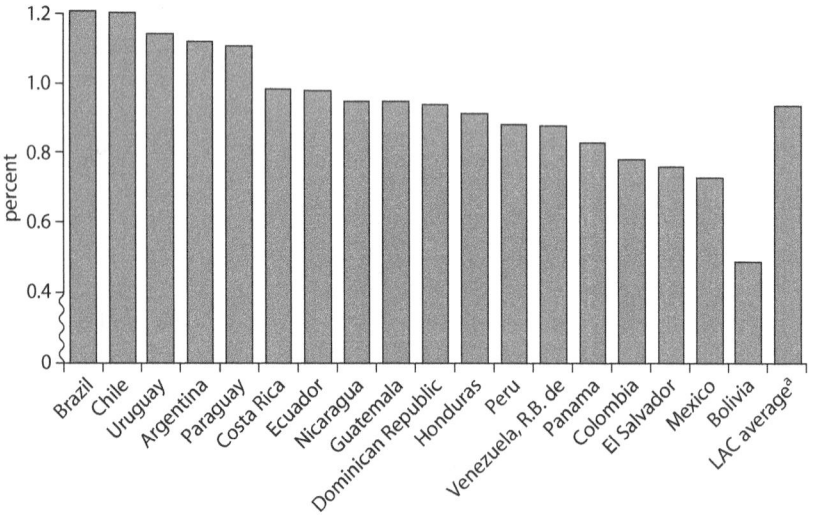

Source: Authors' calculations.
Note: a. Unweighted mean.

the average hourly rate received by young adults. Two groups of countries, however, exhibit a different pattern. In the pro-aging countries—Argentina, Brazil, Chile, and Uruguay—and in Paraguay, hourly wages among the over-60s are higher than the average for young adults. This suggests that for countries where pension coverage is high, only individuals with well-remunerated jobs will remain in the labor market after reaching pension-able age. In the anti-aging countries—Colombia and Mexico—and in Bolivia and El Salvador, wages for the over-60s are drastically lower than for young adults.

Finally, figure 3.16 presents the labor income of the aging as a percent of the income of those aged 25–59. Brazil is the only country in which the over-60 workers have, on average, higher labor incomes than young adults. Argentina, Chile, Guatemala, Paraguay, and Uruguay are the other countries where the labor income of the aging reaches a proportion higher than the 90 percent of the labor income of adults. On the other hand, Bolivia (49 percent), Colombia (61 percent), El Salvador (61 percent), and Mexico (62 percent) are the countries where the labor income of the working aging is a lower proportion of the labor income of adults.

Figure 3.16   Labor Income of the Aging as a Percentage of Income of Those Aged 25–59

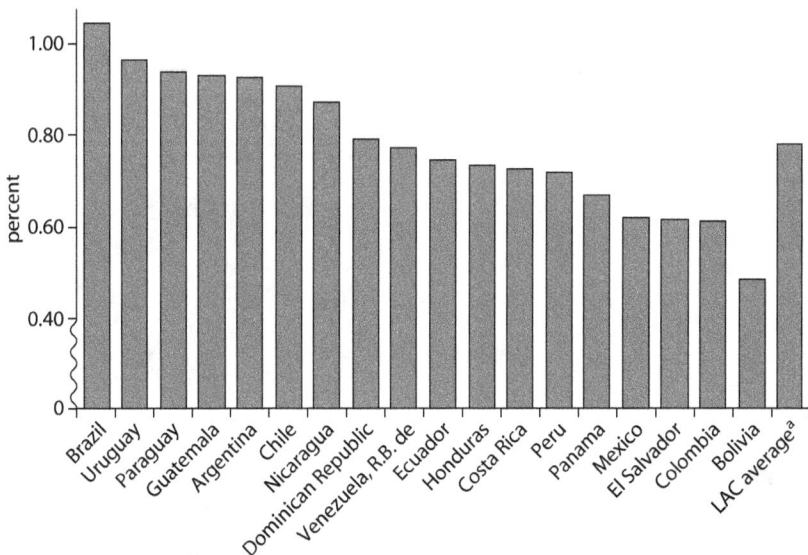

Source: Authors' calculations.
Note: a. Unweighted mean.

Inequality among the Aging

Is income inequality higher among the aging than among the nonaging population? Table 3.12 presents Gini coefficients for household per capita income distribution, comparing inequality between the over-60 population and young adults aged 25–59. The table makes two comparisons, one excluding zero incomes (which are more common among the aging) and another including zero incomes. The results show that inequality among the aging is lower than among young adults only in the four pro-aging countries with large and generous pension systems—Argentina, Brazil, Chile, and Uruguay. Greater inequality exists among the aging than among young adults in many of the other countries (in many of these countries the result is found only if zero incomes are included in the estimation).

Given that Argentina, Brazil, Chile, and Uruguay are the countries in which pension system coverage is high, and relative income inequality among the aging is low, it is important to understand the role played by

Table 3.12   Gini Coefficient: Household Per Capita Income

Country	With zero income		Without zero income	
	60+	25–59	60+	25–59
Argentina	0.445	0.481	0.437	0.475
Bolivia	0.591	0.565	0.590	0.562
Brazil	0.517	0.551	0.509	0.542
Chile	0.508	0.531	0.503	0.525
Colombia	0.670	0.612	0.602	0.586
Costa Rica	0.525	0.495	0.511	0.490
Dominican Republic	0.552	0.512	0.552	0.511
Ecuador	0.562	0.557	0.553	0.550
El Salvador	0.492	0.510	0.486	0.502
Guatemala	0.627	0.550	0.624	0.548
Honduras	0.590	0.564	0.579	0.558
Mexico	0.587	0.513	0.563	0.507
Nicaragua	0.551	0.545	0.551	0.542
Panama	0.556	0.543	0.550	0.536
Paraguay	0.553	0.526	0.550	0.522
Peru	0.555	0.500	0.547	0.485
Uruguay	0.425	0.456	0.420	0.451
Venezuela, R.B. de	0.472	0.446	0.446	0.433
LAC average (unweighted)	0.543	0.525	0.532	0.518

Source: Authors' compilation.

the pension system and other transfers in reducing or increasing income inequality among the aging.

Figure 3.17 presents estimations of the Gini coefficient of household per capita income including and excluding from it income received from pensions and transfers. This exercise constitutes a first approximation of the analysis of the importance of different income sources in reducing or increasing income inequality. The results show the importance of the income transferred by the pension system in reducing inequality among the aging. Pensions and transfers have an equalizing role everywhere. This is especially marked in the four pro-aging countries, but also in Bolivia. In all these countries, this result is robust to the inclusion or exclusion of zero incomes.

We noted above that in Bolivia, where there is large coverage of noncontributory pensions, despite the relatively small size of the benefit, the noncontributory pensions have a significant impact on poverty reduction. In addition, figure 3.17 shows that the Bolivian noncontributory pensions also have a noticeable impact on reducing inequality among the aging.

The results in figure 3.17 show transfers are also important in reducing income inequality among the aging, particularly in most of the countries with a high percentage of the aging receiving transfers: the Dominican Republic, El Salvador, Guatemala, and Paraguay.[13]

Living Arrangements of the Aging and Familial Transfers

Cross-national comparisons of older people's living arrangements reveal substantial differences between developed and developing regions. A major difference is that older people in developed countries tend to live on their own (alone or with a spouse), while living with kin—either children or with extended family—is still the norm in most of the developing world. Studies throughout the developing world have consistently shown the predominance of older people residing with adult children and/or grandchildren. These studies also show that older people rely heavily on family members for their well-being and survival (Bongaarts and Zimmer 2002 and Zeng and George 2000; cited by Kinsella and He 2009). Living arrangements have a profound impact on welfare and on economic behavior. They have been found to affect people's life satisfaction, health status, health-care-seeking behavior, and chances of institutionalization. In addition to social norms that place the responsibility of caretaking with children, the choice of living arrangements depends on various personal characteristics, including marital status, availability of kin, personal wealth, health status, and individual preferences. The availability of transfers of

Figure 3.17   Gini Coefficients of Income of the Aging (with and without pensions and transfers)

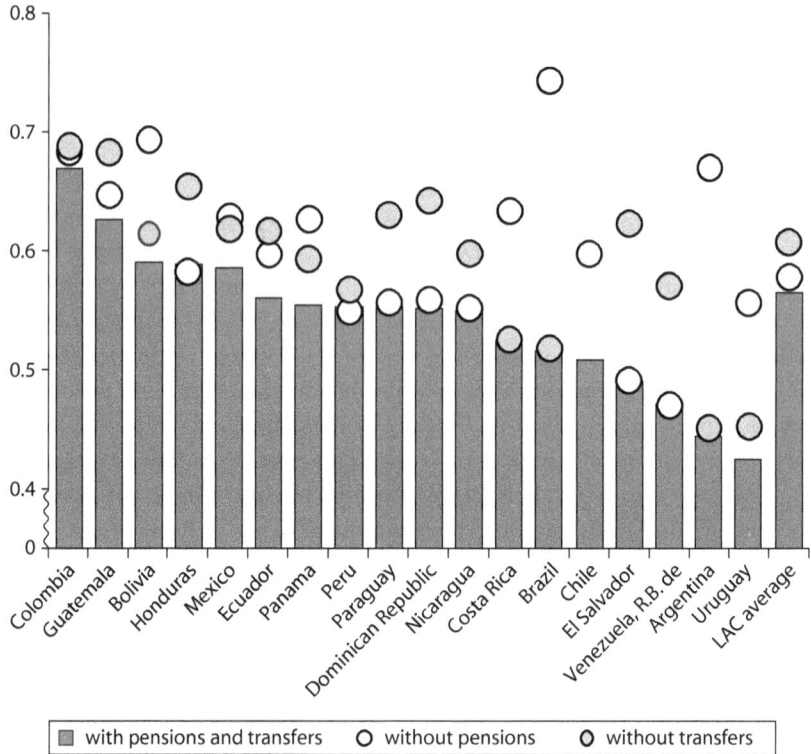

| with pensions and transfers   ○ without pensions   ○ without transfers |

Source: Authors' calculations.

money, space, and time is also important in this choice (Kinsella and He 2009). This section discusses the living arrangements of the aging in LAC, specifically examining the impact on living arrangements of the availability of kin, age, access to pensions, income, and gender. The section also includes a discussion of the direction of transfers across the generations.

Studies of living arrangements in the developed world show that multigenerational coresidence is on the decline. This has been documented for Greece and Japan, where the extended family structure has historically been a prominent feature of social life. The proportion of older Japanese living with children dropped from 87 percent in 1960 to 56 percent by the end of the century and is expected to drop to 42 percent by 2010. It is unclear whether this trend is due to the existence of increasing resources of older people, to the existence of social protection programs that enhance old-age security, which facilitated their independent living, or both. An alternative view is that the trend is mainly due to increasing opportunities for the young combined with declining parental control over their children.[14]

In Latin America, most of the aging live in multigenerational households, but there are significant differences among countries. Figure 3.18 shows the percentage of aging who live on their own (alone or with their spouse). The young Central American countries have the least number of aging living on their own (between 10 and 23 percent). At the other extreme, in two of the older countries—Uruguay and Argentina—about half of the aging live on their own. It should be noted that older countries by definition have a smaller proportion of people in the younger generations than the younger countries. One may think of this as a "supply effect," while choices by the aging related to income, wealth, or other factors may be a "demand effect." Figure 3.19 suggests that availability of kin is a relevant determinant of living arrangements.

Figure 3.20 exhibits nonparametric (kernel) estimates of the proportion of people living alone by age in each Latin American country. It shows a rising trend in single-generational families starting at about age 50 and rising until age 75 to 80 and then decreasing sharply. This is likely to suggest that in Latin America, as in the developed countries, the old become more dependent on their families, but this becomes marked only after age 75.

The tendency to move back with the extended family is very different by gender. Women reaching age 80 move back with their extended family

Figure 3.18   Percentage of Aging Living Alone or with a Spouse

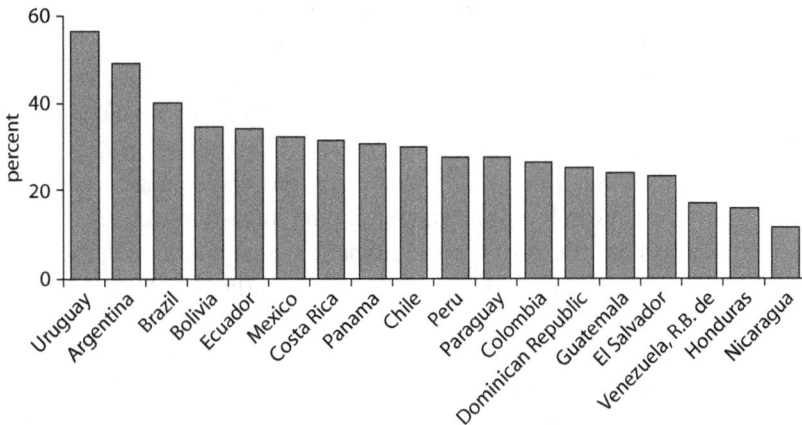

Source: Authors' calculations.

Figure 3.19   Percentage of Aging Living Alone and Availability of Children, National Level

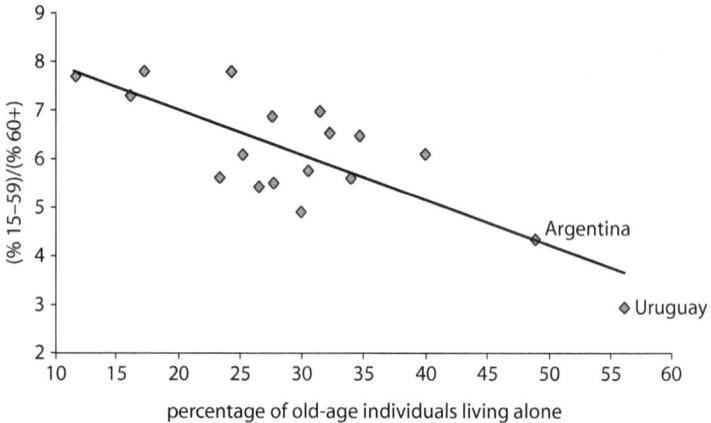

Source: Authors' calculations.

in 12 of the 18 countries while men show no such tendency, instead they become slightly more independent (figure 3.21). This difference is partly due to differences in longevity—women tend to survive their spouses and rejoin the extended family after becoming widows. It partly reflects a greater ease of women to reenter extended family living arrangements.

How do personal income and wealth influence decisions about living arrangements? Does greater income lead to less multigenerational co-residence? Would the aging prefer to live on their own if they had the means? How do risk and security influence living arrangements?

Figure 3.22 compares the incidence of poverty among the aging living independently and those in multigenerational living arrangements. In 13 of the 18 countries, the poverty headcount is higher or similar among the aging in a multigenerational coresidence than among those living alone. Poverty is much less common among those living alone in Argentina, Bolivia, Brazil, Chile, and Uruguay (all high-pension-coverage countries), and in the Dominican Republic and Nicaragua (high-remittance-coverage countries). By contrast, poverty is significantly greater among those living alone in the anti-aging countries identified earlier in the chapter—Colombia, Costa Rica, and Mexico.

Table 3.13 shows that in all countries (except Nicaragua and Paraguay) the aging living on their own have higher average incomes than those coresiding. It seems that the aging with higher incomes choose to live independently while those less fortunate coreside. Does this mean that

Figure 3.20 Percentage of People Living in Single-generation Households

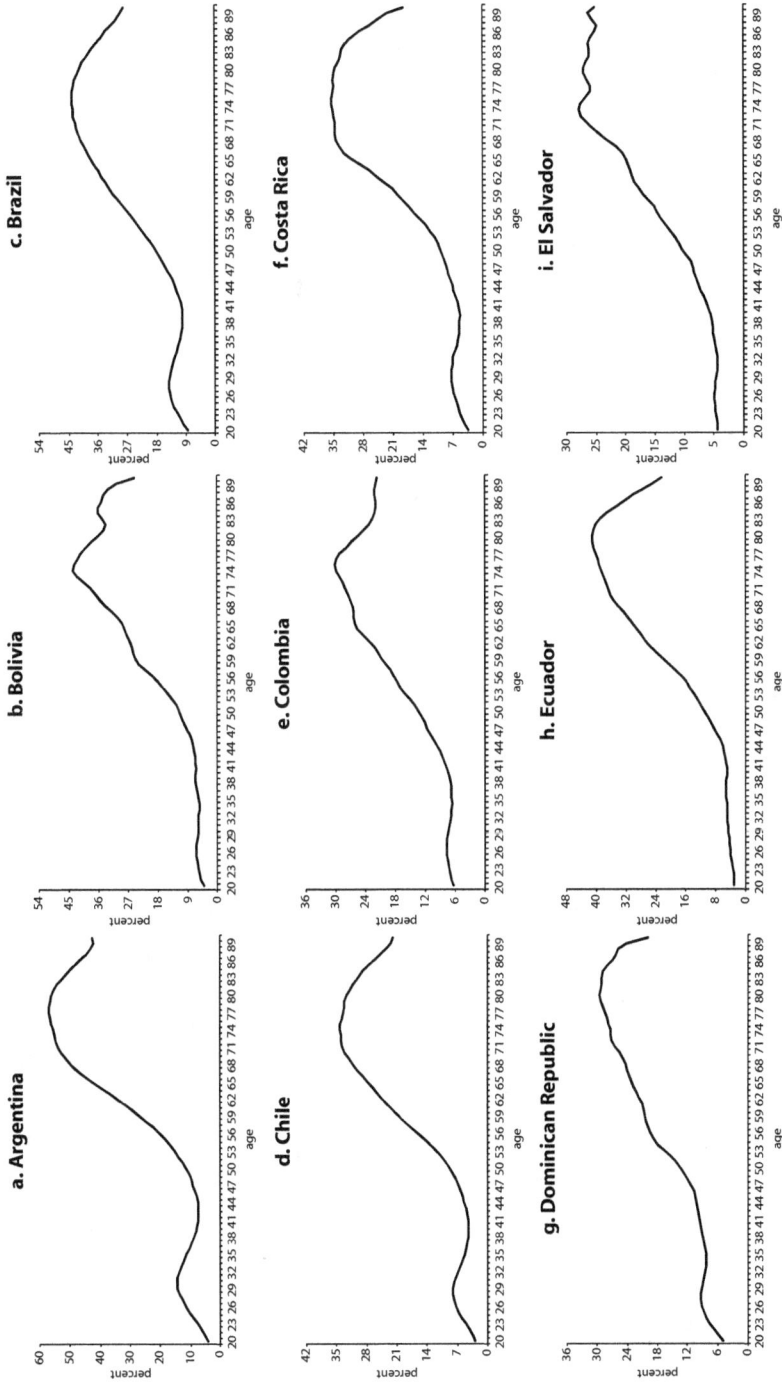

a. Argentina

b. Bolivia

c. Brazil

d. Chile

e. Colombia

f. Costa Rica

g. Dominican Republic

h. Ecuador

i. El Salvador

(continued)

123

Figure 3.20   Percentage of People Living in Single-generation Households *(continued)*

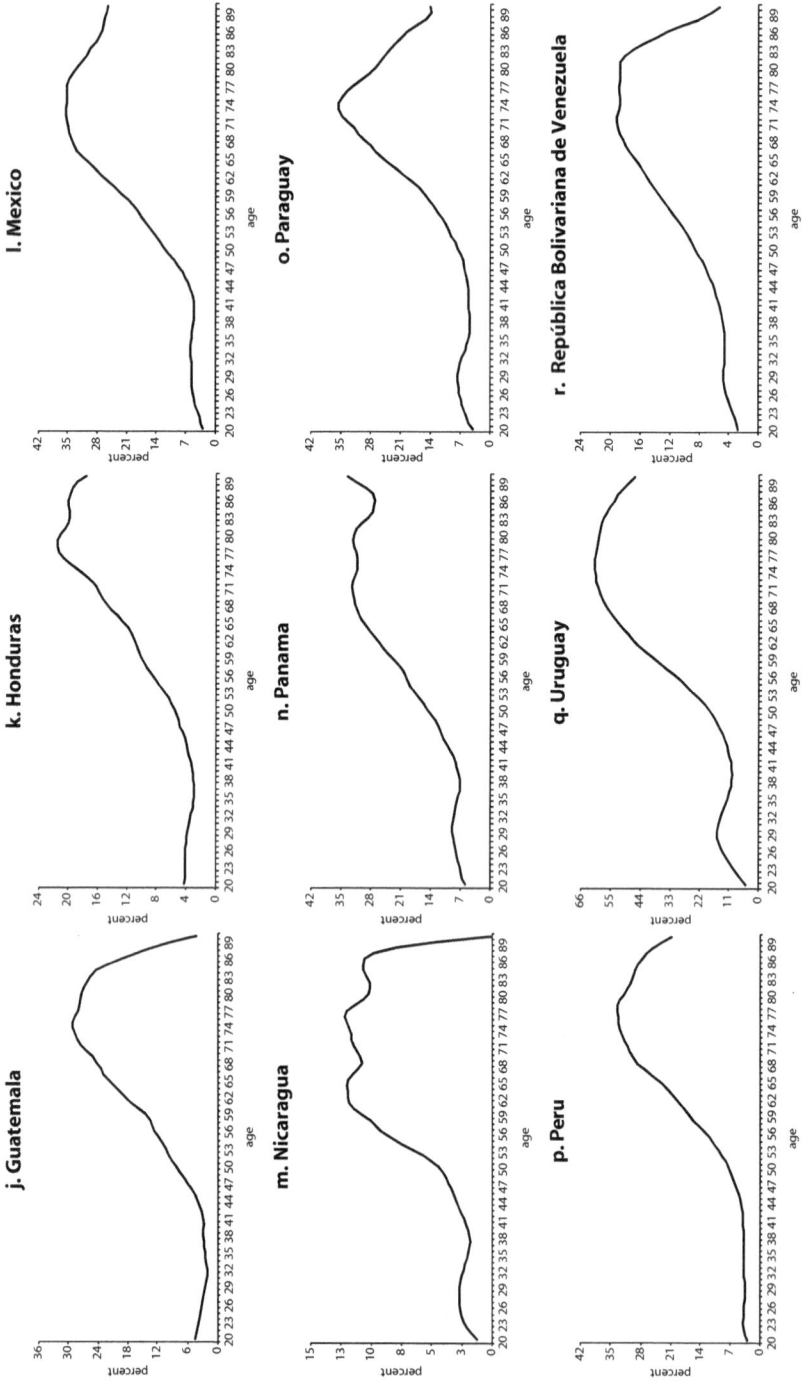

j. Guatemala

k. Honduras

l. Mexico

m. Nicaragua

n. Panama

o. Paraguay

p. Peru

q. Uruguay

r. República Bolivariana de Venezuela

Source: Authors' calculations.

Figure 3.21   Males Living Alone or with a Spouse and Females Living Alone or with a Spouse, Percent

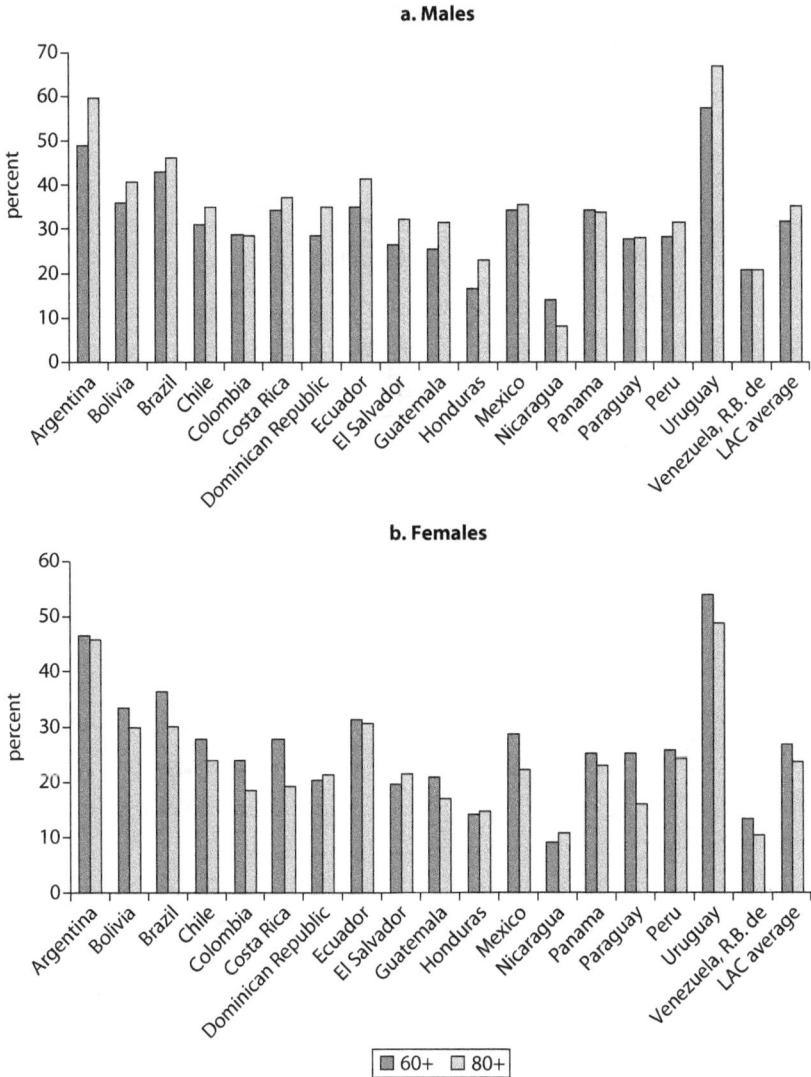

a. Males

b. Females

■ 60+   □ 80+

Source: Authors' calculations.

Figure 3.22   Poverty among the Aging by Living Arrangements, Percent

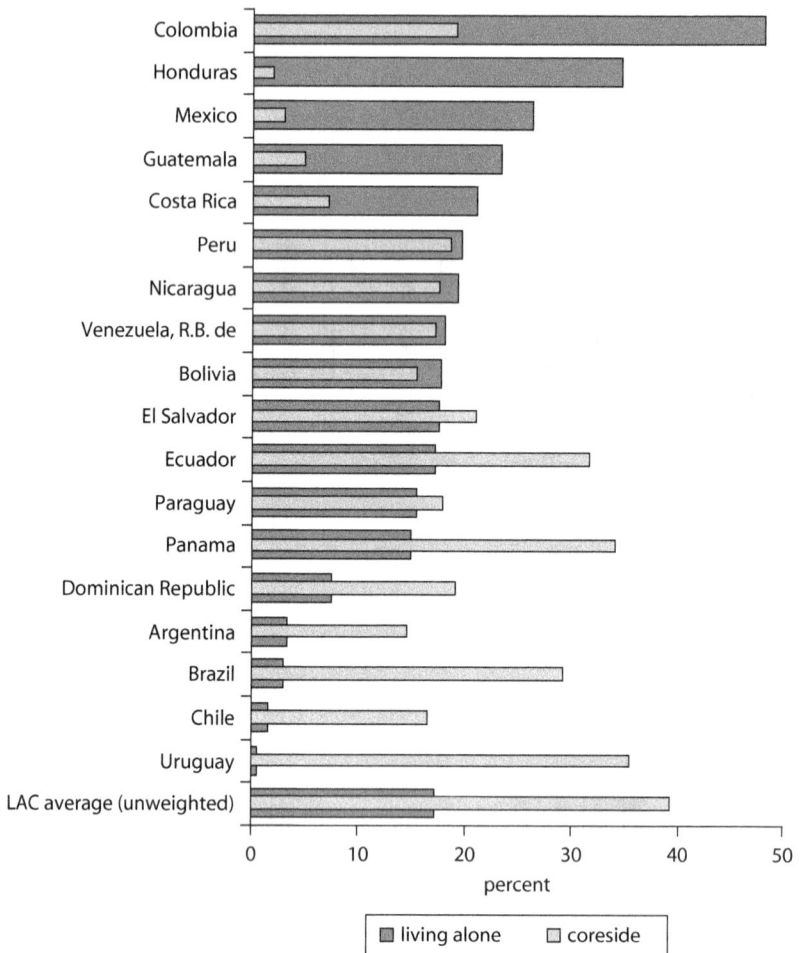

Source: Authors' calculations.

the aging destitute live with their children and grandchildren to benefit from their higher income? Could it be that in LAC—where most of the aging lack pension coverage—they are net receivers of transfers?

In countries with well-established pension and social security programs, many older adults provide support to their adult children and grandchildren. This support may include financial help, shelter, and care for spouses, older parents, and grandchildren. Data from the ongoing Health and Retirement Study in the United States confirm that older

Table 3.13   Average Income of the Aging

	Individual income			Household per capita income		
	Coreside (local currency)	Living alone (local currency)	Differential (%)	Coreside (local currency)	Living alone (local currency)	Differential (%)
Argentina	603	790	31	525	790	51
Bolivia	778	819	5	551	819	49
Brazil	869	963	11	654	963	47
Chile	210,137	231,768	10	166,738	231,768	39
Colombia	245,967	341,831	39	252,162	341,831	36
Costa Rica	94,952	111,852	18	97,811	111,852	14
Dominican Republic	6,550	7,807	19	5,300	7,807	47
Ecuador	196	213	8	170	213	25
El Salvador	1,011	1,189	18	985	1,189	21
Guatemala	1,484	1,532	3	1,169	1,532	31
Honduras	2,567	2,607	2	1,920	2,607	36
Mexico	2,348	3,077	31	2,307	3,077	33
Nicaragua	1,633	1,461	−11	1,214	1,461	20
Panama	243	318	31	209	318	52
Paraguay	1,080,386	933,590	−14	739,463	933,590	26
Peru	544	558	2	412	558	35
Uruguay	7,240	7,874	9	5,661	7,874	39
Venezuela, R.B. de	427,513	486,478	14	352,849	486,478	38

Source: Authors' compilation.
Note: local currency used.

parents are more likely to provide time, money, and shelter to their children than to receive such transfers. This is reversed only for unmarried people over age 80, who are more likely to receive support than to provide it (NIA 2009). The same pattern was found in the United Kingdom for people up to age 75 and in other European countries where net transfers to children remain positive, but decline at very old ages.

The picture for developing countries is less clear. Older people in developing countries are known to make substantial contributions to family well-being through housekeeping, grandchild care, and socialization. There is less evidence about the direction of transfers in developing countries. A new generation of studies is attempting to measure intergenerational transfers, including, in developing countries, to understand the direction of wealth flows and how they may shift with changes in economic development. This is being measured with the introduction of age into national accounts (Mason and others 2009).

The household surveys used in this chapter are not ideally suited to measure flows between the generations because they do not contain information about unpaid work and have imperfect information about how income is shared inside households. However, some interesting patterns are reported below. Are the elderly net receivers of transfers in LAC?

Table 3.13 suggests that is not the case. The table shows how much income the aging "bring into the household" (that is, their individual income) and compares it with the average income of the household. In 12 countries, the individual income of older people in coresidence is higher than the average income of the household. The only exceptions are Colombia and Costa Rica, (where they bring less than the average), and Ecuador, El Salvador, Mexico, and Panama where they bring an amount very close to the average. In other words, in LAC, assuming income is shared equally among all household members, the aging are making net transfers to the other generations with whom they reside.

It seems that the aging with higher incomes choose to live independently, while poorer aging Latin Americans tend to coreside. Possible reasons explaining this pattern include: (a) greater altruism among the less fortunate; (b) a greater importance of economies of scale for those close to the poverty line; and (c) multigenerational coresidence provides a form of insurance against risks, and the lower-income aging are more risk averse than their wealthier counterparts.

Table 3.14 presents econometric results that largely confirm the descriptive results discussed above. For each of the 18 countries, the probability of the aging living on their own is regressed against indicators of age, income, gender, and urban/rural location.[15] Income is measured as a continuous variable, and a dummy for poverty is also included to test for discontinuities. The key results are as follows:

- *Age:* This is included in two variables, age and age squared, to test for the inverted U shape discussed above. In all countries the signs are as expected, and in 16 of the 18 countries both variables are statistically significant.
- *Urban or rural location:* The probability of the aging living on their own is smaller in urban locations; this result is significant in 7 of the 16 countries for which data are available.
- *Gender:* Worldwide, men are more likely than women to live on their own; this pattern is also found in our sample for LAC—the gender dummy has a positive sign in all countries, and it is significant in 13 of the 18 countries.

Table 3.14 Probability of the Aging Living on Their Own

Country	Individual income dF/dx	z	Poverty dummy dF/dx	z	Pensions dummy dF/dx	z	Remittances dummy dF/dx	z	Gender dummy dF/dx	z	Age dF/dx	z	Age² dF/dx	z	Urban dummy dF/dx	z	Observations
Argentina	0.0001	[5.13]**	-0.1334	[3.52]**	0.0291	[1.56]	0.1186	[3.65]**	0.0119	[0.73]	0.1734	[11.03]**	-0.0011	[10.76]**	—	—	10,556
Bolivia	0.0000	[0.21]	-0.2237	[6.09]**	0.0657	[1.46]	0.1029	[2.72]**	0.0260	[0.82]	0.0135	[0.35]	-0.0001	[0.31]	-0.1908	[5.49]**	1,395
Brazil	0.0000	[5.09]**	-0.3007	[15.81]**	0.0142	[1.67]	0.1885	[7.30]**	0.0796	[13.55]**	0.0774	[13.44]**	-0.0005	[13.32]**	0.0003	[0.04]	35,389
Chile	0.0000	[2.02]*	-0.1818	[5.19]**	-0.0086	[0.98]	—	—	0.0368	[4.32]**	0.0723	[8.94]**	-0.0005	[8.70]**	-0.0270	[3.54]**	33,215
Colombia	0.0000	[1.80]	-0.0747	[2.89]**	-0.0600	[2.24]*	0.0809	[2.72]**	0.0505	[2.21]*	0.0576	[2.60]**	-0.0004	[2.47]*	-0.0225	[0.79]	5,902
Costa Rica	0.0000	[1.46]	0.1235	[5.26]**	0.0131	[0.68]	-0.0414	[0.50]	0.0490	[2.62]**	0.0979	[5.38]**	-0.0007	[5.31]**	-0.0375	[2.16]*	3,658
Dominican Republic	0.0000	[0.26]	-0.1498	[6.22]**	0.0338	[1.11]	0.1027	[5.34]**	0.0951	[4.90]**	0.0321	[2.18]*	-0.0002	[2.05]*	-0.0107	[0.55]	2,641
Ecuador	0.0000	[0.29]	-0.0135	[0.64]	0.0409	[1.66]	0.0583	[2.99]**	0.0335	[1.86]	0.0594	[3.94]**	-0.0004	[3.49]**	-0.0341	[1.98]*	5,995
El Salvador	0.0000	[0.19]	-0.0253	[1.23]	0.0272	[1.11]	0.1663	[9.55]**	0.0908	[5.46]**	0.0387	[2.86]**	-0.0002	[2.72]**	0.0256	[1.49]	6,650
Guatemala	0.0000	[0.69]	-0.0603	[2.54]*	-0.0787	[2.40]*	0.0809	[3.14]**	0.0537	[2.07]*	0.1123	[4.62]**	-0.0007	[4.36]**	0.0676	[2.85]**	3,377
Honduras	0.0000	[1.73]	0.0013	[0.09]	0.0188	[0.90]	0.0075	[0.54]	0.0445	[3.36]**	0.0312	[2.70]**	-0.0002	[2.09]*	0.0074	[0.52]	4,111
Mexico	0.0000	[3.14]**	0.0562	[1.91]	-0.0157	[0.71]	0.0392	[1.46]	0.0460	[2.23]*	0.0790	[4.20]**	-0.0005	[4.04]**	-0.0035	[0.14]	4,873
Nicaragua	0.0000	[1.40]	-0.1033	[4.36]**	-0.0421	[1.32]	0.0551	[2.27]*	0.0622	[2.47]*	0.0289	[1.46]	-0.0002	[1.43]	-0.0457	[1.73]	1,644
Panama	0.0000	[4.13]**	-0.0368	[1.75]	0.0197	[1.03]	0.0982	[5.50]**	0.0864	[5.49]**	0.0487	[3.23]**	-0.0003	[3.20]**	-0.0531	[3.21]**	5,159
Paraguay	0.0000	[0.35]	0.0143	[0.43]	0.0782	[1.70]	0.1406	[5.21]**	0.0359	[1.45]	0.1375	[5.29]**	-0.0009	[5.28]**	0.0246	[0.96]	1,769
Peru	0.0000	[1.80]	-0.0801	[5.47]**	0.0151	[0.66]	0.0596	[3.79]**	0.0220	[1.53]	0.0930	[7.58]**	-0.0006	[7.30]**	-0.2212	[15.17]**	8,565
Uruguay	0.0000	[2.86]**	-0.2887	[10.59]**	0.0040	[0.55]	0.0990	[13.43]**	0.0271	[4.66]**	0.1067	[19.70]**	-0.0007	[19.34]**	-0.0348	[5.64]**	48,517
Venezuela, R.B. de	0.0000	[2.68]**	-0.0198	[2.25]*	0.0106	[0.87]	0.1050	[8.82]**	0.0777	[8.94]**	0.0370	[4.44]**	-0.0003	[4.47]**	—	—	11,251

Source: Authors' compilation.

Note: * = Significant at 10%.

** = Significant at 5%.

— = Data not available.

- *Income:* We tested this variable on its own and with the inclusion of dummy variables for poverty, pensions, and remittances. The table presents the results, which include all these variables. Income is always positive, but when accompanied by a poverty dummy it is significant in only 7 of 18 countries. The poverty dummy, however, is negative (less likely to live on their own when poor) in all countries and significant in 11 of the 18 countries.

Conclusions

This chapter describes poverty levels at different points in the life cycle in 18 Latin American countries. Poverty levels vary widely across countries in the region and there is a high correlation between national poverty and poverty in any age group. Children have poverty rates that are between one-and-a-half and two times the national average (even after adjusting for adult equivalence and economies of scale). In five countries, the poverty rate of the young is more than twice the average for the rest of the population—these are the pro-aging countries (Argentina, Brazil, Chile, Uruguay) with the large pension systems mentioned above and the Dominican Republic.

In LAC, there is a widespread assumption that poverty is particularly common among the aging. Much of the ongoing debate about social pensions is justified by this assumption. The evidence presented in this chapter suggests that the population over 60 is not more likely than the rest of the population to be poor (with the exception of Colombia, Costa Rica, and Mexico). A greater problem of poverty and vulnerability exists in the population over 80.

What explains the relative poverty ranking of the aging? The aging depend on a greater variety of sources of income than the rest of the population. Everywhere, pensioners have significantly lower poverty rates than nonpensioners, and even in the low-coverage countries, simple simulations suggest that pensions are a significant source of income for their beneficiaries. But in most countries, pensions are not a significant source of income for most over-60s, since less than 40 percent of the aging receive pensions. Pensions are significant in the four pro-aging countries and in Costa Rica and Bolivia. In two of the anti-aging countries, pension coverage is especially low (Colombia and Mexico).

Other transfers, especially remittances from international migrants, are also a significant source of income for would-be poor aging people in many countries. In six countries, poverty among the aging would increase by 10 percent if these remittances were to abruptly cease (in three of these countries poverty would increase by almost 20 percent). International remittances are also important for the young, but their impact on poverty among the young is significant in only three countries, and in all countries the poverty-reducing impact of transfers is larger among the aging than among the young.

Labor market income is also significant for the aging, especially for those not receiving pensions or other transfers. Among nonpensioners, typically over 40 percent of the over-60s remain active in the labor market. A significant proportion continue to work beyond age 80. The aging work long hours—over 80 percent of the average hours worked by younger workers. Unemployment is very low among the aging, possibly suggesting that those without the option of ceasing to work rapidly downgrade into lower-paying jobs.

Hourly wages for the aging show varied patterns. In the low-pension countries, wages for the aging are a fraction of the wages received by younger adults. The extreme cases are a group of countries that includes two low-income and two middle-income countries: Bolivia and El Salvador, together with Colombia and Mexico. In the high-pension-coverage countries, the aging work only if paid attractively; wages for the aging are higher than for younger adults.

Living arrangements are determined by a variety of factors, including the age, marital status, and availability of kin of the aging. We investigated the significance of the income levels of the aging population and found that the aging tend to coreside with their extended families when their incomes are close to the poverty line, while the aging with higher levels of income tend to live on their own. Since independent living of the aging may impact health care, long-term care of the aging, child care arrangements for working mothers, and other aspects with possible fiscal implications, policies directed to the aging should take these incentive effects into account.

Notes

1. No survey data are available for Cuba, the country with the oldest population in the region.

2. The different patterns found could be related to age selectivity of migration or to differential rural-urban survival rates. The testing of these hypotheses is beyond the scope of this paper.

3. The same pattern is found in rural and urban areas.

4. The Argentine household survey does not have rural coverage. In Mexico, there is an important difference in poverty incidence between urban and rural areas—9.7 percent compared to 28.4 percent, respectively.

5. Defining the aging as those older than age 60 or those older than age 65 does not make a significant difference.

6. Costa Rica also shows this pattern, but with an overall poverty rate that is very low.

7. The exercise borrows an idea developed by Paes de Barros and others (2001) to simulate the impact of demography on poverty in Brazil; in their article, they impose the demographic structure of a previous generation on a new generation to investigate the impact of demography on poverty.

8. We do not have data on private transfers for Chile.

9. In January 2008, the original BONOSOL program was replaced by *Renta Dignidad*. The new program pays US$25 monthly. While this program is not enough to eradicate poverty among elderly pensioners, it does reduce their poverty rate substantially.

10. We do not have data on private transfers for Chile.

11. It is a counterfactual exercise with the same characteristics of the exercise presented in the previous section. In this sense, it constitutes a first approach to estimate the direct short-run effects of transfers on poverty and does not consider the likely behavioral changes that would be expected.

12. If the aging are more likely than the young to permanently leave the labor force after a period of unemployment, policy makers should be made aware that unemployment among the elderly may have larger long-term effects than among the young.

13. This is also true in Ecuador and Honduras but only when zero incomes are included in the estimation.

14. For the latter view, see Engelhardt, Gruber, and Perry (2005).

15. Unfortunately, the significance of the availability of kin could not be estimated because the surveys do not report on family members not living in the household.

References

Barrientos, A. 2000a. "Work, Retirement, and Vulnerability of Older Workers in Latin America. What Are the Lessons for Pension Design?" *Journal of International Development* 12: 495–506.

———. 2000b. "Comparing Pension Schemes in Chile, Singapore, Brazil and South Africa." Paper No. 67. University of Manchester, Institute for Development Policy and Management, Manchester, England.

————. 2002. "Old Age, Poverty, and Social Investment." *Journal of International Development* 14: 1133–41.

Barrientos, A., M. Gorman, and A. Heslop. 2003. "Old Age Poverty in Developing Countries: Contributions and Dependence in Later Life." *World Development* 31 (3).

Bongaarts, J., and Z. Zimmer. 2002. "Living Arrangements of the Elderly in the Developing World: An Analysis of DHS Household Surveys." *Journal of Gerontology* 57B (3): S145–57.

Bourguignon, F., and S. Chakravarty. 2002. "Multi-dimensional Poverty Orderings." Working Paper 2002-22, DELTA, Paris.

Bourguignon, F., M. Cicowiez, J. Dethier, L. Gasparini, and P. Pestieau. 2006. "What Impact Would a Universal Minimum Pension Have on Old Age Poverty in Developing Countries?" Unpublished manuscript, World Bank.

Buhmann, B., G. Rainwater, G. Schmaus, and T. Smeeding. 1988. "Equivalence Scales, Well-being, Inequality and Poverty: Sensitivity Estimates across Ten Countries Using the Luxembourg Income Study Database." *Review of Income and Wealth* 34: 115–42.

Deaton, A., and C. Paxson. 1995. "Measuring Poverty among the Elderly." National Bureau of Economic Research Working Paper No. 5296, Cambridge, MA.

————. 1997. "Poverty among Children and the Elderly in Developing Countries." Research Program in Development Studies, Princeton University, Princeton, NJ.

————. 1998a. "Economies of Scale, Household Size, and the Demand for Food." *Journal of Political Economy* 106 (5): 897–930.

————. 1998b. "Poverty among the Elderly." In *Inquiries in the Economics of Aging*, ed. D. Wise. Chicago: Chicago University Press for the National Bureau of Economic Research.

Deaton, A., and S. Zaidi. 2002. "Guidelines for Constructing Consumption Aggregates for Welfare Analysis." Living Standards Measurement Survey Working Paper 135, World Bank, Washington, DC.

Engelhardt, G. V., J. Gruber, and C. D. Perry. 2005. "Social Security and Elderly Living Arrangements: Evidence from the Social Security Notch." *Journal of Human Resources* 40: 354–72.

————. 2006. "A Guide to the SEDLAC: Socio-Economic Database for Latin America and the Caribbean." Centro de Estudios Distributivos Laborales y Sociales (CEDLAS) and the World Bank, La Plata and Washington, DC.

Gasparini, L., J. Alejo, F. Haimovich, S. Olivieri, and L. Tornarolli. 2007. "Poverty among the Elderly in Latin America and the Caribbean." Centro de Estudios Distributivos Laborales y Sociales (CEDLAS) Working Paper No. 55, La Plata.

Kakwani, N., and K. Subbarao. 2007. "Poverty among the Elderly in Sub-Saharan Africa and the Role of Social Pensions." *Journal of Development Studies* 43 (6): 987–1008.

Kinsella, K., and W. He. 2009. *An Aging World: 2008 International Population Reports*. P95/09-1. Washington, DC: U.S. Government Printing Office.

Lanjouw, P., B. Milanovic, and S. Paternostro. 1998. "Poverty and the Economic Transition: How Do Changes in Economies of Scale Affect Poverty Rates for Different Households?" World Bank Working Paper No. 2009, World Bank, Washington, DC.

Mason, A., R. Lee, A.-C. Tung, M.-S. Lai, and T. Miller. 2009. "Population Aging and Intergenerational Transfers: Introducing Age into National Accounts." In *Developments in the Economics of Aging*, ed. David A. Wise. National Bureau of Economic Research. Chicago: The University of Chicago Press.

NIA (National Institute on Aging). 2009. "Growing Older in America: The Health and Retirement Study." National Institutes of Health, U.S. Department of Health and Human Services, Washington, DC.

Paes de Barros, R., S. Firpo, and R. P. Guedes Barreto. 2001. "Demographic Changes and Poverty in Brazil." In *Population Matters*, ed. N. Birdsall, A. C. Kelley, and S. W. Sinding. New York: Oxford University Press.

Ravallion, M., S. Chen, and P. Sangraula. 2008. "Dollar a Day Revisited." Policy Research Working Paper No. 4620, World Bank, Washington, DC.

Ravallion, M., D. Gaurav, and D. Van de Walle. 1991. "Quantifying Absolute Poverty in the Developing World." *Review of Income and Wealth* 37: 345–61.

United Nations. 2009. "World Population Prospects: The 2008 Revision." Department of Economic and Social Affairs, Population Division. Highlights. Working Paper No. ESA/P/WP.210, United Nations, New York.

Zeng, Y., and L. George. 2000. "Family Dynamics of 63 Million (in 1990) to More Than 330 Million (in 2050) Elders in China." *Demographic Research* 2.

CHAPTER 4

How Age Influences the Demand for Health Care in Latin America

André C. Medici

Introduction

One of the most dramatic changes worldwide in the last 50 years is the population aging process, which is associated with the demographic effects of decreasing fertility and increasing lifespan. This process started early in developed countries and was followed in developing countries; however, the pace of the process accelerated in certain regions, including Latin America and the Caribbean (LAC). Population aging, when combined with other economic, labor market, health status, and health care trends, points to a number of socioeconomic and policy challenges in the decades ahead.

The incidence of chronic diseases increases with aging, as does the number of medical visits, medicines consumed, and hospitalizations, with great impact on the aging adult's family budget. The health care costs for people age 65 and older are several times greater than the cost for young people in many developed countries, and chronic diseases disproportionately affect older adults and are associated with disability and diminished quality of life.

Demographic changes associated with aging demand a new health policy agenda, with implications for the supply and demand sides. On the supply side, the biggest challenge is how to face the fiscal impacts of aging in order to provide funds to finance more and expensive health services. On the demand side, the challenge is to implement policy measures to promote healthy behaviors and other preventive actions among older adults, and to achieve affordable costs for health insurance plans, drugs, and medical procedures.

Despite these challenges, poor health is not an inevitable consequence of aging. Many successful policies to prevent diseases and disabilities in developed countries are providing better coverage and quality of health care to the aging. Controlling risk factors such as high blood pressure, obesity, and diabetes, and promoting healthy behaviors by reducing smoking, alcohol consumption, and a sedentary lifestyle, could help prevent the early consequences of chronic diseases in older adults. Public health interventions could help stem the rising costs of health care by promoting the use of effective preventive measures to make healthy aging a reality.

The social and economic circumstances of the aging, such as late retirement, improvement of health and functional ability, and public and private policies that influence individual well-being are in a state of continuing evolution and transition. Understanding the complexities of this situation and the relationship among demographics, policy, social behavior, economics, and health is essential to improve the design of social policies and to guarantee a better quality of life for the aging.

Objectives, Data, and Concepts

This chapter describes the impact of the aging process on health in Latin America through a discussion of how it affects health profiles, health needs, and the utilization of health facilities. Trends in the impact of aging on health costs and their implications will be discussed using Disability-Adjusted Life Years (DALYs)[1] data on health profiles and health needs. DALY estimations in LAC are available at the regional level in the World Health Organization (WHO) databanks and at the disaggregated level in some of the LAC countries.

Health utilization information is available in some countries from data sources such as household surveys and administrative records aggregated at the country level by major heath institutions. Health costs by age are not often estimated in LAC countries, but some public and private health insurance institutions have current information that could be used to estimate aggregated health costs.

Given the lack of systematic information related to most of the relevant variables, this chapter uses selected information on health needs, health utilization, and health costs to discuss the economic implications of aging on the demand for health services, including the financial gaps in financing these services.

Figure 4.1 illustrates how demographic aging affects health demand, by increasing health needs, health utilization, and health costs. Health needs increase because the prevalence of chronic diseases is higher among the aging. Increasing health needs lead to higher utilization of health services, but international experience shows that the level of utilization does not increase as fast as the perceived health needs, generating gaps in health services utilization when compared with health needs.

On the other hand, health costs associated with aging and increased health utilization by the aging are higher than health costs among other age groups because health problems in older groups, associated with degenerative and chronic diseases, requires diagnostics, treatments, and medicines that are more complex and expensive than those required to attend the medical needs of the younger population. The combination of increasing health costs and higher health care utilization, without managerial measures to improve the efficiency of health care delivery, leads to higher health financing needs, which are not financed by the current health budgets, generating health financial gaps.

Thus, aging could lead to gaps in health utilization and health financing. Health gaps could generate future economic losses associated with reduced human capital, since health is an essential element of economic wealth and productivity.[2] If the current level of health expenditure is not

Figure 4.1   Economic Implications of Aging on Health Demand

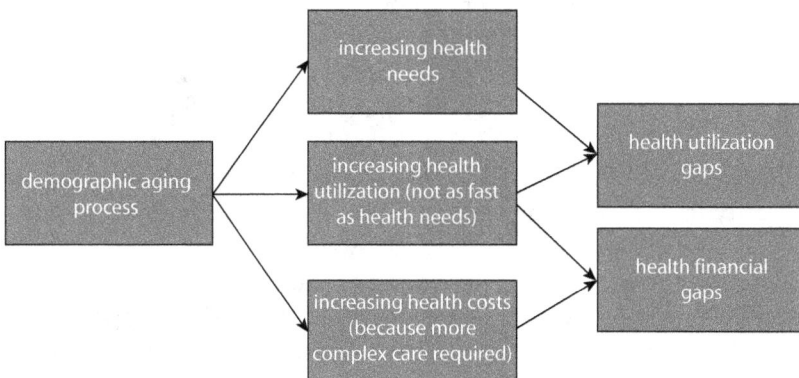

Source: Author.

enough to fill all health needs[3] at an acceptable level of efficiency, the society would have a potential health financial deficit, which reflects the difference between the cost of the estimated health needs and the current levels of health expenditure.

Health needs is a complex and tricky concept with many dimensions. However, for practical purposes, health needs must consider diseases and health conditions for which there are effective interventions (prevention or treatment) the effect of which can be measured, allowing the assessment of health gains to be based on evidence. Massive data based on trials and tests must be available to prove whether the existing evidence is enough to assure that health interventions could generate health gains.

Health Needs in LAC

DALYs: Basic Concepts and Criticism

Observing trends in mortality and morbidity patterns[4] enables us to obtain definitions, estimations, and measurements regarding health issues. Both variables—mortality and morbidity—affect the collective human potential to benefit society. Early mortality eliminates the possibility of realizing human potential, and morbidity can severely compromise a person's ability to contribute to and partake of all that makes a full life—study, work, leisure, and communication with family, friends, and community.

An approximation of the implications of mortality and morbidity is the burden of disease (BOD) approach. Variables such as Disability-Adjusted Life Years should be used as an expression of a stock of health needs existing in one region or country.

DALYs is a synthetic health indicator used to measure the consequences of premature death, or Years of Life Lost (YLL), and disability, or Years Living with Disability (YLD), in the average lifetime of the population (DALYs = YLL + YLD). The YLL are calculated based on life expectancy at birth and YLD are calculated based on the incapacity severity level and on the time spent incapacitated. Both components of DALYs (YLL and YLD) are age-weighted according to studies related to the economic contribution of age groups and social preferences surveys. A discount rate should be applied to components of DALYs (generally 3 percent), indicating that future years will be less valued than current years.[5]

Health Needs and Mortality Trends in LAC

Mortality is an important component of the BOD study. The World Health Organization mortality data estimations for 2004 were improved over previous BOD data, especially for causes more difficult to measure, such as communicable diseases and injuries. Data on mortality were also improved due to better estimations of mortality for children under age 5 and to the review of models used to estimate coverage of death registrations in all countries.

The weight of mortality in the BOD study varies according to development level. The development process, associated with the progress in health systems coverage and quality, brings longer and more productive lives to the entire population. In this context, the weight of mortality is reduced and the weight of morbidity (YLD) in the BOD grows. Data from 2004 show that in high-income countries, the mortality component of the DALYs (YLL) accounted for only 55 percent of the BOD, but in the poorest region of the world—Sub-Saharan Africa—the mortality component was substantially higher (85 percent).

The weight of mortality in the BOD in LAC was 59 percent in 2004, which is closer to the YLL participation in the BOD found in developed countries. Figure 4.2 shows the YLL as a share of the BOD in the LAC region by age and gender in 2004. The participation of the YLL in the

Figure 4.2   Mortality as a Share of DALYs in LAC by Age and Gender, 2004

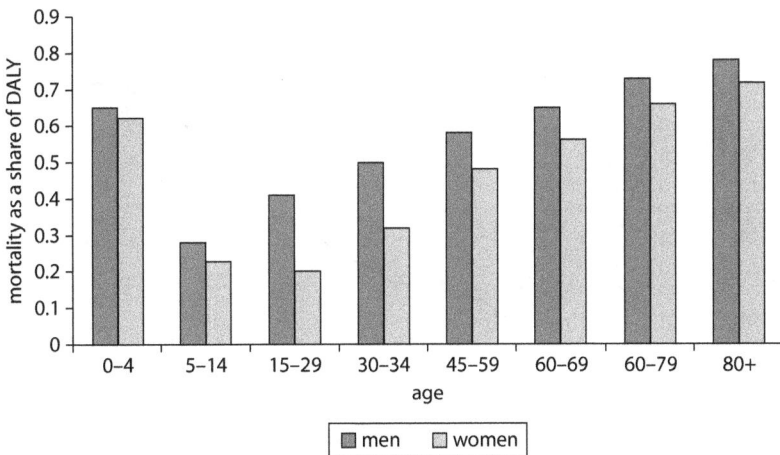

Source: Author's calculations based on World Health Organization 2008.

BOD varies according to age. It is higher for men in all age groups and increases according to the aging process—after age 14 for men, and after age 29 for women. On average, mortality represents 53 percent of the men's DALYs and only 42 percent of women's DALYs.

In certain age-specific groups—0–4 for both genders and after age 30 for men and age 60 for women—mortality is the most important component of the BOD in the LAC region. In the other groups morbidity prevails.

Per capita YLL by gender and age in LAC countries are presented in figure 4.3. The data show that health needs associated with mortality are higher for men than for women because men are always disproportionately affected by mortality in all age groups. The per capita rates of YLL increase continuously after ages 5–14. This fact has relevant policy implications for the way health systems and health policies need to be shaped in LAC to address the aging process from a gender perspective.

Health Needs and Morbidity Trends in LAC

Morbidity is the new frontier in the study of the burden of disease transposing health losses not associated with mortality but related to constraints on quality of life to the same common denominator used to

Figure 4.3   YLL per 1,000 Inhabitants in LAC by Age and Gender, 2004

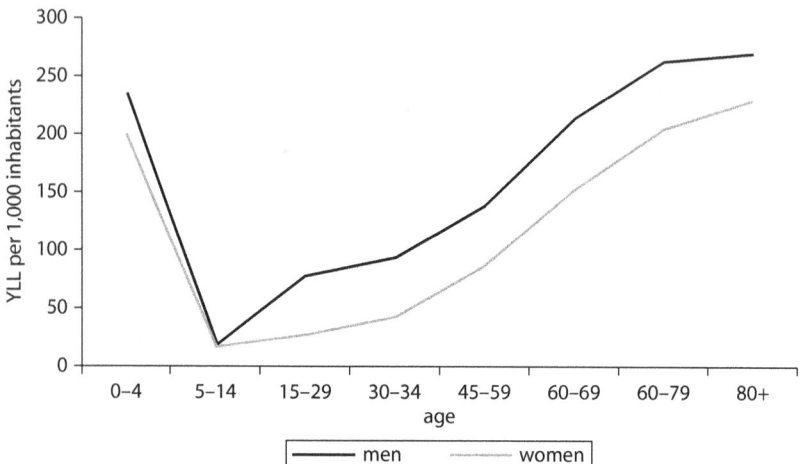

Source: Author's calculations based on World Health Organization 2008.

measure mortality losses—years of life. Information related to morbidity is progressively improving in developed and developing countries, allowing better estimates. In the 2004 updated study, morbidity data were improved for 52 causes, including diabetes, alcohol-related disorders, low vision and blindness, injuries, heart disease, HIV-AIDS, cancer, vaccine-preventable diseases, and malaria.

In high-income countries, people of different ages have higher survival rates and more escape the mortality trap more often due to less exposure to risk factors, extensive coverage by health plans, and better quality of health care systems. In addition, lower fertility rates; better living conditions; good social indicators; and affordable, quality health care lead to lower levels of mortality and morbidity rates in young age groups. The combined effect of these factors reduces mortality in higher proportion than morbidity, because lower mortality feeds the aging process and creates pressure to increase morbidity in the older ages.

Consequently, the quantities of YLD and YLL per capita are lower in high-income countries than in middle- and low-income countries. However, the distribution of DALYs in YLL and YLD between high-income and middle- and low-income countries is totally different. YLL represent a high proportion of the DALYs in lowest-income countries, but YLD correspond to almost half of the BOD in high-income countries. In regions such as LAC (consisting of mostly middle- and high-income countries), the weight of YLD in the BOD tends to be closer to that of high-income countries. In fact, YLD represent 45 percent of the DALYs in high-income countries and 41 percent in LAC compared with 15 percent in Sub-Saharan Africa.

Figure 4.4 shows the distribution of the YLD per capita in LAC in 2004. The data show that the number and distribution of YLD in LAC did not follow the same pattern of the YLL by age, which increases consistently according to the aging process. YLD per capita is higher in the 15–29 age group and declines in the 30–34 age group for both genders. It increases again for man ages 60–69, and after age 70, per capita YLD begins to decline.

On the other hand, the YLD per capita for men and women have almost the same profile until the 30–34 age group. Women's morbidity is significantly higher for the 45–59 age group, and it is slightly lower at ages 60–79. The higher proportion of YLD for women in the older ages is probably associated with the lower female mortality in this age group, meaning that women live longer but are sicker than surviving men.

Figure 4.4   YLD per 1,000 Inhabitants in LAC by Age and Gender, 2004

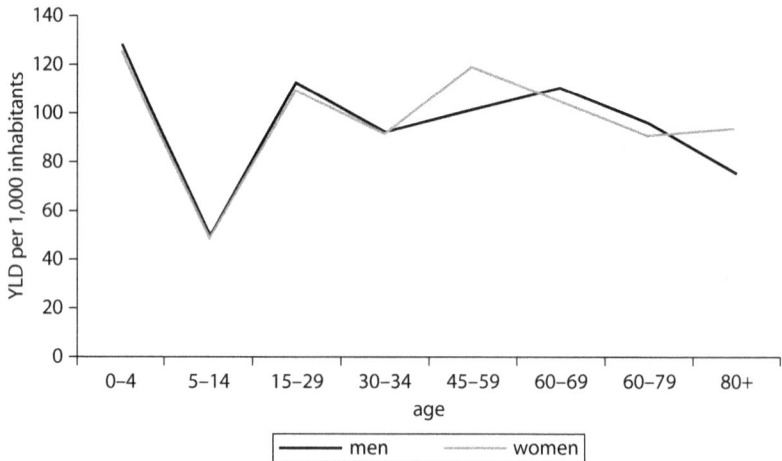

Source: Author's calculations based on World Health Organization 2008.

Burden of Disease by Causes across the Life Cycle

DALYs, as explained, is an aggregated expression of mortality (YLL) and morbidity (YLD). Analysis of figure 4.5, representing the weighted addition of data presented in figures 4.3 and 4.4 for the LAC region in 2004, leads to the following conclusions:

- The burden of disease expressed in per capita DALYs losses, is higher for men in all age groups.
- Men's per capita DALYs are higher than women's per capita DALYs for the age group 15 and older and follow the same trends found in the behavior of YLL per capita.
- Average mortality weights disproportionately higher for men and average morbidity weights more heavily for women than for men.
- Morbidity weights are higher in intermediate age groups and mortality rates are higher in the youngest and oldest age groups.

The age patterns of the BOD are also influenced by the distribution of the DALYs by causes. The 2004 Global Burden of Disease (GBD) study classifies all causes of mortality and morbidity into three major groups: Group 1, composed of communicable diseases, nutrition-related conditions, and maternal and perinatal conditions; Group 2, composed of noncommunicable diseases; and Group 3, related to injuries.

Figure 4.5   DALY per 1,000 Inhabitants in LAC by Age and Gender, 2004

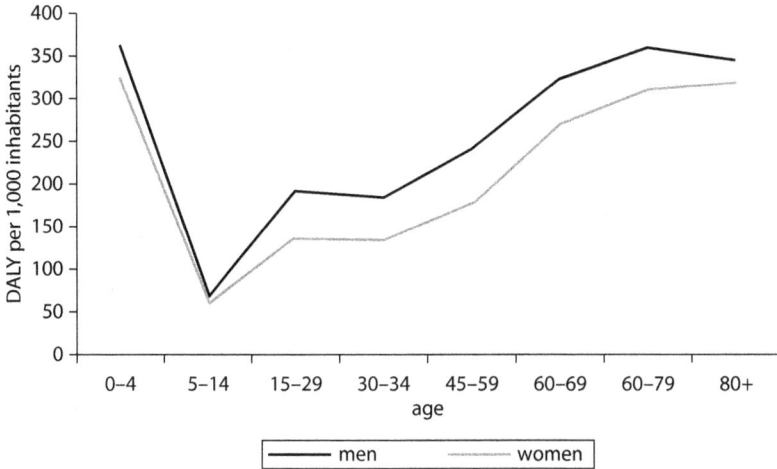

Source: Author's calculations based on World Health Organization 2008.

Compared with other regions, the weight of the BOD in LAC is closer to developed countries than to developing countries. Figure 4.6 shows that in 2004, the BOD per 1,000 inhabitants in LAC was 46 percent higher than in developed countries but 70 percent lower than in Sub-Saharan Africa.[6] However, the weight of morbidity in the BOD in LAC is higher than in any other developing region and closer to the high-income countries.

Figure 4.7 shows that, different from the Sub-Saharan Africa and South Asia patterns, the BOD in LAC is closely related to noncommunicable diseases, which are associated with the population aging process. According to the current literature (Lopez and others 2006), in developed countries, around 80 percent of older adults have at least one chronic condition and 50 percent have at least two. These conditions can cause years of pain and loss of function. Public health efforts can help avoid preventable illness and disability as the population ages. Many specialists maintain that poor health is not an inevitable consequence of aging, given that effective public health strategies could help older adults remain independent longer, improve their quality of life, and potentially delay the need for long-term care.

Aging and Chronic Diseases
Chronic diseases disproportionately affect older adults and are associated with disability and diminished quality of life. They are often associated

Figure 4.6   DALY Losses per 1,000 Inhabitants by World Bank Regions, 2004

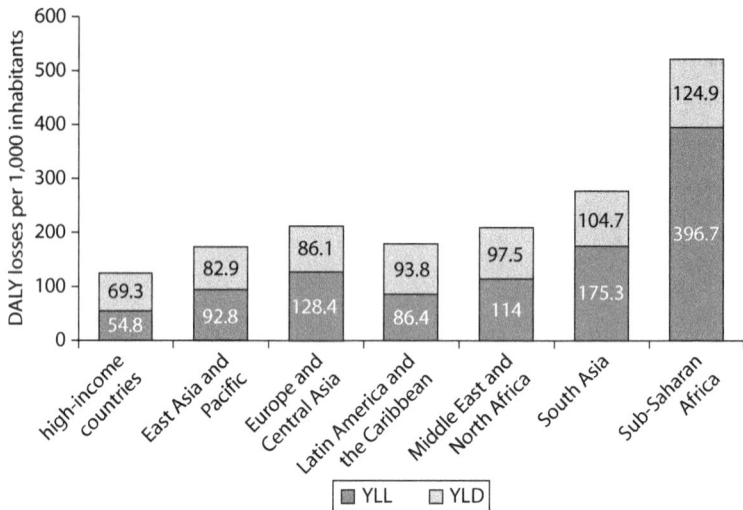

Source: Author's calculations based on World Health Organization 2008.
Note: EAP = East Asia and Pacific; ECA = Europe and Central Asia; LAC = Latin America and the Caribbean; MENA = Middle East and North Africa; SA = South Asia; SSA = Sub-Saharan Africa.

with increasing health care facility needs and expensive long-term-care costs. These facts have been known for a long time.[7] Figure 4.8 presents the prevalence of a set of chronic conditions by age in the Brazilian population in 1998, according to a Brazilian household survey. The data show that the incidence of several chronic conditions increases along the aging process, except asthma, which is also high in the early ages.

The natural aging of the population increases the weight of chronic health conditions in the BOD, but the high impact of chronic diseases on health costs, which was accepted as a given in past decades, has become increasingly controversial in recent years. In fact, chronic diseases—differently from acute health episodes—undermine a long and continuous process of using health facilities and spending on medicines, exams, and medical visits. Health conditions such as stroke, heart disease, fractures and osteoporosis, Alzheimer's, and the results of diabetes such as blindness and amputations increase with the aging process and their treatment and use of health facilities is continuous and expensive. Frequently, the high technology used in treatment and medical exams and the consumption of expensive medicines by the aging are singled out as a major factor leading to higher health expenditures during the aging process. It creates a stepwise effect in the health expenditure curve by age, which is often considered in future budgetary estimations based on demographic forecasting.

Figure 4.7   Distribution of DALY Losses by World Bank Regions according to Groups of Causes, 2004

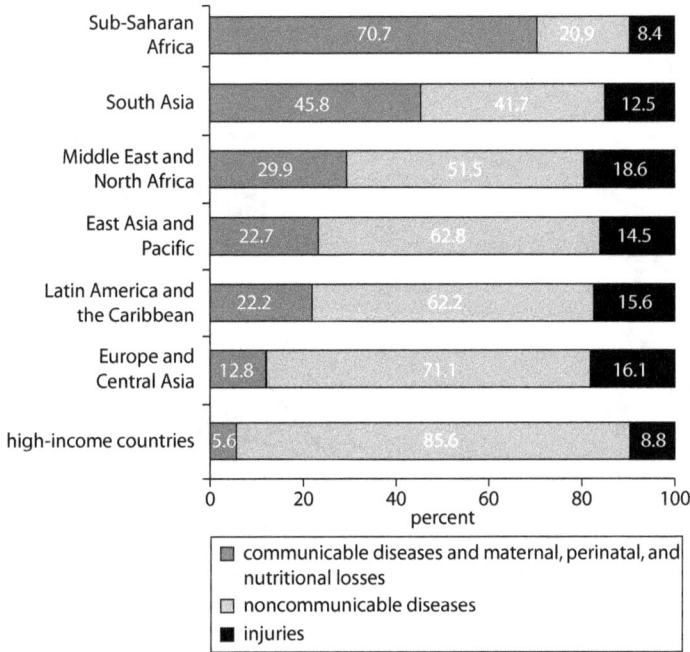

Source: Author's calculations based on World Health Organization 2008.
Note: SSA = Sub-Saharan Africa; SA = South Asia; MENA = Middle East and North Africa; EAP = East Asia and Pacific; LAC = Latin America and the Caribbean; ECA = Europe and Central Asia;.

However, a new debate is behind these arguments. Many policy makers and governmental agencies, such as the Centers for Disease Control (CDC) in the United States, maintain that health systems centered on the use of medical technology, without sound health promotion and prevention policies, tends to spend more on health care during the aging process without achieving good outcomes. A better integration among public health, preventive care, and less aggressive treatments should enable the older population to live longer, more healthy lives with lower personal and institutional health spending. In the United States, for example, the intensive use of medical technology, especially for treatments associated with old age, is one of the factors that led to a per capita health expenditure of US$7,290 in 2007 compared with US$3,601 in France, US$3,588 in Germany, and US$2,992 in the United Kingdom. However, life expectancy at birth in the United States in 2007 was behind these countries: 78.1 years, compared with 79.5 years in the United Kingdom, 80.0 years in Germany, and 81.0 years in France.

Figure 4.8   Incidence (per 100 Inhabitants) of Risk Factors and Chronic Diseases in Brazil by Age Group, 1998

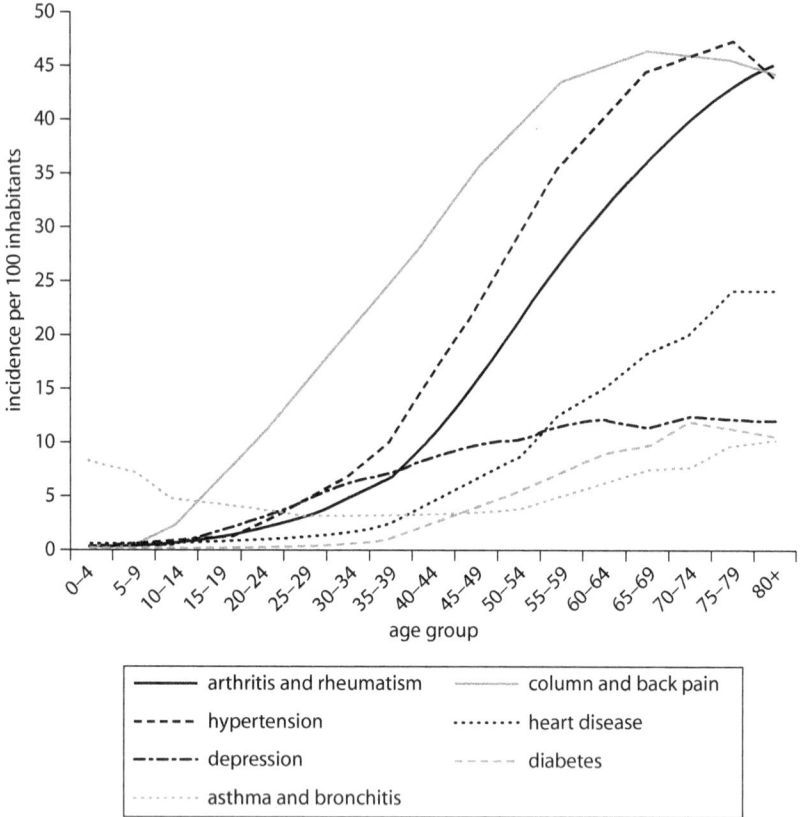

Source: Kilsztajn and others 2003 based on National Household Survey (PNAD) data 1998.

The increasing prevalence of chronic diseases in an aged population also implies a higher burden of disability. Information about old-age disability as a consequence of chronic diseases has been collected in seven Latin America and the Caribbean cities (Buenos Aires, Bridgetown, Havana, Mexico City, Montevideo, São Paulo, and Santiago) by the Survey on Health, Well-being and Aging in Latin America and the Caribbean (*Salud, Bienestar y Envejecimiento en America Latina y el Caribe,* SABE).[8] According to the survey, for all considered cities, only 20.7 percent of the population aged 60 and older declared they were in good health during 1999–2000.

Figure 4.9 shows the data related to health conditions for the average of the population aged 60 and older in the seven cities. Most of the aging

(77 percent) according to the SABE survey live with disease, and a considerable proportion of this population (44 percent) has comorbidities.

Nineteen percent of the population claim to have disabilities, and a larger proportion of the aging lives with the combined effects of disability and disease (17 percent) and disability and comorbidity (12 percent). This indicates that disability in old age is mostly a consequence of chronic diseases and comorbidities, and the prevention of risk factors that lead to chronic conditions could reduce the burden of disability in the aging, resulting in increased quality of life and reduced health expenditures along the aging process.

Some governmental agencies, such as the CDC, argue, based on research reviews, that health promotion activities, such as education and counseling interventions, could improve preventive health behaviors among the aging. Although these studies focused on prevention in healthy people, there is an increasing consensus that behavioral techniques such as self-monitoring, personal communication with health care providers, and viewing audiovisual materials contribute to successful change in behaviors such as quitting smoking, controlling alcohol consumption, improving nutrition, and weight control.

The SABE survey also shows that seven diseases and chronic conditions disproportionately affect the health status of the population aged

Figure 4.9   Health Status of Population Aged 60 and Older in Seven LAC Cities according to the SABE Survey, 1999–2000

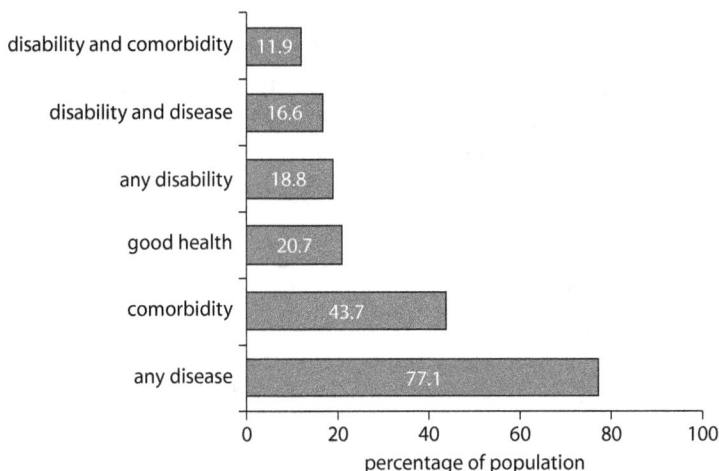

Source: SABE Survey on Health, Well-being, and Aging in Latin America and the Caribbean 1999–2000.

Figure 4.10   Prevalence of Selected Diseases and Chronic Conditions in the Population Aged 60 and Older in Seven LAC Cities according to the SABE Survey, 1999–2000

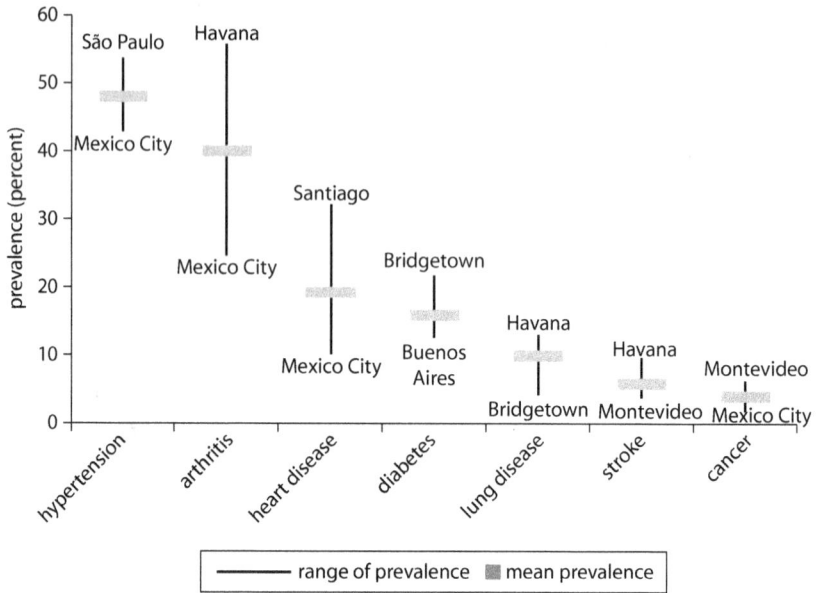

Source: SABE Survey, on Health, Well-being, and Aging in Latin America and the Caribbean 1999–2000.

60 and older in LAC. Figure 4.10 presents additional information related to these diseases in the seven surveyed cities during 1999–2000.

Hypertension (high blood pressure) is more a chronic condition than a disease. It is more common in men, and women are more likely to develop high blood pressure after menopause. Hypertension could lead to several other chronic conditions such as heart disease and kidney failure. Hypertension has the highest prevalence compared with other chronic conditions among elders in the seven cities surveyed (Table 4.1).

Almost half of the population aged 60 and older has hypertension. São Paulo has the highest prevalence (54 percent) and Mexico City the lowest (43 percent). Despite that, hypertension appears to have less association with disability for the aging than other chronic conditions such as arthritis. In fact, many studies, as related by Lima and others (2009), reveal that hypertension can have a long and asymptomatic progression, with no great impact on the quality of life of patients, despite the fact that it affects a large number of aging individuals.

Table 4.1   Prevalence of Diseases or Chronic Conditions in LAC

Diseases or chronic conditions	Prevalence (%)	Highest score (%)	Lowest score (%)
Hypertension (high blood pressure)	48.1	53.7	42.8
Arthritis	40.1	55.8	24.6
Heart disease (cardiovascular disease)	19.3	32.2	10.0
Diabetes	15.9	21.7	12.4
Lung disease	9.9	12.9	4.1
Stroke	5.9	9.7	3.7
Cancer	4.0	6.3	1.9

Source: SABE Survey, on Health, Well-being, and Aging in Latin America and the Caribbean 1999–2000.

Relevant risk factors linked to hypertension are obesity and being overweight, followed by the absence of physical activity; tobacco use; and diet, including the overconsumption of sodium and alcohol and low potassium and vitamin D. Stress and other chronic comorbidities, such as high cholesterol, diabetes, and kidney failure also contribute to increasing blood pressure.

Obesity is the highest risk factor for hypertension but also for other chronic conditions such as type 2 diabetes. Risks associated with hypertension are early mortality by stroke, heart disease, and certain kinds of cancers. Andrade (2006), using SABE survey data, pointed out that the current levels of obesity in LAC appear to be very high, especially for women. Current levels of obesity among the aging require changes in lifestyle and diet, and increases in physical activity, but in many cases professional help is necessary to reduce body weight. Some studies developed on the basis of other surveys (Lima and others 2009) demonstrated that hypertension was more prevalent among the poor and less-educated population. This fact changes the traditional perception that correlates poverty with communicable diseases in LAC. It also shows how important it is to tackle chronic conditions as a way to reduce poverty in the region.

Arthritis is an inflammation of one or more joints, such as the knee, wrist, or spinal column. The two most common types of arthritis are osteoarthritis and rheumatoid arthritis. Joint pain and stiffness are the main symptoms of this disease. Rheumatoid arthritis is primarily a bone and joint disease, but it occasionally damages other parts of the body, including the eyes and lungs.

Arthritis is ranked the second-most-common highly prevalent chronic condition or disease in the seven LAC cities surveyed. Forty percent of the population aged 60 and older has arthritis. A higher prevalence was found in Havana (56 percent) and a lower prevalence was found in Mexico City (25 percent). Self-reported pain among people with arthritis across all countries ranged from 30.7 percent in older Mexican Americans to 83.7 percent in Santiago. Arthritis is more prevalent among aging women and its risk factors are associated with family history and smoking. Arthritis causes other problems among which is joint damage that can be both debilitating and disfiguring, making it difficult or impossible to perform daily activities.

Heart disease (cardiovascular disease, CVD) is a broad term used to describe a range of diseases that affect heart conditions, and in some cases, blood vessels. The various diseases that fall under the umbrella of heart disease include diseases of blood vessels, such as coronary artery disease; heart rhythm problems (arrhythmias); and congenital heart defects. Heart disease is prevalent in 19 percent of the aging in the seven LAC cities surveyed. The highest rates of CVD were found in Santiago (32 percent) and the lowest in Mexico City (10 percent). The risk factors for CVD are the same for men and women. They include inactivity, overweight and obesity, poor diet and nutrition, smoking, high blood pressure, high blood cholesterol, and diabetes. The most common consequences of CVD are heart attack and stroke.

The population of Latin America has remarkably higher proportions of abdominal obesity, high blood cholesterol, and hypertension, according to the results of a study published in the March 6, 2007, edition of the American Heart Association's journal, *Circulation*. The study analyzed data from the six Latin American countries that participated in the INTERHEART international study.[9] In Argentina, Brazil, Chile, Colombia, Guatemala, and Mexico the population-adjusted risk for abdominal obesity was 48.6 percent compared to 31.2 percent in the 46 other countries that participated in INTERHEART. For high blood cholesterol, the risk was 42 percent compared to 32 percent in the other countries. For hypertension, the risk was 29.1 percent compared to 20.8 percent in the other countries. At 48.1 percent, the population-adjusted risk for tobacco smoking was about the same for both the Latin American and the nonLatin American countries.

Diabetes is a condition in which the body either does not produce enough, or does not properly respond to, insulin, a hormone produced in the pancreas. Insulin enables cells to absorb glucose in order to turn it into energy. A malfunction in this ability causes glucose to accumulate in the blood, leading to various potential complications, among them the risk of heart attack, stroke, blindness, kidney failure, and gangrene. The two types of diabetes are type 1 (failure to produce insulin) and type 2 (insulin resistance). The latter is commonly associated with aging.

The SABE survey estimates that 16 percent of the aging LAC population has diabetes. Higher scores were found in Bridgetown (22 percent) and lower scores were found in Buenos Aires (12 percent). Consistent with other studies, older adults with less than three years of education were twice as likely to report having diabetes as other older adults, showing a strong correlation between diabetes and poverty among older people. The study also reveals that in the group aged 60–74, among those reporting diabetes, at least 60 percent also reported problems seeing well with or without eyeglasses, and 20 percent had difficulty with at least one activity of daily living (ADL). In the nondiabetic group of the same age group, only 13 percent reported difficulties with ADLs.

Chronic lung disease (chronic obstructive pulmonary disease, COPD) is a group of progressive respiratory disorders with diffuse abnormalities of gas transport and exchange. The aging are subject to COPD due not only to the biological process of aging, which includes decreased pulmonary tissue elasticity, but to prolonged exposure to pollutants or occupational environment. Cigarette smoking is a major factor in the development of COPD. Environmental exposure to sulfur dioxide, asbestos, and cotton dust are causative factors that predispose the respiratory tract to chronic infection. Repeated pulmonary infections can result in the alteration of lung structure and the destruction of pulmonary tissue. The disease is more prevalent in men than in women.

According to the SABE survey, 10 percent of the population aged 60 and older reported it had COPD, varying from 13 percent (Havana) to 4 percent (Bridgetown) in the seven cities surveyed. The Latin American Project for the Investigation of Obstructive Lung Disease examined the prevalence of post-bronchodilator airflow limitation (Stage I: Mild COPD and higher) among people over age 40 in five major Latin American cities, each in a different country—Brazil, Chile, Mexico, Uruguay, and República Bolivariana de Venezuela. In each country, the prevalence of Stage I:Mild COPD and higher increased steeply with age, with the highest prevalence among those over age 60, ranging from a low of 18.4 percent in Mexico City, Mexico, to a high of 32.1 percent in Montevideo, Uruguay. In all cities/countries the prevalence was appreciably higher in men than in women.

Stroke (cerebrovascular disease) occurs when the blood supply to a part of the brain is interrupted or severely reduced, depriving brain tissue of oxygen and nutrients. Within a few minutes, brain cells begin to die. Stroke is a medical emergency, and prompt treatment is crucial. Early treatment can minimize brain damage and potential stroke complications. Strokes can be treated, and a much smaller number of people in high-income countries die of stroke than 20 or 30 years ago. Improvement in the control of major risk factors for stroke—high blood pressure, smoking, and high cholesterol—is likely responsible for the decline. Stroke is one of the leading disability factors in the aging.

On average, 6 percent of the aging in LAC suffer a stroke, varying from 4 percent in Montevideo to 10 percent in Havana, among the seven surveyed cities. According to Lavados and others (2007), stroke mortality in LAC is higher than in developed countries, but rates are declining. Population-based studies show variations in incidence of stroke—lower rates of ischemic stroke and similar rates of intracranial hemorrhage compared with other regions. A significant proportion of strokes in these populations can be attributed to a few preventable risk factors. Some countries have published national clinical guidelines, although much needs to be done in the organization of care and rehabilitation. Even though the burden of stroke is high, there is a paucity of information for implementing evidence-based management.

Cancer is a class of diseases in which a group of cells display uncontrolled growth (division beyond the normal limits), invasion (intrusion into and destruction of adjacent tissues), and sometimes metastasis (spread to other locations in the body via the lymph system or blood). Cancer affects people at all ages with the risk for most types increasing with age. Cancer caused about 13 percent of human deaths worldwide in 2007 (7.6 million). According to Hansen (1998), based on data from cancer registries in 51 countries on five continents, contrary to the pattern in younger age groups, in which annual cancer rates are almost equally distributed between both genders, aging men have twice the cancer incidence rate as aging women. For all major specific cancer sites except testicular cancer, the incidence rate is significantly higher among the aging than among any groups of younger and middle-aged persons. Among aging men, the most common kinds of cancer are prostate, lung, and colon cancers, and among aging women they are breast, colon, lung, and stomach cancers.

According to the SABE survey, cancer has a prevalence of 4 percent in the seven LAC cities surveyed, varying from 2 percent in Mexico City to 6 percent in Montevideo. Although cancer in the aging is extremely common, few oncology health professionals are familiar with caring for some kinds of cancer in senior patients. Surgery is at present the first choice but is frequently delivered in a suboptimal way, with a huge range of poorly tested protocols. In some cases, undertreatment is justified by concerns about unsustainable toxicity, while overtreatment is explained by the lack of knowledge about optimizing preoperative risk assessment.

Disability and Other Dimensions of Health Needs in an Aging Context

Healthy aging is not only the absence of disease (Rose and others 2008). In fact, through experience, seniors know that an increase in the burden of disease along the aging process is unavoidable. However, other dimensions of healthy aging have been investigated and incorporated in recent years, such as the absence of disability, engagement in social activities, and maintenance of high physical and cognitive function. Self-perception of a healthy life by the aging goes beyond the notion of lack of disease and disability to incorporating concepts such as the ability to be actively engaged in community activities.

The SABE study explored, besides health indicators, other variables related to disability[10] and activity engagement in the community for the seven cities in LAC during 1999–2000. This section will explore the relationship between aging, disease, disability, and active engagement in the community. The analysis will start with the relationship among aging, disease, and disability (figure 4.11).

Figure 4.11   Prevalence Rates of Disease and Disability in the Population Aged 60 and Older by Age Groups in Seven LAC Cities according to the SABE Survey, 1999–2000

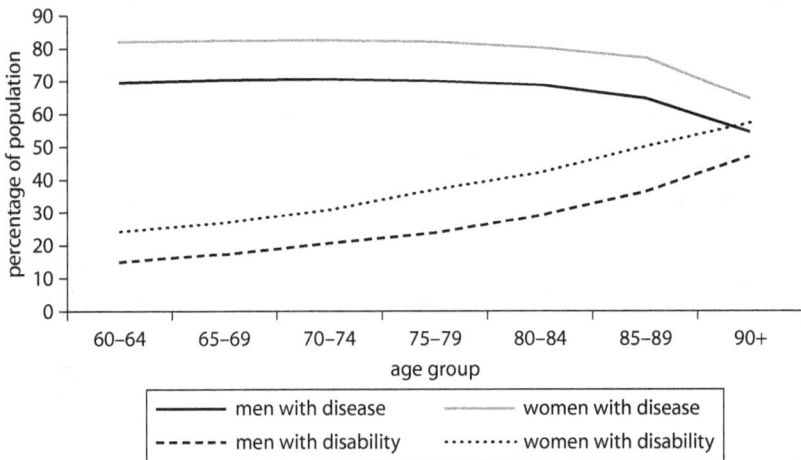

Source: SABE Survey on Health, Well-being, and Aging in Latin America and the Caribbean 1999–2000.

As discussed in the previous section, the prevalence of chronic disease among the aging leads to the prevalence of disability, but along the aging process, considering the age group 60 and older, the prevalence of disability tends to increase while the prevalence of disease tends to decrease (table 4.2).

There is a significant negative linear correlation between the prevalence rates of disease and the prevalence rates of disability for both men ($R2 = -0.92$) and women ($R2 = -0.83$) along the aging process. People surviving into their 60s will live with lower disease rates in their 70s, 80s, and 90s. The young seniors suffering from chronic conditions in their 60s will die and the surviving seniors should have better health conditions, leading, eventually, to lower health expenditures and less aggressive treatments in their final days due to less capacity to survive acute health crises provoked by chronic conditions. However, the data also show that both men and women aged 60 and older probably will have greater disability rates along the aging process. The disability rate, according to the SABE data (table 4.2), increases from 16 percent in the age group 60–64 to 47 percent in the age group 90 and older for men and from 24 percent to 57 percent for women in the same age groups, respectively.

The level of community engagement[11] of the aging in LAC, according to the SABE survey, is relatively high. Less than 9 percent of women and 5 percent of men were in contact with their community at least once a week (the lowest level of engagement). Seventy-four percent of women and 77 percent of men were actively engaged in their community (the two highest levels of engagement were active help and voluntary or paid employment). In all cities, approximately one-third to one-half of all men maintained the highest level of active engagement (having paid or voluntary employment). In contrast, between one-fifth and one-third of women in all cities had this level of engagement,

Table 4.2   Prevalence of Disease among the Aging in LAC

Age group	Men with disease (%)	Women with disease (%)	Men with disability (%)	Women with disability (%)
60–64	69.5	81.9	15.5	23.9
65–69	70.6	82.4	17.6	26.7
70–74	70.2	82.7	20.7	30.7
75–79	69.9	82.0	23.7	36.8
80–84	68.6	80.2	29.0	42.0
85–89	64.7	77.4	36.0	50.0
90 and older	54.2	64.2	47.0	57.1

Source: SABE Survey on Health, Well-being, and Aging in Latin America and the Caribbean 1999–2000.

except in Havana, where less than one-tenth of women were paid or were engaged in voluntary employment.

Community engagement decreases strongly with older age. Compared with those aged 60–64, older age groups were less likely to report high levels of participation in the community. A statistically significant gender difference was also found. The presence of disease and comorbidity further limits community engagement more in men than in women.

Given that mortality affects more men than women in all age groups, there is a trend to increase female participation in the population along the aging process.[12] The fact that women tend to outlive men and that women face disadvantages in the labor market, such as informality, lower wages, and lack of labor protection schemes, means that more women will be on their own than men, and they will face limitations in accessing pensions and affordable health coverage. Otherwise, strong income barriers limit access to long-term care and other expensive health coverage systems for the aging living alone in LAC.

Exploring the Burden of Disease Data in LAC Countries

Most LAC countries have not developed studies on burden of disease. Several have, however, providing some country-specific information about the impact of aging on health needs. BOD studies have been done totally or partially in Brazil (1998, 2008[13]), Chile (1993, 2008), Colombia (2005), Costa Rica (2004), Mexico (2003), and Peru (2004). Selected data from these studies are presented in figure 4.12. They reflect the potential use of the BOD studies in evaluating health needs.

The Brazilian Study presents details on the BOD according to DALYs on a per capita basis, comparing the richest (South) and the poorest (Northeast) regions. The differentials reflect the heavy weight of infant mortality in the earlier ages between the poorest and the richest regions, but the DALY differentials for the groups aged 5 and older do not appear to be significant.

Chile (2008) and Peru (2004), also using per capita data and per 1,000 inhabitants, respectively, show the DALYs distribution by age and gender. Even presenting the same trends on the DALYs distribution by age, configured in a J curve, the studies do not appear to be comparable and some methodological effort has to be made to explain differences in the quantities of DALYs found.

The Costa Rican Study highlighted the specific BODs (DALYs per capita for some related risk factors such as traffic injuries and alcoholism by age), demonstrating how these risk factors disproportionately affect youth and mature populations, but not the aging.

Figure 4.12   Selected Data on the Studies of Burden of Diseases in LAC Countries

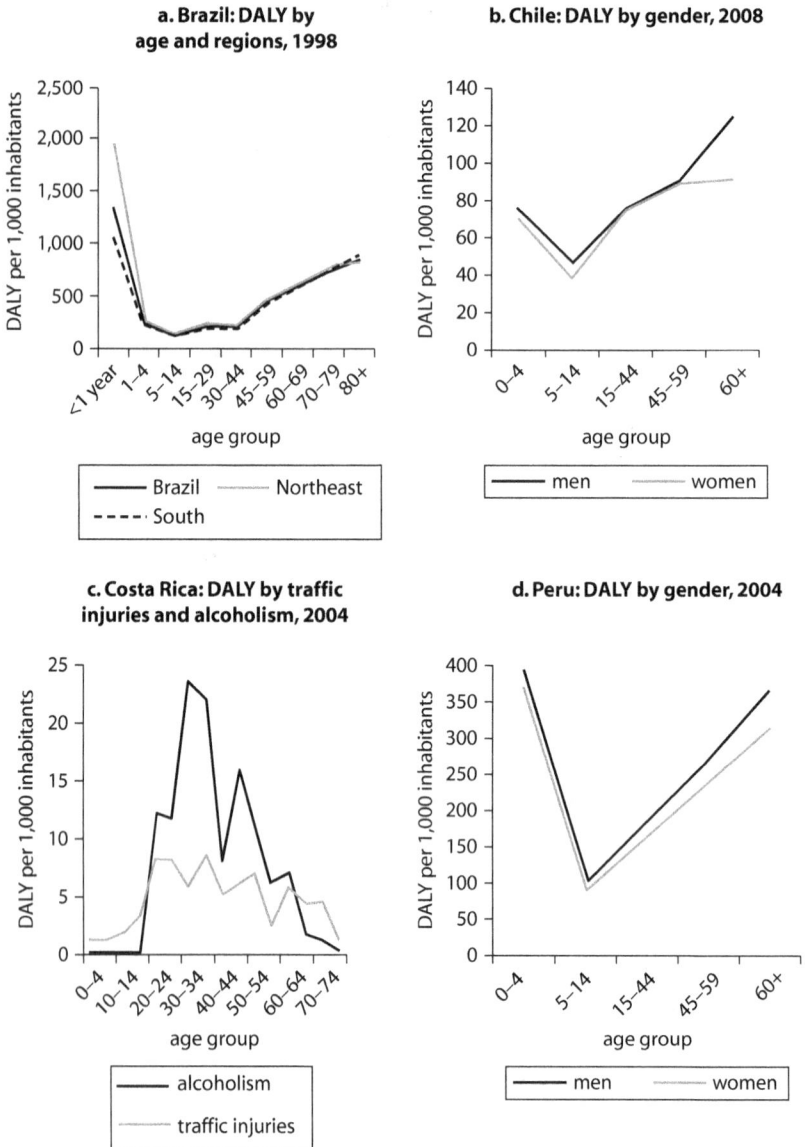

a. Brazil: DALY by age and regions, 1998

b. Chile: DALY by gender, 2008

c. Costa Rica: DALY by traffic injuries and alcoholism, 2004

d. Peru: DALY by gender, 2004

Sources: Brazil: FIOCRUZ; Chile and Peru: Ministries of Health; Costa Rica: SANIGEST Survey.

The country studies of BOD also provided a detailed analysis of the epidemiological profiles at the subregional level, providing additional information about different health conditions of the aging in different patterns and exploring urban-rural, geographic, and social differences.

Despite the high potential of the use of BOD studies to evaluate the health effects and determinants of the aging process in Latin America, the studies are still scarce and no systematic evaluation comparing them has been conducted. Consequently, the methodology and data treatment present some comparability problems, and concepts, methods, data sources, and results need to be harmonized to enable better utilization of the information in order to establish trends and find patterns.

WHO has made efforts to do this, and recently so has the Institute of Health Metrics and Evaluation of Washington State University, sponsored by the Gates Foundation, which is updating GBD surveys and increasing the amount of data, particularly for developing countries. These studies, based on 2005 data, will include a comprehensive and consistent revision of disability weights.

Facing the Aging Process in LAC: Health Needs in the Next 20 Years

This section discusses trends in the burden of disease by age and gender between 2004 and 2030, according to DALY projections developed by WHO (WHO 2008). During this period, a fast reduction of the DALYs per capita is expected for those aged 0–4 and for those aged 60 and older, due to changes in the demographic structure of the population because of the demographic transition.

Given that the reduction of DALYs per capita among children and youth under age 15 will be disproportionately higher than in the group aged 60 and older, health needs will be progressively more concentrated among the aging population. Figure 4.13 presents the progressive effect of aging on per capita DALYs between 2004 and 2030.

The aging effects in the BOD will disproportionately increase the BOD for women, given that the DALYs for women age 60 and older could represent one-third of the total DALY losses by 2030. As a result of the aging process, the shape of the total DALYs per capita curve will be progressively flatter after the age group 30–44 due to longer and healthier life perspectives for both genders. Another result is the fast increase in noncommunicable diseases in the regional BOD. From 2004 to 2030, it will increase from 62 percent to 74 percent, representing almost three-quarters of the total DALYs (WHO 2008).

Figure 4.13   The Individual Weight of the Burden of Diseases by Age: DALYs Per Capita in the LAC Region, 2004–30

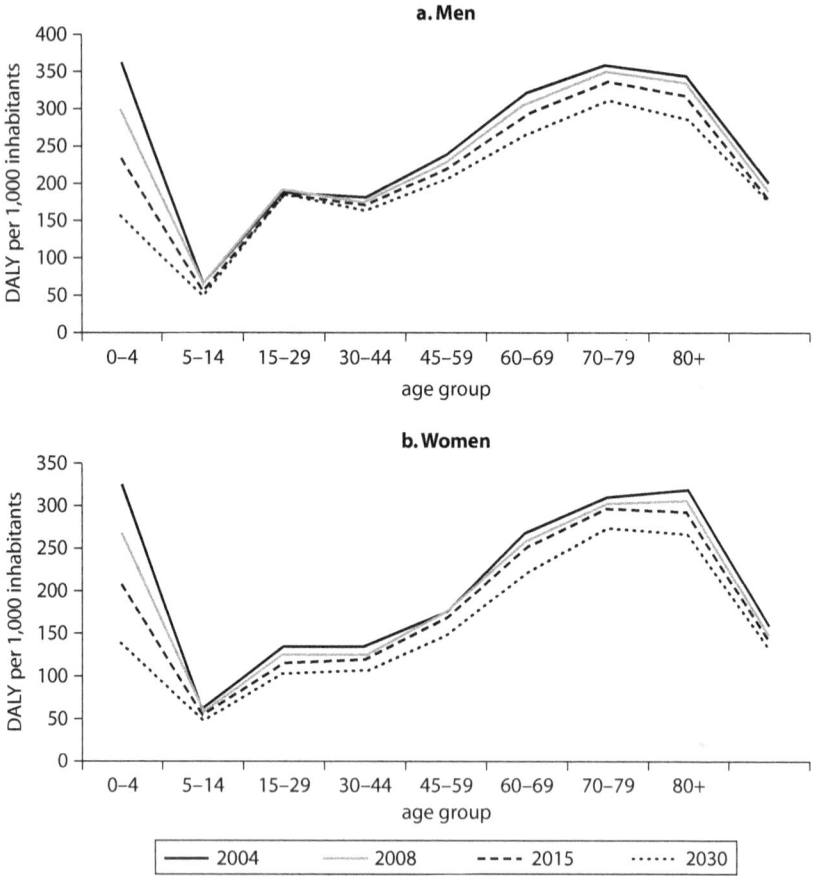

a. Men

b. Women

Source: Author's calculations based on World Health Organization 2008.

Even considering the large structural heterogeneity among countries and social groups in LAC, the increasing potential demand for promotion, prevention, and treatment of chronic diseases, principally in the poorest groups, is unavoidable and needs to be tackled in all countries in the region. According to a recent Pan-American Health Organization report, four out of five deaths from chronic diseases in the Americas occur in low- and middle-income countries. The incidence of early mortality by stroke, for example, is inversely related to per capita gross domestic product (GDP) in the Americas and is highly concentrated in the poorest countries. Early mortality by stroke in 2006 varied from 9 percent to 16 percent in countries like the United States and Canada to 32 percent to 39 percent in countries like Bolivia, Ecuador, El Salvador, Guatemala, Guiana, Haiti, Peru, and Suriname (PAHO 2009).

A study of the municipalities of the Santiago Metropolitan Region (figure 4.14), using data from 1994–96 and 1999–2001 BOD surveys of adults over age 20 by income level (Sanchez, Albala, and Lera 2005), concluded that the poorest quintile suffers from higher early mortality than the richest quintile due to chronic diseases such as endocrinal diseases (82 percent higher), mental disorders (96 percent higher), cardiovascular disorders (25 percent higher), genital–urinary disorders (61 percent higher), respiratory disorders (54 percent higher), gastrointestinal disorders (114 percent higher), and trauma (119 percent higher). Figure 4.15 shows that DALY losses are higher for the poorest income quintiles for both men and women.

This study also reveals that between the two surveys the early mortality due to chronic conditions in the poorest quintile increased faster than in the richest quintile. The decreasing provision of good health care services to the poor aging population during the 1990s, among other factors, could explain the increasing gap between the rich and the poor in mortality due to chronic conditions. In other

Figure 4.14   Chronic Disease Prevalence in Santiago, Chile, Poorest Quintile to Richest Quintile, Ratio, 1999–2001

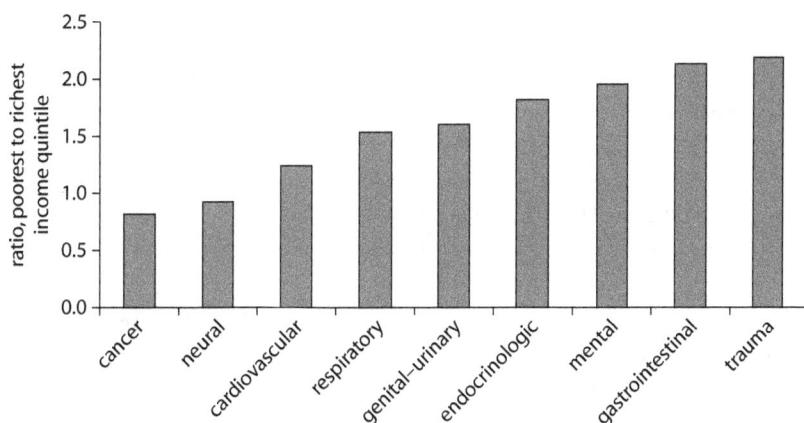

Source: Sanchez, Albala, and Lera 2005.

Figure 4.15   DALY Losses per 1,000 Inhabitants in Santiago, Chile, by Gender and Income Quintile, 1999–2001

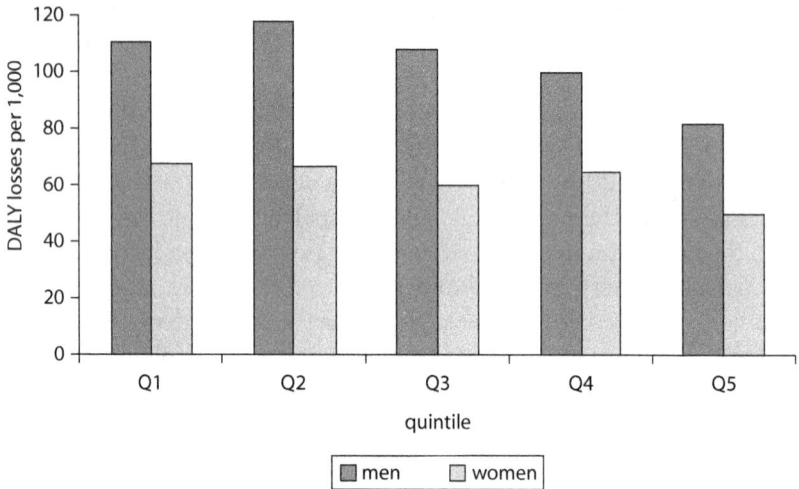

Source: Sanchez, Albala, and Lera 2005.

words, the early mortality due to chronic diseases in the poorest income quintile compared to the richest quintile was associated with the lack of access to middle- and high-technology interventions and treatments by the aging poor. That could explain why, in 2000, the Chilean government implemented a universal health plan (*Plan de Atención Universal con Garantías Explícitas*, AUGE) with explicit guarantees of access to health care for the aging poor. It was decided that increasing free universal access for 56 specific medical interventions related to the most frequently occurring chronic conditions was the fastest way to reduce the chronic disease coverage gap and improve the quality of life of the aging poor.

Finally, most of the disparities between developed and developing countries in rates of early mortality due to chronic disease are due to poor risk factor control, poor quality of health care, and scarce supply of crucial medical interventions. Based on this, any poverty or inequality reduction policy in LAC countries should consider early interventions in promoting, preventing, controlling, and treating chronic diseases as crucial aspects to enhance the quality of life and extend the life expectancy of the poor in a regional aging context.

Trends in Health Care Utilization by Age in LAC

Health Needs Compared to Perceived Health Needs

In developing countries, due to several factors such as lack of information about how to obtain health services, nonexistence of services, distance to the services, or family budget constraints, only part of the health needs is converted to health demand. Health needs perceived by individuals do not necessarily coincide with medical or clinical health needs, given that some subjectivity, lack of correct information, and feelings and perceptions could drive individuals to demand health services when they are not necessary or to avoid demanding them when health prevention or treatment should be required. For this reason epidemiological health needs and perceived health needs do not necessarily match.

Health demand is the collective expression of individual perceived health needs, and health utilization rates reflect the part of the health demand that was met by the population attended by health services. Figure 4.16 is a schematic presentation of how perceived health needs should be converted into health utilization.

Household surveys in LAC measure health utilization as a share of perceived health needs. To identify perceived health needs, household surveys ask whether a person had health problems in a given period of time (a week or a month, for example). People who reply that they do have health problems are asked whether they sought health services. Those who answer yes are asked whether they were provided with service or not.

Figure 4.16   How Health Needs Convert to Health Utilization

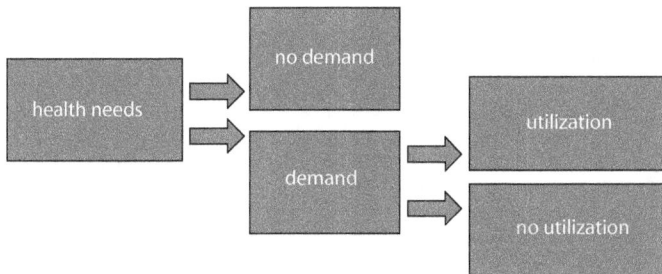

Source: Author.

The Program for the Improvement of Surveys and the Measurement of Living Conditions in Latin America and the Caribbean (MECOVI) is a joint initiative of the World Bank, the Inter-American Development Bank, and the Economic Commission for Latin America and the Caribbean. The purpose is to adequately generate better and more information regarding the living conditions of the LAC region's population and to improve the estimation and analysis of the social indicators obtained from the household surveys, maintaining, improving, and updating a databank of household surveys from all countries in the region, to make socioeconomic data accessible to users.

According to MECOVI data, 12 LAC countries collected information in their household surveys related to perceived health needs and health services utilization, presented by age group. Tables 4.3 and 4.4 show perceived health needs as a share of total population for different age groups (childhood, youth/adult, and the aging) in the poorest and richest quintiles during 1997–99.

As can be seen, in most cases, perceived health care needs are higher in childhood, decline during youth and adulthood, and increase again in the aging. This confirms the same trend observed regarding health needs by age according to epidemiological health. Given that childhood health needs registered in household surveys are perceived primarily by mothers, higher levels of mothers' education lead to a more accurate assessment of children's perceived health needs.

Table 4.3   Percentage of People with Perceived Health Needs as a Share of Total Population, Poorest Quintile, 1997–99

	Men (%)			Women (%)		
Country	Childhood	Youth/adult	Aging	Childhood	Youth/adult	Aging
Argentina	33	18	25	33	24	43
Bolivia	12	17	47	11	29	52
Brazil	38	18	36	29	23	38
Chile	28	15	34	27	21	38
Colombia	14	12	19	12	15	24
Ecuador	44	40	57	42	51	68
El Salvador	38	23	31	37	24	34
Jamaica	11	3	25	8	6	30
Nicaragua	31	30	47	32	36	48
Panama	23	28	46	23	38	52
Paraguay	71	27	46	67	33	52
Peru	26	40	27	26	25	44

Source: MECOVI Household Surveys 1997–99.

Table 4.4   Percentage of People with Perceived Health Needs as a Share of Total Population, Richest Quintile, 1997–99

Country	Men (%)			Women (%)		
	Childhood	Youth/adult	Aging	Childhood	Youth/adult	Aging
Argentina	38	18	27	32	21	44
Bolivia	7	12	43	16	12	48
Brazil	35	17	19	29	17	31
Chile	31	16	25	29	21	43
Colombia	18	20	31	22	21	35
Ecuador	43	35	47	48	46	60
El Salvador	42	19	26	42	22	32
Jamaica	16	6	20	15	8	33
Nicaragua	30	29	46	37	34	63
Panama	35	25	29	39	39	42
Paraguay	64	22	23	57	28	36
Peru	27	22	26	28	22	30

Source: MECOVI Household Surveys 1997–99.

The data for the 12 countries included in tables 4.3 and 4.4 show that perceived health needs vary widely within and among age groups and among income quintiles. Among children, perceived health needs vary from 7 percent in boys (Bolivia's richest quintile) to 71 percent in boys (Paraguay's poorest quintile); among youth/adults, from 3 percent in men (Jamaica's poorest quintile) to 51 percent in women (Ecuador's poorest quintile), and among the aging, from 19 percent in men (Colombia's poorest quintile and Brazil's richest quintile) to 68 percent in women (Ecuador's poorest quintile).

Figure 4.17 displays perceived health needs according to age, gender, and income quintile. As can be seen, perceived health needs increase from adulthood to aging in all 12 countries, in both genders and in the poorest and richest quintiles, except for men in Peru.

Figure 4.18 shows that perceived health needs are higher for youth/adults and seniors in the poorest quintile compared to the richest, but not among children where, in many cases, children's perceived health needs in the richest quintile are higher than in the poorest quintile, probably because the poorest mothers have less information with which to diagnose problems in their children's health status than the richest mothers. Poor families need assistance from health services, such as health agents or household visitors, family doctors, and other professionals in order to increase their health information and allow them to better diagnose health problems among children.

Figure 4.17   Population with Perceived Health Needs in LAC as a Percentage of Total Population by Age Clusters, Gender, and Income Quintiles, 1997–99

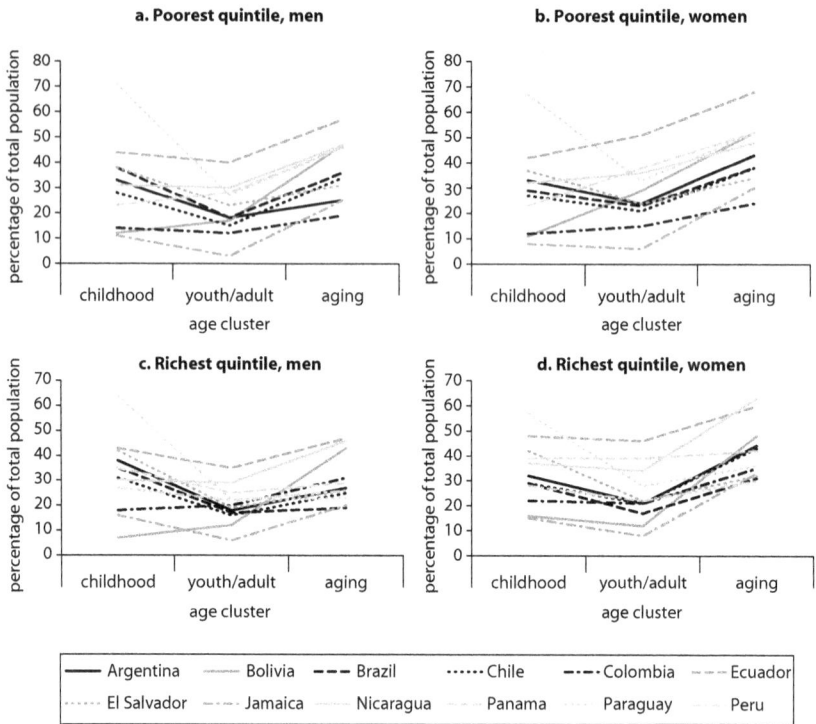

Source: MECOVI household surveys 1997–99.

The data also show that aging women have a higher perception of health problems than aging men in both the poorest and richest income quintile, and this is also reflected in health utilization.

Perceived Health Needs Compared to Health Services Utilization

Health utilization is strongly related to perceived health needs. Given that health utilization is voluntary, the population tends to use health services when it perceives some dysfunction that could affect its present or future health. However, as mentioned, due to several factors related to the availability of health services or the financial resources to afford them, part of the population (particularly the poor) could experience problems accessing health services when they perceive health needs. Table 4.5 and table 4.6 show MECOVI data about health utilization as

Figure 4.18   Persons Who Declared Health Problems as a Percentage of Total Population, by Age Clusters, Gender, and Income Quintiles, Average of 12 LAC Countries, 1997–99

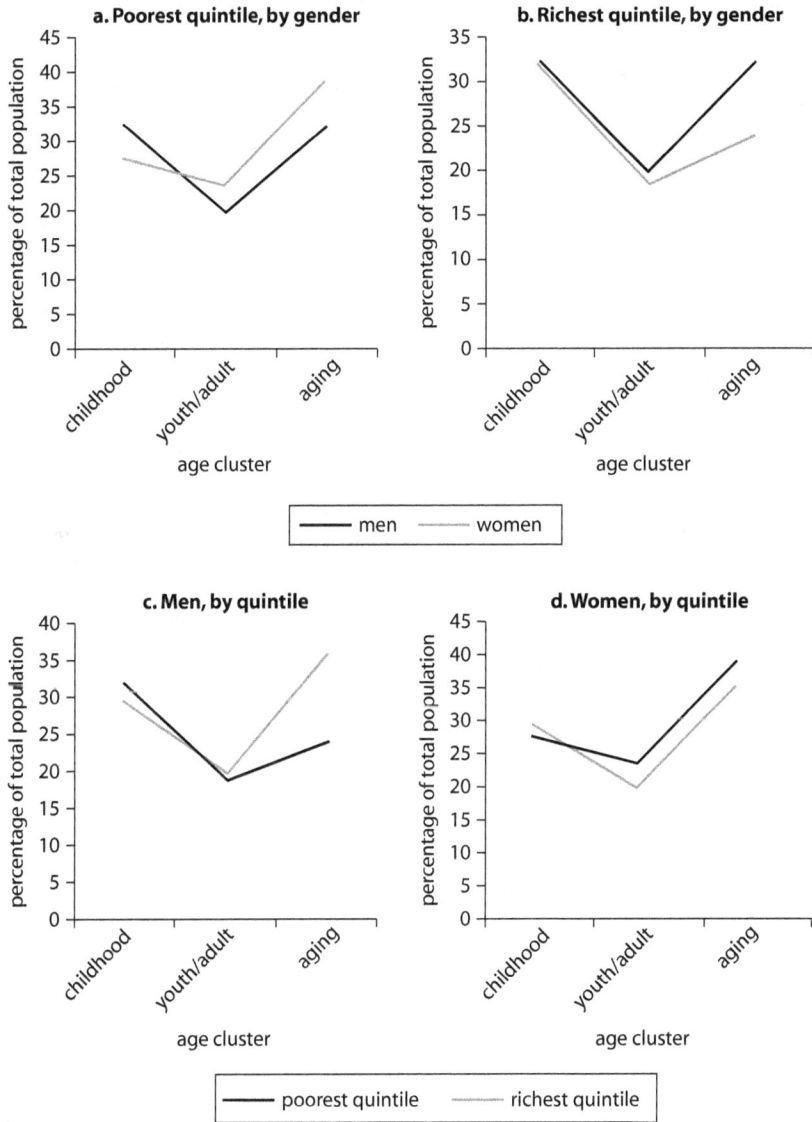

Source: MECOVI household surveys 1997–99.

Table 4.5   Percentage of People Who Received Health Care among Those Who Were Reported as Having Perceived Health Needs, Poorest Quintile, 1997–99

Country	Men (%)			Women (%)		
	Childhood	Youth/adult	Aging	Childhood	Youth/adult	Aging
Argentina	88	60	71	89	71	83
Bolivia	26	29	27	25	38	28
Brazil	86	44	45	88	54	48
Chile	80	59	74	80	70	77
Colombia	51	56	57	57	73	69
Ecuador	31	29	36	23	31	37
El Salvador	48	23	26	49	32	35
Jamaica	64	57	54	53	61	63
Nicaragua	21	22	34	18	29	34
Panama	34	33	36	41	38	52
Paraguay	16	23	32	19	31	43
Peru	35	23	36	29	26	26

Source: MECOVI Household Surveys 1997–99.

Table 4.6   Percentage of People Who Received Health Care among Those Who Were Reported as Having Had a Health Problem or an Accident, Richest Quintile, 1997–99

Country	Men (%)			Women (%)		
	Childhood	Youth/adult	Aging	Childhood	Youth/adult	Aging
Argentina	87	65	87	94	83	87
Bolivia	62	82	76	75	86	72
Brazil	93	79	81	93	67	75
Chile	84	79	90	87	79	86
Colombia	90	81	90	89	87	92
Ecuador	64	51	64	60	51	69
El Salvador	87	53	72	86	61	74
Jamaica	91	52	62	77	62	78
Nicaragua	55	49	49	51	50	54
Panama	72	55	61	67	61	80
Paraguay	72	65	67	74	66	87
Peru	81	34	66	66	45	64

Source: MECOVI Household Surveys 1997–99.

a share of perceived health needs in the 12 LAC countries distributed by gender, age group, and income quintile.

As can be seen, health utilization among children varied from 16 percent of the perceived health needs for boys in the poorest quintile in Paraguay to 94 percent for the richest quintile of girls in Argentina; in youth/adulthood, it varied from 22 percent for men in Nicaragua in the poorest quintile to 87 percent for women in the richest quintile in Colombia; and for the aging it varied from 26 percent in the poorest quintile for men in El Salvador and for women in Peru to 92 percent in the richest quintile of women in Colombia.

Despite the fact that health utilization by age has patterns similar to perceived health needs, the gap in health services utilization levels between the poorest and the richest quintile is huge. For this reason, in the poorest countries in LAC, such as Nicaragua and Paraguay, health services utilization is under 20 percent of the perceived health needs, but in the richest quintile the lowest level found is 45 percent for young/adult women in El Salvador. Figure 4.19 shows the differences among the 12 LAC countries in health services utilization as a share of health needs, comparing

Figure 4.19   Persons Attended by Health Services as a Percentage of the Population Who Declared Health Problems by Age Clusters, Gender, and Income Quintiles, Average of 12 LAC Countries, 1997–99

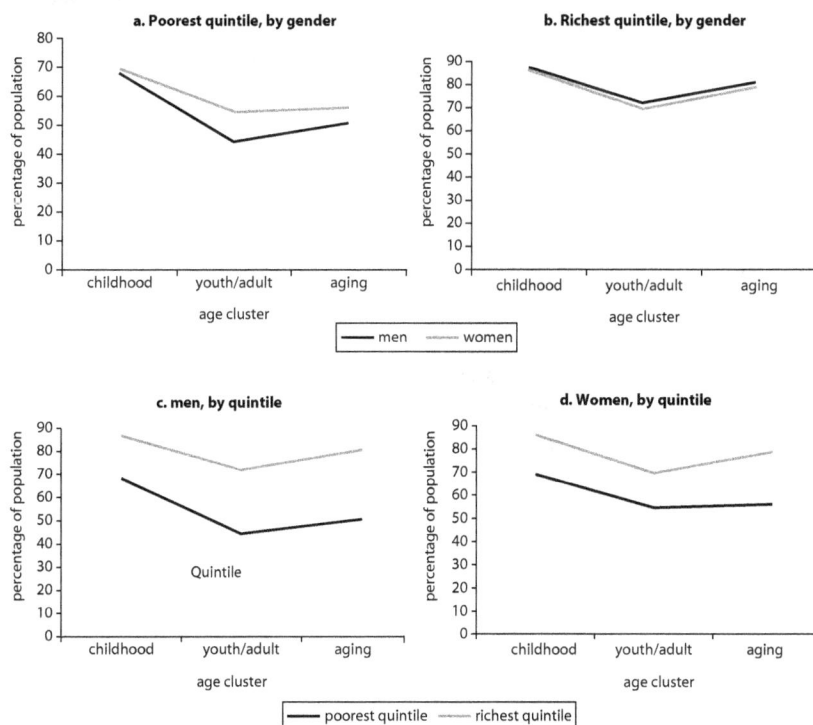

Source: MECOVI household Surveys 1997–99.

the poorest and richest income quintiles. As can be seen, the gap in health services utilization between the poorest and the richest quintile is close to 30 percent in all ages for men and women.

Health Services Utilization in Brazil: Gaps between Public and Private Coverage

Despite having a universal single health system (SUS) with free health care access for all citizens, the Brazilian population has some complaints about the quality of and access to health care. Health indicators show that, besides the fast and huge improvements brought about by SUS, some inequality in access to health care and differential health outcomes between the poor and the rich still exist. The upper and middle classes in Brazil do not use SUS as often as lower-income groups. Besides SUS, a large voluntary private health insurance scheme provides health care to 25 percent of the Brazilian population, with a higher satisfaction among users.

A study based on the 1998 Brazilian household survey (Ribeiro 2005) found that: (a) the population insured by private voluntary health plans was more satisfied with their health status than the population who depended on SUS; and (b) for both groups (with and without private voluntary health plan coverage), health status worsened as the population aged, and the incidence of chronic conditions increased.

Many determinants, such as higher income or educational level, could explain why the population covered by private health plans is more optimistic about their health status than the population covered by SUS. However, men covered by private health plans use ambulatory facilities 50 percent more often than men covered by SUS, and women covered by private health plans use ambulatory facilities 30 percent more often than women covered by SUS. In addition, the number of medical visits for private health plan users is 13 percent higher for men than in SUS and 17 percent higher for women. On one hand, private health plan beneficiaries have fewer hospitalizations than SUS users. So, a positive perception of one's own health status could be associated with higher coverage in medical visits, and eventually promotion and prevention provided by the private health plans.[14] On the other hand, a negative perception of health status is commonly associated with the higher use of acute health care facilities, such as hospital emergency rooms.

Figure 4.20 shows that the number of medical visits for the population affiliated with private health plans is substantially higher than the number for SUS users. Otherwise, despite the huge differentials in the

Figure 4.20   Utilization Rates of Medical Visits as a Percentage of the Population for SUS Beneficiaries without Private Health Plans and Beneficiaries with Private Health Plans by Gender and Age, Brazil, 1998

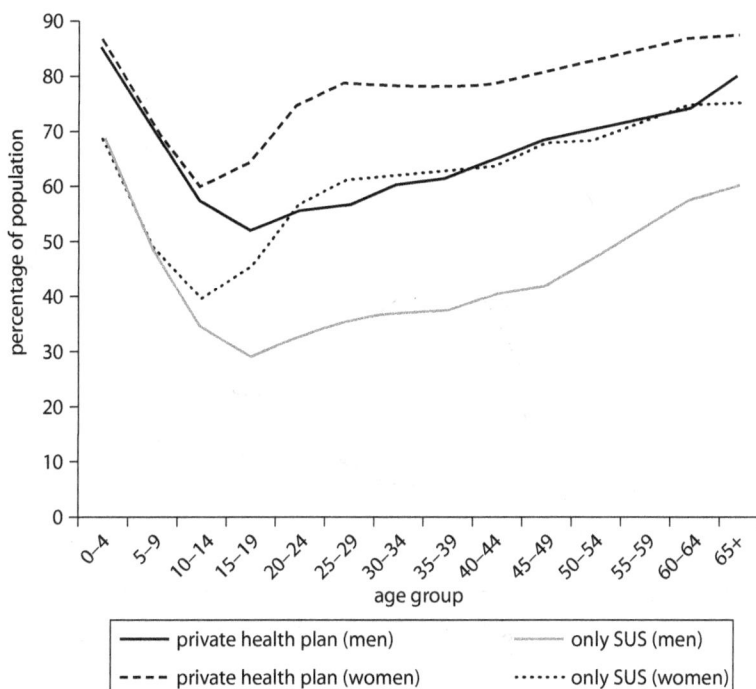

Source: Brazil National Household Survey (PNAD) 1998.

medical visits utilization rates between men and women over age 13, the gaps in medical visits between women covered by SUS and women covered by private health plans is almost the same in all age groups.

The gap in access to medical visits between the two population groups is higher than the gap in hospitalization. Figure 4.21 shows the level of hospitalization for SUS and private health plan users according to the same variables discussed above.

Hospitalization rates associated with private health plan beneficiaries are a little higher than SUS hospitalization rates for both men and women in most age groups, indicating easier access to hospital care for those with private health plans, particularly among the aging. In the population aged 17–25, females using SUS have higher hospitalization rates than those

Figure 4.21   Hospitalization Rates as a Percentage of the Population for SUS Beneficiaries without Private Health Plans and Beneficiaries with Private Health Plans by Gender and Age, Brazil, 1998

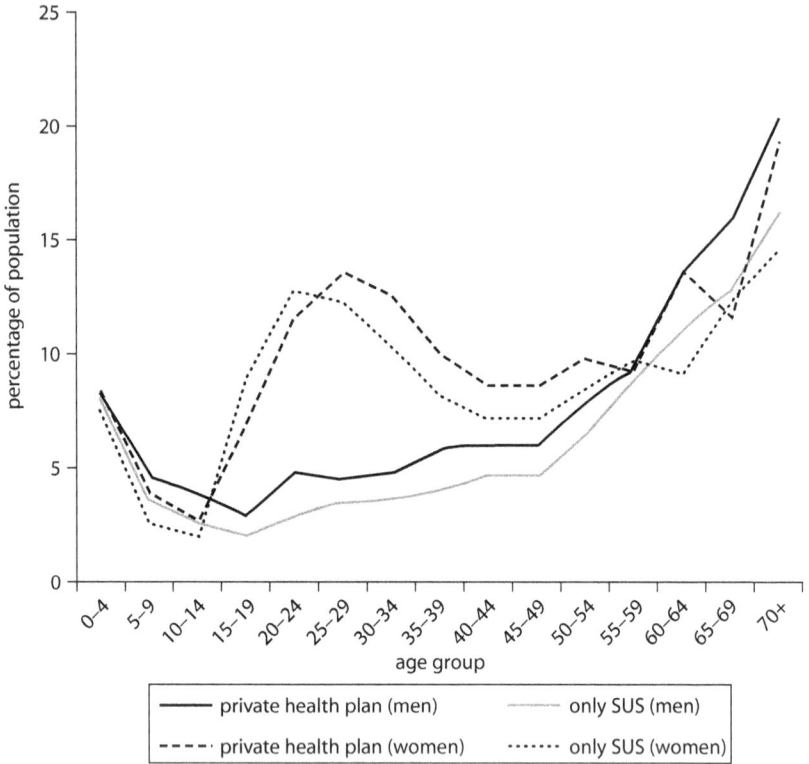

Source: Brazil National Household Survey (PNAD) 1998.

using private health plans due to higher fertility rates in early ages for the lower-income population.

Narrowing the Health Services Utilization Gaps

MECOVI data reveal the huge gaps in health services utilization and perceived health between rich and poor. Apparently, there are few age gaps between health needs and the utilization of health services. Gaps between needs and utilization are higher for both men and women in adulthood than in children and the aging. The gaps in the access of the aging to health services are associated mostly with income and not with age, but there are few studies that show in detail the nature of age gaps between health needs and health utilization. Some of these studies, like one conducted in Mexico, reveal that this gap increases with age and is higher among the aging (Lozano and others 2006). MECOVI data (table 4.5) also show that the aging poor in Bolivia present higher gaps between health needs and health utilization than children and adults.

However, given the LAC region's heterogeneity, levels of utilization of health services vary socially and geographically. Differences in the rates of usage are also associated with organizational structures and the distribution of public and private health facilities and geographic aspects of health care systems.

Perceived health needs are also linked to social and environmental conditions. If the services are not accessible, the perception of health needs is reduced, but the accessibility of services stimulates an increasing perception of health needs. That is one of the reasons developed countries create economic incentives to moderate the demand and utilization of health care in a context of increasing health expenditures.

MECOVI data do not provide information about the nature of the health services demanded or used (whether for promotion, prevention, treatment, or rehabilitation, for example). Increased utilization of preventive services among the aging has been associated with improved health status by combining quality care with decreased medical costs.

Provision of health information for the aging in developed countries has shown to have positive effects on health measures such as compliance with medication therapy, quality of life, and utilization of health services. However, health promotion and prevention services are not perceived as important by the aging population. Thus, it is necessary to share health knowledge and to promote better preventive behavior among the aging. It is also important to increase access to preventive services and medical visits to the aging poor in order to improve their perception of health needs and guarantee better information to use existing health services.

Universal health policies and single health systems,[15] if not well structured to reduce inequalities and promote active and informed health demand, are not able to close the health utilization gaps among the rich and poor. For example, even considering universal provision and free access to health care in Brazil, there is still some degree of inequity. A study (Mendoza-Sassi, Beria, and Barros 2003) conducted in Rio Grande do Sul State concluded that the poorest and least-educated groups still use health services to a lesser extent. Since more education can improve access and diminish the inequity of this underserved group, it may be that the problem is lack of information about accessing and gaining entry into the universal health system.

Together with obvious structural changes necessary to improve education profiles, other specific policies and strategies should be implemented to improve health services utilization in the underserved group, such as communication campaigns about when and how to get access to the health system. Furthermore, having a regular source of care (a doctor or site, for example) should be encouraged, especially among the poorest groups, as a means to reduce the health services utilization gaps and improve the quality of health care systems.

Health Expenditures and Health Costs by Age

Trends in Health Spending

Health care spending has been increasing quickly, particularly in developed countries. Data from Organization for Economic Co-operation and Development (OECD) countries show that health expenditures' share of GDP has grown systematically since the 1960s in these countries. However, some countries in other regions have not followed the same trajectory. Figure 4.22 shows the pace of growth of health expenditures as a share of GDP. In OECD countries, many factors (including the aging process), are associated with the continuous growth of health spending. In LAC, health expenditure growth was reversed in Brazil, Costa Rica, and República Bolivariana de Venezuela during the 1990s, and in Bolivia, Chile, Colombia, and Uruguay during the 2000s, partially because of the adoption of macroeconomic adjustment policies to reduce inflation and public spending and partially due to the recession at the end of the last decade. In addition, income constraints did not allow a faster increase in health expenditures by families.

In recent decades, aging has been the most important factor in increasing health costs. In fact, the few data that exist on health costs by age show that older adults spend much more on health than the young due to the following previously discussed factors: (a) the progressive weight of the burden of disease along the aging process, (b) the high levels of perceived health needs among older adults, and (c) the elevated levels of utilization of both ambulatory and hospital care among the aging.

In fact, health expenditures tend to grow due to a set of health sector internal determinants such as cost inflation (health-related prices increase

Figure 4.22   Trends in Health Care Spending in OECD and LAC Countries

a. OECD countries, 1960–2007

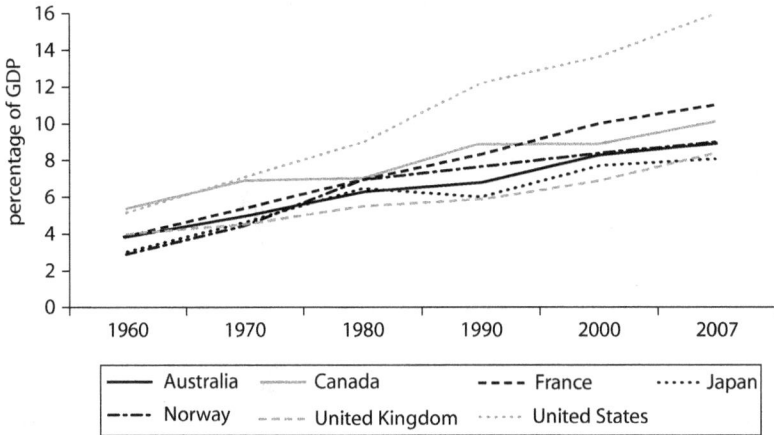

b. LAC countries, 1985–2007

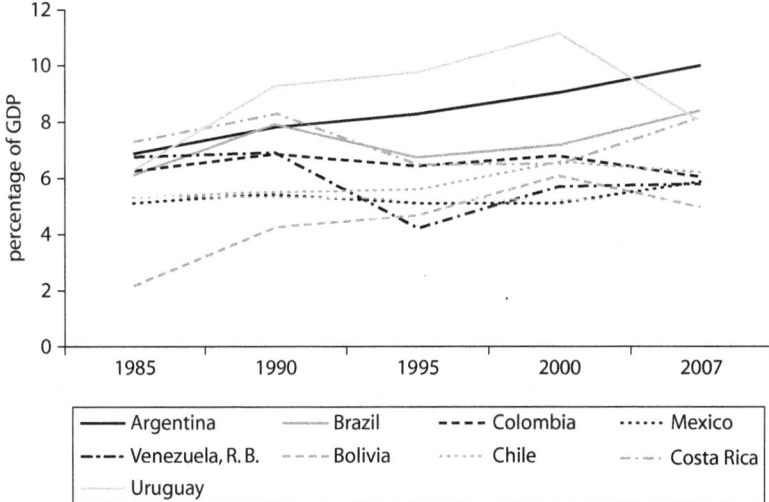

Source: WHO (World Health Survey Database 2010); PAHO (Health Indicators in the Americas 1999).

over the general price indexes), imperfect competition (barriers to competition, inefficiencies brought by third-payer systems, information asymmetry), and incorporation of medical technology.

In addition, certain external determinants, such as the income effect and the aging effect, lead the volume of health provisions to increase faster than economic growth. Regarding the income effect, it has been demonstrated that health spending is moderately inelastic when income reduces but tends to increase when income grows.

In developed countries, government health care expenditures have been growing much more rapidly than GDP. Kotlikoff and Hagist (2005) published a study comparing health care costs in 10 OECD countries. According to this study, between 1970 and 2002 these expenditures grew 2.3 times faster than GDP in the United States, 2.0 times faster than GDP in Germany, and 1.4 times faster than GDP in Japan. But the main message of this study is that aging alone is not responsible for increasing government expenditures on health. To prove this argument, the study decomposes the 1970–2002 growth in each country's health care expenditures into growth in benefit levels and changes in demographics.

The main conclusion is that growth in health benefit levels has been remarkably high and represents 89 percent of overall health care spending growth in the 10 countries. However, the new benefits distribution has disproportionately benefited the older age groups, due to increases in the fraction of individuals covered in each age group and the generation of new benefits. Recent benefits in the United States, such as the Medicare D prescription drug coverage benefit, designed to make prescription drugs more affordable for retired Americans, are examples of newly incorporated benefits. Figure 4.23 shows health care benefit-age levels in the 10 OECD countries included in the study. The figure uses the age-specific health spending constant through time and normalizes age profiles of average expenditures by dividing by average expenditures of the age group 50–64.

However, independently of the determinants of the increase in health care expenditures along the aging process, as population age structures change in the coming decades, the costs of publicly provided health care will change dramatically if current trends continue.

Data produced by the National Transfer Accounts (NTA) project on the generational economy, directed by Professors Ronald Lee (University of California, Berkeley) and Andrew Mason (University of Hawaii), and conducted by a research network of academic centers worldwide, have enabled estimations on age-specific expenditures for various public services according to the trends in the demographic transition.

According to several studies using the NTA methodology (Miller, Mason, and Holz 2009), the aging effects are going to increase over

Figure 4.23   Health Care Benefits Age Profile in OECD Countries, 2000–05

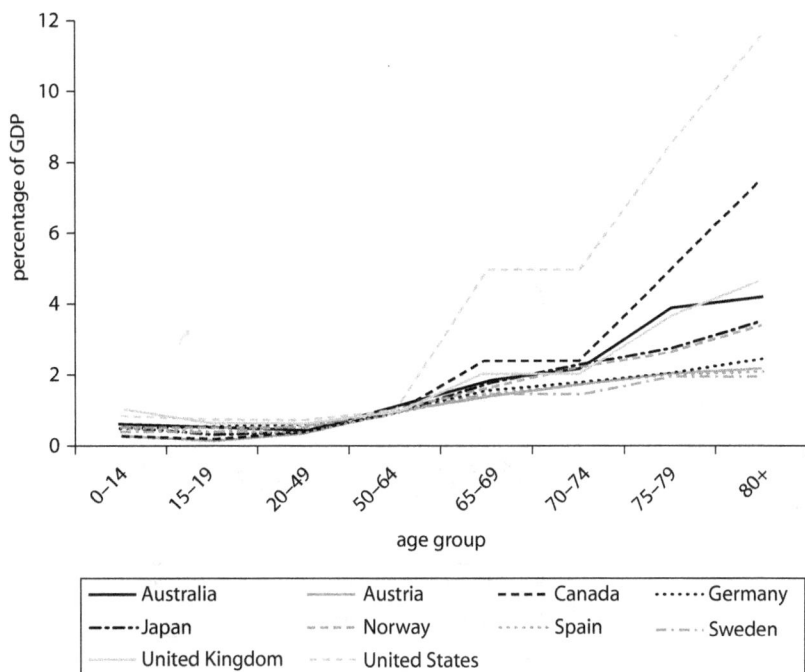

Source: Kotlikoff and Hagist 2005.

time, but they account for only a part of the increase in health care expenditures as a share of GDP. Most of the studies found that growth in nondemographic factors seems more important, especially, as demonstrated by Kotlikoff and Hagist (2005), the inclusion of new, costly benefits such as long-term care and the high costs of technology in health care, particularly in the last years of life. Figure 4.24 shows estimations of health care expenditures as a share of per capita GDP by age in six OECD countries. As can be seen, the proportion of health expenditures in the per capita GDP grows along the aging process, and health expenditures in advanced ages represent four or five times the health expenditures associated with teenagers.

Similar studies for Latin America using the NTA methodology have been developed by CELADE/ECLAC (Miller, Mason, and Holz 2009)

Figure 4.24   Health Expenditures Age Profile in 6 OECD Countries, 2005

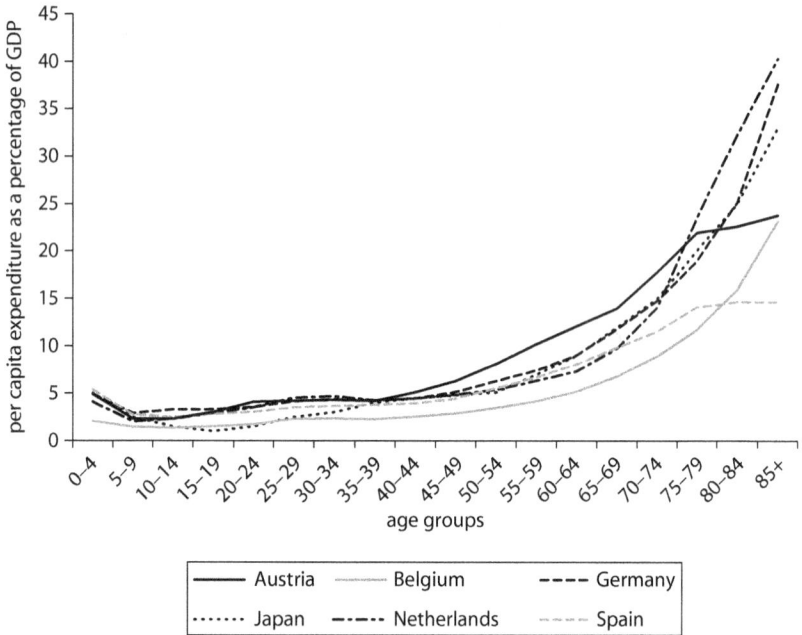

Source: OECD Health Database 2005.

that separate the aging effect from the benefit generosity effect, which measures the relative generosity of the benefit by comparing the health benefit to GDP per working-age person. This study also produced projections of future health spending by countries in order to estimate the future fiscal impacts of health care in the region.

The projections also estimate the effect of benefit generosity levels on health spending from 2005 to 2050. The main findings show that population aging alone will bring moderate increases in health spending to all countries in the region—an average increase of 1 percentage point of GDP by 2050. However, based on observations of currently wealthy and older societies in OECD countries, it is not reasonable to expect age-specific expenditures to remain constant in LAC countries. Considering the benefit generosity effect, public health expenditures as a share of GDP should increase on average by 1.9 percentage points and 4.3 percentage points by 2050, which is comparable to what is currently happening in OECD countries. Figure 4.25 shows estimations of health care expenditures per capita as a share of GDP per worker for a set of LAC countries included in the NTA project.

Health Costs by Age

Information about health costs is fragmented and difficult to integrate, particularly in developing countries. In LAC, household surveys or family budget surveys can provide information about out-of-pocket health expenditures by age but not costs associated with family health spending.

Cost information needs to be obtained through direct research in health institutions and health networks, and its aggregation is a difficult task. In addition, most health public accounting information systems do not use age as a variable to inform payments for procedures or costs in

Figure 4.25   Health Care Expenditures per Capita by Age as a Share of GDP per Worker in Selected LAC Countries, 2005

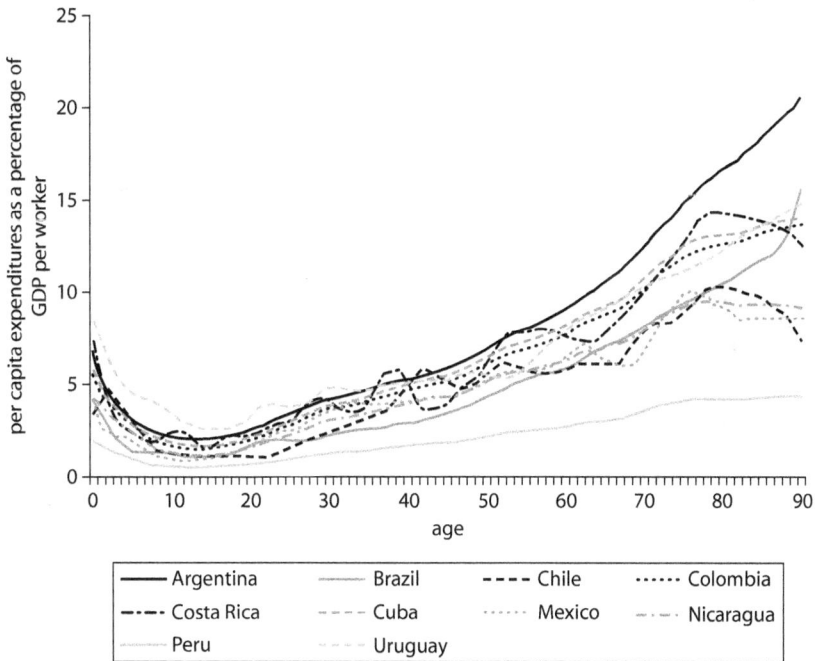

Source: Calculations based on Miller, Mason, and Holz 2009.

publicly owned hospitals. These difficulties limit the use of cost information as a way to estimate aggregate health expenditures by age.

Several examples of health costs by age could be shown in Latin America
in public and private institutions, but most of the health institutions in LAC
do not systematically collect this information. Figure 4.26 presents hospital

Figure 4.26   Hospital Health Costs in Brazil and Uruguay by Age and Gender

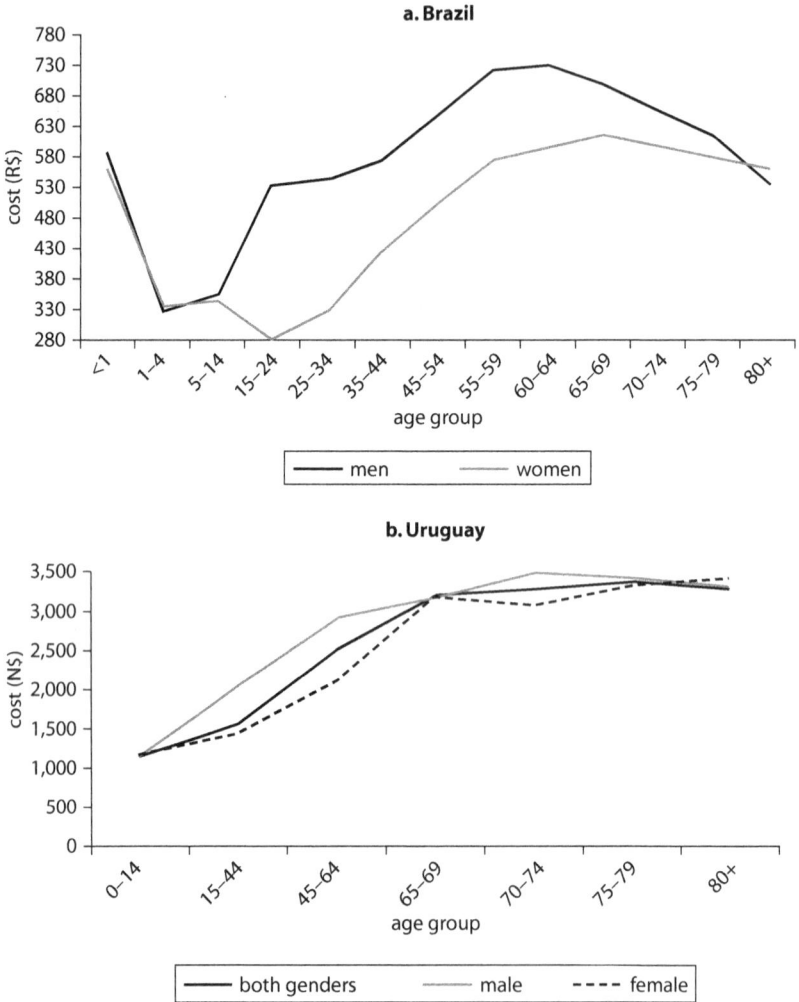

Sources: For Uruguay; Micklin and others 1993; for Brazil: DATASUS-AIH 2003.

health costs by age in a health maintenance organization in Brazil and in SUS in Uruguay.

The data show that health costs follow epidemiological needs and hospital utilization levels, as presented at the beginning of this chapter. They also show the extra burden of hospital utilization for women due to reproductive health functions in all age groups over age 15. Some studies developed in the Federal University of Minas Gerais/*Centro de Desenvolvimento e Planejamento Regional de Minas Gerais* (UFMG/CEDEPLAR) in Brazil (Ribeiro 2005) demonstrated that, discounting the hospitalizations associated with reproductive health functions, the hospital utilization profile for both genders is similar.

Health costs also vary according to different epidemiological profiles. The heterogeneity of regions like LAC is evidenced by countries, states, and provinces with different levels of epidemiological needs and health utilization profiles. This heterogeneity reflects different health cost structures by age. A recent study of SUS hospital health costs in Brazil in different metropolitan regions shows that in two Brazilian metropolitan regions, one poor (Belem) and one rich (Curitiba), the health costs should be different (figure 4.27), and these differences should be explained not only by the utilization-level profiles but also by different prices and referral costs, given that the richest regions expend more on health production factors, especially labor.

Another aspect worthy of note is the period of an individual's life associated with health spending or health cost. The health economics literature provides several examples of how the end of life absorbs a substantial part of an individual's health spending. A UFMG/CEDEPLAR study in Brazil (Berenstein, Nascimento, and Machado 2008) shows how hospitalization expenditures associated with patient interventions resulting in death are much more expensive than interventions in patients who survive after hospitalization (figure 4.28).

However, along the aging process, the hospitalization cost difference between patients who die and patients who survive is substantial. For this reason, the association between catastrophic hospitalization costs and older adults is not correct, despite the fact that it happens more often with older persons. The costs of hospitalization for children and young adults when interventions result in death are associated with conditions such as injuries and trauma, which imply higher costs than those linked with older adults, which are associated mostly with chronic conditions.

Figure 4.27   Inpatient Rates and Correspondent Costs for Men in Two Brazilian Metropolitan Regions (Belem and Curitiba), Brazil, 2005

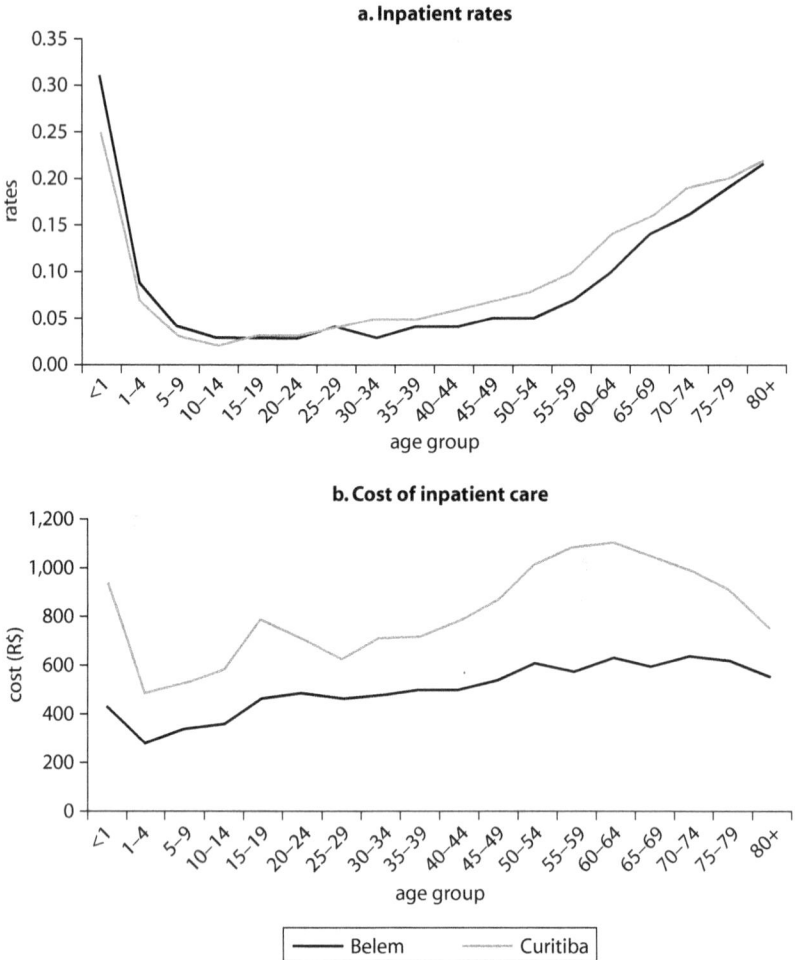

a. Inpatient rates

b. Cost of inpatient care

—— Belem   —— Curitiba

Source: Berenstein and Wajnman 2008 based on DATASUS-AIH.

Conclusions

We can draw the following conclusions from the information presented in this chapter. First, the quality of data on health status and health utilization for the aging in LAC needs to be improved. Most LAC countries do not conduct burden of disease studies and the epidemiological data need to be enhanced. Second, few countries have created benefit

Figure 4.28   Hospital Costs Per Capita according to Life Status (Death or Survival) by Age and Gender, Brazil Minas Gerais State, 2005

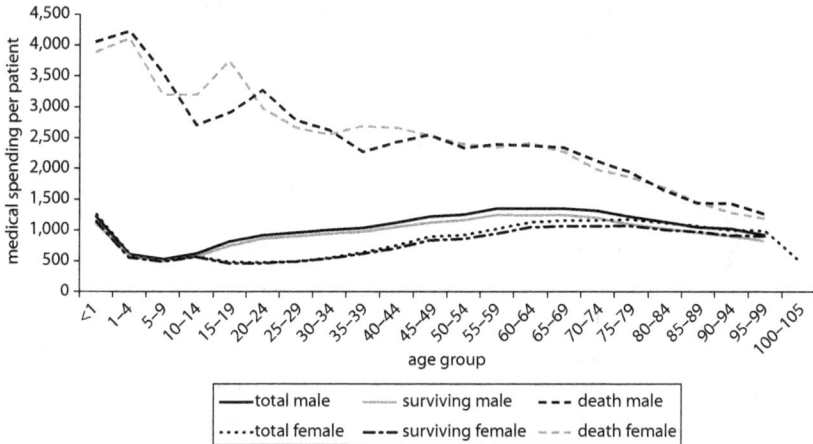

Source: Berenstein, Nascimento, and Machado 2008 based on DATASUS-AIH.

packages that allow seniors to access better health promotion, prevention, and treatment. Efforts like the AUGE Plan in Chile have improved the aging's access to high-cost interventions, but policies to enhance promotion and prevent illness and risk factors still need to be promulgated. There is also an absence of insurance policies, including in the private sector, that could protect seniors from overspending on catastrophic treatments, exams, and drugs associated with the aging process.

So, how does age influence the demand for health care in Latin America?

The greatest influence is the higher level of epidemiological needs and perceived health needs of older adults. Data presented in this chapter show that older adults potentially and effectively consume medium- and high-technology health services more often than youths and adults. Thus, the aging process in LAC will certainly expand the demand for health care in the region.

The second influence is the incorporation of new health benefits and the generosity level of the health benefits, as Kotlikoff and Hagist (2005) and Miller, Mason, and Holz (2009) show in their studies. Most LAC countries are increasing health entitlements, not only by extending coverage through the creation of universal health systems, but also by the progressive incorporation of new procedures into the current health packages.

The strong influence of corporatism and leftism in LAC governments during the 2000s is ensuring the fast incorporation of more generous health benefits, despite probable future fiscal constraints. Other factors that could contribute to supporting policies to increase the generosity of health benefits in the region are the fast-rising income levels in LAC countries and the inelasticity of health spending.

The implications of the increasing demand for health care associated with the aging process for national health expenditures will depend on several factors such as (a) increasing health promotion and prevention of chronic conditions, (b) regulation of the use of medical technology and health insurance markets, (c) incentives to increase price competition in the sector, and (d) the pace at which new health benefits are incorporated into public programs.

But it also depends on government priorities and what populations are willing to pay. As figure 4.22 showed, health spending in LAC fell as a share of GDP in certain countries during the early 2000s—even in those at a very advanced stage of the demographic transition, such as Uruguay. This happened as a response to the economic crisis at the beginning of the decade and led to a decrease in health coverage (including for older adults), caused a number of national health maintenance organizatons to go broke, and led Uruguay to search for new arrangements to increase health protection and cut health costs, resulting in a reduction in health spending from 11 percent to 8 percent of GDP between 2000 and 2005.

Regarding medical care costs, everything depends on the changing mix and cost of the production factors used to deliver health services. Health professionals, like physicians, are distributed in many specializations. Their training is costly and their ability to generate demand, such as ordering medical exams and prescribing extensive use of high-cost therapies, is huge. Medical research and technology is one of the largest fields of innovation, and the structures of the big industries associated with health, such as pharmaceuticals and medical equipment, are big and cartelized. These industries have no difficulty placing new products in the world market and defining the market price for their products.

The bottom line is that the future size of the aging population is only one important determinant of the costs of health age-related programs. The health status of the aging (and consequently of the whole population, because everyone who survives will age) is another factor. Demographic projections are needed to assess the long-term fiscal impact of population aging, but they are also important to predict the health status of future cohorts of older people since this status relates to both their ability to continue working at older ages and their use of health services. Plus, better regulation of other determinants of health spending (the income effect, the use of technology, the generosity of benefits, and the imperfect market structure of the health sector) need to be addressed in order to realize savings in the public programs and to shape health care policy into one that will ensure affordable health care for the aging and for future generations.

Notes

1. The World Health Organization, which developed the concept of DALYs, defines the term as the sum of years of potential life lost due to premature mortality and the years of productive life lost due to disability.

2. Existing economic analysis shows that bad health status, especially if associated with chronic illness, undermines current productivity and probably future losses in output. Good health improves the capacity to learn and work and consequently improves income and welfare at the household level. Effects at the aggregated level, however, may be hard to discern (Spence and Lewis 2009).

3. Health needs have been approached from philosophical, human rights, and health economics perspectives. At the individual level, health needs include whatever is required for health or comfort, including personal and social care, health care, accommodation, finance, education, use of time on employment and leisure, and access to transportation. At the individual level, these are perhaps subjective needs. But at the collective level, these needs are perhaps more objective and include achieving, maintaining, and restoring an acceptable level of health that allows social independence and good quality of life.

4. Mortality and morbidity affect the human lifespan at different stages of the life cycle according to the incidence of communicable and noncommunicable diseases and injuries.

5. DALYs are an elegant formulation, but it has measurement and subjectivity problems. Although considered controversial, the WHO Global Burden of Disease (GBD) study gave less weight to a year of healthy life lived during young and older ages than a year of life lived during the working ages, based on several studies on social preferences. This weighting has not been accepted by many who consider the contribution of individuals at all ages to be equal. DALYs are also criticized for the subjectivity of the definitions used to measure severity of disability levels related to the YLD calculations and the fragility of existing data and estimations. However, others,

including Murray and Evans (2003) and Lopez and others (2006), refute this criticism. Given these disparate views, DALYs-based estimations must be viewed as a rough and indicative methodology and not an absolute measure of the BOD. The DALY data used in this chapter are updated from the WHO GBD estimations for 2004, which builds on the previous GBD for 2002. This information updated, among other things, mortality estimations for communicable diseases and AIDS, wars, civil conflicts, and natural disasters in 192 countries; the latest death registration in 112 countries; and revised estimations of disability for 52 causes in all countries. More on the updated information in the 2004 estimations can be found in WHO (2008).

6. This paper uses the World Bank classification of regions by development level: High-Income Countries (HIC), East Asia and Pacific (EAP), Latin America and the Caribbean (LAC), Europe and Central Asia (ECA), Middle East and North Africa (MENA), South Asia (SAR), and Sub-Saharan Africa (SSA).

7. Jean Downes, in a remarkable article written in 1941, pointed out that "The seriousness of the problem of the chronic diseases characteristic of middle and old age has been judged by their rank as leading causes of death. The amount of and need for institutional and other community facilities for the treatment and care of cases of chronic illness, such as cancer, heart disease, mental disease, and tuberculosis has been another measure of their importance. Both of these criteria imply an unusual risk of complete incapacity and death for the chronic-disease sufferer" (Downes 1941).

8. The SABE was a survey of over 10,500 older adults (age = 60 in 1999) conducted in the following seven cities in LAC during 1999–2000: Buenos Aires (Argentina), Bridgetown (Barbados), São Paulo (Brazil), Santiago (Chile), Havana (Cuba), Mexico City (Mexico), and Montevideo (Uruguay). The study, which received technical support from PAHO, comprised a research team that included members from PAHO, the University of Wisconsin–Madison, and local investigators from each collaborating city. The survey collected comprehensive information on health, functional ability, and social support networks. Data from this survey have been available to the public for free download since January 2005 from the National Archive of Computerized Data on Aging, and details about the methodology of the SABE study have already been published. The SABE questionnaire response rates were 63 percent in Buenos Aires, 65 percent in Montevideo, 80 percent in Bridgetown, 84 percent in Santiago, 85 percent in São Paulo and Mexico City, and 95 percent in Havana.

9. Sheps and others (2004) describe the INTERHEART study as follows: "INTERHEART was a standardized case-control study of acute myocardial infarction conducted in 52 countries. . . The study was designed to examine the

relationship of smoking, history of hypertension or diabetes, waist-hip ratio, dietary patterns, physical activity, consumption of alcohol, blood apolipoproteins and *psychosocial factors* to myocardial infarction."

10. The SABE survey defined "disability" as difficulty performing at least one of the six activities of daily living (dressing, eating, bathing, walking across a room, getting into/out of bed, and using the toilet).

11. The community engagement levels considered by the SABE survey are the following: (1) See or speak with offspring, siblings, other family, or friends less than once a week; (2) See or speak with offspring, siblings, other family, or friends at least once a week; (3) Giving money or things (like food, clothing, etc.) to offspring, siblings, other family, or friends; ± Level (2); (4) Helping offspring, siblings, other family, or friends with services (such as transportation, housework, etc.), or childcare; ± Level (2), ± Level (3); (5) Provided services for free (to social services, children's home, senior citizens' center, college or university, health center, church, hospital, or other place), or worked for free or for payment in the past week; ± Level (2), ± Level (3), ± Level (4). Active engagement was then defined as a combination of Levels (4) and (5).

12. According to CELADE data, in 2004, the estimated gender ratio (number of men per women in a given age group) in the LAC region was 1.04 in the age group 0–4, 0.89 in the age group 60–69, and 0.72 in the age group 80 and older.

13. This study is still in progress.

14. Despite that, there are many complaints that private health plans in Brazil do not provide enough health promotion and preventive care.

15. Single health systems are those in which there is only one public structure that offers health programs to the entire population of a region or country, like the National Health Services in the United Kingdom and SUS in Brazil.

References

Abrego, G. R., J. E. de La Peña, B. Zurita, and T. de Jesús Ramírez. 2007. "Muerte prematura y discapacidad en los Derechohabientes del Instituto Méxicano de Seguridad Social." *Salud Pública de México* 49 (2) (Mar–Abr): 143. México.

Alves, D. 2001. "Gastos em saúde: Uma análise por domicílios para a cidade de São Paulo." 2001. *Pesquisa e Planejamento Econômico*, IPEA 31 (3): 479–94, Dez. Rio de Janeiro.

Andrade, F. C. D. 2006. "Obesity and Central Obesity in Elderly People in Latin America and the Caribbean—Are We Fat?" Paper presented at the XV Meeting of the Brazilian Population Studies Association (ABEP), Caxambu (MG-Brazil), September.

Andrade, M. V., and M. B. Lisboa. 2002. "Determinantes dos gastos privados e pessoais com saúde no Brasil." Texto para Discussão No. 75. CEDEPLAR/UFMG, Belo Horizonte, Agôsto.

Audisio, R. A., F. Bozzeti, R. Gennari, M. T. Jaklitsch, T. Koperna, W. E. Longo, T. Wiggers, and A. P. Zbar. 2004. "The Surgical Manager of Elderly Cancer Patients: Recommendations of the SIOG Surgical Task Force." *European Journal of Cancer* 40 (7) (May): 926–38.

Berenstein, C. K., R. Nascimento, and C. J. Machado. 2005. "O Perfil etáreo dos custos de internação na saúde Pública no Brasil: Uma análise para as capitais das regiões metropolitanas do Brasil em 2000." Ed. CEDEPLAR/UFMG, Dissertação de Mestrado apresentada ao CEDEPLAR, Belo Horizonte.

————. 2008. "Viver ou Morrer: o que explica o aumento dos gastos com saúde no Brasil." Trabalho apresentado no IIIo. Congresso da ALAP. Córdoba, Argentina, Setembro.

Berenstein, C. K., and S. Wajnman. 2008. "Efeitos da estrutura etárea nos gastos con internação no sistema únido de saúde: Uma análise de decomposição para duas áreas metropolitanas Brasileiras." *Cadernos de Saúde Pública* 24 (10): 2301–38. ENSP-FIOCRUZ, Rio de Janeiro.

Campos, A. C. 2001. "O envelhecimento da população e os gastos em saúde." *Economia da Saúde* 19 (1) (Jan–Jun). Lisboa.

CELADE/CEPAL (Latin American and Caribbean Centre for Demography/ Economic Commission for Latin America and the Caribbean). 2005. "dinámica demográfica y desarrollo en América Latina y el Caribe." CEPAL Seria Población y Desarrollo No. 58, Santiago de Chile, Febrero.

————. 2008a. "Tendencias demográficas y protección social en América Latina y el Caribe." CEPAL Seria Población y Desarrollo No. 82, Santiago de Chile, Febrero.

————. 2008b. "Demographic Changes and Its Influence on Development in Latin America and the Caribbean." Document presented at the Thirty-Second Session of ECLAC, Santo Domingo, Dominican Republic, June 9–13.

Dachs, N., M. Ferrer, C. E. Florez, A. J. D. Barros, R. Narváez, and Martín Valdivia. 2002. "Inequalities in Health in Latin America and the Caribbean: Descriptive and Exploratory Results for Self-Reported Health Problems and Health Care in Twelve Countries." *Pan-American Journal of Public Health* 11 (5/6): 335–55. Washington, DC.

Diseases Control Priorities Project—DCP2. 2007. *Marco prioritario de salud en el Cono Sur: Acciones necesarias sobre los factores de riesgo del estilo de vida.* DCP2, Washington, DC.

Downes, J. 1941. "Chronic Disease among Middle and Old-Age Persons." *The Milbank Memorial Fund Quarterly* 19 (1) (January): 5–25. Blackwell Publishing on behalf of Milbank Memorial Fund.

Gadelha, A. M. J., and others. 2002. *Relatorio final do projeto estimativa da carga de doença no Brasil 1998.* Ed. FENSPTEC/FIOCRUZ, Rio de Janeiro.

García, J. R., ed. 2008. *Carga de enfermedad Colombia 2005: Resultados alcanzados.* Documento Técnico ASS/1502, Pontificia Universidad Javeriana y CENDEX. Bogotá, Octubre.

GOLD (Global Initiative for Chronic Obstructive Lung Disease). 2006. "Global Strategy for the Diagnosis, Management and Prevention of Chronic Obstructive Pulmonary Disease." World Health Organization. http://www.who.int/respiratory/copd/GOLD_WR_06.pdf.

Hansen, J. 1998. "Common Cancers in the Elderly." *Drugs & Aging* 13 (6) (December): 467–78.

Kanamura, A. H., and A. L. D. Viana. 2007. "Gastos elevados em planos de saúde: Com quê e em quê?" *Revista de Saúde Pública* 41 (5): 814–20. FSP/USP, São Paulo.

Kilsztajn, S., A. Rossbach, M. B. Camara, and M. S. N. Carmo. 2003. "Serviços de saúde, gastos e envelhecimento da população Brasileira." *Revista Brasileira de Estudos de População* 20 (1) (January–June), Rio de Janeiro.

Kotlikoff, L. J., and C. Hagist. 2005. *Who Is Going Broke? Comparing Health Care Costs in Ten OECD Countries.* National Bureau of Economic Research, Working Paper No. 11833, Cambridge, MA.

Lavados, P. M., A. J. Hennis, J. G. Fernandes, M. T. Medina, B. Legetic, A. Hoppe, C. Sacks, L. Jadue, and R. Salinas. 2007. "Stroke Epidemiology: Prevention and Management Strategies at a Regional Level: Latin America and the Caribbean." *The Lancet Neurology* 6 (4) (April): 362–73.

Lee, R. 2001. *The Fiscal Impact of Population Aging: Testimony Prepared for the State Budget Committee.* University of California, Berkeley, February.

Lee, R., and T. Miller. 2002. "An Approach to Forecasting Health Expenditures, with Application to the U.S. Medicare System." *Health Services Research* 37 (5) (October): 1365–86.

Lima, M. G., M. Berti de Azevedo Barros, C. L. Galvão César, M. Goldbaum, L. Carandina, and R. Mesquita Ciconelli. 2009. "Impact of Chronic Diseases on Quality of Life among Elderly in the State of São Paulo, Brazil: A Population-based Study." *Pan-American Journal of Public Health* 25 (4). Pan-American Health Organization, Washington, DC.

Lopez, A. D., C. D. Mathers, M. Ezzati, D. T. Jamison, and C. J. L. Murray, eds. 2006. *Global Burden of Diseases and Risk Factors.* Disease Control Priorities Project, Oxford University Press and World Bank, Washington, DC.

Lozano, R., P. Soliz, E. Gakidou, J. Abbott-Klafter, D. Feehan, C. Vidal, J. P. Ortiz, and C. J. Murray. 2006. "Benchmarking of the Performance of Mexican States with Effective Coverage." *The Lancet* 368 (9548): 1729–41.

Massardo, L., M. H. Cardiel, A. R. A. Levy, I. Laurindo, E. R. Soriano, E. Acevedo-Vázquez, A. Millán, C. Pineda-Villaseñor, C. Galarza-Maldonado, C. V. Caballero-Uribe, R. Espinosa-Morales, and B. A. Pons-Estel. 2009. "Management of Patients with Rheumatoid Arthritis in Latin America: A Consensus Position Paper from Pan-American League of Associations of Rheumatology and Grupo Latino Americano De Estudio De Artritis Reumatoide." *Journal of Clinical Rheumatology* 15 (4): 203–10, June.

Medici, A. C. 2009. "Salud: de pacientes a ciudadanos." In F. H. Cardoso and A. Foxley, eds. *A medio camino: Nuevos desafíos de la democracia y del desarrollo en América Latina*. Uqbar y CIEPLAN, Santiago de Chile, Marzo.

Mendoza-Sassi, R., B. U. Beria, and A. J. Barros. 2003. "Outpatient Health Service Utilization and Associated Factors: a Population-Based Study." In *Revista de Saude Pública* 37 (3): 372–78. FSP/USP, São Paulo, Setembro.

Micklin, M., H. Wong, and S. Heinig. 1993. *The Effects of Population Aging in Health Care Utilization and Costs*. For the *Centro de Asistencia del Sindicato Medico de Uruguay—CASMU*. Bethesda, MD, August.

Miller, T. 2001. "Increasing Longevity and Medicare Expenditures." *Demography* 38 (2) (May): 215–26.

Miller, T., C. Mason, and M. Holz. 2009. *The Fiscal Impact of Demographic Change in 10 Latin American Countries: Projecting Public Expenditures in Education, Health and Pensions*. CELADE/ECLAC, Santiago.

Ministerio de Salud, Chile. 1996. *Estudio de carga de enfermedad en Chile—Informe Final*. Ministerio de Salud, Santiago de Chile.

———. 2008. *Estudio de carga de enfermedad y carga atribuible, Chile 2007—Informe Final*. Ministerio de Salud, Santiago de Chile.

Ministerio de Salud, Costa Rica. 2005. *Medición de la carga de enfermedad en Costa Rica, Año 2005*. Ministerio de Salud, San José.

Ministerio de Salud, Peru. 2006. *Estudio de carga de enfermedad en el Perú 2004*. Dirección General de Epidemiologia, Lima, Julio.

Murray, C. J. L., and D. B. Evans, eds. 2003. *Health Systems Performance Assessment: Debate, Methods and Empiricism*. World Health Organization, Geneva.

Nunes, A. 2005. *O envelhecimento populacional e a despesa de saúde no Brasil*. Diretoria de Estudos Sociais do IPEA, Brasilia.

PAHO (Pan-American Health Organization). 2006. *The State of Aging and Health in Latin America and the Caribbean*. Washington, DC.

———. 2009. *Premature Mortality due to Cerebrovascular Disease (CeVD)*. In *Health Situation in the Americas: Basic Indicators 2009*. Washington, DC.

Pellikaan, F., and E. Westerhout. 2005. *Alternative Scenarios for Health, Life Expectancy and Social Expenditure: The Influence of Living Longer in Better*

Health on Health Care and Pension Expenditures and Government Finances in the EU. ENEPRI Research Report No. 8, June 2008. http://www.enepri.org.

Ribeiro, M. M. 2005. *Utilização de serviços de saúde no Brasil: Uma investigação do padrão etário por sexo e cobertura por plano de saúde.* Tese de Mestrado apresentada ao CEDEPLAR/UFMG, Belo Horizonte.

Rose, A. M. C., A. J. Hennis, and I. R. Hambleton. 2008. "Sex and the City: Differences in Disease- and Disability-free Life Years, and Active Community Participation of Elderly Men and Women in 7 Cities in Latin America and the Caribbean." *BioMed Central Public Health* 8: 127. Available at: http://www.biomedcentral.com/1471-2458/8/127.

Saad, P. M. 1998. *Impact of Pension Reform in the Living Arrangements of Older Persons in Latin America.* Population Division of the United Nations, New York.

Sanchez, H., C. Albala, and L. M. Lera. 2005. "Años de vida perdidos pro muerte prematura en adultos del gran Santiago: ¿Hemos ganado con equidad?" *Revista Médica de Chile* 133: 575–82, Santiago.

Sheps, David S., Nancy Frasure-Smith, Kenneth E. Freedland, and Robert M. Carney. 2004. "The INTERHEART Study: Intersection between Behavioral and General Medicine." *Psychosomatic Medicine, Journal of Biobehavioral Medicine* 66: 797–98.

Spence, M., and M. Lewis, eds. 2009. *Health and Growth.* Commission on Growth and Development, World Bank, Washington, DC.

Turra, C. M., and M. Holz. 2009. *Who Benefits from Public Transfers? Incidence across Income Groups and across Generations.* World Bank, Washington, DC.

WIIO (World Health Organization). 2008. *The Global Burden of Diseases Update 2004.* Geneva.

Zucchi, P., C. Del Nero, and A. M. Malik. 1998. "Gasto em saúde: Os fatores que agem na demanda e oferta dos serviços de saúde." *Revista de Administração Pública* 32 (5): 124–47, Rio de Janeiro.

CHAPTER 5

The Economics of Happiness and Health Policy: How Health Norms Vary across Cohorts in Latin America

Carol Graham

Norms of health vary a great deal across countries and cohorts, and the variations often have little to do with objective health conditions. Yet these norms influence the demand for health care across countries and cohorts, and may help explain why demand is low in many contexts where objective health conditions are very poor. Satisfaction with the health care respondents have access to in the Latin America and the Caribbean (LAC) region, for example, is remarkably high given the objective conditions, and is the same in Guatemala as it is in Chile, even though objective health indicators are markedly worse in the former than in the latter[1] (figure 5.1). Health satisfaction is highest among the elderly and lowest among the middle aged in the region, mirroring age-related trends in happiness.

This chapter reviews the literature, including the results of my research with several colleagues, on health and happiness and, in particular, the role of different norms of health in explaining variance in health satisfaction across cohorts, countries, and health conditions. This literature relies on novel methods from the economics of happiness. This method is utilized to attach relative weights to the values that individuals place on different health

Figure 5.1   Average Country Health Satisfaction Scores

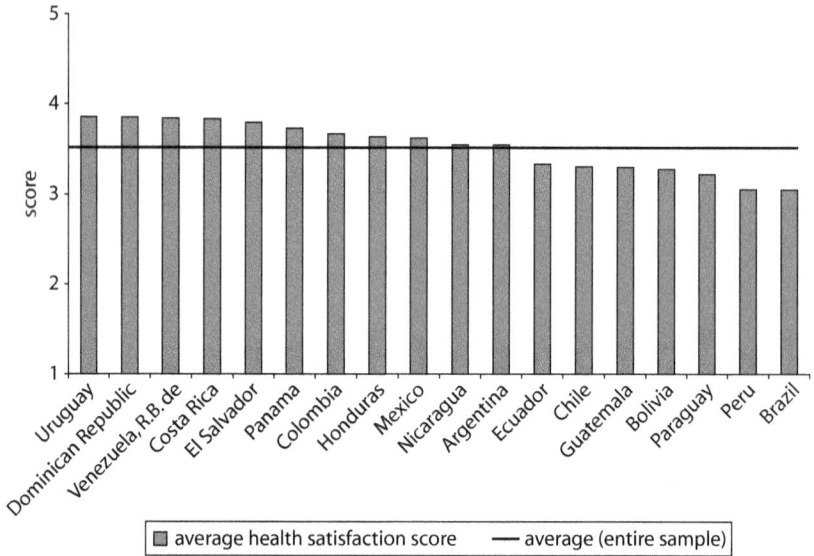

Source: Latinobarometro data, reported in Graham and Lora (2009).
Note: This is based on the Latinobarometro question, "Generally speaking, how satisfied are you with the health care that you have access to?" The question mixes respondents' evaluations of their own health conditions with their access to health care.
1 = No access.
2 = Not satisfied at all.
3 = Not very satisfied.
4 = Satisfied.
5 = Very satisfied.

conditions and to assess how those weights vary across cohorts. The results for Latin America and the Caribbean relied on a novel data set for the region, which combines the standard questions from the Gallup World poll for 2007—including life and health satisfaction—with responses to the Euro-quality Five Dimensions (EQ-5D) index, a measure of physical and mental health that has been used to value different health conditions in the United States and Europe. The data are available for roughly 18,000 respondents across 18 countries in Latin America and the Caribbean.

There is significant variance in health satisfaction across countries, which is more important than the variance across cohorts. There also exists significant variance in the life and health satisfaction effects of various health conditions, with some conditions having markedly stronger effects than others. The modest cross-cohort variance that exists depends on each cohort's ability to adapt to those conditions.

Norms of health—for example, the level and quality of health that people are accustomed to—seem to play a role in determining how much
tolerance people have for poor health.

The Economics of Happiness

In the past few years there has been a burgeoning literature on the economics of happiness. While happiness has been a topic for philosophers
and psychologists for decades, it is a novel one for economists. Early economists and philosophers, ranging from Aristotle to Bentham, Mill, and
Smith, incorporated the pursuit of happiness in their work. Yet as economics grew more rigorous and quantitative, more parsimonious definitions of welfare took hold. Utility was taken to depend only on income as
mediated by individual choices or preferences within a rational individual's monetary budget constraint (revealed preferences). Most economists
shied away from survey data (expressed preferences), under the assumption that there is no consequence to what people say in surveys, while
consumption choices pose concrete tradeoffs.

This focus on revealed preferences has been a powerful tool for
answering many questions and has allowed for a more parsimonious and
quantitative approach to economics. Yet it does not do a good job of
explaining certain kinds of questions, particularly those in contexts where
choice is constrained. These include the welfare effects of institutional
arrangements that individuals are powerless to change; choices that are
made according to perceptions of fairness or other principles; situations
where individuals are constrained in their capacity to make choices; and
seemingly nonrational behaviors that are explained by norms, addiction,
and self-control. Happiness surveys provide us with a novel metric.

Happiness surveys are based on questions in which the individual is
asked, "Generally speaking, how happy are you with your life?" or "How
satisfied are you with your life?" The answers are given on a four-to-seven-
point scale. Answers to happiness and life satisfaction questions correlate
quite closely.[2] Still, the particular kind of happiness question that is used
matters to the results. For example, respondents' income level seems to
matter more to their answers to life satisfaction questions than it does to
their answers to questions that are designed to gauge the innate character
component of happiness (affect), as gauged by questions such as "How
many times did you smile yesterday?"

Happiness questions are also particularly vulnerable to order bias—
that is, to where they are placed in a survey. Bias in answers to happiness

surveys can also result from unobserved personality traits and related errors that affect how the same individuals answer a range of questions. (These concerns can be addressed via econometric techniques if panel data are available.) Related concerns about unobservable variables are common to all economic disciplines and are not unique to the study of happiness. For example, a naturally cheerful person may respond to policy measures differently and/or put more effort into the labor market than the average person would.

Despite the potential pitfalls, cross-sections of large samples across countries and over time find remarkably consistent patterns in the determinants of happiness. Psychologists, meanwhile, find validation in the way that people answer these surveys based in physiological measures of happiness, such as the frontal movements in the brain and in the number of "genuine"—Duchenne—smiles (Diener and Seligman 2004).

The data in happiness surveys are analyzed via standard econometric techniques, with an error term that captures the unobserved characteristics described above.[3] Because the answers to happiness surveys are ordinal rather than cardinal, they are best analyzed via ordered logistic or probit equations. These equations depart from standard regression equations, which explore a continuous relationship among variables, and instead explore the probability that an individual will place himself or herself in a particular category, typically ranging from unhappy to very happy. These regressions typically yield lower R-squares than economists are used to, reflecting the extent to which emotions and other components of true well-being are driving the results, as opposed to the variables that we are able to measure, such as income, education, and employment status.

While it is impossible to measure the precise effects of independent variables on true well-being, happiness researchers have used the coefficients on these variables as a basis for assigning relative weights to them.[4] They can estimate how much income a typical individual in the United States or the United Kingdom would need to produce the same change in stated happiness that comes from the well-being loss resulting from, for example, divorce (US$100,000) or job loss (US$60,000) (Blanchflower and Oswald 2004.).

In his original study of happiness, Richard Easterlin revealed a paradox that sparked interest in the topic but is as yet unresolved.[5] While most happiness studies find that *within* countries wealthier people are, on average, happier than poor people, studies across countries and over time find very little, if any, relationship between increases in per capita income and average happiness levels. On average, wealthier countries (as a group) are happier than poor countries (as a group); happiness seems to rise with income up to a point, but not beyond it. Yet even among the less happy, poorer countries, there is not a clear relationship between average income and average happiness levels, suggesting that many other factors—including cultural traits—are at play (figure 5.2).

Figure 5.2   Health Satisfaction in Latin America by Cohorts

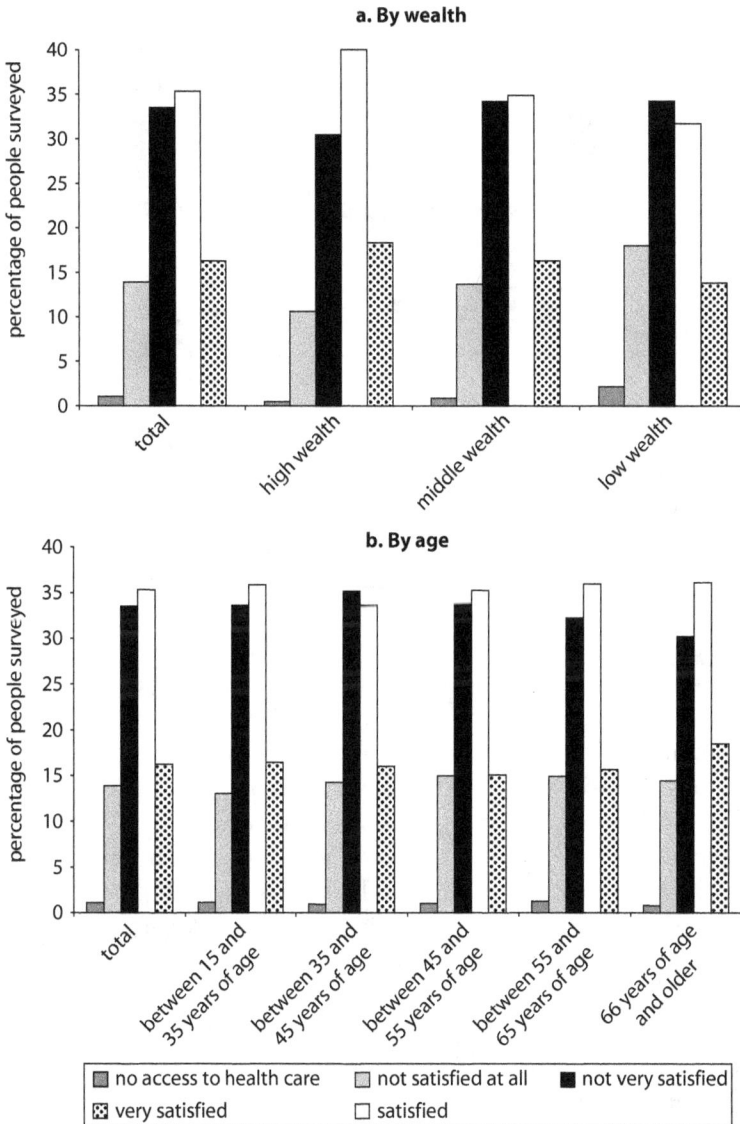

a. By wealth

b. By age

| no access to health care | not satisfied at all | not very satisfied |
| very satisfied | satisfied | |

(continued)

Figure 5.2   Health Satisfaction in Latin America by Cohorts *(continued)*

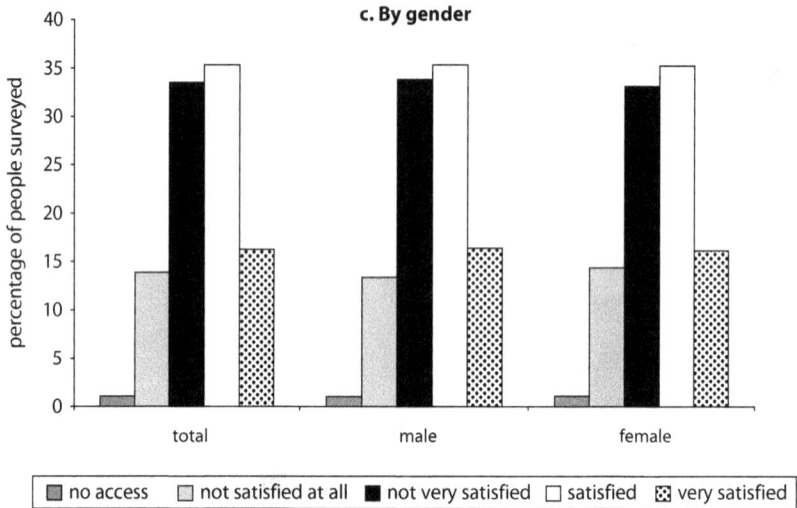

c. By gender

Source: Author's calculations based on Latinobarometro data for 2007.

More recently, there has been renewed debate over whether there is an Easterlin paradox or not. Why the discrepancy? For a number of reasons—many of them methodological—the divergent conclusions may each be correct. The relationship between happiness and income is mediated by a range of factors that can alter its slope and/or functional form.[6]

There is much less debate about the relationship between income and happiness within countries. Income matters to happiness (Oswald 1997). Yet after basic needs are met other factors such as rising aspirations, relative income differences, and the security of gains become increasingly important, in addition to income.[7] Happiness studies find that a number of variables have a consistent relationship with happiness, across countries and across development levels. Income, health, and employment are good for happiness; unemployment, divorce, and crime victimization are consistently bad for happiness. Age and happiness have a U-shaped relationship, with happiness typically declining until the middle-aged years (from early to late 40s, depending on the country), and then increasing monotonically after that, controlling for health and having a stable partner.[8]

The correlates of happiness in Latin America fit the standard pattern, including the U-shaped relationship between happiness and age (figure 5.3). The low point for happiness in Latin America is in the late 40s, while in the United States and Europe it is in the early to mid-40s. One

Figure 5.3   Happiness and Health Satisfaction by Age in Latin America

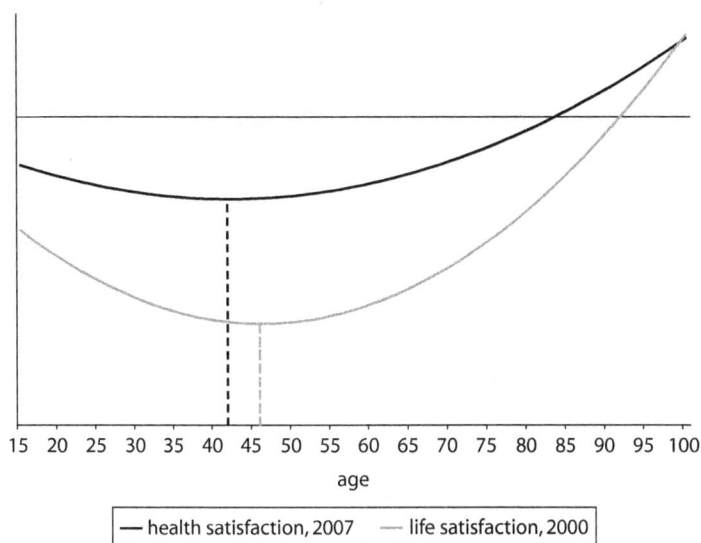

age

| — health satisfaction, 2007   — life satisfaction, 2000 |

Source: Graham and Pettinato (2002) for Life Satisfaction, and author's calculations based on Latinobarometro data 2007 for Health Access Satisfaction.
Note: Age of Minimum Life Satisfaction: 45.83 years. Age of Minimum Health Access Satisfaction: 41.69 years.

difference between Latin America and the United States and Europe, though, is self-employment. While the self-employed are happier than the average in the United States and Europe, they are less happy than the average in Latin America. In the former context they are likely self-employed by choice, while in the latter context they are likely in the informal sector due to lack of stable employment opportunities (Graham and Pettinato 2002).

The coefficients that result from these sorts of estimations reflect statistical associations or correlations and cannot be interpreted in a causal manner. The information that is reported by individuals can be biased by their inherent personality traits. This can be corrected to some extent by the construction of an individual bias or "optimism" variable, which is calculated based on each respondent's responses to questions across several quality-of-life domains, and the latent correlation among them—for example, that which is not explained by socioeconomic and demographic traits.[9]

While the debate over happiness and income has received much attention, an equally important variable—health—correlates more closely with happiness than income.[10] Good health is linked to higher happiness levels, and health shocks—such as serious diseases or permanent disabilities—have negative and often lasting effects on happiness. At the same time, a number of studies find that happier people are healthier. Causality seems to run in both directions, most likely because personality traits or other unobservable variables are linked to better health and higher happiness levels.

As noted, numerous studies have explored the income-happiness relationship and attempt to explain the nonlinearities and apparent paradoxes (Clark and Oswald 1994; Biswas-Diener and Diener 2002; Helliwell 2003; Leigh and Wolfers 2005). There is some evidence that the happiness-health relationship displays trends similar to the Easterlin paradox, although less is known about it. Clearly, there is adaptation: health standards have been improving over time and people come to expect them. There may also be diminishing marginal returns in some sense: once certain levels of longevity are reached, its benefits are weighed against other objectives, such as better quality of life. Even less is known about the happiness-health relationship among the very poor, who typically have lower expectations and different norms of health, and, as a result, underreport health problems. We explore the role of different norms of health in greater detail in the sections that follow.

Norms of Health: The Example of Obesity

Different norms of health—for example, the level, nature, and quality of health conditions and health care that societies or cohorts within them are accustomed to—seem to play a role in determining health behaviors and health satisfaction. My own research with several colleagues certainly suggests that is the case, as does some work by others (see Graham 2008; Deaton 2008; Graham and Lora 2009). This difference in norms of health helps explain cross-country and cross-cohort differences in the levels of demand for health services, among other things. One example of this is the variance in obesity rates—and differences in their effects on happiness—across socioeconomic and racial cohorts in the United States.

Andrew Felton and I assessed the well-being costs associated with obesity in the United States and Russia, based on data from the U.S. National Longitudinal Survey of Youth and the Russian Longitudinal Monitoring Survey. We found that obese people are, on average, less happy than the nonobese. But those well-being costs are mediated by social norms. The unhappiness associated with obesity in the United States is much greater in socioeconomic and professional cohorts where obesity is *not* the norm, such as in white-collar professions, and is much lower among poor blacks and Hispanics, where obesity rates are typically higher (Graham 2008). These unhappiness costs are additional to the objective health consequences associated with obesity and lower happiness levels. Higher levels of stigma may make people more aware of the health consequences of their condition.

In Russia, in contrast, where obesity rates are highest among wealthy men, we found that the condition is associated with higher happiness levels. The relationship only turns negative at extreme levels of obesity (Body Mass Index > 33), when the health consequences become more difficult to ignore. At lower levels, there is limited awareness of the health consequences.

Figure 5.4 shows how the impact of obesity on depression varies among demographic groups in the United States. The base impact of obesity on happiness is 0.57; that is, white obese people with income in the middle quintile living in the East (the default/left-out region in figure 5.2) in a nonurban area who have not graduated from high school are 0.57 standard deviations higher on the depression scale than their nonobese counterparts. In contrast, obese people who fit the same demographic characteristics but are in the fourth income quintile are 0.33 (0.57–0.24) standard deviations more depressed than their nonobese counterparts.

Figure 5.4   Norms and Obesity in the United States

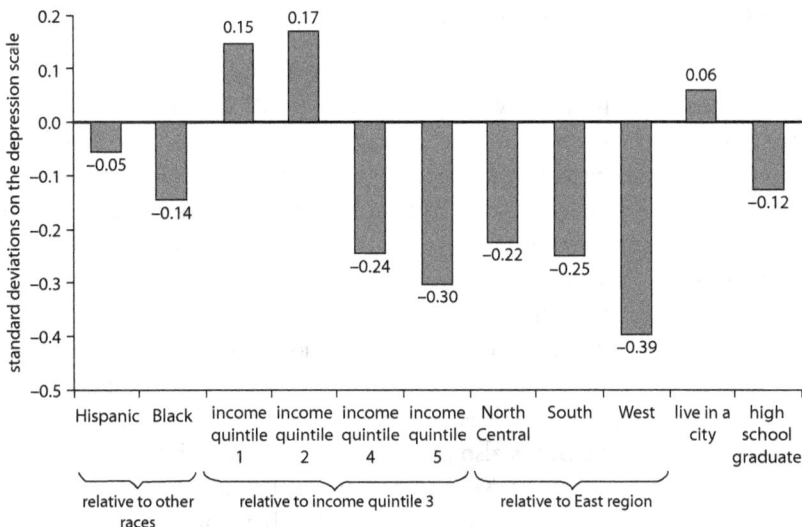

Source: Graham 2008.

The well-being costs of obesity are highest for low-income whites who live in the East, live in a city, and have not graduated from high school. We posit that obesity serves as a type of physical marker that distinguishes them from wealthier, more educated, higher-status whites. The same norm does not seem to apply to obese blacks and Hispanics in lower-income cohorts.

The well-being costs of obesity are even higher for those who depart from the norm for their rank/status cohort. Because obesity prevalence is so much lower in high-status occupations, it likely carries higher stigma. Other studies find that the perceived discrimination associated with obesity increases with professional status. Norms about appearance seem to be stronger across occupation and status than they are across income and racial groups.

Obesity also brings difficulties in the job market. We find that the obese are 29 percent less likely than the nonobese to move up an income quintile in any given year; accounting for education, gender, race, and other demographic factors, the obese are still 12 percent less likely to experience upward mobility. We do not know whether this is due to lower expectations and less effort or to greater job discrimination. We do know that conforming to higher weight norms is condemning a significant part of society to inferior outcomes in both professional and health arenas, and to lower levels of happiness.

Health Satisfaction in Latin America

Health satisfaction in the LAC region is remarkably high given objective conditions, and displays several paradoxes. Health satisfaction is assessed by a standard question in the Gallup Poll which asks respondents, "Generally speaking, how satisfied are you with your health?" Possible answers range from very satisfied to not at all satisfied, on a four-point scale. Respondents in Chile are less satisfied with their individual health than are those in Guatemala, even though objective indicators are much better in Chile than they are in Guatemala. Worldwide, based on the Gallup Poll, national average health satisfaction is only weakly correlated with gross domestic product per capita and is negatively correlated with the economic growth rate. It is weakly and positively correlated with life expectancy at birth, But is also positively correlated with the infant mortality rate. Respondents in Kenya, meanwhile, are as satisfied with their health as are those in the United States. Variables that capture cultural differences seem to matter more to health satisfaction than the expected indicators do (Graham and Lora 2009).

Within countries, the rich are clearly more satisfied with their health than are the poor, but the gaps between their attitudes are much smaller than the gaps between their outcomes. On average, for the 18 countries in LAC, the health satisfaction gaps between the richest and the poorest quintiles are only 7 percentage points, while the gaps among objective health indicators, access to health care, and incomes across quintiles are much greater.

Graham and Lora (2009) looked more closely at satisfaction with health care in LAC, based on data from the 2007 Latinobarometro survey, and on a question that asks respondents how satisfied they are with the health care they have access to. They find that a majority of respondents in the region—51 percent—are either satisfied (35 percent) or very satisfied (16 percent) with the health care they have access to, which is rather surprising given both objective indicators and the state of public health care in much of the region.

Based on an ordered logit regression, with the health satisfaction question in the Latinobarometro as the dependent variable, they find that the relationship between age and health satisfaction mirrors that between age and happiness, although the low point for the former is slightly earlier— at 43 years of age (figure 5.3).

When the sample is broken into high-, middle-, and low-wealth cohorts modest differences in satisfaction are found with the health care that individuals have access to, with the satisfaction of the rich being slightly higher than the other groups. Fifty-eight percent of the high-wealth group is satisfied or very satisfied with health care access, while 51 percent of the middle-wealth group is, and 46 percent of the low-wealth group is. Analysis by age cohort reveals a remarkable lack of difference in satisfaction across ages, with a modest *increase* in satisfaction among older cohorts. Finally, men and women are equally satisfied with their health.[11] (See figure 5.2.)

Given that objective health indicators vary a great deal across cohorts, as does access to health care, the lack of variance in health satisfaction is rather surprising. It suggests that different norms of health—and therefore expectations of health care access and quality—play an important role and may help explain lack of demand among underserved populations.

Valuing Different Health Conditions in Latin America Based on the EQ-5D

Do the health standards and conditions of those around you affect your own life and health satisfaction? Should we attach more policy weight to particular diseases or conditions? To mental or physical health? Do the old and the young—or the poor and the wealthy—rate health conditions the same way? There is substantial debate over how to make these decisions, not least because it is difficult to attach values to different health states. In a paper coauthored with two colleagues, we developed a new method for doing so, based on comparisons between individuals' reporting suffering (or not) from an index of specific health conditions on the one hand, and their life and health satisfaction scores on the other.[12]

Our empirical work was based on a unique data set, which combines health and life satisfaction assessments with a widely accepted measure of health—the EQ-5D index, which captures various aspects of physical and mental health. The EQ-5D consists of five dimensions. Respondents are asked if they have problems with mobility, self-care, usual activities, pain/discomfort, and anxiety/depression. The "usual activities" variable pertains to respondents' typical daily routine—going to work and school, enjoying leisure time, and so on. For each dimension, respondents can answer that they have no problems, moderate problems, or extreme problems. While the EQ-5D is based on self- reports, it has been widely used as a tool to assess health status in both Europe and the United States (Dolan 1997; Shaw, Johnson, and Coons 2005). Our data set—the Latin America subset of the Gallup World poll for 2007—covers respondents in 18 countries in Latin America and includes the EQ-5D.

We explored the effects of individual health conditions and variance across income, gender, and age cohorts. Our basic model used life and health satisfaction as dependent variables, and sociodemographic traits, individual-level income, the EQ-5D as a measure of objective health, and controls for shared country-level characteristics as right hand-side-variables. (The full equations are in Graham, Higuera, and Lora [2009]).

Respondents' EQ-5D scores were strongly and significantly correlated with both subjective health status and life satisfaction. Given the consistent relationship between happiness and health in most studies, and that the EQ-5D seems to be a robust instrument for reporting objective health status, this is not surprising. The effect is larger for the health scores than it is for life satisfaction. Thus, health status is more closely correlated with health satisfaction than it is with life satisfaction, which is surely influenced by health status, but also by a wide range of other variables. In contrast, material goods, such as assets and telephones, are more important to life satisfaction than they are to health satisfaction.

We also explored the effects of the individual EQ-5D conditions on our subjective variables. The (expected) negative effects of extreme conditions in self-care and mobility on both life satisfaction and health satisfaction disappear when a control for personal optimism is included. It is likely that people adapt to these conditions, and the importance of inherent character traits in maintaining happiness or satisfaction is more important than (irreversible) objective conditions. In contrast, extreme pain, extreme anxiety, and the usual activities continue to have negative effects on health satisfaction when the optimism control is included, suggesting that even naturally optimistic people cannot adapt to these conditions. It is likely that people are less able to adapt to the unpredictability of some health conditions than they are to the unpleasant certainty of others. The well-being of paraplegics, for example, typically reverts to the level before their trauma, while many epileptics face a lifetime of uncertainty about when they will have seizures. A number of studies of the quality of life of epileptics find that age—and in particular higher age of onset—posed significant and negative effects on health-related quality of life. Adapting to the uncertainty may be more difficult later in life, when social, economic, and psychological dimensions are more established (Lua and others 2007).

We find that age moderates the unhappiness associated with difficulties doing usual acts—perhaps since older people expect to have these difficulties—but makes anxiety worse. Income moderates the effects of extreme pain on life satisfaction—perhaps because wealthy people can better afford treatments and medicine, yet another example of the extent to which access to good health care is regressively distributed in the region. At the same time, wealthy people likely have higher expectations about their health and therefore their ability to maintain self-care. Finally, gender moderates mobility and anxiety problems: men seem to feel the negative effects of mobility problems more than women do, while the latter suffer worse effects from anxiety.

As a means to attach relative weights to the effects of our health conditions, we calculated life satisfaction equivalents for each of the EQ-5D conditions for our sample. We find that the negative effects of some of the health conditions are very high compared to those of other important variables, such as the loss of income or friendships. Baseline/initial median per capita household income in U.S. purchasing power parity dollars is US$93.70 per month, which is the average income of the sample taken for these calculations.

The amount of income needed to compensate an individual for the life satisfaction drop associated with moderate problems with the usual acts is 2.1 times average per capita income (figure 5.5). Problems with self-care and with mobility, meanwhile, had insignificant effects. Pain and anxiety are the most "expensive" in life satisfaction terms: having extreme pain is equivalent to a loss of 4.8 per capita incomes, while extreme anxiety

Figure 5.5   Income Equivalences of Health Conditions in the EQ-5D

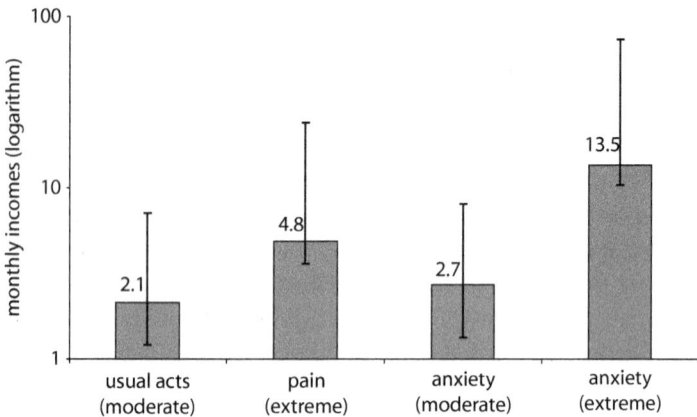

Source: Graham, Higuera, and Lora 2009.
Note: Direct equivalences are calculated on the basis of the effect of each health component on life satisfaction. The EQ5 equivalences are based on the effect of changes in the EQ5D index, derived from changes in each health component. Vertical bars represent a 95% confidence interval.

is worth 13.5 incomes. Moderate anxiety is worth 2.7 incomes. These ratios reflect orders of magnitude; they are based on self-reports and in some cases are larger than the available income that respondents could realistically trade off (for example, giving up income equivalent to 13 times its size in order to reduce anxiety would place most in extreme debt and poverty). They provide us, though, with a means to attach relative weights to the various conditions.

We also tested for the effects of reference group norms. We define a reference group as the subsample of individuals of the same country and area of residence (rural or urban), of the same gender, the same age group (within a 10-year interval), and with a similar education level. In the regressions for reference groups we tested whether the mean EQ-5D of the reference group was associated with life or health satisfaction of the individual, controlling also for mean income for the reference group.

Both the mean EQ-5D score and mean income for the reference group were positively and significantly correlated with health satisfaction. Thus the effects of health were above and beyond those of mean income for the reference group. This is an interesting contrast with the effects of reference group income on economic and other forms of satisfaction. Mean income of the reference group has negative effects on economic, job, and housing satisfaction in the region, for example (*Beyond Facts* 2008, table 3.3). More generally, previous studies in the United States,

Europe, Latin America, and Africa find that comparison effects in the income domain tend to be negative (Alesina, DiTella, and MacCulloch 2004; Luttmer 2005; Graham and Felton 2006).

Comparison effects in the health arena may provide more positive signals than do those in the income realm. How important they are, meanwhile, likely depends on the size and the nature of the reference group. These, in turn, may vary across countries. In Chile, for example, the poor may compare themselves to everyone else, while in Guatemala, the poor compare themselves to the poor if and when it is the only relevant reference group they have or know.

To the extent that the latter is an empathy or solidarity finding, it seems to cross various nonmaterial domains. Several researchers have found that the negative effects of divorce, unemployment, and obesity are less severe in contexts where the rates for these respective phenomena are higher. This is likely due to less stigma and greater solidarity.[13] In contrast, there is a wide body of research that suggests that concerns for relative incomes go up as incomes are higher, and that the signaling effects of higher comparison incomes are negative for life satisfaction (see Graham and Felton 2006; *Beyond Facts* 2008, chapter 3; and Luttmer 2005). For health the literature suggests the existence of a positive effect of good health among peers. It is more enjoyable to be surrounded by healthy people.

The actual balance of investments in different health policies is a question that must be resolved at the level of particular societies. Yet our method can inform such decisions by assigning relative weights to the well-being effects of particular conditions. Better understanding of how anxiety and pain undermine quality of life, for example, and of how that varies across cohorts, countries, and cultures—in large part depending on norms of health—might go a long way toward improving well-being in general.

Lessons for Policy

This chapter explored the relationship between health and happiness and, in particular, the role of different norms of health in explaining variance in health satisfaction across cohorts, countries, and health conditions. Norms of health seem critical to creating public demand for better health care in contexts where there is high tolerance for poor objective conditions. We know little about tipping norms, the complex process whereby enough people change either their expectations or their behavior at the same time so as to shift society-wide paradigms, such as the appropriate age to retire, the level of demand for health care, or acceptable rates of crime. The positive role that we (and others) find for peer effects and health suggest that social networks may be a good place to start thinking about how these processes work, with potential spillover effects across age and income cohorts. Challenging cross-country norms of health is a more difficult problem.

A related issue is adaptation. Human beings have a remarkable capacity to adapt to all sorts of bad things and maintain their natural cheerfulness. This is likely a good thing from an individual psychological perspective. However, it may also result in collective tolerance for bad equilibrium, such as poor health. Our research suggests that, at least in the health arena, individuals are better at adapting to unpleasant certainty than they are to the unknown and to constant uncertainty. Thus they can adapt better to some health conditions than to others, with some variance across cohorts; the elderly, for example, are better at adapting to mobility problems than are the young (perhaps because the elderly expect to have them), but are less good at adapting to anxiety and other kinds of uncertainty.

This suggests an additional challenge in thinking about changing norms: People may prefer the certainty of a bad but tolerable system to the uncertainty associated with change and reform. While this finding does not translate easily into a policy recommendation, it does suggest that better understanding of what individuals can and cannot adapt to could help us understand why some kinds of poor health seem more tolerable than others, and why there is remarkable persistence in collective tolerance for poor conditions in general.

This chapter is a foray into a new and difficult area. Identifying differences in norms—much less measuring them accurately—is rife with methodological challenges. Happiness surveys give us a tool—albeit an imperfect one—to help get at the question. What we find by using this tool is that differences in norms help explain surprising tolerance for poor health in some contexts and surprising dissatisfaction with good health in others. Happiness surveys may also help explain differences across sociodemographic cohorts. At the least, our results suggest that a further look at these questions could yield better policy design and/or a better understanding of why there are such differences in the reaction to health policy interventions across countries and cohorts.

Notes

1. This question is not ideal, because it asks respondents how satisfied they are with the health care they have access to, mixing their views of their own

health conditions with their access. Nevertheless, it is the only health satisfaction question in that particular survey.

2. The correlation coefficient between the two—based on research on British data for 1975-92, which includes both questions, and Latin American data for 2000–01, in which alternative phrasing was used in different years— ranges between .56 and .50 (Graham and Pettinato 2002; Blanchflower and Oswald 2004).

3. Micro-econometric happiness equations have the standard form: $W_{it} = a + \beta x_{it} + \varepsilon_{it}$, where W is the reported well-being of individual i at time t, and X is a vector of known variables including sociodemographic and socioeconomic characteristics. Unobserved characteristics and measurement errors are captured in the error term.

4. The coefficients produced from ordered probit or logistic regressions are remarkably similar to those from ordinary least square (OLS) regressions based on the same equations, allowing us to substitute OLS equations for ordered logit or probit and then to attach relative weights to them. For an extensive and excellent discussion of the methodology underpinning happiness studies and how it is evolving, see Van Praag and Ferrer-i-Carbonell (2004).

5. A number of scholars, such as Angus Deaton, and Betsey Stevenson and Justin Wolfers, have published papers demonstrating a clear relationship between per capita incomes and average happiness levels, with no sign that the correlation weakens, either as income levels increase or over time. This is with a log-linear specification (Deaton 2008; Stevenson and Wolfers 2008).

6. These include the particular happiness question that is used, the specification on the income variable (log or linear), and the sample of countries/time-frame that is used. For details on this debate, see Graham, Chattopadhyay, and Picon (forthcoming).

7. The behavioral economics literature, meanwhile, shows that individuals value losses more than gains. Easterlin argues that individuals adapt more in the income or financial arenas than in nonincome-related arenas, while life-changing events, such as bereavement, have lasting effects on happiness (Kahneman, Diener, and Schwarz 1999).

8. For details on variance across countries, see Graham (2009).

9. For details on the method, see Graham and Lora (2009).

10. For a review, see Graham (2008).

11. When Graham and Lora (2009) run their basic regression with the sample split by gender, they find that the age effect holds for women but not for men, suggesting that men are slightly less positive about their health as they age— or are less able to adapt to worsening health—than are women.

12. This section is based on Graham, Higuera, and Lora (2009).

13. For divorce, see *Beyond Facts* (2008, chapter 4); for unemployment, see Clark (2003) and Eggers, Gaddy, and Graham (2006); and for obesity, see Graham (2008).

References

Alesina, A., R. DiTella, and R. MacCulloch. 2004. "Inequality and Happiness: Are Europeans and Americans Different?" *Journal of Public Economics* 88: 2009–42.

Beyond Facts: Understanding Quality of Life in Latin America. 2008. Washington, DC: Inter-American Development Bank, table 3.3.

Biswas-Diener, R., and E. Diener. 2002. "Making the Best of a Bad Situation: Satisfaction in the Slums of Calcutta." *Social Indicators Research* 55 (3): 329–52.

Blanchflower, D., and A. Oswald. 2004. "Well-being over Time in Britain and the USA." *Journal of Public Economics* 88: 1359–87.

Clark, A. 2003. "Unemployment as a Social Norm: Psychological Evidence from Panel Data." *Journal of Labor Economics* 21.

Clark, A., and A. Oswald. 1994. "Unhappiness and Unemployment." *The Economic Journal* 104 (424): 648–59.

Deaton, A. 2008. "Income, Health, and Well-Being around the World: Evidence from the Gallup World Poll." *Journal of Economic Perspectives* 22 (2): (Spring).

Diener, E., R. Lucas, and E. Suh. 2003. "The Relationship between Income and Subjective Well-being: Relative or Absolute?" *Social Indicators Research* 28: 195–223.

Diener, E., and M. E. P. Seligman. 2004. "Beyond Money: Toward an Economy of Well-being." *Psychological Science in the Public Interest* 5 (1): 1–31.

Dolan, Paul. 1997. "Modeling Valuations for Health States." *Medical Care* 11: 1095–1108.

Eggers, A., C. Gaddy, and C. Graham. 2006. "Well-Being and Unemployment in Russia in the 1990's: Can Society's Suffering Be Individual Solace?" *Journal of Socioeconomics* 35.

Graham, C. 2008. "Happiness and Health: Lessons—and Questions—for Policy." *Health Affairs:* January–February.

———. 2010. *Happiness around the World: The Paradox of Happy Peasants and Miserable Millionaires.* Oxford: Oxford University Press.

Graham, C., and J. C. Chaparro. 2009. "The Linkages between Insecurity, Health, and Well-being in Latin America: An Initial Exploration Based on Happiness Surveys." The Brookings Institution, Washington, DC.

Graham, C., S. Chattopadhyay, and M. Picon. 2010. "The Easterlin Paradox Revisited: Why Both Sides of the Debate May be Correct." In *International*

Differences in Well-being, ed. E. Diener, J. Helliwell, and D. Kahneman. Oxford: Oxford University Press.

Graham, C., and A. Felton. 2006. "Inequality and Happiness: Insights from Latin America." *Journal of Economic Inequality* 4 (1): 107–22.

Graham, C., L. Higuera, and E. Lora. 2009. "Valuing Health Conditions: Insights from Happiness Surveys across Countries and Cultures." IDB Working Paper Series No. 100, Research Department, Inter-American Development Bank, Washington, DC.

Graham, C., and E. Lora. 2009. "Health Satisfaction in Latin America." In *Paradox and Perception: Measuring Quality of Life in Latin America,* ed. C. Graham and E. Lora. Washington, DC: The Brookings Institution Press and the Inter-American Development Bank.

———. 2009. *Paradox and Perception: Measuring Quality of Life in Latin America.* Washington, DC: The Brookings Institution Press.

Graham, C., and S. Pettinato. 2002. *Happiness and Hardship: Opportunity and Insecurity in New Market Economies.* Washington, DC: The Brookings Institution Press.

Helliwell, J. F. 2003. "How's Life? Combining Individual and National Variables to Explain Subjective Well-being." *Economic Modeling* 20 (2): 331–60.

Kahneman, D., E. Diener, and N. Schwarz. 1999. *Well-being: The Foundations of Hedonic Psychology.* New York: Russell Sage.

Leigh, A., and J. Wolfers. 2005. "Happiness and the Human Development Index: Australia Is Not a Paradox." Center for Economic Performance Discussion Paper No. 5476, Sydney.

Lua, L., H. Haron, G. Cosmos, and N. H. Nawi. 2007. "The Impact of Demographic Characteristics on Health-Related Quality of Life: Profile of Malaysian Epilepsy Population." *Applied Research in Quality of Life* 2.

Luttmer, E. 2005. "Neighbors as Negatives: Relative Earnings and Well-Being." *Quarterly Journal of Economics* 120 (3): 963–1002.

Oswald, A. 1997. "Happiness and Economic Performance". *Economic Journal* 107: 1815–31.

Shaw, J. W., J. A. Johnson, and S. J. Coons. 2005. "U.S. Valuation of the EQ-5D Health States: Development and Testing of the D1 Valuation Model." *Medical Care* 43 (3): March.

Stevenson, B., and J. Wolfers. 2008. "Economic Growth and Subjective Well-Being: Re-assessing the Easterlin Paradox." Brookings Panel on Economic Activity. Washington, DC.

Van Praag, B., and A. Ferrer-i-Carbonell. 2004. *Happiness Quantified: A Satisfaction Calculus Approach.* Oxford: Oxford University Press.

CHAPTER 6

Who Benefits from Public Transfers? Incidence across Income Groups and across Generations in Brazil and Chile

Cassio M. Turra, Mauricio Holz, and Daniel Cotlear

Introduction

Who benefits from public transfers? The study of the distribution of public expenditures across income groups is now a standard feature of public expenditure studies in Latin America and the Caribbean (LAC). Less is known about the distribution of public expenditures across generations. Even less is known about how decisions to allocate funds across generations may impact their distribution across income groups (or vice-versa). Policies derived from benefit incidence analyses across income groups naturally emphasize allocation decisions in that dimension. During the last two decades, this emphasis has led to an intense debate about whether governments should aim to target social expenditures to the poor or if a model of "universality" may be more appropriate.

This chapter attempts to link the analysis of the distribution of public expenditures across income groups with the analysis of the distribution of these expenditures across generations in Brazil and Chile. The chapter advances two arguments: (a) that much of the regressive nature of public expenditures across income groups in Brazil and Chile is due to generational allocations, and (b) that the role of the public sector in redistributing across generations varies in different parts of the world.

Much of the debate concerning social policy in LAC relates to the incidence of public expenditures across income groups. Almost every country in the region has conducted studies about how public expenditures, specifically in education, health, and social assistance, are distributed between the poor and the rest. In the last two decades, most countries in the region have established instruments and institutions designed to target expenditures to the poor. In the 1990s, the region was at the forefront in the development of geographic poverty targeting for social infrastructure through social investment funds, and during the 2000s, about a dozen countries have developed proxy means tests to identify and target the poor with conditional cash transfer programs.

Beyond the question of incidence and equity across income groups, public transfers also play an important role in redistributing resources from the working-age population to both children and the elderly (Lee 2003). Recent studies have also documented an increase in public expenditures among old-age dependent groups, driven by the expansion of retirement and health care public programs, both in developed countries and in some emerging economies. Becker and Murphy (1988), along with others, have argued that this expansion compensates tax payments that current elderly were asked to make earlier, when they were working-age adults, for the development of public education. Others have blamed political lobbying for favoring the elderly to the detriment of children (Preston 1984). While this has not been a central feature in the policy debate in LAC, as population aging proceeds in LAC, it is reasonable to expect the question of generational equity to become more prominent, as it already is in Organisation for Economic Co-operation and Development countries. This tendency is already clear in relation to pension reforms: while in many countries there is an undisputed need to reform public pensions for fiscal reasons, it is hard to introduce reforms partly because they are seen as being unfair to current generations, especially those near retirement. Also, most people agree that it is not possible to judge the fairness of the distribution of pension benefits without considering the history of personal contributions to the system.

The rest of this chapter is organized as follows: Section 2 describes the methods employed to estimate incidence of public expenditures by sector. Section 3 describes the patterns found in education, health care, and pensions. Section 4 describes the aggregate patterns and explores further the relation between income and generational patterns. Section 5 compares the support patterns of the elderly and of children found in Chile and Brazil with support patterns from other countries and regions in the world. Section 6 provides concluding remarks.

Methods

Below we look into how public expenditures are allocated for pensions, education, and health care across age groups and across income quintiles. This is done by combining individual data from household surveys with administrative records to estimate per capita age profiles of public expenditures by income quintiles and by age.

For Brazil, the data used to construct the age profiles of public health originate from a supplement of the 2003 *Pesquisa Nacional por Amostra de Domicilios* (Brazil's National Household Survey, PNAD), a nationally representative household survey collected every year (except census years) since the end of the 1970s. The supplement estimates both hospital and outpatient utilization rates by age and income groups. Since information about the costs of public health services was not collected by the PNAD, the average costs for each type of health condition/attention are based on administrative data from the Ministry of Health in Brazil. For Chile, utilization rates are estimated based on data from the 2003 *Encuesta de Caracterización Socioeconómica Nacional de Chile* (Chile's National Survey for Socioeconomic Classification of Households), a nationally representative household survey collected biannually since 1985. As in Brazil, the costs by type of attention (hospitalization, operation, and so forth) and by modality (no-charge and copayment) are based on administrative data.

To estimate the age profiles of public expenditures on education, administrative data were used to input expenditures per beneficiary and level of education for each survey data set, and micro data were used to estimate the enrollment rates and the mean values of payment per beneficiary by income quintiles and five-year age groups.

For Brazil, we also examine the conditional cash transfer program *Bolsa Familia*, a conditional public cash transfer program created in 2003 that provides a monthly stipend per child attending school, to a maximum of three children, to families living in poverty, and an additional monthly flat stipend for families living in extreme poverty. The program is of particular interest for this analysis because it targets a large fraction of the young population, and has expanded significantly over the last five years. Incidence of public expenditures with *Bolsa Familia* per age and income group was estimated using the PNAD. In 2004, the PNAD collected information on beneficiaries of social insurance programs in Brazil including *Bolsa Familia*. The data were originally reported on a household basis and did not include information about benefits. Therefore, two assumptions had to be made to estimate the age profiles: children are assumed to be the only beneficiaries of *Bolsa Familia* and payments are assumed to be the same for all beneficiaries.

The age-income profiles of expenditures with public pensions are based on responses about retirement benefits received during the survey's month of reference. However, we do not distinguish between types of benefits (that is, survivor vs. old-age benefits), or among systems (for example, civil servants vs. private workers in Brazil) to estimate the profiles. In addition, to account for discrepancies between the weighted sum of benefits in each household survey and the actual costs of the pension programs, all responses are adjusted by the same percentage to yield the aggregate numbers.

Before describing the results, it is important to note some weaknesses in the data. Ideally, an analysis of the incidence of public spending would be combined with an analysis of the incidence of taxation. That step has been left for future work. The interpretation of pension data should be done with special care. From an individual standpoint, the analysis of pension benefits ignores the history of contributions to old-age social security and equates the benefits received by retirees who made contributions during their working life with social pensions, which do not require a history of contributions. From a fiscal standpoint, benefit incidence analyses of pay-as-you-go systems often make a distinction between pension benefits financed from contributions of the current labor force (which are implicitly assumed to have an actuarial relation with past contributions of today's beneficiaries) and the subsidy that taxpayers provide to finance any deficit in pensions. This distinction, however, has been left for future work on this matter.

Another weakness is that comparisons of the benefits received by each generation for intergenerational equity purposes should take into account the timing in the life cycle when they are received. Bommier and others (2010) show for the United States that doing this can reverse the conclusions of the analysis regarding what generations are the winners and what generations are the losers of intergenerational transfers. They argue that for the United States, the benefits of public education are received on average about 30 years earlier than the average age of paying taxes, which is in turn about 30 years earlier than the average age of receiving old-age benefits. Each 30 years of discounting at 3 percent introduces a discount factor of 0.4, so that of education received as a child carries a relatively great weight in the longitudinal accounts. It is 2.5 times greater than the taxes paid for education later in life and six times greater than of benefits received in old age. Taking survival probabilities into account, a dollar of educational benefits can easily be worth of old-age benefits.

Benefit Incidence by Sector

In this section we analyze the distribution of public benefits across income groups and across age groups. The analysis is based on three sets of figures, each of which compares Brazil and Chile on five dimensions: (a) the incidence of public expenditure by income quintiles with (b) the incidence of public expenditures by age. To clarify the relations between the two, the incidence by age is then shown (c) for the top and bottom quintiles. This is then further disaggregated looking at (d) the utilization rate and (e) the cost per beneficiary. The main patterns found for each sector are described below. We also describe the incidence for *Bolsa Familia* in Brazil.[1]

As shown in figure 6.1, in education, public spending is neutral in relation to income; it is similarly divided among all quintiles both in Chile and in Brazil. Most education funds are benefiting children and adults younger than 30 in both countries, although in Brazil some public education funds reach adults in their 30s. Comparing spending in education for the bottom and top quintiles, we find in both countries that expenditures in the bottom quintile are focused on children and adults under age 20, while education funds for the top quintile peak in the early 20s, suggesting that the bottom quintile is mainly benefiting from public financing for basic education while the top quintile benefits mostly from public expenditures at the tertiary level. The difference between the bottom and top quintiles is not mainly a reflection of utilization rates, since even in the top quintile the utilization rate for publicly financed higher education is small. The source of the difference is in the costs per user, suggesting that university students from the top quintile attend more expensive public universities; presumably this higher cost reflects a higher quality.

The incidence of public pensions is shown in figure 6.2. In pensions, public spending is concentrated in the higher-income groups and is highly skewed in favor of the richest quintile. Expenditures on pensions are highly concentrated at ages above 50 but appear to increase faster with age in Brazil than in Chile, probably because of the more generous eligibility rules that exist in Brazil. The top quintile receives a much higher

Figure 6.1   Education: Incidence of Public Expenditures in Brazil and Chile

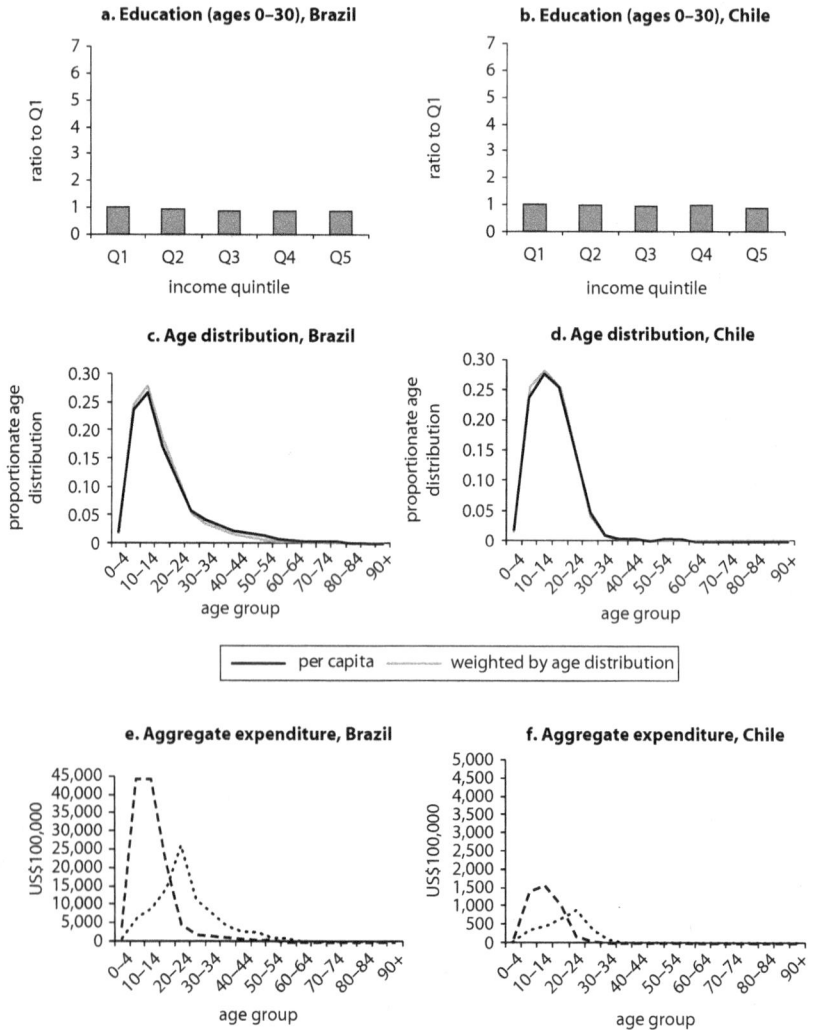

a. Education (ages 0–30), Brazil

b. Education (ages 0–30), Chile

c. Age distribution, Brazil

d. Age distribution, Chile

per capita   weighted by age distribution

e. Aggregate expenditure, Brazil

f. Aggregate expenditure, Chile

(continued)

Figure 6.1   Education: Incidence of Public Expenditures in Brazil and Chile
(continued)

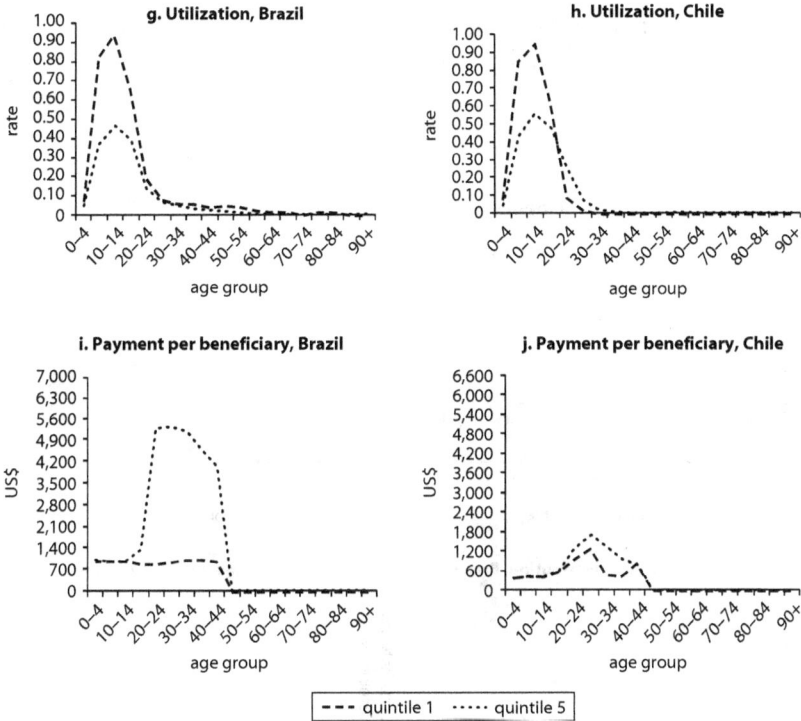

g. Utilization, Brazil

h. Utilization, Chile

i. Payment per beneficiary, Brazil

j. Payment per beneficiary, Chile

--- quintile 1   ····· quintile 5

Source: Authors' calculations.

share of the pension benefits than does the bottom quintile. This difference is many times higher in Brazil than it is in Chile. The difference between the top and bottom quintiles is not mainly a function of coverage since in both countries there is a high coverage of pensions for the elderly at all income levels. The main difference is in the value of the benefits, which are much higher in the top quintile than they are in the rest. Chile has reformed its pension system to prefund individual accounts. The results of the reform are not yet apparent in the analysis because the transition is still at an early phase and most pension benefits paid today belong to the "old" public system.[2]

Figure 6.3 shows the incidence of public expenditures in health care. Public spending is slightly higher in the lower quintiles in both countries.

The per capita age profile has a J shape, suggesting high public health costs in infancy, which then decrease for the young and then increase again in middle age. For the aggregate, however, the estimates of this study suggest that they decline, reflecting the age composition of the population. In health care, in both countries, the poor make a more intensive use of public health care services than the rich at all ages. The age pattern

Figure 6.2   Pensions: Incidence of Public Expenditures in Brazil and Chile

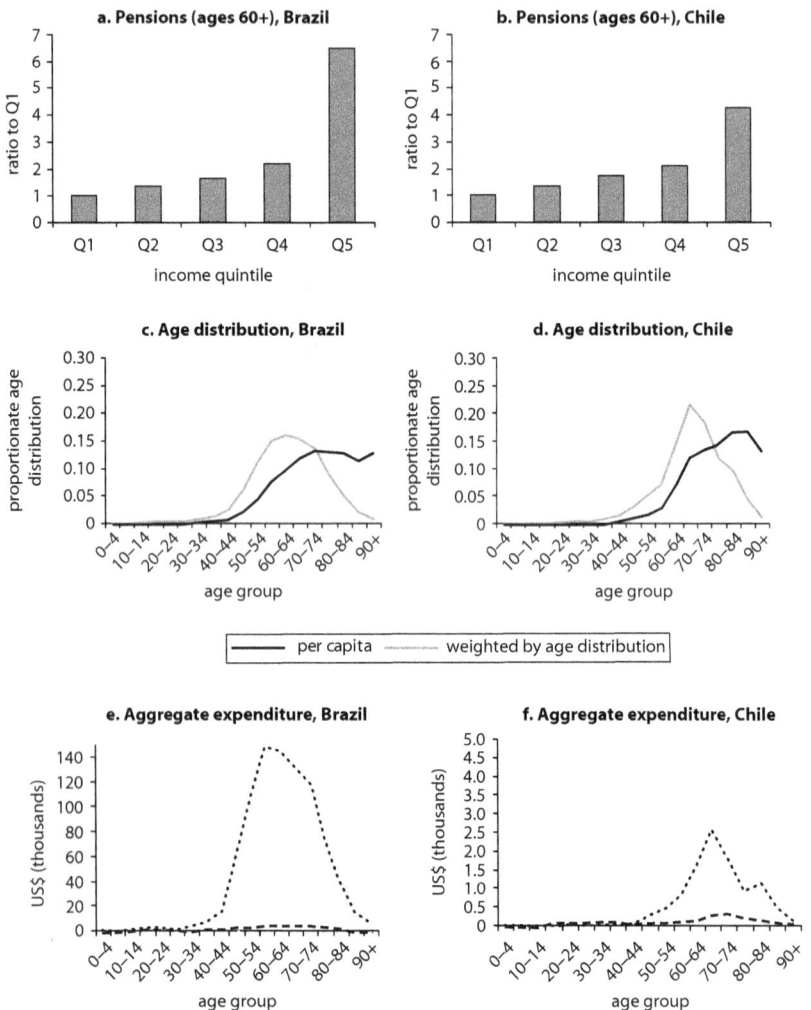

(continued)

Figure 6.2   Pensions: Incidence of Public Expenditures in Brazil and Chile *(continued)*

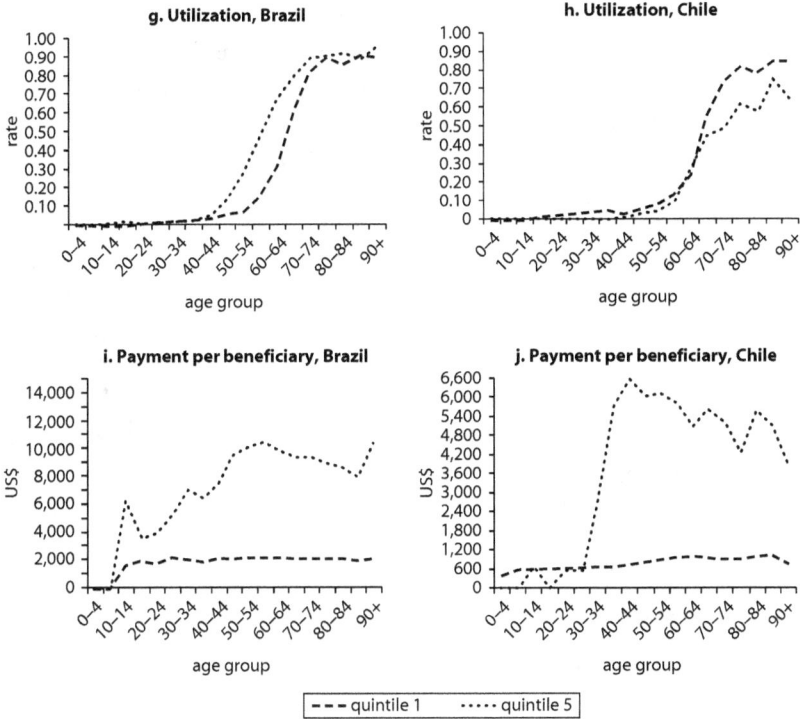

g. Utilization, Brazil

h. Utilization, Chile

i. Payment per beneficiary, Brazil

j. Payment per beneficiary, Chile

- - - quintile 1   ····· quintile 5

Source: Authors' calculations

of use of health care also differs by quintile. The poor use public services for infants and for young adults in their 20s and 30s much more than the rich. This is likely related to child and maternal services, which the rich prefer to have in a private setting rather than in a public one. The rich use public health services mostly in old age.

In Brazil, where the incidence of *Bolsa Familia* is examined, the program is found to have a strongly progressive pattern of spending, with most expenditures concentrated in the first and second quintiles (figure 6.4).

When each of the sectors is analyzed independently we find very different patterns in the incidence of spending across sectors, while within each sector, we find surprisingly similar patterns across countries. In the next section we examine the patterns of incidence for social expenditures in the aggregate.

The Incidence of Aggregate Public Expenditures

Figure 6.5 shows an aggregate view of the distribution of social expenditures (education, health care, pension benefits and, for Brazil, *Bolsa Familia*) across income groups and across age groups. The expenditures considered include those examined independently in the previous section—education, health care, pension benefits and (for Brazil) *Bolsa Familia*. The comparison of income quintiles for Brazil shows a growing proportion of public expenditures going to each subsequent quintile as income increases. The concentration of public expenditures in the top quintile is particularly striking in Brazil, where they are 3.6 times higher than in the bottom quintile. The shape of the aggregate is driven by the shape of pensions which, at 12 percent of gross domestic product, accounts for a large part of total public expenditures in the social sectors. In Chile, the expenditures are more equitable across the bottom four quintiles; however, the top quintile still absorbs 1.5 times the public expenditure of the bottom.

Figure 6.3   Health Care: Incidence of Public Expenditures in Brazil and Chile

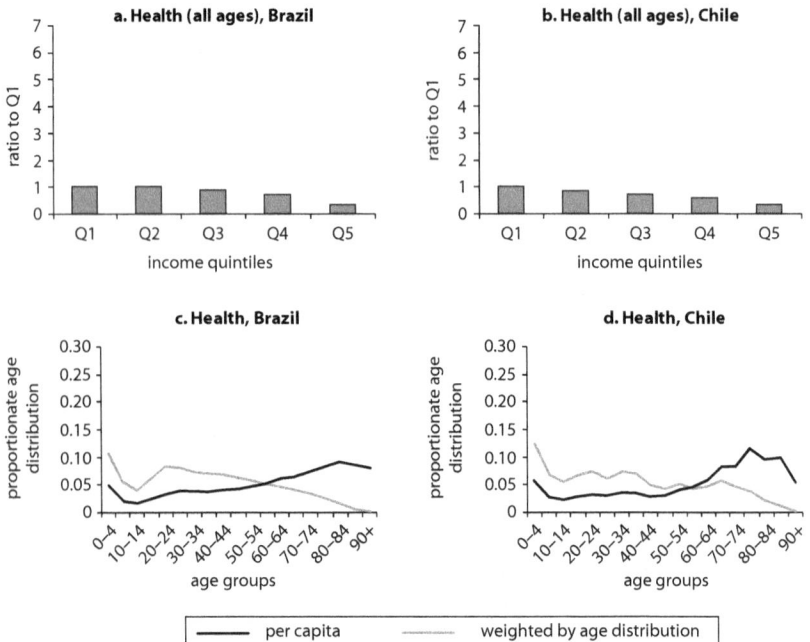

(continued)

**Figure 6.3   Health Care: Incidence of Public Expenditures in
Brazil and Chile** *(continued)*

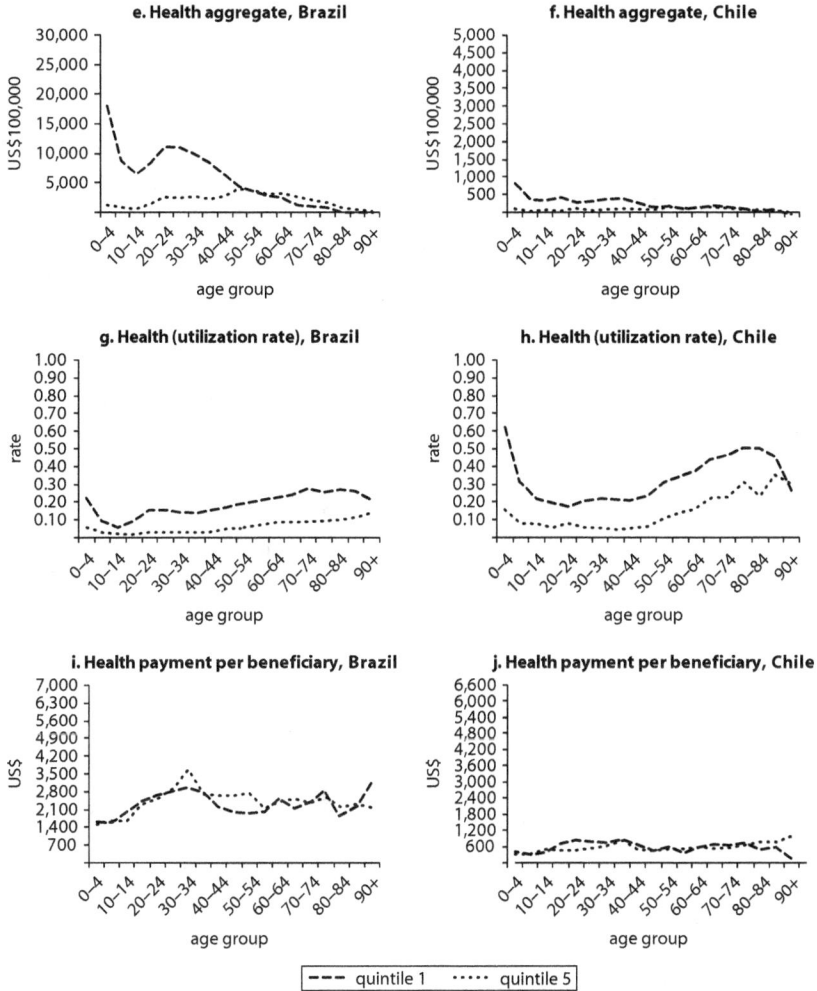

e. Health aggregate, Brazil

f. Health aggregate, Chile

g. Health (utilization rate), Brazil

h. Health (utilization rate), Chile

i. Health payment per beneficiary, Brazil

j. Health payment per beneficiary, Chile

--- quintile 1   ····· quintile 5

Source: Authors' calculations.

The comparison by age shows a per capita age profile and an aggregate distribution estimated by weighting the per capita profiles by the
age distribution. In Brazil and in Chile, the per capita profiles have a
small bulge among children and young adults and then fall to grow
steeply at around age 50. The per capita profiles also reflect the weight
of pensions; in both countries public spending on an individual elderly
person is several times higher than public spending on an individual child.

Figure 6.4   Bolsa Familia: Incidence of Public Expenditures in Brazil

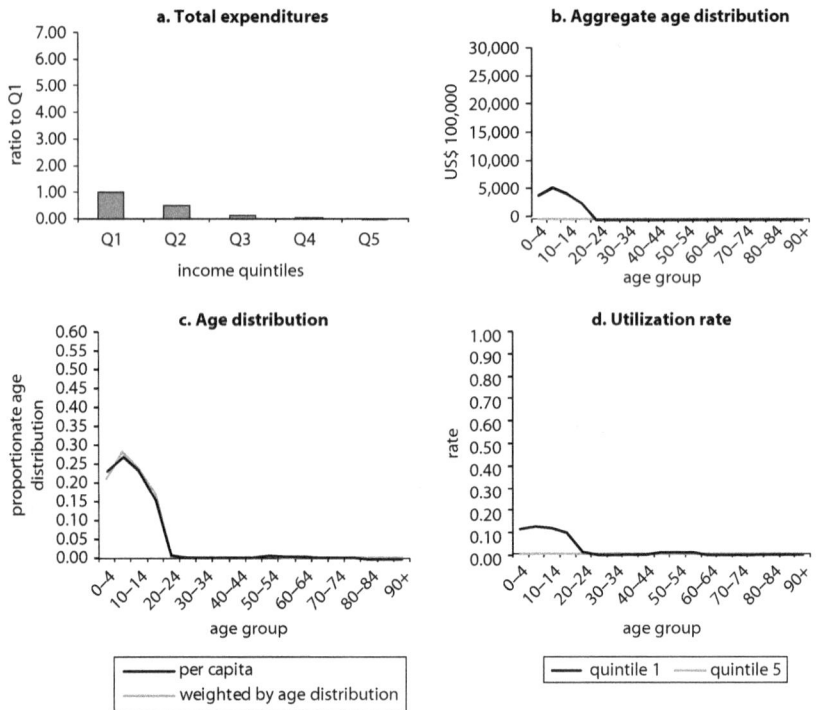

Source: Authors' calculations.

When the overall distribution of the population is taken into account the aggregate public expenditures on the elderly and the young become more balanced, especially for Chile, but remain strongly biased toward the elderly in Brazil.

But why is there such a strong association between public spending on the rich and public spending on the elderly? Figure 6.6 shows the distribution of the age groups between income quintiles for Brazil and Chile. It shows that in both Brazil and Chile the young are concentrated in the lower-income groups, and the elderly are concentrated in the higher-income groups[3] though the degree of concentration is greater in the former. What explains this pattern? Some hypotheses are presented below; unfortunately the testing of these hypotheses is beyond the scope of this paper.

Why are the elderly concentrated in the top quintiles? Two different, though not mutually exclusive, explanations can be offered. The elderly

Figure 6.5   Distribution of Total Public Expenditures by Income and Age Groups, Brazil (2006) and Chile (2000)

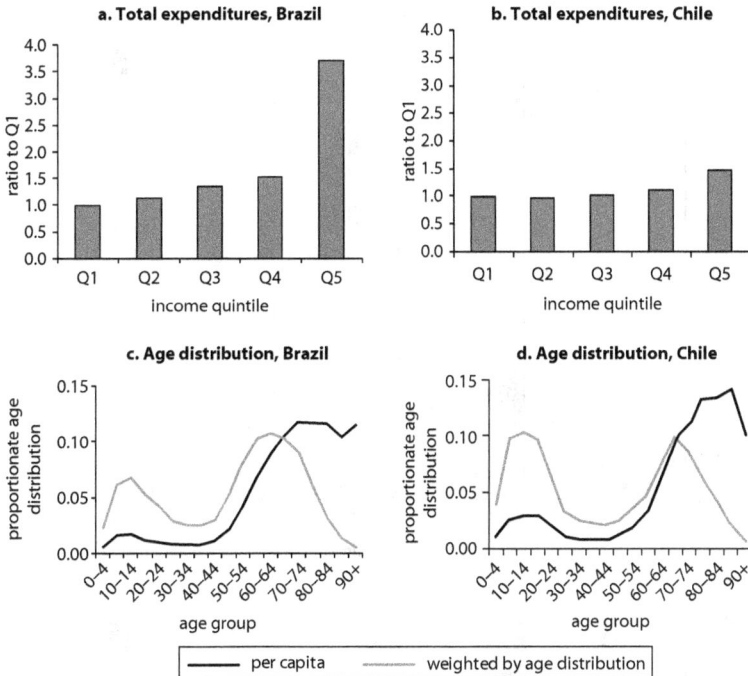

Source: Authors' calculations.

may have achieved higher incomes through life cycle savings, accrued public pensions, and perhaps receive private transfers from their children. In both Brazil and Chile, pension systems include minimum guarantees for former contributors and social pensions for elders with no history of contribution. This in itself may be enough to raise their incomes beyond the threshold of the bottom 40 percent of incomes. In addition, chapter 3 showed that the elderly live in smaller families, so they may have higher incomes because they share their incomes with fewer family members. The second hypothesis is that the majority of the poor are unlikely to live long enough to become elderly and so there is a selection process determined by different life expectancies across income groups.[4]

The concentration of children in the bottom quintiles may likewise be explained by several complementary reasons. The poor have higher levels of fertility. There may also be a life cycle element by which children are

Figure 6.6   Distribution of Large Age Groups by Income Quintiles, Brazil and Chile, 2003

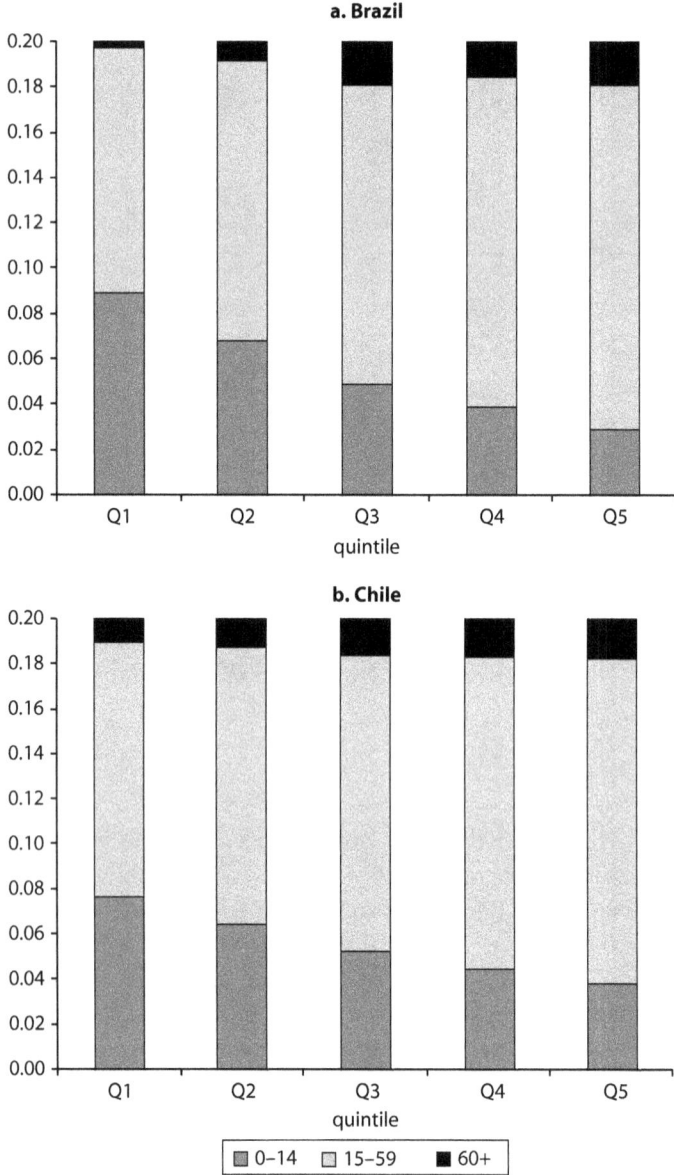

a. Brazil

b. Chile

0–14   15–59   60+

Source: Authors' calculations.

concentrated in households with young parents who have recently entered the labor market and are at an early phase of labor market insertion, with correspondingly low salaries. There is also an element of definition; per capita incomes are estimated by dividing the incomes of family members by the total number of family members, and two families with identical incomes but where one family has more children will show the larger family with lower per capita income.[5]

Larger Support for One Generation: Is there a Global Model?

The previous sections concluded that in Brazil and Chile public spending per older person is significantly higher than public spending per child. This could suggest a pattern of a society where the public sector is responsible for the sustenance of the elderly and where the families remain responsible for the sustenance of children. Is this a fair description of countries in LAC? Early studies for Brazil (Turra 2000; Turra and Rios-Neto 2001; Turra, Queiroz, and Rios-Neto, forthcoming) have shown that the consumption of old people depends largely on public health care services and pensions. Is this perhaps a "normal" pattern found in other regions of the world? To answer this question we turn to a set of data produced by the National Transfer Accounts (NTA) project. This project has developed a consistent methodology to measure comparable life cycle flows based on data from household surveys and from the National Income and Product Accounts. The NTA project is producing data for about 30 countries around the world. Some of the data are already available and were used to compare the importance of public transfers as a proportion of the consumption of elders and of children; these data are shown in figures 6.7 through 6.11. Notice that in what follows, "consumption" is defined to include, in addition to private consumption of goods and services purchased by the household, in-kind services in education and health care. Methodological notes on the NTA project can be found on its Web site.[6]

The importance of public transfers in financing the consumption of the young and of the elders is found to vary widely across countries and regions. Figure 6.7 shows that in Europe a full two-thirds of elderly consumption is financed from public transfers. At the other end of the spectrum, public transfers to the elderly are very small in the Republic of Korea and Taiwan, China (other Asia in figure 6.7). Japan is in the middle of the spectrum, with about half of the consumption of the elderly

Figure 6.7   Elderly: Public Transfers as a Percentage of Total Consumption

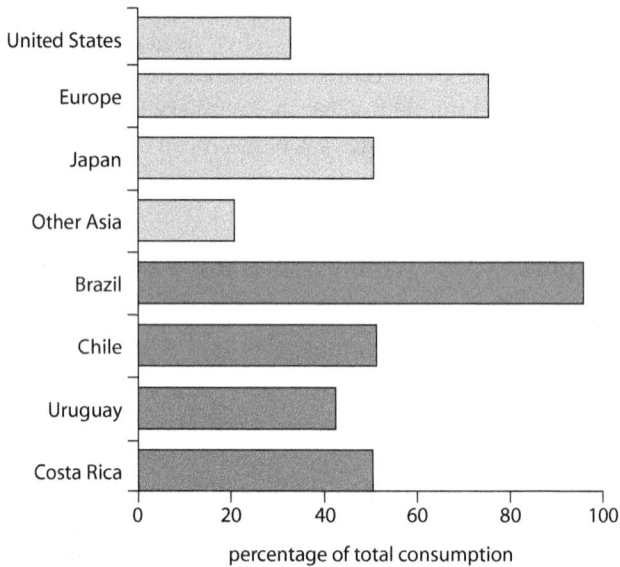

Source: National Transfer Accounts Project (www.ntaccounts.org).

financed by public pensions. Data are available for four countries in LAC. Chile, Costa Rica, and Uruguay are in the middle of the spectrum, as is Japan, and Brazil stands out in LAC, with pension benefits equivalent to over 95 percent of the consumption of the elderly.[7]

Figure 6.8 shows that public transfers also finance a significant fraction of children's consumption through cash transfers and through in-kind provision of services such as education and health. Public financing for children is highest in Europe and Japan, where it constitutes over half of children's total consumption. In LAC and other Asia (Korea and Taiwan, China) it is smaller but not insignificant, at about a third of children's total consumption. Brazil has different patterns than Chile, Costa Rica, and Uruguay in the differential treatment it applies to children and the elderly. In all four LAC countries, public expenditures finance about a third of the consumption of children.

Is the public sector more important to the financing of consumption of children or of the elderly? There is no global pattern. In the United States and in Asia, public expenditures finance a larger fraction of the consumption of children than the consumption of the elderly. In Europe and the four LAC countries for which data are available,

Figure 6.8   Children: Public Transfers as a Percentage of Total Consumption

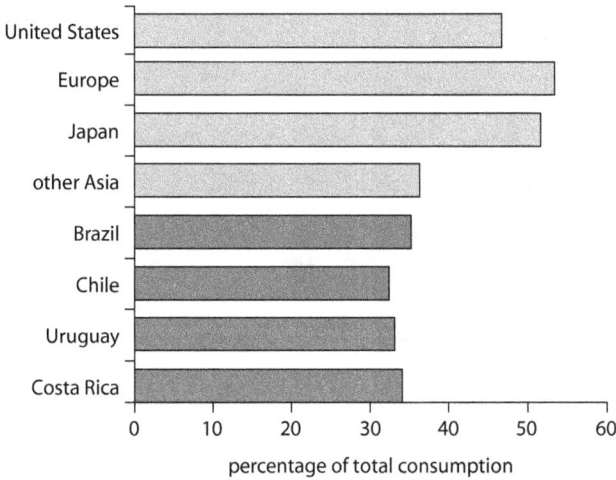

Source: National Transfer Accounts Project (www.ntaccounts.org).

public expenditures finance a larger fraction of the consumption of the elderly.[8]

Figure 6.9 shows that education is a substantial part of the value of the consumption of children. Here, too, there are significant variations across countries. The cost of education (public and private) as a percentage of total consumption of children is highest in Japan (37 percent), followed by Europe (about a third), the United States (a bit over a fourth), and other Asia, with the four LAC countries trailing behind all these international comparators. Figure 6.10 shows that most of the cost of education is publicly financed in the richer countries. Other Asia has the lowest public financing of education. Within the four LAC countries, Chile and Costa Rica have relatively higher levels, while Brazil and Uruguay have the lowest levels.

Figure 6.11 shows familial private transfers as a proportion of the consumption of the elderly. It is usually thought that elderly parents are helped by "upward transfers" (private transfers from their children). The NTA data show that this is only observed in Asia. In Europe, the United States, and LAC the pattern observed is of net "downward transfers"— from the elderly to their children and grandchildren. These downward transfers are particularly large in Brazil and Uruguay. In these two countries it seems that the elderly receive significant transfers from public pensions and pass some of these funds to their children and grandchildren.

Figure 6.9   Children: Education as a Percentage of Total Consumption

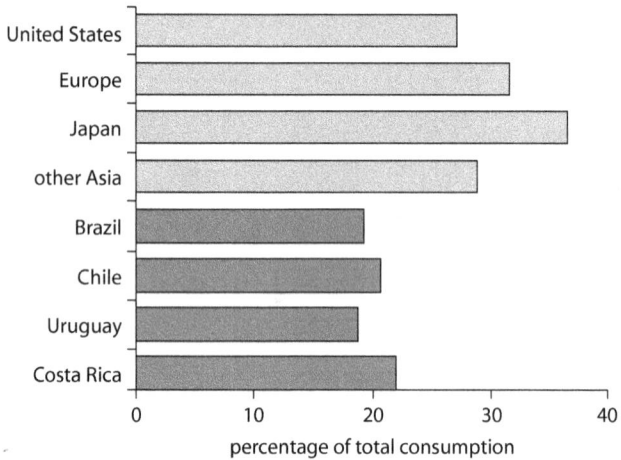

percentage of total consumption

Source: National Transfer Accounts Project (www.ntaccounts.org).

Figure 6.10   Public Funding of Education as a Percentage of Total Cost

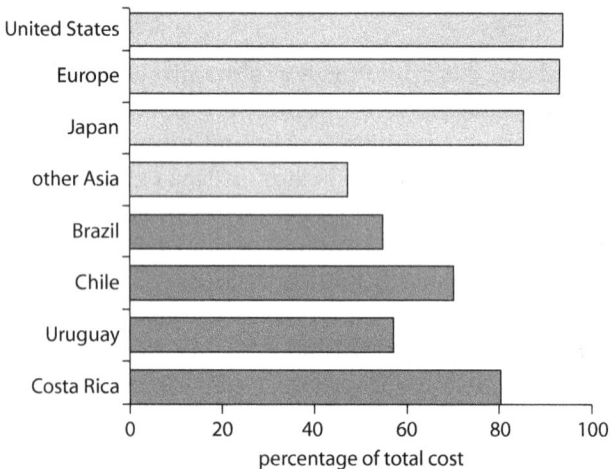

percentage of total cost

Source: National Transfer Accounts Project (www.ntaccounts.org).

Conclusions

In conclusion, who benefits from public transfers? This chapter suggests that the answer to that question varies by sector and by region. It also shows that the incidence across income groups is influenced by allocations across generations and age groups.

Figure 6.11   Elderly: Private Transfers as a Percentage of Total Consumption

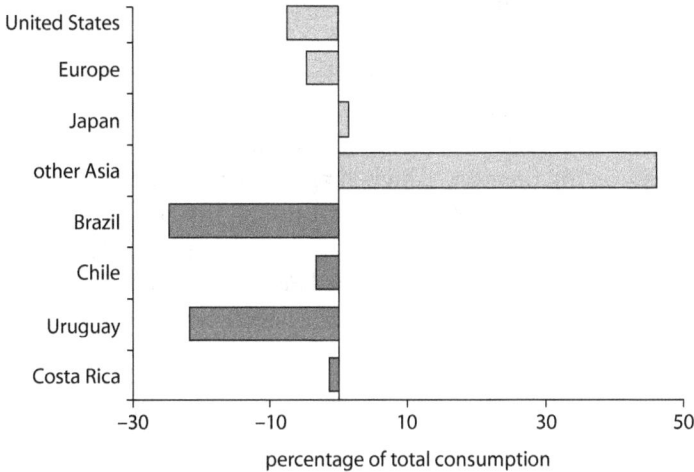

percentage of total consumption

Source: National Transfer Accounts Project (www.ntaccounts.org).

The comparison of Brazil and Chile showed interesting regularities by sector. The incidence of public spending was found to be neutral in education, lightly progressive in health care, and strongly regressive in public pensions.[9] Given the large size of pension benefits compared with expenditures in health and education, the incidence of the total social expenditure is defined by the incidence of pensions.

Many LAC countries have developed conditional cash transfers directed mostly to families with young children in the bottom income quintiles. One of the largest such programs is Brazil's *Bolsa Família*. This program was shown to be targeted to the bottom income groups. The relative size of *Bolsa Família* compared with the pension benefits implies that inclusion of this program barely reduced the regressive nature of total expenditures.

Brazil and Chile have achieved a high level of pension coverage for their elderly populations. If that is the case, why is the incidence of pension benefits regressive across income groups in both countries? Part of the answer has to do with inequality in the size of the pension benefits and part has to do with differences in the demographic makeup of income groups. Children are concentrated in the lower-income groups while the elderly are concentrated in the high-income groups. An exploration of the reasons for this is beyond the scope of this paper, but we hypothesize that the correlation of income and age may reflect the accumulation of wealth over the life cycle or it may reflect higher mortality among the poor.

The comparison of Brazil and Chile to other countries studied by the NTA project shows that there is no global model for the distributional role of the public sector across age groups. In Asia and the United States the public sector finances a higher proportion of the consumption of children than of the elderly, while in Europe, Brazil, Chile, Costa Rica, and Uruguay the public sector finances a higher proportion of the consumption of the elderly. For the four LAC countries this pattern is the result of both large public pension systems and comparatively low spending on education.

Notes

1. Recent studies of income distribution in Brazil have found the distribution to improve significantly and have emphasized the role of *Bolsa Familia* in this improvement. See for example Barros and others (2006).

2. See a more detailed discussion of this in chapter 7.

3. Chapter 3 describes how this pattern is observed in most Latin American countries.

4. We know of no data that measure this differential in life expectancy by income group for LAC. This relationship is well established in developed countries (see Cutler, Deaton, and Lleras-Muney 2006).

5. The estimation of per capita incomes uses as the denominator "equivalized adults," a concept discussed in chapter 3 that takes into account the fact that children have lower consumption needs than adults.

6. See www.ntaccounts.org. The NTA project is based on the demo-economic models developed by Lee (1980, 2000, 2003): and Lee and Mason (2004).

7. Draft estimates also exist for Mexico; we have excluded them because the large role of incomes financed by oil revenues in that country raises issues of classification that could not be resolved by the time this chapter was completed.

8. We should not generalize the patterns found in Brazil, Chile, Costa Rica, and Uruguay to the rest of Latin America. As shown in chapter 3, these countries (together with Argentina) have by far the largest pension systems in the region.

9. Note that this conclusion is reached without reference to the history of contribution to pension systems.

References

Becker, G., and K. Murphy. 1988. "The Family and the State." *Journal of Law and Economics* 21.

Bommier, A., R. Lee, T. Miller, and S. Zuber. 2010. "Who Wins and Who Loses? Public Transfer Accounts for U.S. Generations Born 1850 to 2090." *Population and Development Review* 36 (1) (March): 1–26.

Cutler, D. M., A. S. Deaton, and A. Lleras-Muney. 2006. "The Determinants of Mortality." National Bureau of Economic Research Working Paper Number 11963, Cambridge, MA. http://ssrn.com/abstract=877468.

Lee, R. 1980. "Age Structure, Intergenerational Transfers and Economic Growth: An Overview." In *Revue Economique: Special Issue on Economic Demography,* ed. G. Tapinos 31 (6): 1129–56.

———. 2000. "A Cross-Cultural Perspective on Intergenerational Transfers and the Economic Life Cycle." In *Sharing the Wealth: Demographic Change and Economic Transfers between Generations,* ed. A. Mason and G. Tapinos, 17–56. Oxford: Oxford University Press.

———. 2003. "Demographic Change, Welfare, and Intergenerational Transfers: A Global Overview." *Genus* LIX (3–4) (July–December): 43–70.

Lee, R., and A. Mason. 2004. "Macroeconomic Demography of Intergenerational Transfers." Grant Proposal, National Institute on Aging, Bethesda, MD.

Mason, A., and others. 2005. "Population Aging and Intergenerational Transfers: Introducing Aging into National Accounts." Paper presented at the Annual Meeting of the Population Association of America, Philadelphia.

———. 2009. *National Transfer Accounts Manual.* Draft Version 1.0. March.

Paes de Barros, R., M. N. Foguel, and G. Ulyssea. 2006. *Desigualdade renda no Brasil: uma analise da queda recente.* Volume 1. Instituto de Pesquisa Econômica Aplicada.

Preston, S. H. 1984. "Children and the Elderly: Divergent Paths for America's Dependents." *Demography* 21 (4).

Turra, C. M. 2000. "Contabilidade das geracoes: riqueza, sistema de transferencias e consequencias de mudancas no padrao demografico." Master's thesis, CEDE-PLAR/UFMG.

Turra, C. M., B. L. Queiroz, and E. Rios-Neto. Forthcoming. *Idiosyncrasies of Public Transfers in Brazil.* First NTA book.

Turra, C. M., and E. Rios-Neto. 2001. "Intergenerational Accounting and Economic Consequences of Aging in Brazil." Paper presented at the XXIV IUSSP General Population Conference, Salvador, Brazil.

CHAPTER 7

The Fiscal Impact of Demographic Change in Ten Latin American Countries: Projecting Public Expenditures in Education, Health, and Pensions

Tim Miller, Carl Mason, and Mauricio Holz

Introduction

As population age structures change in the coming decades, the costs of publicly provided education, health care, and pension benefits will change dramatically. In this chapter we project the costs of education, health care, and pension programs in 10 Latin American countries and calculate the increased fiscal burdens that countries are likely to face as a result of both demographic and policy changes. This work relies extensively on data on age-specific expenditures for various public services produced by the National Transfer Accounts (NTAs) project on the generational economy[1]; however, the driving force behind these projections is the *demographic transition*. In Latin America, the effects of this inexorable process will vary in timing and magnitude owing to the different stages of the demographic transition of each country. But the general pattern will be the same in all countries.

Against a backdrop of declining mortality and fertility, Latin American countries are set to experience both increased income (as the proportion of the population in productive ages increases), but also substantial increases in public costs (as population aging ultimately leads to increases in demand for pensions and health care).

While demography alone can explain a substantial share of future cost trajectories, public policy also plays a critical role. In this chapter, we eschew country-specific policy forecasts, not only because we lack the necessary detailed understanding of each country's unique circumstances, but also because our goal is to produce projections that are comparable across countries in understandable ways. Consequently, our results should not be seen as forecasts but as illustrative estimates of what these social programs will cost under a fairly restricted set of assumptions.

These long-range fiscal projections are useful to policy makers and analysts for the following reasons:

- Demographic change is one of the most important forces shaping the outcome of social policy, but it cannot be observed in the short term. Its impact is readily apparent in medium- and long-term projections of the sort we present here. Mindful of the impact of population aging, a number of governments have begun to issue official long-term budget projections: Australia (Australia, The Treasury, 2007), the European Union (European Commission Directorate General for Economic and Financial Affairs, 2006), New Zealand (New Zealand, The Treasury, 2006), and the United States (U.S. Congressional Budget Office, 2009). The work presented in this chapter on long-term expenditure forecasts is novel in the context of Latin America and is an important step toward long-term budget forecasts for the region.

- The challenges and opportunities that demographic change brings to education, health care, and pension programs are sometimes compounding and sometimes offsetting. Projecting all three expenditure paths with a comparable methodology will provide insight into the interconnections and tradeoffs available to national policy makers. Too often, policy reforms of pension, health care, and education systems are debated, analyzed, and implemented in isolation from each other without considering the fiscal links among these systems.

- Projections made on the basis of a common methodology with the same underlying assumptions about demographic, economic, and policy change permits inter-country comparisons. As we will see, the fiscal impact of population aging varies considerably among countries in the region and is as much a product of policy differences as demographic ones.

The Influence of Demography and Policy on Current Levels of Public Spending

The Example of Secondary School Expenditures in Nicaragua and Japan

Before presenting our projection model, a simple back-of-the-envelope analysis would be useful in defining the main themes of the analysis. In this section, we analyze the current situation of public spending in 10 Latin American countries compared with Organisation for Economic Co-operation and Development (OECD) countries, highlighting the importance of population age distributions. The amount of resources societies devote to public education, health care, and pensions is the result of both political decisions and the demographic situation of each country.

As shown in Equation 1, we can decompose public spending on education, pensions, and health care into the product of three factors: benefit costs per participant, the participation rate, and the demographic dependency ratio for each sector.

Equation 1

Expenditure/GDP = benefit costs per participant * participation rate * demographic dependency ratio, or

$$E/Y = [(E/P) / (Y/W)] * [P/B] * [B/W],$$

where E = aggregate expenditures, Y = GDP, P = participants (for example, students), W = working-age population (aged 20–64), and B = population at risk of benefit (for example, student-age population).

For example, expenditures on secondary education as a percent of gross domestic product (GDP) are the product of the cost per student, secondary school enrollment rate, and the ratio of the secondary school-age population to the working-age population. Table 7.1 compares secondary school spending in Japan and Nicaragua. As can be seen, the countries have similar levels of spending on secondary schooling: 1.6 percent of GDP in Japan and 1.7 percent of GDP in Nicaragua. Of course, the productivity and wealth of these economies are vastly different: the GDP per capita in Japan is 40 times larger than that of Nicaragua, so the nominal amounts spent on education are vastly different. But in this chapter we are concerned

Table 7.1   Spending on Public Secondary Education in Japan and Nicaragua, 2000

	Japan	Nicaragua
Aggregate spending (% GDP)	1.6	1.7
Spending per student (% GDP per working-age adult)	17.0	10.0
Gross enrollment rate (% secondary school-age population enrolled)	102.0	66.0
Dependency ratio (school-age population/working-age population)	10.0	26.0

Source: Authors' compilation.

with the relative efforts made by each society, so our measures of social effort control for productivity differences between the economies.

The decomposition of aggregate spending on public secondary schools according to the three factors of Equation 1 is shown in table 7.1. The first two factors are policy/economic variables and the third one is demographic. Spending per student in secondary school is very different in the two societies. In Japan, spending for one year of secondary schooling is nearly double that of educating a student in Nicaragua (about 17 percent of GDP per working-age adult compared to 10 percent). The higher relative cost of schooling in Japan is some combination of these factors: teaching may be a relatively high-paid occupation in Japan, class size may be smaller, and capital investments may be higher.

The second policy/economic factor is the gross enrollment rate, which is the number of secondary school students divided by the potential number of students (those in the official age groups for secondary schooling). Gross enrollment rates in Japan are nearly double those of Nicaragua (102 percent compared to 66 percent).

The final factor is demographic: the ratio of the secondary-school-age population to the working-age population. In Japan, the school-age population is 10 percent of the working-age population—that is, for every potential secondary student there are 10 workers who can provide financial support. In Nicaragua, each potential student can only rely on 4 workers. The demographic burden of supporting students in Nicaragua is more than double that of Japan. It is this higher demographic burden that explains why Nicaragua is spending the same share of GDP on secondary education as Japan but with vastly different outcomes in terms of spending per student and enrollment rates. Given its current demography, if

Nicaragua were to raise its relative spending per student and enrollment rates to Japanese levels, its aggregate spending on education would have to be more than double that of Japan.

Due to past and future changes in fertility and mortality, the age structure of the Nicaraguan population is projected to change fundamentally in the coming decades, with large declines in the proportion of children. The resulting decline in demographic burden in supporting the secondary population could lead either to steep declines in aggregate spending or alternatively allow for large increases in investment in education. A recent Economic Commission for Latin America and the Caribbean study of the impact of demographic change on secondary school education showed that future reductions in education dependency ratios throughout the Latin American region will substantially ease demographic constraints on educational financing, bringing within reach universal secondary education in virtually all Latin American countries. In addition, more ambitious educational goals such as reaching OECD-country levels of investment per student are also increasingly within reach for a growing number of countries (ECLAC 2009).

The Influence of Demography and Policy on Public Education

This section presents an overview of public spending on education in 10 Latin American countries and selected OECD countries. For the purposes of this simple analysis, we can measure the contribution of economics/policy via a single variable: the Benefit Generosity Ratio (BGR)—which is the product of two policy variables—participation rates and benefits per participant. The BGR is the relative cost of benefits per person at risk. For example, the BGR for secondary education is the cost of educating a student aged 12–17. The BGR measures the generosity of the benefit in each country relative to the average productivity of the working-age population (GDP/working-age population). The BGR can be thought of as roughly the fraction of the average worker's income that is consumed by the average person who is in the appropriate age range for consuming education, health care, or pension benefits. The numerator of the BGR is obtainable from the NTA data on expenditure by age of recipient.

The influence of demography on aggregate spending is reflected in the sector dependency ratio, defined as the ratio of the population "at risk" of receiving the benefit (education, pensions, and health care) to the working-age population. Aggregate spending is the product of these two factors, as seen in Equation 2.

Equation 2

Expenditure/GDP = benefit generosity ratio * sector dependency ratio, or

$$E/Y = [(E/B) / (Y/W)] * [B/W],$$

where E = aggregate expenditures, Y = GDP, W = working-age population (aged 20–64), and B = population at risk of benefit (for example, student-age population).

Current levels of BGRs and dependency ratios for public education for selected countries are shown in table 7.2. Estimates of aggregate expenditures in public education are taken from UNESCO (2009) and estimates of sector dependency ratios are calculated based on population estimates from CELADE (2007). The BGR is derived as a residual.

The current level of educational spending in Latin America contrasted with OECD countries is presented in figure 7.1 and table 7.2. The education sector dependency ratio is defined as the school-age population as a percentage of the working-age population and is shown on the x-axis in figure 7.1. At one extreme is Nicaragua, where the school-age population exceeds the working-age population. Japan and Italy lie at the opposite extreme, where the school-age population is about one-third that of the working-age population. On average, the school-age population is about three-quarters the size of the working-age population in Latin America,

Table 7.2   Public Education: Aggregate Spending, Benefit Generosity Ratio, and Dependency Ratio, 2005

Country	Aggregate spending (% GDP)	Benefit generosity ratio (% GDP per working-age adult)	Dependency ratio (% working-age population)
Cuba	9.8	20.6	47
Mexico	5.5	6.9	80
Nicaragua	4.9	4.4	112
Colombia	4.8	5.7	84
Brazil	4.5	6.2	72
Costa Rica	4.5	5.7	79
Argentina	3.7	5.3	70
Chile	3.4	5.2	65
Uruguay	2.8	4.5	62
Peru	2.7	3.2	84
Median, LAC	4.5	5.5	75
Mean, LAC	4.7	6.8	76
Mean, OECD	4.9	12.0	41

Source: Authors' compilation.

Figure 7.1   Percent of GDP Spent on Public Education, Disaggregated by Education Dependency Ratio and Benefit Generosity Ratio, 2005

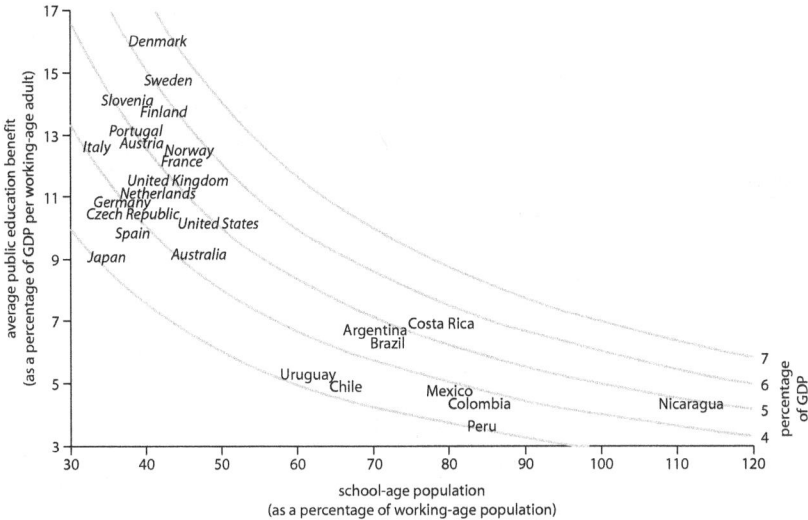

Source: Authors' calculations.

whereas among our OECD sample, the school-age population is about 40 percent of the working-age population. Thus, the two groups face very different demographic burdens in educating the next generation.

The y-axis of figure 7.1 shows the BGR. Mean education spending per youth in OECD countries is 12 percent of GDP/worker, while most countries in Latin America invest half that amount. This large difference is a reflection of differences in both enrollment rates and spending per student. (For a detailed analysis of these differences in secondary education, see CELADE [2008]). Spending isoquant curves show all the possible combinations of BGRs and sector dependency ratios that yield a given level of aggregate spending. The isoquant curves shown in the figure range from 4 percent of GDP to 7 percent of GDP. On average, both groups are devoting the same relative amount of resources to educate the next generation (about 5 percent of GDP), but with vastly different amounts of investment per youth due to the high proportions of children in most Latin American societies.

Population aging in Latin America will result in a substantial reduction of the fiscal burden associated with financing education and make possible significant increases in educational investment in youth. Educational dependency ratios have been falling and will continue to decline over the next few decades. Figure 7.2 contrasts the trajectories for three Latin American countries, Costa Rica, Cuba, and Nicaragua. In the early phases of the demographic transition, the dependency ratio peaks at more than 100 percent, with the school-age population exceeding the working-age population. As the transition proceeds, the ratios fall, generally to around 40 percent, a level currently observed in most OECD countries. By 2050, our group of Latin American countries will reach an average dependency rate of 44 percent, suggesting that educational investment would reach OECD levels by that date if aggregate spending levels are maintained.

The Influence of Demography and Policy on Public Pensions

The current levels of public pension spending in Latin America contrasted with those of OECD countries is presented in figure 7.3 and table 7.3. Aggregate values for spending on public pensions are derived from the National Transfer Accounts (NTA 2009) of the respective countries, when available, and are otherwise taken from OECD estimates (OECD 2009). The pension sector dependency ratios are calculated based on population estimates from CELADE (2007). The BGR is calculated as a residual.

Figure 7.2   Estimates and Projections of Education Dependency Ratio in Nicaragua, Costa Rica, and Cuba, 1950–2050

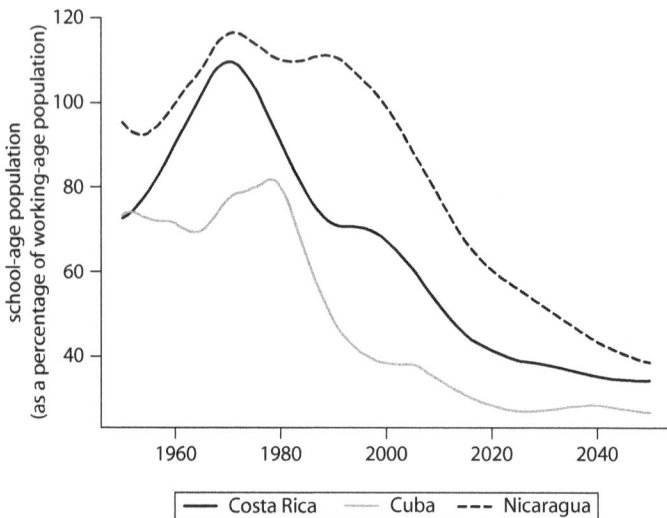

Source: Authors' calculations.

Figure 7.3   Percent of GDP Spent on Public Pensions, Disaggregated by Pension Dependency Ratio and Benefit Generosity Ratio, 2005

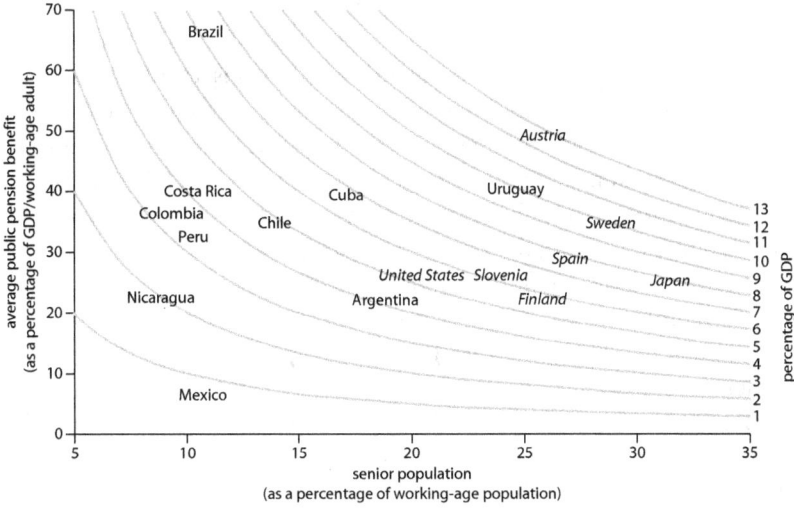

Source: Authors' calculations.

Table 7.3   Public Pensions: Aggregate Spending, Benefit Generosity Ratio, and Dependency Ratio, 2005

Country	Aggregate spending (% GDP)	Benefit generosity ratio (% of GDP per working-age adult)	Dependency ratio (% of working-age population)
Uruguay	9.8	40.5	25
Brazil	7.0	66.5	11
Cuba	6.8	39.7	17
Argentina	4.2	22.3	19
Costa Rica	4.2	40.0	11
Chile	3.5	35.1	14
Peru	3.2	32.8	10
Colombia	3.0	36.5	9
Nicaragua	2.0	22.6	9
Mexico	0.7	6.5	11
Median, LAC	4.2	35.8	11
Mean, LAC	4.4	34.2	14
Mean, OECD	8.0	30.4	26

Source: Authors' compilation
Note: Pension expenditures figures for Brazil include only the General Pension Program (RGP). These figures do not include civil servant retirement programs (RPPs).

As was the case with education, these two groups face vastly different demographic constraints. The pension sector dependency ratio is defined as the ratio of the senior population (aged 65 and older) to the working-age population (aged 20–64) and is shown on the x-axis of figure 7.3. At one extreme is Japan, where the senior population is about one-third the size of the working-age population. Nicaragua, Colombia, and Peru lie at the other extreme, where the senior population is less than one-tenth the size of the working-age population. A few societies in Latin America are strikingly different, with high proportions of seniors (Uruguay, Argentina, and Cuba). On average, the senior population is about 14 percent the size of the working-age population in Latin America, whereas among our OECD sample, the senior population is about 26 percent of the working-age population. Thus, the two groups face very different demographic burdens in providing pensions to seniors.

The BGR for public pensions is shown on the y-axis of figure 7.3. Mean public pension benefits per senior in OECD countries is 30 percent of GDP/worker, while the average in Latin America exceeds that figure at 34 percent of GDP per worker. This surprising result does not, however, imply that most retirees in Latin America are better off than their OECD cousins. Most retirees in Latin America receive modest pensions if they receive any pension at all. BGRs in Latin America are high because low coverage rates are offset by above-average pension generosity since the wealthiest workers are most likely to be covered by the contributory public pensions. Even in countries with high coverage rates, the benefits paid closely mirror the high degree of inequality in income distribution. (See Turra and Holz [2009] for evidence on Brazil and Chile.)

The spending isoquant curves in figure 7.3 show the combinations of benefit generosity ratios and sector dependency ratios that yield a constant share of GDP spending at levels from 1 percent to 13 percent. There is large variation among countries, with Mexico devoting less than 1 percent of GDP to public pensions and Austria more than 12 percent. On average, the Latin America group is spending about 5 percent of GDP on pensions while the OECD group is spending about 8 percent. Spending is lower in the Latin American group mainly because of its young population age structure; the average generosity of pension benefits (BGR) in the Latin American group exceeds those of the OECD group.

The demographic history of Latin America has meant that these relatively generous pension systems were developed and expanded over decades in which there was very little demographic pressure on costs. For most of Latin America, until quite recently, pension dependency ratios were largely flat; however, dramatic increases are expected in the coming decades. For example, Costa Rica, Cuba, and Nicaragua are shown in figure 7.4. Dependency ratios are set to more than double in most of the 10 countries. Brazil and Mexico will see the steepest growth, while Argentina and Uruguay, which are further along in the demographic transition, will see less-severe increases. For the Latin American group, the average senior population will reach 37 percent of the working-age population by 2050, exceeding the proportion currently observed in Japan, the oldest OECD country. If current pension generosity were maintained, these demographic changes would lead to large increases in GDP devoted to public pensions. But many countries in Latin America have introduced pension reforms with the introduction of prefunded contributory systems. The likely impact of these reforms in the face of demographic change is discussed later in the chapter.

The Influence of Demography and Policy on Public Health

The current levels of public health care spending in Latin America are contrasted with those of OECD countries in figure 7.5 and table 7.4. Aggregate values for spending on public health care are derived from the National Transfer Accounts (NTA 2009) of the respective countries,

Figure 7.4   Estimates and Projections of Pension Dependency Ratios in Costa Rica, Cuba, and Nicaragua, 1950–2050

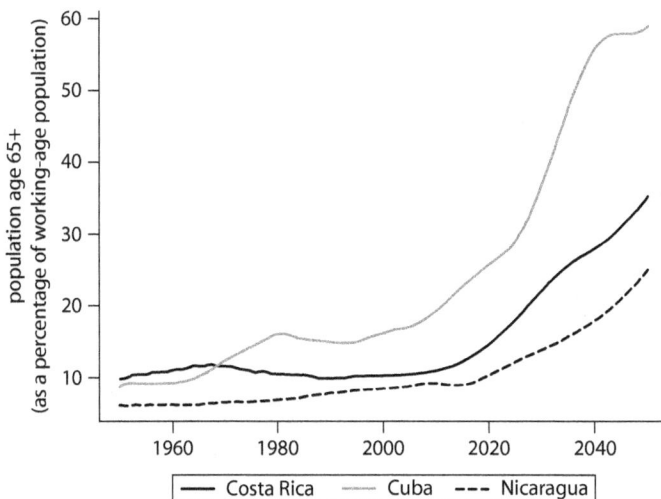

Source: Authors' calculations.

Figure 7.5   Percent of GDP Spent on Public Health, Disaggregated by Near-death Dependency Ratio and Benefit Generosity Ratio, 2005

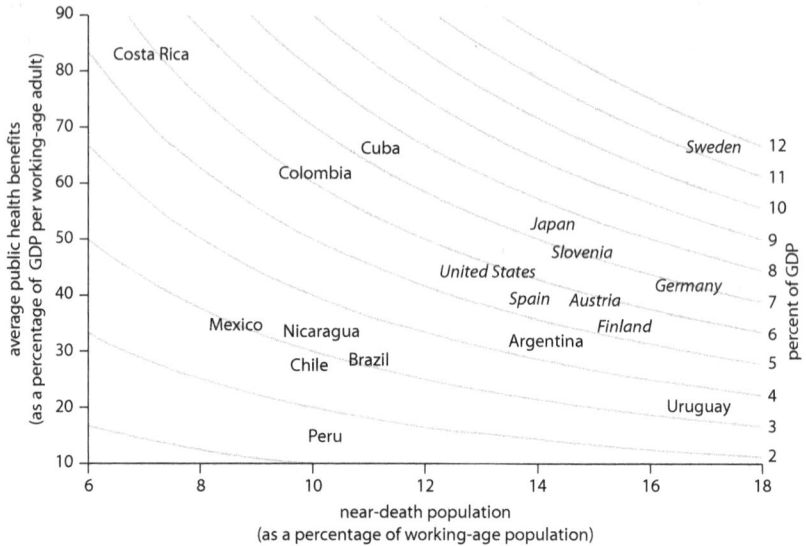

Source: Authors' calculations.

Table 7.4   Public Health Care: Aggregate Spending, Benefit Generosity Ratio, and Dependency Ratio, 2005

Country	Aggregate spending (% GDP)	Benefit generosity ratio (% of GDP per working-age adult)	Dependency ratio (% of working-age population)
Cuba	7.4	66	11
Colombia	6.2	62	10
Costa Rica	5.9	83	7
Argentina	4.5	32	14
Nicaragua	3.4	33	10
Uruguay	3.4	20	17
Brazil	3.1	28	11
Mexico	3.0	35	9
Chile	2.8	31	9
Peru	1.5	15	10
Median, LAC	3.4	34	10
Mean, LAC	4.1	38	11
Mean, OECD	6.9	46	15

Source: Authors' compilation.

when available, and are otherwise taken from World Health Organization estimates (WHO 2009). The health sector dependency ratios are calculated based on population estimates from CELADE (2009). The benefit generosity ratios are calculated as a residual.

To illustrate the importance of changes in age structure on demand for health care, we can measure the ill health of the population using a demographic measure—the number of people near death. The health sector dependency ratio is defined as the number of persons close to death in the population divided by the working-age population (aged 20–64). To estimate the number of persons close to death in the population we multiply the annual number of deaths by 10. This is a good approximation of the number of people within 10 years of death. Many studies of OECD countries have shown that most health costs for individuals occur in the final decade of life, and in that decade, in the final year of life (Zweifel and others 1999; McGrail and others 2000; Miller 2001; Lubtiz and others 2003). That is, most health systems devote a large percentage of their resources to curative and palliative services rather than preventive services.

The x-axis in figure 7.5 shows the health sector dependency ratio defined as the population near death as a percentage of the working-age population (aged 20–64). At one extreme are countries like Germany, Sweden, and Uruguay, where the near-death population is 17 percent of the size of the working-age population. At the other extreme are countries like Chile, Costa Rica, and Mexico, where the near-death population is about 7 or 8 percent of the working-age population. On average, the near-death population is about 11 percent the size of the working-age population in Latin America, whereas among our OECD sample, the near-death population is about 15 percent of the working-age population. Thus, the two groups face very different demographic burdens in terms of health care. It may be surprising for nondemographers to learn that the proportion of people near death is higher in OECD countries than in Latin American countries. This is a result of the older population age distributions in OECD countries. Although mortality rates are lower at each age in OECD countries compared to most Latin American countries, their older age structures mean that a greater proportion of their populations is closer to death.

The BGR for public expenditures on health is shown on the y-axis. Countries in Latin America with similar demography as measured by the health sector dependency ratio (~7 to 10 percent) have very different generosity levels and overall spending levels. For example, Colombia,

Costa Rica, and Cuba have relatively high generosity levels and spend in excess of 6 percent of GDP on public health, but countries like Brazil, Chile, Mexico, and Nicaragua have much less generous public health systems and are spending roughly 3 percent of GDP on health. Similarly, in Europe we observe countries with similar demography and vastly different levels of spending on health care. Sweden stands out with more than 11 percent of GDP devoted to health care.

As countries move through the demographic transition, the health sector dependency ratio follows a U-shaped curve, a result of the changes in the relative importance of rate versus composition effects. Initially, declines in mortality rates lead to declines in the proportion of the population near death. As evident in the case of Nicaragua as shown in figure 7.6, such declines can be quite rapid and substantial. The near-death population was about half the size of the working-age population in 1950 in Nicaragua. Over five decades, the near-death population declined to

Figure 7.6   Estimates and Projections of Health Dependency Ratio in Costa Rica, Cuba, and Nicaragua, 1950–2050

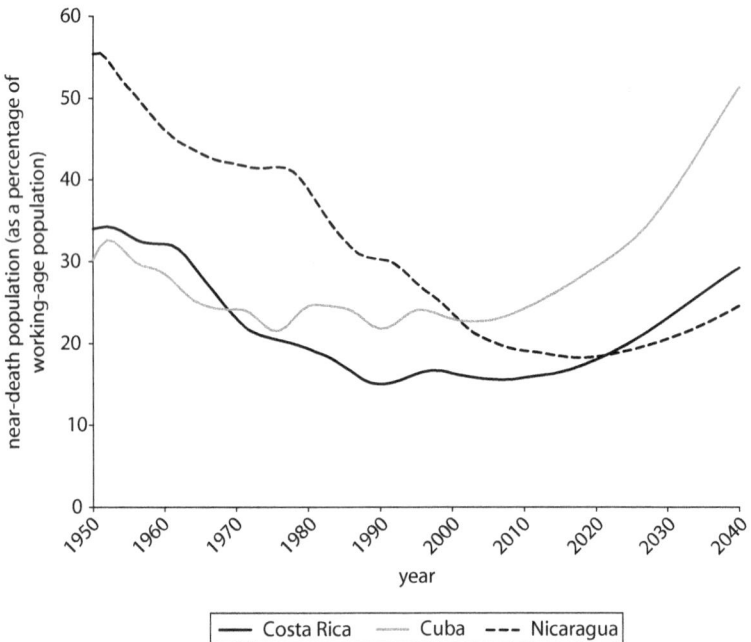

y-axis: near-death population (as a percentage of working-age population)

x-axis: year

Legend: —— Costa Rica   ----- Cuba   - - - Nicaragua

Source: Authors' calculations.

about one-tenth the size of the working-age population. Eventually as the demographic transition proceeds, the age structure of the population shifts substantially toward older persons and the near-death population begins to increase relative to the working-age population. Virtually all Latin American countries are set to experience relative increases in the near-death population, which will increase the fiscal burden associated with financing health care. As we will discuss later, this simple model of health costs greatly understates likely future increases in costs.

The Influence of Demographic and Policy Change on Future Public Spending on Education, Pensions, and Health Care

An Age-based Approach

We now turn to a more complete model of spending based on age, rather than broad age groups. This model forms the basis of our projections. The decomposition of aggregate spending shown in Equation 3 is the single-age version of Equation 2.

Equation 3

$$E(t)/GDP(t) = Sum\ over\ x\ \{b(x,t) * P(x,t)/P(20\text{--}64,t)\},$$

where

$$b(x,t) = [E(x,t)/P(x,t)] / [GDP(t)/P(20\text{--}64,t)],$$

and where $E(t)$ = expenditure in year t on education, health care, or pensions; and $P(x,t)$ = population aged x in year t.

That is, the proportion of GDP spent on education, health care, or pensions equals the sum over all ages of the expenditure per person of age x relative to GDP per working-age population divided by the ratio of people age x to the working-age population.

$b(x,t)$ is the BGR expressed by single year of age x in year t and $P(x,t)/P(20\text{--}64,t)$ is the dependency ratio expressed by single year of age x in year t.

To project $E(t)/GDP(t)$, we specify scenarios in terms of $b(x,t)$ for $x = 0$ to 90 and $t = 2005$ to 2050. We use official CELADE population projections (CELADE 2007) for the values of $P(x,t)$.

For Brazil, Chile, Costa Rica, Mexico, and Uruguay, initial $b(x,t)$ values are readily calculable from data collected by the NTA Project. In the case of Argentina, Colombia, Cuba, Nicaragua, and Peru, initial $b(x,t)$ values had to be estimated.

Education: Initial age profiles of benefits, $b(x,t)$, for education programs were constructed from United Nations Educational, Scientific and

Cultural Organization statistics (UNESCO 2009). Gross enrollment rates for preprimary, primary, secondary, and tertiary education were taken as coverage rates. $b(x,t)$ was derived from total public expenditure on each education level divided by the number of students.

Since the underlying data for education expenditures are tabulated in terms of primary, secondary, and tertiary, and the age ranges associated with each level vary from country to country, it was necessary to standardize the age ranges.

Also, owing to the categorization of education into levels, expenditures over ages within a single category do not vary and neither can the ratio of public-to-private expenditure. Since we know only the total public and private expenditures on secondary education for a given country, we must assume that public (private) expenditure per enrolled 12-year-old is the same as that for each enrolled 16-year-old.

Health Care: Initial $b(x,t)$ values for health care are available for countries that participate in the NTA project. For the non-NTA countries, however, it was necessary to estimate these initial values. To do so, we used a singular value decomposition (SVD). SVD can be thought of as a way of simultaneously interpolating all of the $b(x,t = 2005)$ values for a non-NTA country based on the shape of the $b(x,t = 2005)$ of the NTA countries and on the country's GDP per working-age population relative to those of the NTA counties.[2]

The results of the SVD estimations and the NTA derived $b(x,t = 2005)$ curves are shown in figure 7.7. The strong U-shaped pattern is evident in all the curves. Not surprisingly, those taken from the NTA are less smooth than those that are estimated using SVD.

For the five non-NTA countries (Argentina, Colombia, Cuba, Nicaragua, and Peru) it was necessary to use aggregate expenditure data to apportion estimated spending between public and private sources. So while the public share of total expenditure on health care varies by age in the NTA countries, the available data do not allow us to model that aspect of health care expenditures for non-NTA countries. Consequently, each non-NTA country has a constant share of public expenditure across all ages.

Pensions: The same SVD procedure described above was used to estimate the initial $b(x,t)$ values for pension programs in non-NTA countries.

Three Scenarios for Expenditure Trajectories
We consider three scenarios for the age-specific patterns of expenditures as summarized in table 7.5.

Figure 7.7   Initial Average Expenditures on Health Care by Age as Proportion of GDP/Worker: Estimated and Observed

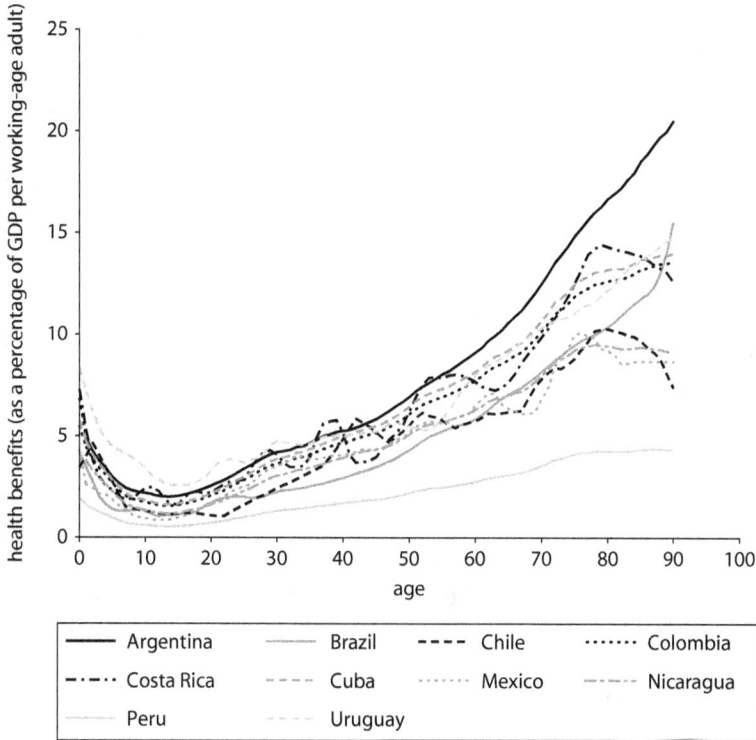

Source: Authors' calculations.

Table 7.5   Assumptions Underlying the Scenarios

Aging-only scenario	Aging and economic change scenario
Changing age structure	Changing age structure
Legislated pension reforms	Legislated pension reforms
No change in benefits; age-specific benefits that rise with productivity growth	Age-specific benefits that move toward OECD averages as income per capita rises (for education and pensions, benefits stop- rising once OECD targets are reached; for health care, benefits continue to rise, exceeding current OECD target levels)

Source: Authors' compilation.

"Aging Only Scenarios for Education, Pensions, and Health Care." In these scenarios, only changes in the age structure of the population through 2050 are allowed. Age-specific expenditure patterns are held constant relative to GDP per working-age person throughout the forecast. That is, age-specific benefits are assumed to increase at the rate of productivity growth (in step with wages). Pensions are an exception. In those countries in which structural reforms in pensions have been introduced, we account for the future reductions in legislated benefit coverage that will accompany the shift away from public sector pensions toward prefunded individual accounts.

"Aging and Economic Change Scenario for Education and Pensions." In these scenarios for education and pensions, the age profile of spending, $b(x,t)$ evolves toward the pattern observed today in a set of mostly European NTA countries as GDP per working-age population increases (at 2.5 percent per year over the projection period). More specifically, in each year t, $b(x,t)$ is a linear combination of the country's initial $b(x,t = 2005)$ and median $b(x,t = 2005)$ of the rich countries, $b^{rich\_countries}(x,t = 2005)$, with weight determined by the country's projected GDP/worker in year t as a fraction of corresponding value for rich countries in 2005.

Under these scenarios, the countries' $b(x,t)$ values converge to the median $b(x,t = 2005)$ of rich countries when their GDP/worker reaches the current median of the OECD, approximately US$41,000. In several countries, GDP/worker will exceed the current OECD figure before 2050. In these scenarios, we hold the spending pattern constant at that point. After current OECD levels of income are attained, future growth in aggregate expenditures in education and pensions is caused only by demographic changes.

"Aging and Economic Growth Scenario for Health Care." In these scenarios, age-expenditure profiles are based on singular value decomposition estimations very much like the one proposed by Lee and Carter (1992):

$$b(x,t) = b(x,t = 2005)) + \beta x * [k(t) - k[1]],$$

where βx is the first right singular vector of the SVD of a matrix whose rows are $b(x,t = 2005)$ of NTA countries logged and ordered by GDP/worker, and where $k(t)$ are values derived from a regression of GDP/worker on the first left singular vector from the above SVD. The values of $k(t)$ are fitted values based on an assumed GDP/worker growth rate of 2.5 percent per year. Age-specific benefits for health care are allowed to increase beyond levels currently observed in OECD countries.

GDP is assumed to result from a Cobb-Douglas aggregate production function; by this assumption the proportion of GDP that accrues to labor is constant, as are the returns to scale, total factor productivity, and the output elasticity of labor and capital. Therefore, forecasts of the wage bill are sufficient to determine GDP. In this analysis, those forecasts are driven by increases in the number of working-age people and by the rate of productivity growth, which is assumed to be the same constant rate (2.5 percent per year) in all economies. To reiterate, the projections in this chapter should be considered illustrative examples based on the application of common assumptions across countries. These rates of productivity growth will vary among countries in important ways (many of which are related to investments in human capital) that are not considered here. In addition, population aging will also affect the growth of the wage bill through its impact on the age distribution of the workforce since productivity varies by age.

To summarize the increases in future costs, we calculate two measures: the increase in spending as a percentage of GDP and the actuarial balance, separately for each public program (education, health care, and pensions) and for all programs combined. The actuarial balance represents the present value of the expected shortfall in funding these sectors during 2005–50, expressed relative to present value of future resources. The actuarial balance represents the size of the tax increase (expressed in percentage points of GDP) necessary to fund the increased program costs over the period. It does not consider any of the costs of these programs after 2050.

Equation 4

$$AB(2005) = PV(E.new(t)) - PV(E.old(t)) / PV(Y(t));$$
$$for\ t = \{2005,...,2050\},$$

where PV = present value of future expenditures (or GDP) in years 2005 through 2050, with a real discount rate of 3.5 percent (1 percent above the forecast productivity growth rate).

This summary measure of future costs does not take into consideration future legislated increases in tax rates (for example, as are often undertaken in parametric reforms of pension systems) nor of assets that may have been accumulated. These actuarial balances indicate the amount of an immediate and permanent tax increase needed to meet future costs in these systems.

Caveat Emptor

This chapter provides illustrative projections, not forecasts. They are based on simple extrapolation of trends. Since everyone who will be over age 41 in 2050 is already born, the most important population numbers on which our projections are based will probably hold true (though migration and better-than-anticipated gains in longevity could ruin those). Projecting policy is a much less certain enterprise. Our projections assume that in a broad sense, these 10 Latin American countries are on a path that will lead them to be much like the welfare states of Europe today. In terms of national income this certainly seems plausible. Even under conservative assumptions, by 2050, many Latin American countries will enjoy per capita national incomes that exceed those of today's rich countries. We are less confident, however, that Latin American countries will make the same decisions about spending their higher wealth as the European welfare states of today do. One striking policy difference is that many Latin American countries have moved toward capitalized pension systems.

Our projections are also not based on any notions of equilibrium. We are simply projecting trends and ignoring the interrelationships among them. No doubt public borrowing (or taxation) is necessary to finance the increased expenditures that we project will have an impact on economic growth. No doubt investment in education would lead to increases in productivity. And there is no doubt that increasing (decreasing) public expenditures in these three areas would compete with other public and private sector priorities in important ways. None of these effects are considered in these projections.

Our projections focus on expenditures, ignoring important fiscal issues pertaining to debt and taxation (particularly in the context of pension reform). Further, the projections do not incorporate any information about our uncertainty about future demographic and economic changes (we do not provide prediction intervals for these projections, as is done in Lee and Miller [2002], for example).

The NTA provides good internationally comparable estimates of the receipt of age-specific public benefits in health care, education, and pensions for five of the countries; data were collected as part of the National Transfers Account project for Brazil, Chile, Costa Rica, Mexico, and Uruguay. Our estimates of age-specific benefits for the other five countries (Argentina, Colombia, Cuba, Nicaragua, and Peru) are illustrative and based on patterns present in the NTA countries. Of course, we do have aggregate data on expenditures for all 10 countries, but the lack of age-specific data for these five countries is a serious shortcoming.

Even with these obvious deficiencies, these projections give us a sense of the magnitude of the effects of the demographic changes under way in Latin America and of the differences in these effects across countries in the region.

The Influence of Demographic and Policy Change on Public Education

Four illustrative projections are presented in tables 7.6 and 7.7 that summarize changes in public spending on education from 2005 to 2050. With no change in benefit generosity levels (educational enrollment rate and investment per student), population aging alone will bring significant reductions in educational spending in all countries. In the "Aging only" scenario, spending will fall by 1 to 2 percentage points of GDP over the next 40 years. This easing of financial pressures over the next few decades (on average amounting to 40 percent of current GDP) implies a liberation of resources that could be used to finance other challenges of population aging (growing costs of pension and health systems) or could be reinvested in the education sector.

In the "Aging only" scenario, the benefit levels and enrollment rates do not change; only the age structure changes. We also present three alternative forecasts in which benefit generosity levels change over the

Table 7.6   Public Spending on Education: Percent of GDP

Country	2005 (% of GDP)	2050 (% of GDP)		Change between 2005 and 2050 (% GDP)	
		Aging only	Toward OECD	Aging only	Toward OECD
Cuba	9.8	7.1	5.2	−2.6	−4.6
Mexico	5.5	3	4.7	−2.4	−0.8
Nicaragua	4.9	2.1	3	−2.6	−1.9
Colombia	4.8	2.9	3.8	−1.9	−1
Brazil	4.5	2.4	3.8	−2	−0.7
Costa Rica	4.5	2.6	6.1	−1.8	1.6
Argentina	3.7	2.5	5	−1.2	1.3
Chile	3.4	2.3	3.4	−1	0
Uruguay	2.8	2	5.8	−0.7	3
Peru	2.7	1.5	3.5	−1.2	0.8
Median	4.5	2.5	4.3	−1.9	−0.4
Mean	4.7	2.8	4.4	−1.7	−0.2

Source: Authors' compilation.

Table 7.7   Public Spending on Education: Actuarial Balance, 2005–50
(Percent of GDP)

Country	Aging only	Aging and economic change	OECD 2050	OECD now
Uruguay	−0.4	1.9	1.3	3.1
Argentina	−0.5	0.9	0.4	1.7
Costa Rica	−0.9	0.3	0.2	1.8
Peru	−0.5	0.1	0.7	2.3
Chile	−0.6	0.1	−0.2	0.4
Colombia	−0.8	−0.5	−0.4	0.1
Mexico	−1.2	−0.5	−0.5	0.4
Brazil	−1.1	−0.5	−0.5	0.2
Nicaragua	−1.0	−0.8	−0.4	0.6
Cuba	−2.0	−2.8	−3.2	−4.4
Median	−0.9	−0.2	−0.3	0.5
Mean	−0.9	−0.2	−0.3	0.6

Source: Authors' compilation.

projection period: "Aging and economic change," "OECD in 2050," and "OECD Now."

In the "Aging and economic change" scenario, both the enrollment rates and the benefit levels grow toward current OECD levels as income per worker rises. It is assumed that GDP/worker grows at 2.5 percent per year in all countries, and once a country reaches the mean OECD income/worker, benefit levels remain constant.

Since benefits are measured in terms of GDP/worker, achieving OECD target levels means achieving similar spending per student as reflected in teacher salaries (relative to country-specific wage levels) and student/teacher ratios. Neither OECD benefit levels nor OECD levels of enrollment will strain national budgets. As table 7.6 indicates, reductions in numbers of students will for all countries more than offset expenses associated with raising enrollment levels. For most countries, this remains true even if benefit levels are immediately increased.

Part of the reason for this result is that universal primary education has already been achieved in all 10 countries. It is in secondary and tertiary education where there is room for further improvement in coverage. The average enrollment rate for secondary-age students in all 10 countries is 86 percent compared to 108 percent in OECD countries (for which data are available). At the tertiary level the corresponding figures are 40 percent compared to 67 percent.

In terms of expenditures *per enrolled student* (relative to GDP/working-age population), the 10-country average expenditure per enrolled secondary school student (combined public and private) is 12 percent, about one-third lower than the OECD average of 17 percent. At the tertiary level, the 10-country average expenditure per enrolled student is 21 percent (of GDP/working-age population). This is somewhat higher than the OECD target figure of 18 percent. It should be noted that the average is affected by Colombia and Brazil, each of which reports expenditures per tertiary student above 40 percent.

Two other costs scenarios are presented in table 7.7 "OECD 2050" and "OECD now" in which OECD levels of enrollment and expenditures per student are reached either in 2050 or immediately. For most countries, achieving OECD levels of educational investment in youth within a generation has an actuarial balance of zero or less, meaning that tax resources (maintaining current tax rates) over the next 40 years would be sufficient to pay for the investment. Even a more ambitious goal of immediately achieving OECD levels of educational investment in youth would entail only small increases in taxes—less than half a percentage point of GDP for most countries.

While population aging will free up a considerable amount of resources to fund ambitious goals in education, these resources are generated over the course of the demographic transition. So, while the actuarial balance on these ambitious plans is small, they imply a large amount of borrowing. In addition, there will be increasing fiscal demands on governments from pensions and health care systems, which limit the governments' abilities to pursue these ambitious targets.

Finally, many studies point to the key role that investment in education can play in preparing for the challenges of population aging (Lee and Mason 2008; Lutz, Cueresma, and Sanderson 2008). However, in this analysis we treat educational spending as consumption and not as an investment in human capital. Therefore, levels of educational investment have no influence on productivity growth in the national economy (which are all assumed to grow at the same rate). This is an important next step in future development of our model.

The Influence of Demographic and Policy Change on Public Pensions

Pension reforms have figured prominently in Latin America. In our sample of 10 countries, 8 have undertaken major structural reforms to their original pay-as-you-go (PAYGO) financed systems by introduction of a prefunded pillar with mandatory contributions. We do not attempt to model the unique pension systems in each country. Instead, we assume reform to a simple PAYGO system for each country, represented by a percentage hypothetically ranging from zero percent (meaning no participation in public pension systems, either contributory or noncontributory) to 100 percent for each cohort. This value is assigned by age in the year of the reform and is fixed to this cohort as it ages.

As an example, we can consider the case of Chile, which was the first country to undergo structural reform, introducing in 1981 a substitutive model in which a prefunded, defined-contribution system replaced the PAYGO, defined-benefit system (table 7.8). In 1981, those closest to retirement age were assigned a value of 100 percent, meaning that the government recognized the pension benefits owed to this cohort and would pay it out over time. Conversely, those who were just entering the workforce in 1981 were assigned a smaller percentage. If that cohort were entirely excluded from the PAYGO system, they would be assigned a zero in our scheme, indicating that their pensions would be entirely determined by the defined contribution pillar. Recent reforms in Chile, however, have strengthened the noncontributory, PAYGO pillar, so our minimum value is 15 percent (based on an analysis of Chilean pension data).

In the year following the reform, public pension system payouts are exactly as they would have been under the old PAYGO system, but over time the proportion qualifying for benefits under the old PAYGO system declines and eventually the new public system is operating at a level of expenditures 15 percent of what it would have been paying out under the old PAYGO system.

Table 7.8   Pension System Reforms in LAC

Pension system	Country	Year reform began	Public obligation (%)
Substitutive	Chile	1981	15
	Mexico	1997	15
Parallel	Colombia	1994	17
	Peru	1993	17
Mixed	Costa Rica	2001	100
	Uruguay	1996	65
PAYGO	Argentina	—	100
	Brazil	—	100
	Cuba	—	100
	Nicaragua	—	100

Source: Authors' compilation.
Note: — = not available.

Mexico also introduced a substitutive model in 1997. As in Chile, the PAYGO system was replaced by a defined-contribution system, reducing the PAYGO obligations in the future, but not eliminating it entirely. Lacking good data, we assume that Mexico's PAYGO system will also move toward an obligation of 15 percent, as in Chile. Two countries (Peru and Colombia) reformed their system toward a parallel model. Under this model, the PAYGO and defined-contributing systems run in parallel, and workers can choose which system in which to participate. Analysis of workers affiliation from survey data in Colombia suggests that PAYGO system obligations in Colombia would be about 17 percent. Lacking data, we adopt a similar value for Peru. Uruguay and Costa Rica reformed their pension systems toward a mixed model in which workers participate in both systems simultaneously. Consequently, workers will receive pension income from the public PAYGO system and from a defined-contribution system. Analysis of the rules in these mixed systems suggests that the PAYGO system in Uruguay will operate at 65 percent of its previous PAYGO obligation. But in Costa Rica, despite the introduction of a defined contribution pillar, the old PAYGO system continues to provide the same guarantees as prereform and hence operates at 100 percent. The remaining four countries (Argentina, Brazil, Cuba, and Nicaragua) operate PAYGO systems, though two of those countries (Argentina and Nicaragua) reverted to PAYGO systems after failed attempts at structural pension reforms.

The results of our pension projections are presented in tables 7.9 and 7.10. We evaluate two scenarios. *In both scenarios, we account for the changes in public sector obligations based on legislated pension reforms.* In the "Aging only" scenario, costs are driven by increasing the proportion of elderly relative to the working ages, offset by declining public sector obligations in those countries that have enacted pension reforms. In the "Aging and economic change" scenario, benefit generosity moves toward OECD levels with growth in GDP/worker. Under this scenario, OECD levels of benefits are reduced by the pension reforms that have already been enacted and by the fact that OECD levels of BGR are lower than the ones observed for Latin American countries.

In the "Aging only" scenario, 3 of the 10 countries would see reductions in the costs of their public pensions systems by 2050. These countries are the ones that have pension systems that reduce participation of the public sector due to a substitutive or parallel reform. An exception is Peru. Although Peru introduced a parallel reform in 1993, it will offset less of the effect of the aging process in the public spending because Peru

Table 7.9   Public Spending on Pensions with Pension System Reforms
(Percent of GDP)

Pension system	Country	2005	2050		Increase between 2005 and 2050	
			Aging only	Aging and economic change	Aging only	Aging and economic change
PAYGO	Cuba	6.8	23.1	16.6	16.3	9.8
	Argentina	4.2	7.4	8.6	3.2	4.4
	Nicaragua	2	5.6	6	3.6	4
	Brazil	7	25.1	10.1	18.1	3.1
Mixed	Costa Rica	4.2	13.8	9.1	9.6	4.9
	Uruguay	9.8	10.5	6.7	0.7	−3.1
Parallel	Peru	3.2	6.2	5.4	2.9	2.2
	Colombia	3	2.3	1.8	−0.7	−1.2
Substitutive	Mexico	0.7	0.6	2.3	−0.1	1.6
	Chile	3.5	2.1	1.5	−1.4	−2

Source: Authors' compilation.
Note: Pension expenditures figures for Brazil include only the General Pension Program (RGP). These figures do not include civil servant retirement programs (RPPs).

Table 7.10   Public Spending on Pensions: Actuarial Balance, 2005–50
(Percent of GDP)

Pension system	Country	Aging only	Aging and economic change
PAYGO	Cuba	7.5	5.5
	Brazil	5	1.5
	Argentina	0.8	1.3
	Nicaragua	0.7	0.7
Mixed	Costa Rica	2.7	1.5
	Uruguay	0	−1.9
Substitutive	Mexico	0	0.8
	Chile	−0.6	−1
Parallel	Peru	0.7	0.5
	Colombia	0	−0.2

Source: Authors' compilation.

is in an earlier stage of the demographic transition. For countries that maintain PAYGO systems, the fiscal effect of aging will be severe. For these countries, the "Aging only" scenario charts the effects of population aging with current age patterns of benefit costs. Public pension obligations in Brazil and Cuba will triple over the period.

The "Aging and economic change" scenario combines the three effects on pension spending: the reform effect, the aging effect, and an economic/policy effect in which countries move to the actual average of benefit generosity ratios of OECD countries. For some countries, as we will see, moving toward OECD generosity ratios can offset the effect of aging, especially in countries that have a higher BGR and had not introduced reforms to their pensions system. This is because the BGRs of OECD countries are lower.

Table 7.9 shows the widely varying impact of these three effects on the 10 countries. For two countries (Nicaragua and Argentina) the combined effect (shown in the "Aging and economic change" column) is positive (that is, public costs will increase) and higher than the "Aging only" effect. The difference between the "Aging only" and the "Aging and economic change" values is due to more generous pension schemes in the OECD countries than in Argentina or Nicaragua. That these countries have not undertaken pension reform means that these countries will see large increases in public costs of pension systems under *both* scenarios.

In six of the countries the combined effect ("Aging and economic change") is positive, but smaller than that of the "Aging only" scenario. These are countries in which the pension BGR is higher than the OECD mean. Once again the difference between the two scenarios is only in the level of generosity of the pension schemes. Both scenarios account for pension reform in the same way and both of course use identical population projections. Brazil, with a BGR of 66 percent, is the most extreme case. Under the "Aging only" scenario, its public expenditures will rise from 7 percent to 25.1 percent of GDP; by adopting OECD benefit levels, the cost will rise to "only" 10.1 percent.

For two countries (Chile and Colombia) both the "Aging only" and the "Aging and economic change" scenarios produce lower public pension costs (as a fraction of GDP) in 2050 than each is experiencing currently. That the "Aging only" scenario values are low is the result of both countries' aggressive pension reforms. That the "Aging and economic change" scenario produces lower values than the "Aging only" scenario indicates that these countries also have generous pension systems relative to the OECD mean.

Table 7.10 shows the effects of both scenarios on the actuarial balance of the 10 countries. Not surprisingly, substantially higher fiscal debt impacts are projected for those countries that continue with the PAYGO system: Argentina, Brazil, Costa Rica, and Cuba. Countries with a reformed system will be able to largely neutralize the aging effect on fiscal sustainability.

That is, they will be able to continue to fund their pension systems without drastic tax increases. But neutralizing the fiscal consequences is not the same as solving the problem. Though taxpayers will be protected, the numbers and demands of pensioners will still grow. Whether these needs are met publicly or privately is a distributional and generation issue. Nonetheless, countries with a PAYGO pension system will have to deal with the inexorable aging process in the public sphere, meeting vastly increasing public obligations with some form of taxation.

The Influence of Demographic and Policy Change on Public Health Care

In the case of health care, using data from the National Transfer Accounts project, we can observe striking differences in health care expenditures by age in high- and middle-income countries. Figure 7.8 shows public and private expenditures per person of each age as a fraction of GDP per working-age population. The difference between the two lines (high-income

Figure 7.8   Health Benefit Generosity Ratio in High-income and Middle-income NTA Countries

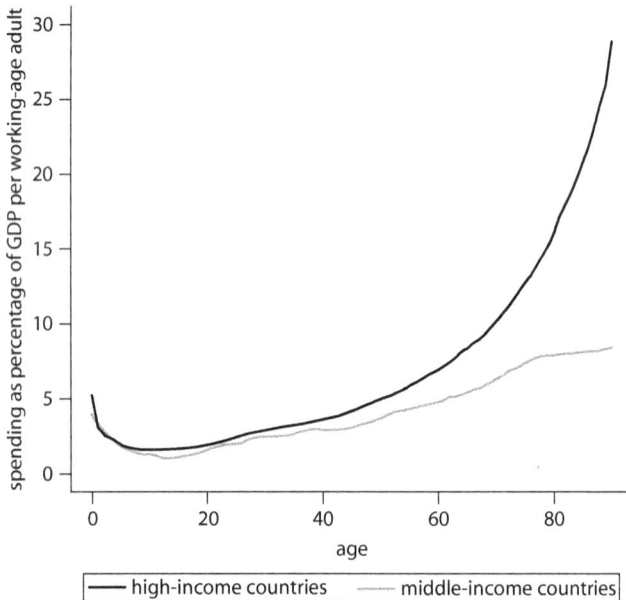

Source: Authors' calculations.
Note: This is public and private combined.

countries and middle-income countries) can be interpreted as "income elasticity." Where the lines in figure 7.8 lie on top of each other, the "elasticity" is 1.0 and health care expenditures per person increase exactly in proportion to increases in GDP per worker. This appears to be the case at ages below 40, with the possible exception of age 0.

Above age 40, the pattern is quite different. There, we see expenditures *per person* in terms of GDP/worker rising significantly as GDP/worker (that is, income) rises. In terms of elasticities, health care for the aged is a "luxury good" whereas health care for those under 40 is a "normal good."

It is very much an open question (and beyond the scope of this chapter) as to why societies seem to choose this path. Some possibilities include:

- Age-biased technological change, wherein advances in medical care favor the sorts of medical problems that older people have.
- Political power; since these are public expenditures, it could represent the rising political power of older people as societies age (and simultaneously become wealthier).
- Past promises; policies with open-ended promises (for older people) may have been set at a time when medical costs were lower.
- Data measurement anomalies; older and wealthier countries may provide some care for senior citizens in the market, whereas in poorer countries such goods are home produced. This is almost certainly the case for Sweden, where NTA project data categorize long-term care as health care.[3]

Whatever the reasons, the shift to higher expenditures in older ages magnifies the effect of population aging, in some cases quite dramatically. Colombia, Nicaragua, and Peru will see their over-40 population grow by a factor of between 2.6 and 3.5 by 2050, whereas wealthier countries such as Argentina, Chile, and Uruguay, will see increases in their over-40 populations of between 44 and 91 percent. Cuba is an exception, as usual.

Two illustrative projections presented for future public health care spending are presented below.

"Aging only." In this scenario, only the population structure changes. The level of expenditure by age for each country remains fixed at their current levels.

"Aging and economic change." In this scenario, the evolution of $b(x,t)$ is determined by the singular value decomposition. The initial $b(x,t)$ values are those observed in 2005 (or estimated by SVD if the country is not

participating in the NTA project). The SVD approach does not require that $b(x,t)$ stop evolving once the mean OECD level of GDP per worker is attained (as is assumed in the case of education and pensions). In general, the SVD produces less-smooth trajectories since it gives more weight to the data from countries at the extremes of the GDP per worker distribution.

Figure 7.9 contrasts the two scenarios for Mexico. The fainter lines refers to later years. The projections assume a large increase in health spending per elderly—more than tripling over the next 40 years. It is the interaction between increasing numbers of elderly and the increased focus of medical systems on the elderly that results in large increases in public health care spending.

Tables 7.11 and 7.12 summarize changes in public spending on health from 2005 to 2050. With no change in benefit generosity levels, population aging alone will bring moderate increases in health care spending to all countries in the region—an average increase of 1 percentage point of

Figure 7.9   Projections of Public Health Care Spending by Age in Mexico

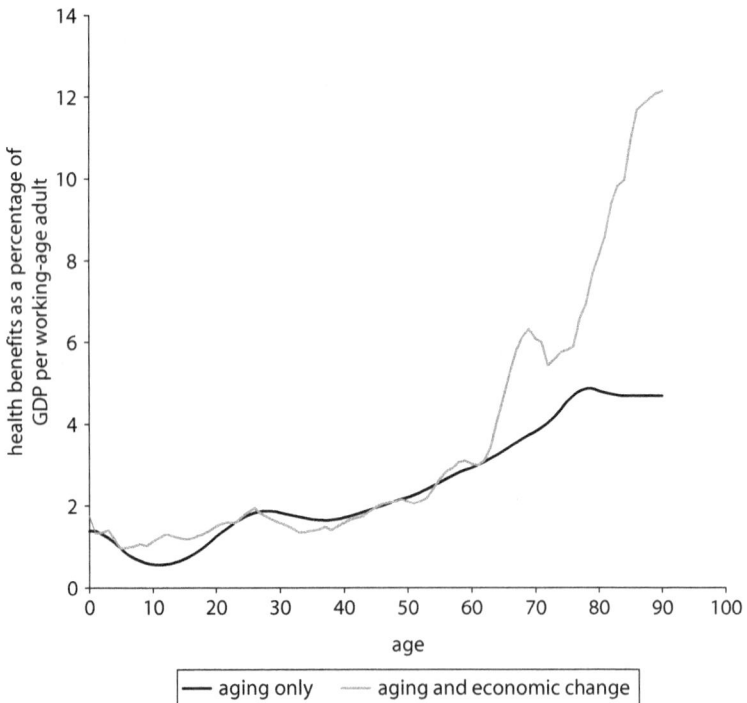

Source: Authors' calculations.

Table 7.11   Public Spending on Health
(Percent of GDP)

| Country | 2005 | 2050 | | Increase between 2005 and 2050 | |
		Aging only	Aging and economic change	Aging only	Aging and economic change
Cuba	7.4	12.4	20	5	12.6
Costa Rica	5.9	8	12	2.1	6.1
Colombia	6.2	8.1	11.8	1.9	5.6
Brazil	3.1	4.6	7.2	1.5	4.1
Argentina	4.5	5.4	8.2	0.9	3.7
Mexico	3	4.1	6.2	1.1	3.2
Chile	2.8	3.7	5.5	0.9	2.7
Nicaragua	3.4	3.9	5.5	0.5	2.1
Uruguay	3.4	3.7	5.4	0.3	2
Peru	1.5	1.9	2.7	0.4	1.2
Median	3.4	4.4	6.7	1	3.5
Mean	4.1	5.6	8.5	1.5	4.3

Source: Authors' compilation.

Table 7.12   Public Spending on Health: Actuarial Balance, 2005–50
(Percent of GDP)

Country	Aging only	Aging and economic change
Cuba	2.2	4.7
Colombia	0.5	1.4
Costa Rica	0.5	1.4
Brazil	0.4	1
Argentina	0.2	1
Mexico	0.2	0.8
Chile	0.3	0.8
Uruguay	0	0.6
Nicaragua	0	0.4
Peru	0.1	0.3
Median	0.3	0.9
Mean	0.4	1.2

Source: Authors' compilation.

GDP by 2050 (table 7.11). As discussed, based on observations of currently wealthy and older societies in the OECD, it is not reasonable to expect age-specific expenditures to remain constant. The "Aging and economic change" scenarios reflect the large increases in health expenditures per elderly as Latin American societies become wealthier and age.

In these scenarios, public health expenditures as a share of GDP increase on average by 4.3 percentage points by 2050. A recent European Union report projected an increase of 3.5 percentage points of GDP in health care spending (medical care and long-term care) during 2005–50. The increases we project for Latin America, while quite large, are similar to those projected for the European Union.

Fiscal Impact of Population Aging in Latin America

These projections draw attention to the policy challenges that governments in Latin America will face as their populations age. In some countries, these effects are likely to be rather modest, and in others, quite severe. Demography plays a large role in driving expenditure growth, but policy choices, especially in the face of demographic change, are vitally important.

The Role of Demographic Change

In most countries, the demographic role is surprisingly benign. With current spending patterns, the cost of education will decline sufficiently to offset the growth in pension costs, *at least in countries that have moved away from PAYGO systems.* In non-PAYGO countries, about 1 percent of the present value of GDP will shift from education to pension programs (see table 7.12). But, of course, focusing on the public sector obscures significant increases in pension obligations that will be met (or not) by the private sector. In countries with minimum pensions guaranteed by the government, the pension obligations not met by the private sector could increase the obligations of the public sector.

Demographic change will result in increases in health care costs in all 10 countries. But the magnitude of the change (at current age-spending levels) is modest. Health care accounted for an average of 4.1 percent of GDP in 2005 (in public expenditures). In 2050, with no change in age profiles of expenditures, that figure will rise to 5.6 percent. Compared to pension costs this is both modest and far less variable.

Projection results for the "Aging only" scenario are presented in tables 7.13 and 7.14. With no change in age profile of expenditures, the fiscal impact of population aging on most countries is neutral, accounting for perhaps 1 or 2 percentage points of GDP over the next 40 years. In a few countries (Chile, Mexico) it is mildly beneficial. It is pension reforms that have shifted and will shift some pension costs off of public budgets more than demography that is at work in these countries.

Table 7.13   "Aging Only" Scenario: Public Sector Spending on Education, Health Care, and Pensions, 2005 and 2050
(Percent of GDP)

		2005	2050			
Fiscal impact	Coutnry	Combined	Combined	Education	Health	Pensions
Detrimental	Cuba	24	42.6	7.1	12.4	23.1
	Brazil	14.6	32.1	2.4	4.6	25.1
	Costa Rica	14.6	24.4	2.6	8	13.8
Neutral	Uruguay	16	16.2	2	3.7	10.5
	Argentina	12.4	15.3	2.5	5.4	7.4
	Colombia	14	13.3	2.9	8.1	2.3
	Nicaragua	10.3	11.6	2.1	3.9	5.6
	Peru	7.4	9.6	1.5	1.9	6.2
Beneficial	Chile	9.7	8.1	2.3	3.7	2.1
	Mexico	9.2	7.7	3	4.1	0.6
	Median	13.2	14.3	2.5	4.4	6.8
	Mean	13.2	18.1	2.8	5.6	9.7

Source: Authors' compilation.
Note: Pension expenditures figures for Brazil include only the General Pension Program (RGP). These figures do not include civil servant retirement programs (RPPs).

Table 7.14   "Aging Only" Scenario: Public Sector Spending on Education, Health Care, and Pensions, Actuarial Balance, 2005–50
(Percent of GDP)

Fiscal impact	Country	Combined	Education	Health	Pensions
Detrimental	Cuba	7.7	2	2.2	7.5
	Brazil	4.3	−1.1	0.4	5
	Costa Rica	2.3	−0.9	0.5	2.7
Neutral	Argentina	0.5	−0.5	0.2	0.8
	Peru	0.3	−0.5	0.1	0.7
	Nicaragua	−0.3	−1	0	0.7
	Colombia	−0.3	−0.8	0.5	0
	Uruguay	−0.4	−0.4	0	0
Beneficial	Chile	−0.9	−0.6	0.3	−0.6
	Mexico	−1	−1.2	0.2	0
	Median	0	−0.9	0.3	0.7
	Mean	1.2	−0.9	0.4	1.7

Source: Authors' compilation.

Brazil, Costa Rica, and Cuba appear to be on quite different trajectories. In these countries, holding policies constant, population aging alone over the next 40 years is set to add between 10 and 18 percent of GDP to public obligations. Once again, future pension obligations are a big part of the story. In these countries, PAYGO systems remain in place, so all of the future expenses are in the government budget.

The Role of Economic Change

We now consider the impact of plausible changes in the age profile of benefits. In education, we project movement toward OECD levels of both enrollment and expenditure as income per worker rises toward current OECD levels. This "Aging and Economic Change" scenario is described above and in Table 7.5.

In pensions, we also focus on a scenario in which countries move toward currently observed OECD benefit levels. For most countries, this means a decline in pension generosity and a particularly large decline for Brazil, Costa Rica, and Uruguay (whose pension BGRs are above .4). For Argentina, Mexico, and Nicaragua, pension benefit levels rise slightly in the "Aging and economic growth" scenario.

In health care, countries move toward and in some cases beyond the current OECD levels of age-specific spending as income per worker rises. Unlike the cases of education and pensions, no upper bound is placed on age-specific costs.

The combined impacts of population aging and expansion of health care and education systems and movement toward OECD pension levels means that all governments will increase social expenditures over the period. For some, the overall increase is mild (Chile and Uruguay), representing an increase in expenditures of less than 2 percentage points of GDP by 2050 (table 7.15). Colombia, Mexico, Nicaragua, and Peru will see moderate increases of about 4 percent of GDP in all three programs combined by 2050. Some countries will face severe fiscal pressures (Argentina, Brazil, Costa Rica, and Cuba). In these countries, public expenses on education, health care, and pensions combined will rise by more than 50 percent, adding between 6.5 and 17.8 percent of GDP to public expenditures (table 7.16).

Thus, the demographic changes of the next 40 years present both challenges and opportunities. By far, the most compelling opportunity is in the educational sphere. These projections imply that rich-country levels of education are possible with moderate increases in spending over the period. Although this chapter ignores the relationship between education and productivity, it is clearly the case that the human capital improvements that follow from investment in education could further offset even the moderate costs that we project.

Table 7.15 "Aging and Benefit Change" Scenario: Public Sector Spending on Education, Health Care, and Pensions, 2005 and 2050
(Percent of GDP)

Fiscal imbalance	Country	2005				2050			
		Combined	Education	Health	Pensions	Combined	Education	Health	Pensions
Severe	Cuba	24	9.8	7.4	6.8	41.8	5.2	20	16.6
	Costa Rica	14.6	4.5	5.9	4.2	27.2	6.1	12	9.1
	Argentina	12.4	3.7	4.5	4.2	21.8	5	8.2	8.6
	Brazil	14.6	4.5	3.1	7	21.1	3.8	7.2	10.1
Moderate	Colombia	14	4.8	6.2	3	17.4	3.8	11.8	1.8
	Nicaragua	10.3	4.9	3.4	2	14.5	3	5.5	6
	Mexico	9.2	5.5	3	0.7	13.2	4.7	6.2	2.3
	Peru	7.4	2.7	1.5	3.2	11.6	3.5	2.7	5.4
Mild	Uruguay	16	2.8	3.4	9.8	17.9	5.8	5.4	6.7
	Chile	9.7	3.4	2.8	3.5	10.4	3.4	5.5	1.5
	Median	13.2	4.5	3.4	3.9	17.7	4.3	6.7	6.4
	Mean	13.2	4.7	4.1	4.4	19.7	4.4	8.4	6.8

Source: Authors' compilation.

Note: Pension expenditures figures for Brazil include only the General Pension Program (RGP). These figures do not include civil servant retirement programs (RPPs).

Table 7.16   "Aging and Benefit Change" Scenario: Change in Public Sector Spending on Education, Health Care, and Pensions, 2005–50
(Percent of GDP)

Fiscal imbalance	Country	Combined	Education	Health	Pensions
Severe	Cuba	17.8	−4.6	12.6	9.8
	Costa Rica	12.6	1.6	6.1	4.9
	Argentina	9.4	1.3	3.7	4.4
	Brazil	6.5	−0.7	4.1	3.1
Moderate	Peru	4.2	0.8	1.2	2.2
	Mexico	4	−0.8	3.2	1.6
	Colombia	3.4	−1	5.6	−1.2
	Uruguay	1.9	3	2	−3.1
Mild	Nicaragua	4.2	−1.9	2.1	4
	Chile	0.7	0	2.7	−2
	Median	4.2	−0.4	3.5	2.7
	Mean	6.5	−0.2	4.3	2.4

Source: Authors' compilation.

The biggest challenge turns out to be health care (tables 7.16 and 7.17). In large part, this is because many countries have already reformed their pension systems in ways that shift future costs away from government budgets. It is important to remember that these reforms do not make pension costs disappear; they merely make them disappear from the public accounts. How successful the new pension schemes are at providing for the growing numbers of elderly remains to be seen. The projected increases in pension expenditures in Latin America (mean of 2.4 percentage points) are very close to those projected for the EU15[4] countries (mean of 2.3 percentage points) (DG ECFIN 2006). However, in the case of the EU15, only one country (Austria) shows a projected decline in pension costs, while in Latin America there are three such cases (Chile, Colombia, and Uruguay).

With health care, government policy is likely to make matters more rather than less expensive for governments. If the trends we observe continue, increases in GDP/worker are going to come with significant growth in health care expenditures on the elderly. The combination of rapidly increasing numbers of elderly with expanding health care benefits at higher ages produces large growth in government budgets.

The impact of population aging on health care in Latin America is projected to be larger than that observed in the European Union. On average, we forecast a 4.3 percentage point increase in public health

Table 7.17   "Aging and Benefit Change" Scenario: Public Sector Spending on Education, Health Care, and Pensions: 2005–50
(Percent of GDP)

Fiscal imbalance	Country	Combined	Education	Health	Pensions
Severe	Cuba	7.4	−2.8	4.7	5.5
	Costa Rica	3.2	0.3	1.4	1.5
	Argentina	3.2	0.9	1	1.3
	Brazil	2	−0.5	1	1.5
Moderate	Mexico	1.1	−0.5	0.8	0.8
	Peru	0.9	0.1	0.3	0.5
	Colombia	0.7	−0.5	1.4	−0.2
	Uruguay	0.6	1.9	0.6	−1.9
Mild	Nicaragua	0.3	−0.8	0.4	0.7
	Chile	−0.1	0.1	0.8	−1
	Median	1	−0.2	0.9	0.8
	Mean	1.9	−0.2	1.2	0.9

Source: Authors' compilation.

spending among the 10 countries considered; a recent EU report found average cost increases of around 3.2 percentage points (DG ECFIN 2006).

Based on these illustrative projections for the 10 Latin American countries, we reach four key conclusions:

- On average, the fiscal impacts of population aging are likely to be as large in Latin America as they are in the European Union.
- However, this average obscures the large amount of heterogeneity in Latin America, due in part to demographic differences among the countries but also to substantial differences due to pension reforms undertaken in many of the countries. For countries that reformed their pension system toward a higher participation of a defined-contribution system, the effect of aging on the public budget will be offset by a reduction in the obligations of the PAYGO system.
- Increases in health care obligations are likely to rival those of pensions. Health care financing should figure prominently in future debates about sustainability of social protection systems in Latin America.
- Population aging reduces the costs of public investment in education and would allow for substantial increases in educational investment per child, allowing the achievement of universal secondary education, OECD levels of investment per child, and other ambitious educational goals in the coming decades.

Notes

1. Directed by Professors Ronald Lee and Andrew Mason. For more information, see: http://www.ntaccounts.org.

2. Our SVD approach is analogous to the method proposed by Lee and Carter (1992) for forecasting mortality rates. In our case, GDP per working-age population plays the role of time in the Lee and Carter procedure.

3. The NTA data for Sweden and the United States include long-term care expenditures as part of health care. This creates some ambiguity and probably means that our estimates overstate health care if narrowly defined but underestimate it if broadly defined. An explicit treatment of long-term care expenditures would be preferred.

4. The EU15 countries are Austria, Belgium, Denmark, Finland, France, Germany, Greece, Ireland, Italy, Luxembourg, the Netherlands, Portugal, Spain, Sweden, and the United Kingdom.

References

CELADE (Latin American and Caribbean Demographic Center). 2007. "Population Projection." *Demographic Observatory for Latin America and the Caribbean* 3 (April).

———. 2008. "Demographic Change and Its Influence on Development in Latin America and the Caribbean." Presented at the 32nd Session of ECLAC in Santo Domingo, Dominican Republic, June 9–13. Document Number LC/G.2378. Chapter III on "The Economic Impact of the Demographic Dividend on Social Sectors."

Commonwealth of Australia. 2007. *Intergenerational Report 2007.* The Treasury, Canberra.

Congressional Budget Office. 2009. *Long-Term Budget Outlook.* Washington, DC.

DG ECFIN (European Commission Directorate General for Economic and Financial Affairs, Economic Policy Committee and the European Commission). 2006. *The Impact of Ageing on Public Expenditures: Projections for the EU25 Member States on Pensions, Health Care, Long-term Care, Education and Unemployment Transfers (2004–2050).* Special Report No. 1/2006. Brussels.

ECLAC (Economic Commission for Latin America and the Caribbean). 2008. "The Demographic Dividend: An Opportunity to Improve Coverage and Progression Rates in Secondary Education." In *Social Panorama of Latin America 2008.*

Lee, R., and L. Carter. 1996. "Modeling and Forecasting the Time Series of U.S. Mortality." *Journal of the American Statistical Association* 87 (419) (September): 659–71.

Lee, R., and A. Mason. 2008. *Fertility, Human Capital, and Economic Growth over the Demographic Transition.* Paper presented at the Annual Meeting of the Population Association of America.

Lee, R., and T. Miller. 2002. "An Approach to Forecasting Health Expenditures, with Application to the U.S. Medicare System." *Health Services Research* 37 (5) (October): 1365–86.

Lubitz, J., L. Cai, E. Kramarow, and H. Lentzner. 2003. "Health, Life Expectancy, and Health Care Spending among the Elderly." *New England Journal of Medicine* 349 (11): 1048–55.

Lutz, W., J. Crespo Cuaresma, and W. Sanderson. 2008. "The Demography of Educational Attainment and Economic Growth." *Science* 319 (February 22): 1047–1048.

Mason, A., and others. 2005. "Population Aging and Intergenerational Transfers: Introducing Aging into National Accounts." Paper presented at the Annual Meeting of the Population Association of America, Philadelphia.

Mason, A., and R. Lee. 2009. *National Transfer Accounts Manual.* Draft Version 1.0. March. Unpublished manuscript.

Mason, A., R. Lee, A.-C. Tung, M.-S. Lai, and T. Miller. 2009. "Population Aging and Intergenerational Transfers: Introducing Age into National Accounts." In *Developments in the Economics of Aging*, ed. D. A. Wise. National Bureau of Economic Research. Chicago: University of Chicago Press.

McGrail, K., B. Green, M. L. Barer, R. G. Evans, C. Hertman, and C. Normand. 2000. "Age, Costs of Acute and Long-term Care and Proximity to Death: Evidence for 1987–88 and 1994–95 in British Columbia." *Age and Ageing* 29 (3): 249–53.

Miller, T. 2001. "Increasing Longevity and Medicare Expenditures." *Demography* 38 (2) (May): 215–26.

Miller, T., C. Martinez, P. Saad, and M. Holz. 2008. "The Impact of the Demographic Dividend on 3 Key Support Systems: Education, Health Care, and Pensions." Paper presented at the Expert Group Meeting on Mainstreaming Age Structure Transitions into Economic Development Policy and Planning, organized by the United Nations Population Fund and the Institute for Future Studies, Vienna, October 7–9.

New Zealand, The Treasury. 2006. *New Zealand's Long-Term Fiscal Position*, Parl. No. B10.

OECD (Organisation for Economic Co-operation and Development). 2009. Social Expenditure Database. Online database available at http://oberon.sourceoecd.org/vl=2355160/cl=17/nw=1/rpsv/ij/oecdstats/1608117x/v135n1/s1/p1, accessed May–June 2009.

Turra, C. M. 2000. "Contabilidade das Geracoes: riqueza, sistema de transferencias e consequencias de mudancas no padrao demografico." Master's thesis, Centro de Desenvolvimento e Planejamento Regional de Minas Gerais/Federal University of Minas Gerais.

Turra, C., and M. Holz. 2009. "Who Benefits from Public Transfers? Incidence across Income Groups and across Generations." Paper presented at author's workshop for Demographic Change and Social Policy: A LAC Regional Study, held at the World Bank, Washington, DC, July 14–15.

Turra, C. M., B. L. Queiroz, and E. Rios-Neto. Forthcoming. "Idiosyncrasies of Public Transfers in Brazil." In *Population Aging and the Generational Economy*, ed. A. Mason and R. D. Lee.

UNESCO (United Nations Educational, Scientific, and Cultural Organization). 2009. UNESCO Institute for Statistics Data Centre. Online database available at: http://stat.uis.unesco.org.

WHO (World Health Organization). 2009. WHO Statistical Information System. Online database available at: http://www.who.int/whosis/en/index.html.

Zweifel, P., S. Felder, and M. Meiers. 1999. "Ageing of Population and Health Care Expenditures: A Red Herring?" *Health Economics* 8 (6): 485–96.

Index

Figures, notes, and tables are indicated with *f*, *n*, and *t* following the page number.

www.ingramcontent.com/pod-product-compliance
Lightning Source LLC
Chambersburg PA
CBHW071837270326
41929CB00013B/2028